German Jew, French Resistance Fighter, British Spy

I Am André is an amazing real-life story of espionage, of courage and resistance, and of friendship and love. It pulls back the veil on the hidden history of the struggle for the identity of the Resistance in France.

The life of 'André' Joseph Scheinmann is more intriguing and compelling than any work of fiction. His true-life story of derring-do starts as a Jewish youth in Munich, whose family moves to France in 1933 to escape the Nazi tide. He joins the French army at the outbreak of WW2 and escapes from a prisoner-of war camp after the bitterly brief fight for France in the summer of 1940.

André becomes a spy and saboteur for the British and Free French whilst working undercover as translator and liaison with the German high command at the Brittany headquarters of the French National Railroads. Summoned by the British, he clandestinely crosses the Channel for initiation and training as an MI6 agent in England.

His network betrayed during his absence, he is arrested on his return to France. André then begins an even more perilous journey with interrogation in Gestapo prisons and the little-known Natzweiler concentration camp in Alsace, before being transferred to Dachau and Allach, ahead of the advancing Allies.

Many vintage photographs and letters from his agents come to illustrate this heart-pounding story of a debonair young man in a broken world who remade himself as a cunning fighter for freedom.

Diana Mara Henry has since 1985 translated and researched the memoirs, assembled a pioneering bibliography, and corresponded with survivors of the Natzweiler-Struthof concentration camp in Alsace, France. In 2004 she created www.natzweiler-struthof.com.

Her video interview of Phillip Maisel is at the USHMM. She has been published in the *Journal for Ecumenical Studies*, reviewed *Resistance in the Second World War* for the *Journal of Military History*. She has also presented at conferences and symposia at the University of Salzburg, the Hebrew University of Jerusalem, The Genocide Studies Progam of Yale University, German Studies Association Summer Workshop at the Freie Universität of Berlin, Birkbeck University of London, Monash University, The 9/11 Memorial and Museum, and others.

Diana's first career, as a photojournalist, was honored with exhibitions including at the National Women's Hall of Fame, Overseas Press Club/NYC, the Organization of American Historians' Centennial Conference, and the Woodrow Wilson Center. Named special collections of her work were purchased by UMass/Amherst, The NY State Museum, the Schlesinger Library at Harvard, and the NY Public Library. Her books of photography are *Women on the Move* and *A Life in Photography* and her art is on display at saatchiart.com.

I AM ANDRÉ

German Jew, French Resistance Fighter, British Spy

By Diana Mara Henry
From the life of André Joseph Scheinmann

Chiselbury

Copyright © 2024 Diana Mara Henry

Every effort has been made to identify and credit other copyright holders. Please bring any inadvertent omission to the attention of the publisher for future editions

Published by Chiselbury Publishing, a division of
Woodstock Leasor Limited 14 Devonia Road, London N1 8JH, United Kingdom

www.chiselbury.com

ISBN: 978-1-916556-56-0 (hardback/dustjacket)

ISBN: 978-1-916556-37-9 (hardback/laminate)

ISBN: 978-1-916556-55-3 (ebook)

A CIP catalogue record for this book is available from the British Library

The moral right of Diana Mara Henry to be identified
as the author of this work is asserted.

This is copyright material and must not be copied, reproduced, transferred, distributed, leased, licensed or publicly performed or used in any way except as specifically permitted by the publishers, as allowed under the terms and conditions under which it was purchased or as strictly permitted by applicable copyright law. Any unauthorised distribution or use of this text may be a direct infringement of the publisher's rights and those responsible may be liable in law accordingly.

Chiselbury Publishing hereby exclude all liability to the extent permitted by law for any errors or omissions in this book and for any loss, damage or expense (whether direct or indirect) suffered by any third party relying on any information contained in this book.

Author photo by Kenric Kite

Cover design by Indra Murugiah

Typeset by Andy Barr

Contents

The life and times of André Joseph Scheinmann 5
Introduction: An Eagle's Eye View 9

Part One: I Am André 27
Chapter I My Story Begins 29
Chapter II Teen Leader 31
Chapter III A New Homeland 38
Chapter IV War Approaches 43
Chapter V Fighting For France 47
Chapter VI Spy For The British 54
Chapter VII By Night To London 76
Chapter VIII Prisoner Of The Gestapo 87
Chapter IX 'NN' At Natzweiler 101
Chapter X Natzweiler – Four Episodes 126
Chapter XI Dachau, Allach, Dachau 133
Chapter XII Freedom and Loss 145
Chapter XIII The Concentration Camp Universe 151
Chapter XIV Conclusion 159
André's Official Reports to the French Government 162
    Report of Captain André Peulevey 163
    Report of 'Joseph dit [called] André Scheinmann' to the French government 167

Part Two: Cher Camarade 169
Introduction: The rest of the story 171
Chapter 1 André's War: Resistance and the SIS 173
Chapter 2 From SIS to a place in French history: André's post-war service to the Resistance 198
Chapter 3 André reframes and reclaims his life 216

A Closer Look 233
Who Betrayed André? 235
André's War Record 240
Trip and Training in England 247
The very controversial Madame Louis 256
André's Agents 260
Records for the murder of Max and Regina in the Holocaust 266

Claire's Story 269

Bibliography... 275

Endnotes 295

Acknowledgements... 337

Index... 343

I AM ANDRÉ

**German Jew,
French Resistance Fighter,
British Spy**

André captured by USC Shoah Foundation – The Institute for Visual History and Education. Interview #24954 of André Scheinmann, 1/27/1997 at Boca Raton, Fl

5/

MRS. ANDRÊ D. SCHEINMANN
44 WILSON STREET, SOUTH DARTMOUTH, MASSACHUSETTS 02748

Attention :
Les Anglais connaissent pas mon nom. Ils m'ont connu sous le nom :
André Maurice PEULEVEY
né le 7/11/1915
matricule I.S. 99421
En Angleterre j'ai suivi un entraînement de parachutiste. j'ai appris comment coder et décoder.
Ils m'ont trouvé important assez pour désigner un opérateur radio pour moi personnellement.
Entretemps en FRANCE le réseau ami qui m'avait aidé avait été infiltré et la GESTAPO m'attendait

NB:

The English don't know my name.

They knew me under the name:

André Maurice Peulevey

Born 7/11/1915

Registration number I.S. 99421

In England, I was given training in parachuting, I learned to code and decode.

They found me useful enough to designate a radio operator for me personally.

Meanwhile in FRANCE the network that had helped me had been infiltrated and the GESTAPO were waiting for me

In his own words and handwriting, in 1999 André provided a CV on his wife's stationery including page 5, where he noted his false identity as he was known to the British, his training, and the betrayal of his network.

André's places, 1915-1945

The life and times of André Joseph Scheinmann

'Fear is the canvas upon which courage paints its masterpiece.'
Rabbi Yisroel Bernath, Associate Chaplain, Concordia University

1914-1918: World War One

Max Scheinmann fights for Germany.

1915: Joseph Scheinmann born 1/28/1915 in Munich to Max and Regina Thorn Scheinmann.

Spends his early childhood in Kempten and his teens in Düsseldorff, Germany.

1921: *Hitler takes leadership of Nazi party.*

1924: *Hitler sentenced to five years for the 'Beer Hall Putsch' attempt to overthrow the German government, spends 8 months in prison writing* Mein Kampf, *his vision for world domination.*

Max Scheinmann begins public speaking against Hitler, takes out visas for France for his family.

1933: *Nazis seize power. Dachau concentration camp opens March 22.*

Max Scheinmann moves his family to Bruay-en-Artois, France.

Military activity

'Giving to horror grace, to danger pride,
Shine martial Faith, and Courtesy's bright star.
Through all the wreckful storms that cloud the brow of War.'
Sir Walter Scott, *The Lady of the Lake*, Canto 5, I.

1938: *Germany moves into Czechoslovakia, takes the Sudetenland. Appeasement at Munich.*

Max and Joseph turn in their German passports and volunteer for duty in the French Army.

1939: *Hitler-Stalin Pact. Germany invades Poland, war declared between Germany, France and Great Britain.*

Joseph Scheinmann is enrolled under his real name and birthplace in the French Army, serving from August, 1939 in the 43rd Infantry Regiment, then is given the name and identity of André Maurice Peulevey, born 7/11/1915 in Gucourt.

1940: *German assault on north-west Europe results in the capture and subjugation of Luxembourg, the Netherlands, Belgium and France. Alsace is retaken into Germany and France is carved up into many zones. Pétain becomes leader of Vichy France.*

André is wounded in action in Belgium, shipped back to hospital in Brittany.

Military hospital in Rennes becomes prisoner of war camp, June 20. André escapes July 26.

Resistance activity

'All warfare is based on deception. Therefore, when capable, feign incapacity; when active, inactivity ... Offer the enemy a bait to lure him ... Pretend inferiority and encourage his arrogance.'
Sun Tzu, *The Art of War*

1940-1942: Hired as interpreter by the SNCF/French national railroad, August, 1940.

Organized sabotage & information-gathering throughout Brittany, October 1940 to January, 1942.

Served in a leading role in the networks La Bête Noire, Aigle, Alexandre.

Aggregated networks La Bande à Sidonie and Groupes Lehmann and Le Dantec to Georges-France/Groupe 31.

Connected with Johnny and Overcloud networks.

Spy work for the British and Free French

1941: Agent #31AQ for Georges-France/Groupe 31, directed by Commander Dunderdale, SIS

Supervised by SIS Thomas H. Greene/'Uncle Tom' under the alias 'Le Neveu/The Nephew'.

Sent weekly intelligence reports to England, Fall, 1940 through December, 1941.

1942: Dispatched to England in the SOE/BCRA 'Overcloud' operation on January 6, 1942.

As SIS/MI6 agent 99942, underwent 'various courses' and parachute training in England.

Sent back to France on February 2 with code name 'Turquoise', entrusted with organizing a new network, funded with an initial 500,000 francs; assigned a personal radio operator to follow.

Arrest and deportation

1942: Arrested by the Feldgendarmerie (German Military police) after his return from England, February 4, 1942.

Incarcerated at Fresnes prison in Paris, 11 months in solitary confinement, subjected to 33 interrogations.

1943: Sent with first convoy of French NN/*Nacht und Nebel*/Night and Fog prisoners to KL Natzweiler. His prisoner no. 4368.

July 9, 1943 - September 1944 at Natzweiler.

1944-1945: Incarcerated at concentration camps Dachau, its subcamp Allach, back to Dachau, prisoner no.101739. Member of International Prisoners Committee and typhus ward 'staff' at Dachau.

Post-War

1945: Liberated from Dachau April 29,1945. On June 22, 1945, received letter of reference from SIS Thomas Greene and returned 500,000 francs receipted by SIS J.E. Gentry.

1945-1949: With rank of Captain, served as *Liquidateur de Réseau* Overcloud, registering agents of his Resistance networks for the French government.

Awarded Legion of Honour (Knight, Officer), Medal of the Resistance, Army Corps War Cross with gold star; registered as DIR (Déporté Interné de la Résistance and FFC (Forces Françaises Combattantes).[1]

Married Claire Dyment Jarrett, 29 December 1946 in New Bedford, MA and 24 January 1948 in Paris.

1951: Granted French citizenship, moved to the US, settling in New Bedford, MA.

Retired from French Army Reserves as Lt. Colonel André Scheinmann.

2001: Died May 13. Buried in Tifereth Israel Cemetery at 1400 Old Plainville Rd. New Bedford, MA.

Manuscript tribute by Charles De Gaulle issued as a printed piece for members of the Forces Françaises Libres, with heading for Captain André Peulevey, dated September 1, 1945. 'Answering the call of France at peril of death, you rallied to Free French Forces. You were of the volunteer team of good Companions who kept our country in the war and in honor. You were in the first rank of those who allowed her to win Victory! At the moment when the goal has been reached, I wish to thank you in friendship, simply, in the name of France!'

Introduction:
An Eagle's Eye View

> 'Anyone who has the opportunity to compare the true image of a writer with what can be deduced from his writings knows how frequently they do not coincide ... But how pleasant and cheering is the opposite case: the man who remains true to himself in what he writes...' Primo Levi: *Moments of Reprieve*.[2]

Standing at my window in Carmel, CA, watching for the taxi that was to take me on the first leg of my journey back to Cambridge, MA, for my 25th college reunion in 1994, I picked up the ringing phone and heard Michel Scheinmann say: 'We were classmates but never met at Harvard, and if you are coming to the reunion, I want to introduce you to my father, André. He was a camper at Natzweiler.' A camper at Natzweiler? I had never heard of a prisoner in a concentration camp described as 'a camper!' Intrigued, I accepted Michel's invitation. He had seen my entry in the autobiographies book published by Harvard for its alumni in the years of their major reunions. Michel had read in my entry that, for the last ten years, I had been studying the Natzweiler-Struthof concentration camp in Alsace, that the Germans named Konzentrationslager Natzweiler /KLNa.[3]

I met André that fall. I came to know that the man and his writing are one. And after all the documentation that has come to light, I have every reason to believe, and 'to make it understood that the man speaking now and the man who was over there are one and the same.'[4]

We hear his silent sob – in breaks in the sentences, in punctuation marks, in the space around the letters ... because the sob is there, hidden in silence, as it interrupts every conversation about the camps, his friends, all the other brave souls he could not reach out to and save. It comes when he speaks of good people, not of hardship.

Above all questions, André struggled with the possibility that his preoccupation with resistance activities may have distracted him from preventing his parents' tragic extinction in the Lublin death camps. Max and Regina were arrested where they had been staying, at the Hotel Paris Rivoli in the Marais section of Paris. Regina's brother Jakob 'Kuba' Thorn's family survived the war hidden in a home in the Paris suburb of Le Vésinet, after his aunt by marriage Regine Madeleine Thorn born Felsen's internment at the Rieucros camp from 1941 to the beginning of 1942.

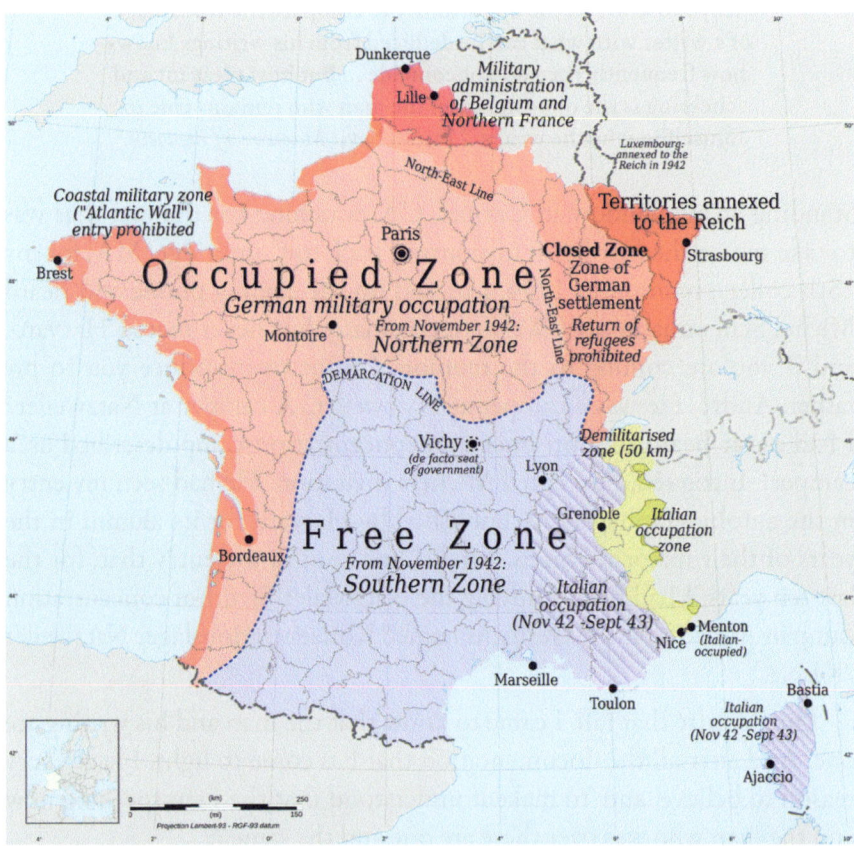

After its defeat in three weeks in 1940, France was divided by the Germans into the Northern Occupied zone; a Southern zone which was administered by the French collaborationist government from the city of Vichy until its occupation by the Germans in November, 1942; forbidden zones along the Atlantic coast and the English Channel, where André and his networks would operate and from which he traveled to England; and separation and ethnic cleansing zones in northeast France. Not only were there armed German forces at barriers at each of these frontiers but also signs prohibiting Jews from crossing them. Image courtesy of Wikimedia Commons.

André's parents were not naïve or inexperienced about being uprooted, having first left Poland of their birth and then Germany in 1933 as soon as Hitler came to power.[5] From the time of the 'beerhall *putsch*' in 1923, his father Max had traveled around Germany to speak out against Hitler to fellow veterans of World War I and at public meetings. As early as 1924, Max took out visas for the family to live in France. In the summer of 1939, Max took his daughter Rosa 'Mady' to the US where she married her cousin, Dr. Sydney Scheinman, M.D.[6] Finally, when the Germans invaded the Pas de Calais, and sectioned it off from 'occupied' France to make it part of the territories under the German Military command of Belgium, they fled again They were assisted by a friendly police chief of the town where they lived and worked, who provided them with passes to get into occupied France from the restricted Northeast zones.[7]

'In 1940,' recalled André, 'when the Germans occupied the country, all the Jews were called to a certain place. The head of the police in Bruay told my parents: "Don't go, it's no good." And he gave them a *laissez-passer* (pass) to go over to the [occupied] zone [of France.] Because Northern France was attached to Belgium by Germany [and became a forbidden zone] and then, the rest was occupied too, but you had to pass like a border [through another zone through which residents could not return] so he gave them – he procured them papers for passage to go to Paris ... We had good relations with the Mayor, with the head of police, with everybody. For holidays, they got a bottle of wine, a bottle of whiskey, whatever, and generally we were considered good people. They warned my family and provided them with contact to the people who could bring them over.'[8]

André spent the last 50 years of his life in New Bedford, MA, the city where his sister also lived. He never spoke of the US State Department's having frustrated Mady and her husband's application for visas to bring their parents to live with them in the US. The heartbreakingly cold bureaucratic letter putting off their son-in law's efforts to obtain asylum for them was dated June 23, 1941. A year and a month later, they were murdered in extermination camps.

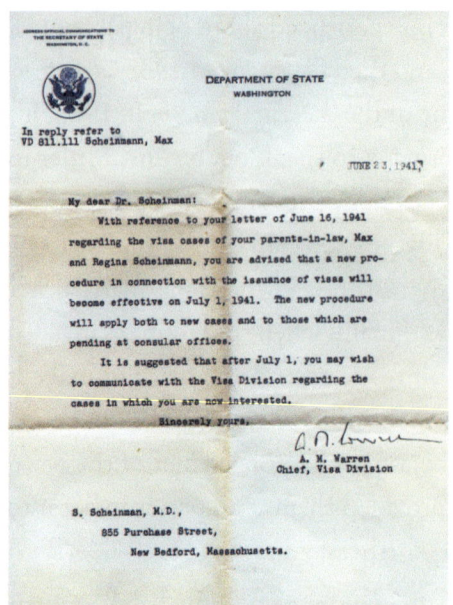

'With reference to your letter of June 16, 1941 regarding the visa cases of your parents-in-law, Max and Regina Scheinmann, you are advised that a new procedure in connection with the issuance of visas will become effective on July 1, 1941...

It is suggested that after July 1, you may wish to communicate with the Visa Division regarding the cases in which you are now interested.

Sincerely yours,

A.M. Warren, Chief, Visa Division.'

Letter from US Department of State to Dr. Sydney Scheinman putting off his visa application for André and Mady's parents to come to the US in 1941. A year and a month later, they were murdered at Auschwitz.

Saving his parents was a paramount goal of André's ambition as a soldier on the battlefield with 'the army of the shadows'. Going to London in January, 1942 on assignment for the Secret Intelligence Service was a major milestone in moving toward that goal. That ambition was inexorably thwarted even before he could reconnect with them; as soon as he returned in February, he was arrested and was held in prison after that.[9] He believed 'they gave up hope' when they learned he had been arrested and they refused to keep moving out of harm's way.[10] André never spoke or wrote about the official French collaboration, expulsions and laws modeled on those of Nazi Germany, and the round ups and transports of their Jewish residents and citizens to the extermination camps.

No one can be certain that André could have saved them, or himself, even had they escaped the 'Rafle of the Vel D'Hiv,' the ignominious roundup of thousands of Jews in Paris by the French police to be turned over to the Germans for extermination in July 1942. One thing is sure: the loss of these gentle people, whom he obviously revered, brought him unbearable pain and remorse.[11]

Regina and Max chaperoning Mady at Le Pré Fleuri, a country restaurant with dancing, 1939. Right: André and Mady in childhood.

During his lifetime, no doubt still respecting his Official Secrets pledge, André was mostly 'mum' on what transpired during his trip to England and did not reveal his secret archive of post-war correspondence with and about the members of his networks.[12] Once an agent, always an agent.

The archives of WWII where his work is recorded were not yet open. He did not know of the many books by survivors that mentioned him. Highlights from these sources and his personal archive frame his connection to the earliest Resistance in France, his deep friendships with members of his networks, and the devotion to their comrades they shared after the war. As *Liquidateur de Réseau* (network registrar), he worked for the Resistance longer after the war than he did while it lasted, to assure its heroes the honors and pensions they deserved. He had to use all his skill and doggedness in navigating the choppy political waters and factions within France after the war that he had used in navigating between the French and British Secret Services in London.

In his memoir, we read how, for 18 months, from summer 1940 to February 1942, in parallel with his job as interpreter liaising with the

Germans in control of the French National Railroads/SNCF hub in Brittany, André, as the boss of a network of 300 saboteurs and informants, poured strategic information to England. Employed seemingly 'against his will,' he toured the German U-boat and air bases, fuel depots, acting as a rather doltish interpreter. 'Just being helpful,' he convinced the German switchboard operators to take their lunch break, then fielded their phone calls to get valuable information from the Luftwaffe, using 'a commanding Prussian voice.'

André connected with the 'handful of extraordinarily brave inhabitants of the occupied nations who started Resistance networks in the early days … [who] deserve the highest admiration for breaking ranks with their cowed fellow-countrymen long before the Allied cause became fashionable.' [13] He also recounts the courageous and often amusing collective actions of defiance by the Bretons, who were the most numerous of all the French to join the resistance, as they taunted the occupiers in the cafés, movie theaters, and on the streets.

He joined a drama class at the local University of Rennes as well as signing up for graduate study of German to explain his excellent command of the language.

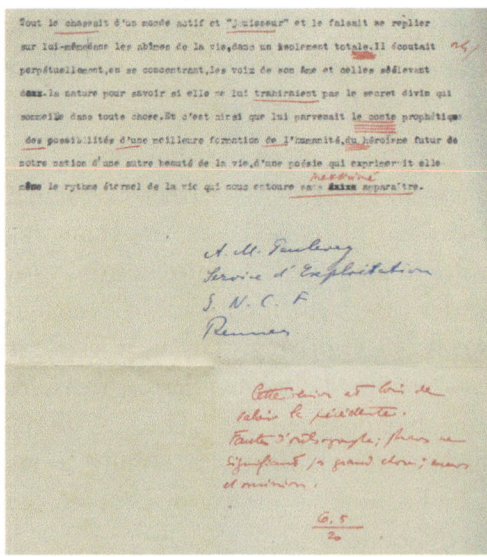

André received a failing grade of 6.5/20 for a paper whose second page begins: 'Everything chased him away from an active and "hedonistic" life and made him withdraw into himself, into the depths of life, in total isolation… A.M. Peulevey, Management, S.N.C.F. Rennes.'

The professor's evaluation: 'This German to French translation is far from as good as your earlier one. Spelling mistakes, fairly meaningless phrases, errors and omissions.'

His girlfriend may have corrected the previous assignment that earned him a better grade – but she had ditched him before he handed in this

Introduction - An Eagle Eye's View

one. He tells how disgusted she had been with his bourgeois refusal to join her resistance network, giving as excuse that he couldn't jeopardize his job security. She never knew that he had turned her down to protect her from his much larger involvement in the Resistance, and that several of his people were coordinators of the Rennes student resistance group, the Comité Rennais des Etudiants.[14] It may have even been after inviting him to one of their dances that she tried to recruit him, carrying out their goal to 'identify individuals capable of acting for us. To that end, these clubs include members who are neutral and ignore the clubs' true goal.'[15] André, who had a talent with women, was also a man of purpose, whatever it cost him.[16]

He spent eighteen months in Gestapo prisons in France where he endured some three dozen interrogations. He shares tale upon tale of daring misdirection including telling the Germans that he had only gone to England to see if a pre-war romance was still viable. André and 55 others, including 10 others from his networks, were then shipped to the Natzweiler concentration camp as NN/*Nacht und Nebel*/Night and Fog prisoners. They were meant never to be heard from and never to return.

> **Secret**
> "It has for a long time been the wish of the Führer that other measures should be found for dealing with offenders in the Occupied Countries against the Reich and the Occupying Powers. The Führer is of the opinion that term sentences or imprisonment for life are a sign of weakness. An effective deterrent is sentence of death or such measures as leave the relations and the peole oblivious of the fate of the offenders. For this reason they should be brought to Germany. The attached directions for the persecution of the offenders interpret the Führer's wishes. They have been approved and accepted by him."
>
>   sgd. Keitel

'Secret' footnote to the first NN Decree signed by Wilhelm Keitel. (Nuremberg trial translation of evidence) Courtesy Arolsen Archives of the International Tracing Service DocID: 82329120

The NNs were political prisoners from Norway, Belgium, the Netherlands, and France. Originally destined for trial in Germany, they were eventually shipped directly to the concentration camps there.[17] The NN Decree was designed not only to eradicate Hitler's political enemies but also to be an instrument of terror when public executions were creating unrest.

> (Nacht und Nebel), and were kept isolated under a regime so severe as to amount to/death sentence. The following order by KRAMER (late Commandant of Belsen), when Commandant of Natzweiler, illustrates this.
>
> (The original text, with Kramer's signature, is in this office.)
>
> Translated from the German.
>
> Waffen SS
> Natzweiler Concentration Camp
> Commandant's Office
>
> Natzweiler, 29 March, 1943.
>
> Ia/Az.: KL 14 d 4 / 3.43/ Kr. / Fi.
>
> Secret Journal No. 60 / 43.
>
> re: Prisoners falling under the "Keitel Decree".
> Ref: o.V.
> Encl: None.
>
> S E C R E T!
>
> To the Chief of the Natzweiler Concentration Camp Office.
>
> You must immediately ascertain from the Political Department which prisoners in the camp fall under the "Keitel Decree". As you are aware, all communication between these prisoners and their families is forbidden. By the non-acceptance of a letter, a prisoner's family were recently enabled to learn that he had died in the camp here. Such negligent performance of duties may lead to grave difficulties in the sphere of foreign politics.
>
> I expect the orders given to be adhered to with the greatest exactitude in the future. You will please give very particular instructions in this matter to the SS members under your control. In the event of further offences they will have to expect certain dismissal and severe punishment. In the case of the few prisoners confined here who come under this decree, it is expected that the orders given by RSHA will be noted and carried out in every case.
>
> KRAMER
>
> SS Hauptsturmführer and
> Commandant.

The United Nations War Crimes Commission,
Summary of Information No. 35, July 1945

In camp André, serving as interpreter once again, stepped up his rescue operations, devising safe zones and assignments to shelter his weaker comrades with all his wiles and insight into the German mind and human needs. He does not describe any brutality to himself, in the camps, but only to others. He mentions that German Shepherd dogs were set to bite others but never shared that he himself had undergone surgery in the camp infirmary for a dog bite.

One finds that in a doctor's report from after the war, tucked away in his files. One has to look to other survivor writings about André to read that the *Kapos* and SS 'flattened him to the wall' and that 'he got the Tamer's boot in the behind.'[18]

The *NN* and the X that *Nacht and Nebel* (Night and Fog) prisoners had to paint on their uniforms identified them as a prime target for the guards. Here, a dog is biting and a prisoner is getting a 'boot in the behind' and Kommandant Kramer, smoking his cigar, is looking on. By Henri Gayot, a resistor and survivor of Natzweiler. Courtesy of the CERD and the family of Henri Gayot.

There is not nearly as much graphic description of cruelty in André's memoirs as there are in others by survivors of torture in Nazi prisons and at Natzweiler/KLNa, which was, like Mauthausen, of the harshest category – Category 3 – of camps according to the Nazis. For instance, he mentions that wounds could never heal, without the descriptions found almost word for word in many of the other memoirs of how SS *Röttenführer* Franz Ehrmanntraut (the SS corporal all the survivors mention by name) used to dig around for the maggots in the flesh of fallen prisoners' open wounds with the metal point of his cane and urinate on them. There is not a single incident of cruelty in André's account that some other eyewitness, or several, have not described in much more graphic and horrible detail.

André chooses instead to focus the reader's attention on the ultimate goal he had in mind: to tell how he and his partners in courage struggled to live to see, after 12 years, the defeat of the '1,000-year *Reich*'.[19] He pauses for several silent sobs when telling about the German career officer who spent twelve years in concentration camps rather than join the SS.

Unshakeable values, flexibility and adaptability combined in him with insight into what made the Nazis and their henchmen 'tick' and how to best manipulate them. Sidestepping ego, he read human nature and used cultural clues to talk to people based on what they knew and let them believe what they expected. He did not assert his true identity if their misguided preconceptions served his purpose.

'Rescuers were able to play various roles and take required actions because, at the deepest level of their beings, it was who they were and what they believed that really mattered ... The rescuer self allowed them to do whatever was needed to save lives. If the role called for lying, stealing, even killing, they did it.[20] There is no indication André killed anyone.

These memoirs offer a reality check to the general impression of rescuers and victims under Nazi occupation. The generally-held view that rescuers were Christian and that the passive recipients of the generous aid provided by the heroes of the resistance were Jewish is confounded in the story of André.

In a grim continuation of his false military identity, André was imprisoned in a concentration camp meant to be exclusively for non-Jews.[21] In fact, there were 10, 427 known Jews among the 52,000 prisoners at the KLNa. The Nazis categorized about half of the Jews they identified as political prisoners. They did not identify secret Jews like André, Henri Rosencher, Gilbert May, and no one knows how many others.[22]

André's story does not take away from the glorious history of Jewish resistance groups in Europe; circumstances simply did not provide him with entrée into those milieus but gave him perfect cover for working with non-Jews, as so he did. The non-Jewish resistance fighters who have written about the Natzweiler experience do not write about rescuing Jews, but only about their pity for the Jews there being even more horribly abused than other prisoners.[23] André, on the other hand, mentions making specific efforts to rescue Jean Lemberger at Natzweiler and Pierre Schillio and his son at Dachau.[24]

Introduction - An Eagle Eye's View

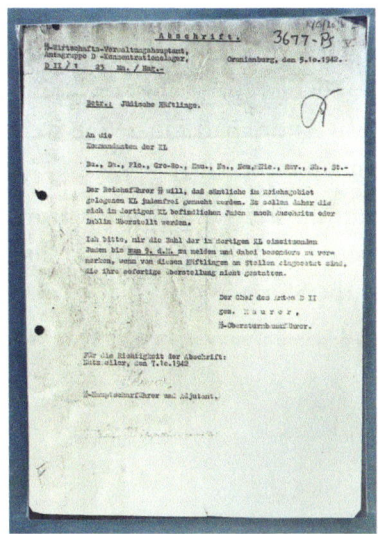

Sent out from Oranienburg, the concentration camp and administrative center of all the camps. *Reichsführer* was Heinrich Himmler's title starting in June 1936.
Microfilm from US National Archives and Records Administration / NARA Item #RG 238, c.174, No-1501; Location 190.12.24.1, box 31 of the series titled Nuernbrg Organization (NO) Documents, March 15, 1947–June 20, 1949 (Record Group 238).

"Copy

SS Economic Direction of the Concentration Camps
Department D

Oranienburg 5.10.1942

D II / 1   23   Ma./   Hag.-

Subj: Jewish prisoners

To the Kommandants of the Concentration Camps
Bu(chenwald), Da(chau) Flo(ssenburg) Gro(ss)-Ro(sen), Mau(thausen), Na(tzweiler), Neu(engamme), Nie(derhagen), Rav(ensbrück), Sh (Sachsenhausen), St(uthof) *

The SS Reichsführer wants all concentration camps situated on reich territory to be cleansed of Jews that are there. All Jews in your camp must therefore be transferred to Auschwitz or Lublin. Please let me know by the 9th of this month how many Jews are in your camp, mentioning specifically if they are employed in a position that would make it impossible to transfer them immediately.

The head of Department D II
Sig(ned) Maurer,
SS-Obersturmbahnnführer

For the accuracy of the copy:
Natzweiler, October 7,1942
[signed] Volkmar
SS-Haupscharführer and second in command [of the KLNa].
[Handwritten note]
on October 7, 1942,
32 Jews noticed for transfer"

Image with English translation side by side] October 5, 1942, official edict of SS *Oberststurmbahnnfüher*: 'SS Reischsführer [Himmler] wants all concentration camps situated on Reich territory to be cleansed of all Jews that are there. All Jews in your camp must therefore be transferred to Auschwitz or Lublin' [to the extermination camps in Poland.]

Although he heard of gassings of Jews and Gypsies at the time of his imprisonment from the camp's sympathetic chief prisoner (*LagerKapo* Willi), André does not write about the Natzweiler gas chamber. People of those two groups were brought in from Auschwitz to be killed, to satisfy Dr. Hirt's never completed 'study of the skulls of Jewish Bolshevik Commissars,' Dr. Haagen's typhus vaccine and Dr. Bickenbach's mustard-gas experiments.[25] André's omission represents his first-hand truth. Most of the other survivors who wrote memoirs, however, included this information which they discovered later from the Nuremberg Trials.[26]

When Franz Ehrmanntraut – the killer mentioned most frequently by André and other prisoners – died, survivors of Natzweiler reacted with horror to his death notice.[27] This man, who after the war stood accused by former deportees of killing more than 340 named prisoners at the KLNa, was depicted as a man of Christian piety and family values. The florid remembrance begins: 'Jesus, I live for You, Jesus, I die for You, Jesus, I am Yours, in life and in death.' André wrote to his widow that she had no idea of the true nature of the man she had married. He never received a reply.

Natzweiler had exterior *Kommandos* (*Aussenkommandos*) or work details, where André and the other Frenchmen 'were not allowed' to work for fear that they might slip away and blend in with the locals whose language they shared. The *Kommandos* André participated in were assigned to specific jobs in and around the main camp.

In the exterior *Kommandos,* slave labor administrative dependencies of the mother camp, non-French nationals were hired out as slave workers called 'pieces' (*Stück*) to private industry by the SS.[28]

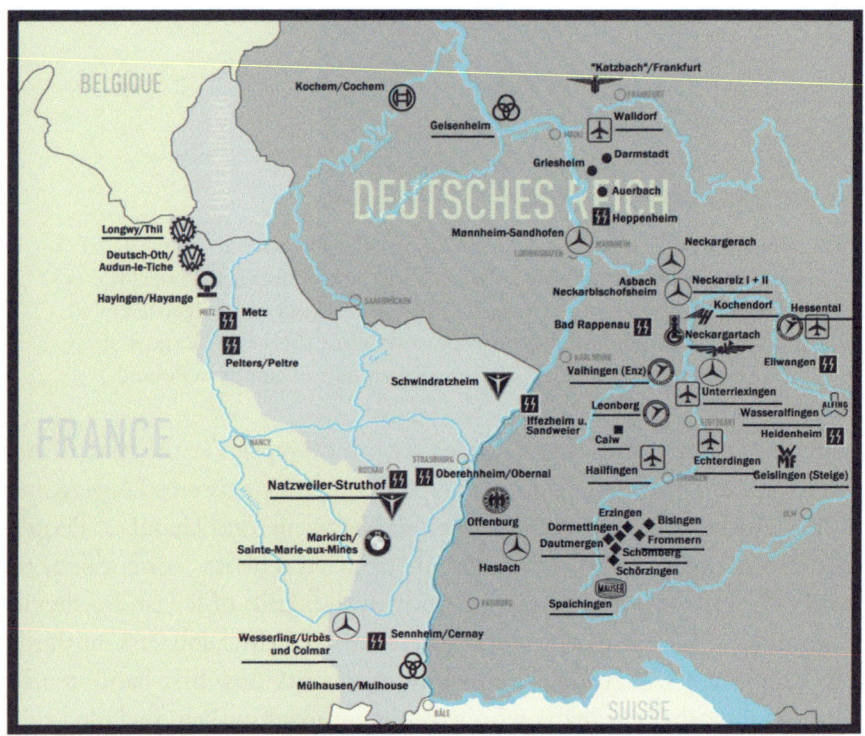

Map of some of the slave labor subcamps of Natzweiler, with the logos of the industries that hired out slaves from the concentration camp. Jewish prisoners slaved at camps underlined by the author. Map courtesy of Arno Huth and KZ-Gedenkstätte Neckarelz, and of the Centre Européen du Résistant Déporté and Robaglia Design

All the major concentration camps had slave labor *Kommandos*. Allach was one where André spent time after he got to Dachau. He states that he never worked for the arms manufacturing (BMW) there and eschewed seeking slave labor reparations after the war.

André, who wore the red badge of political prisoners, explains how he was made *Kapo* for a *Kommando* when their *Kapo* was disciplined and there was no other to be found. Very few prisoners have spoken of being given this role. He says he did not have privileged sleeping arrangements and 'never wore the boots.'

His comrades who knew him in camp only ever call him 'interpreter.' In their book, *1943-1945: La Résistance en Enfer* [Resistance in Hell] three of his fellow prisoners devote a chapter to him ('One of ours is an interpreter!') and offer other sketches throughout the book of his efforts to alleviate their suffering and take abuse in their stead. They also give evidence that, in addition to taking on physical punishment for others, he was not exempt from hard labor despite his role as interpreter.

> 'One of ours is an interpreter!'
>
> *Our jailers, who left nothing to chance when it came to organization, designated an interpreter. André Peulevey saw this task attributed to him. His wasn't a choice part. He was constantly being yelled at by the SS and by the head of the barrack, without ever receiving the slightest reward. Luckily for us, Peulevey showed no zeal in his official function, and never used it in any way against us. On the contrary, each time he could, he spoke German for a little bit longer with the SS or the barrack head, which distracted them for a time from the blows they were handing out. François Faure would say: 'That was a little breather we could appreciate.' (Footnote) André Peulevey was in reality a German Jew. He had been able to conceal his true name: Scheinemann [sic] (p. 88)*
>
> ...
>
> *Our interpreter, André Peulevey, had his hands full ... and 'Big Jak' kept his truncheon within reach to use unsparingly. Jakob Schroeder (Kapo of Barrack 13) a 'green triangle' [criminal prisoner] was experienced. He had held positions of responsibility for a long time, and the SS trusted him. He is known more by the nickname 'Jak' or 'Big Jak.' But, from the first night on, we called him 'The Tamer.' (p. 154)*
>
> ...

> *One day, the SS [in charge of the work detail] came up with an idea to change the routine. He recruited his 'thugs' and began a* furia *[tantrum/rage], quickening the pace of our work under their blows. André Peulevey, who was charged with setting the chocks under the wagon, didn't adjust the wooden shim correctly, and, inevitably, it plunged into the ravine, dragging with it two or three of our comrades. There were two SS guards at bottom, to 'clean things up' in case of an 'escape attempt.' (p. 159)*
>
> ...
>
> *André Peulevey, our interpreter, always got himself into big trouble. He was a good soul, who could always be found running to get anyone who might be late to roll-call to hurry up. Very often, he was the one who got the SS or 'The Tamer's' boot in the behind. (p. 204)* [29]

André's position as interpreter gave him undoubted advantages, which he describes time and again. He did not allow these to include food – which would have been the best of them. His leadership and mediating role did provide options. Asserting moral and ethical choices involved in his everyday kept him going. Much of his narrative invokes resistance as fighting for the army of his choice, living personal and traditional values in the face of danger.

André's situation as a circumcised Jew, like that of other 'secret Jews' who ended up at Natzweiler and other camps because of their resistance activities, was particularly challenging because prisoners were compelled to frequent strips, and nudity revealed their surgical interventions. André handled this dangerous passage with his customary bravado: he simply 'reminded' the SS: 'The best families in France circumcise their children.'

This was in fact borne out by the experience of another secret Jew, Gilbert May, who thought his last hour had come when his group of new arrivals was made to strip. Lo and behold, he found himself next to Prince Xavier of Bourbon-Parme, heir to the French throne, and Monsignor Piguet, the archbishop of Clermont-Ferrand – neither of them Jewish, both circumcised. May asked their permission to squeeze between them and was never questioned as they went down the line for questioning by the SS, who were far more interested in the v.i.p.'s.[30] Dr. Henri Rosencher, André's friend in the camps, told the Nazis he had been operated on following an infection, which was a more frequently-used cover story.

One of the unique aspects of André's story is its abundant documentation in the National Archives of both France and England, shared here. Most agent stories only rely on either one country's or the other's, or memoir alone. André's story is documented by all three as well as by the many references in other agents and resistors' files and memoirs.

A fourth archival source would document his work as well, but the SIS records are permanently sealed.[31] Although SIS censored the Special Operations Executive/SOE documents before they were made public, substantial glimpses of André, only slightly redacted but recognizable, have come to light with the opening of the SOE archives. The SOE was started by Churchill in 1940 to 'set Europe ablaze' and wound up in 1945.[32] It comprised Overcloud, the network headed by Joël and Yves Le Tac, with whom André traveled to England in January, 1942. The Overcloud documents are in the British National Archives because, although the Le Tac brothers operated for the Free French (Bureau Central de Renseignments et d'Action/BCRA) they depended on the SOE and the SIS for transport to cross the English Channel, and for radio messaging and other logistics as well. We share evidence that the SIS considered Yves, like André, to have been their agent since the beginning of the occupation.

André's short and dramatic sortie across the English Channel in January, 1942 is told in several places beside the archives. An eyewitness account is given in *Secret Flotillas*, by Sir Brooks Richards, a Royal Navy Volunteer Reserve/RNVR officer on board the vessel, the MGB 314, that brought André to England from Brittany and back. He also describes André's capture after the February 1 return of what was to be the last Overcloud mission.[33]

This promising trip that held so much hope for its participants and planners, and so much tragedy when these hopes were dashed, is told in planning memos of the Special Operations Executive/SOE, where the liaison and organiser for the various services – BCRA, SOE, and SIS – shows up to be (later Sir) Eric Piquet-Wicks, head of the SOE/RF section at the time. Piquet-Wicks later drew an insightful portrait of 'the little people of France – men who, if captured and executed, would die without a trace, yet France could only exist through their efforts.'[34]

A very humorously peevish account in the archives tells in detail how the night of the return to France played out: who had dinner with whom, how the Le Tacs had done too much shopping and ditched their accompanying officer, and how Thomas Greene, a top honcho of SIS who was André's handler, stayed with him until the last possible moment – all from the report to de Gaulle's high command of the B.C.R.A., the French Secret Services.[35] This book's 'From the Archives' section shares this culmination of a day-by-day of those fraught three weeks in England from the official British and French secret services.

Always respectful, André wrote: 'I was taken in hand by the head of the IS FRENCH section of the I.S. COMMANDER DUNDERDALE AN EXTRAORDINARY MAN.[36] My SUPERIOR was Mr. Thomas Green who minded me when I was in ENGLAND'.[37] Hence his alias *Le Neveu*/the Nephew, of Uncle Tom. Wilfred Dunderdale was head of SIS section for France throughout the war.[38] The powerful people André met with in London had the political and military clout, status and means to help accomplish his objectives. In his Legion of Honor and Army Corps awards, he is never mentioned as an associate or aid to anyone. André was accustomed to being his own boss in the Resistance, despite his nominal hierarchical attachment to the man he worked for both in the Networks and at the French National Railroads/SNCF in Rennes. As the founder, leader or aggregator of the networks he was bringing to the table, André chose the British as much as they chose him.

André criticizes himself acutely for going back into the snakepit of his office at the SNCF, that was under control of the Gestapo, after his return from England, despite being warned that all his coworkers in the networks there had been arrested. Perhaps the time in England and the measure of support and status he enjoyed there gave him a 'high'; he identifies that false confidence as an error that had never previously affected his 15 months-long successful work in intelligence. He was looking forward to the 'important new missions' and 'new network' he had been entrusted to create with the 500,000 francs the Secret Intelligence Service gave him to start operations on his return from England on February 2, 1942.[39]

André had hidden the British bankroll for his missions with (Robert) Lucien Rauch of Rennes before he returned to work and was arrested.

Trésorerie Générale bank receipt for the deposit by Lucien Rauch of the funds André hid in his care during the war on May 25, 1945. The funds were returned to the British a month later by André.

John Edward Gentry wrote the receipt for the return of funds to the SIS on June 22, 1945. 'I CERTIFY having received from Mr. PAULEVEY, Andre Maurice, born 7.11.1915 at Gucourt (Pas-de-Calais) the sum of 500,000 (Five hundred thousand francs) that were entrusted to him on February 1, 1942 to accomplish a resistance mission in Occupied France. — J.E.Gentry, Commander, R.N.V.R. [Royal Navy Volunteer Reserves] O.C. [Officer Commanding] Anglo-French Communications Bureau [cover name for SIS] PARIS.' [40]

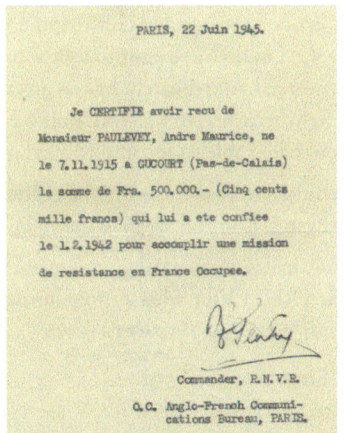 

Receipt from J.E.Gentry, R.N.V.R., for return of funds from André with embossed stamp at top left and at signature. Gentry's passport photo of 16 June 1940, Bordeaux, courtesy of Caroline Babois née Gentry.

On that same day, Thomas Greene gave André the letter of reference he needed for the French government's *Direction générale des études et recherches/D.G.E.R.* (Intelligence Agency) to establish his service with the Résistance. Beside its intrinsic value as a rare confirmation of SIS service, it might have been a life-saver in the chaotic and hyper-emotional atmosphere of post war France. Anyone whose behavior was circumspect during the war could be suspected of collaboration, although there is no indication that André was ever challenged on that account.[41]

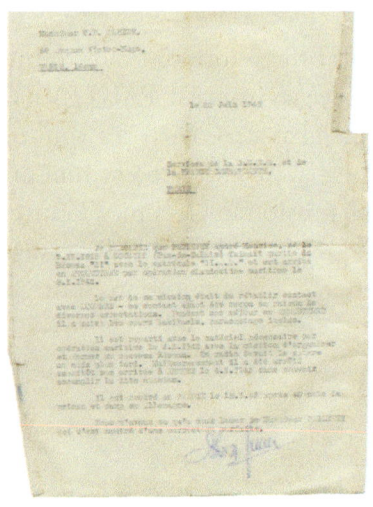

Mr. T.H.Greene
69 Ave. Victor-Hugo, PARIS 16
22 June 1945
Offices of the D.G.E.R. and of The Fighting French. PARIS.

I CERTIFY that PAULEVEY André Maurice, born 7/11/1915 at GUCOURT (Pas-de-Calais) was part of Network "31" with the ID "31.A.Q." and that he arrived in ENGLAND by clandestine maritime operation on 8.1.1942.

The goal of his mission was to reestablish contact with LONDON – that contact having been broken because of various arrests. During his stay in ENGLAND he followed the usual courses, including parachuting.

He left with the necessary equipment by maritime operation on 2/21942 with the mission of organizing and constituting a new Network. I radio was meant to follow him a month later. Unfortunately, he was arrested as soon as he returned to RENNES on 4.2.1942 without being able to accomplish said mission.

He returned to France on 18.5.1945 after 40 months in prison and camp in Germany.

We only had reason to congratulate ourselves for Mr. PAULEVEY who showed himself to be perfectly behaved. *Thomas Greene*

Thomas H. Greene 22 June 1945 letter of recommendation for André and transcript of it.

Both Greene and Dunderdale appear in André's little black book of addresses for his operations after the war both in France and for his trip back to England in December of 1945. The purpose of André's trip back to London, as well as to US Army Intelligence operations in Southern France and for a French Enemy Crimes Commission after the war remain a mystery. After reading his story, one can imagine what might have been.

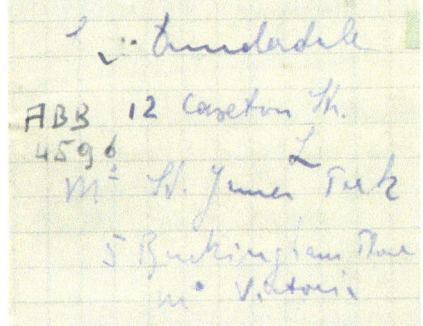 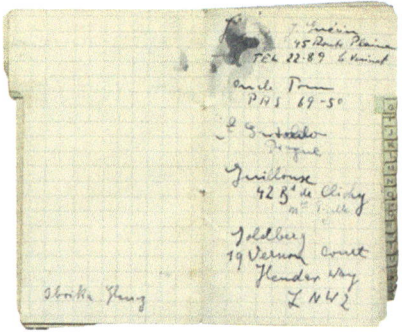

From André's post-war (conjectural date) little black book. Left: Commander Wilfred 'Biffy' Dunderdale's telephone number and addresses at Caxton St. and Buckingham Pl. with the 'tube' (métro) stations closest to them. According to Nigel West, '12 Caxton Street was an SIS locale which accommodated Dunderdale's Polish cryptographers. There were several such offices in the area around Victoria, such as Buckingham Place, and they were used as an expedient to avoid visitors coming to the headquarters at Broadway.' Right: His handler 'Oncle Tom' [Greene] and his Paris phone number on the 'G' page of address book.

'Cher Camarade' (Part Two) raises questions and documents answers to what André didn't tell, including how he managed to get exactly what he wanted from his trip to England in meetings at the highest levels of the Secret Services of France and Great Britain, in neither of which he held citizenship … and identify some of those who betrayed his networks as well as his agents and comrades.

From his private papers and those in the French National Archives we can now see how his skills served him when he came back from the concentration camps. He immediately had to navigate the structures and dictates of the government that de Gaulle had put in place in Paris almost a year before André was liberated. Being *Liquidateur de Réseau* (registrar for the Overcloud network) was not as humdrum as it sounds – André had to use as much wit, understanding, flexibility and savvy in the poleshift of politics in post-war France. as he had in managing his war, the resistance, and politics in London.

De Gaulle, whose world view magnified the role of uniformed forces compared to that of the underground, finally established, from England in July, 1942, the criteria for recognition of the Resistance within France under the rubric of Forces Françaises Combattantes.[42],[43] That Decree 366 is referenced in one of the first stages of André's being officially registered as a Resistor, his 'Attestation' of August 29, 1945.[44]

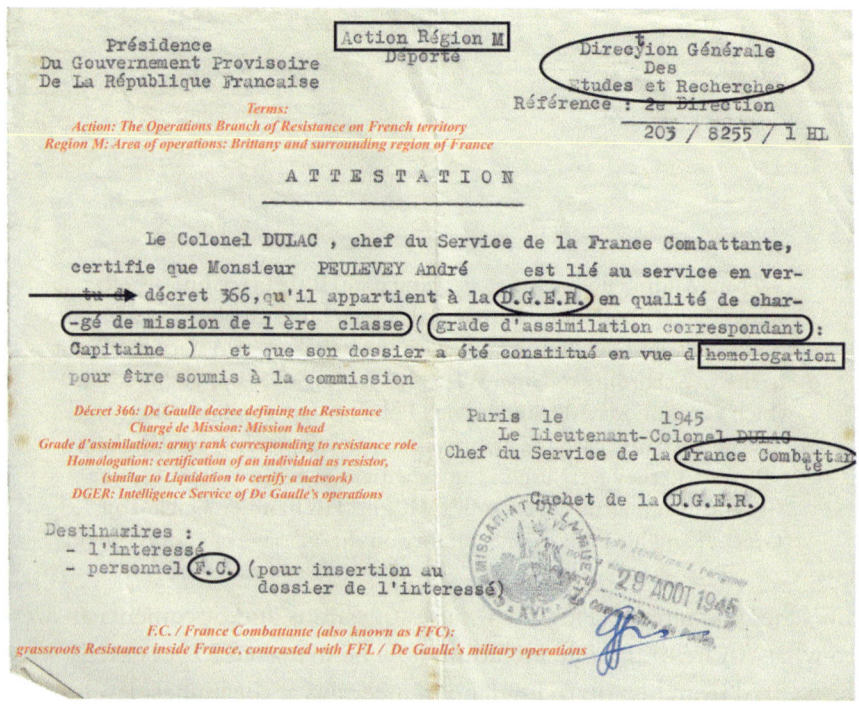

August 28, 1945: Confirmation with the seal of the D.G. E.R. (De Gaulle's Secret Services) that André's dossier has been put together for admission to the ranks of F.C. (FFC /Forces Françaises Combattantes) as 'Chargé de Mission 1ère classe' in the Resistance, by virtue of which he attained the rank (*grade d'assimilation*) of Captain.

Amazingly, eighty years after they played their parts, there is still much to discover of his service and that of his comrades. 'These redacted lives need to be viewed in the context of Free France toward the British Secret Service. A voluminous dossier in the archives of the SOE in London, titled "Persecution of Agents and sympathisers by their political enemies and measures taken for their protection" indicates that, already during the conflict, the English authorities were anticipating problems as to how their agents would be recognized and treated.'[45]

To some extent, SIS agents and networks were less vulnerable to these suspicions than those of the SOE, because 'in 1942, SIS's closest links with France were with the pre-war Intelligence Service, many of whose members were serving Vichy.'[46] This was nevertheless a dubious credential in Gaullist France after D-Day. Such was the snarl of rivalries between all the services both during and after the war that André had to cut through in the phases of his war, from 1939 to 1950...

Having returned to service after the war, André eventually signed himself out of the French Army with his commanding officer's stamp, as a preemptive measure to avoid assignment to Vietnam. A higher-up in the French Armed Forces, meeting him a bit later, was puzzled, and asked him about his departure. André shared that the procedure had been 'non-conforming'. We have in his archive a carbon copy of his July 12, 1949 answer about 'regularising my situation' to Monsieur le Géneral Vangenhuchten's letter of March 28. Thus was André's last known act of derring-do given official *imprimatur*.[47] He continued to serve as Lt. Colonel in the French Army Reserves for years after he came to the U.S.

André loved to tell how, when he first had a chance to meet his future wife Claire at his aunt and uncle's house after the war, he had so much trouble attracting her attention that he deliberately spilled a cup of tea in her lap. As he was making a thousand excuses and offering to pay for her to have her suit cleaned, she asked him: 'What do you want of me?' André answered, 'I want to marry you!'

Tim Austin's summary of Claire's career highlights her work as a Royal Air Force linguist assigned to listen to radio signals transmitted in all seven languages that she spoke. Her reports were sent for decoding to SIS operations at Bletchley Park, and now, thanks to Tim's outreach and research, she is included on the Roll of Honour there.[48]

As an operative in the British 'spoofing and jamming' Operation Corona, she was tasked with impersonating Luftwaffe (German Air Force) operators to confuse German pilots as they conducted their air fights with the RAF. This took nerves of steel. Her strength and courage must have made her a marvelous partner in marriage, as André's devotion bears out.

André and Claire come to the US on the S.S. Washington, December 1946.

Brought up in an observant home mostly for the sake of his visiting grandparents, André continued to attend synagogue occasionally and was extremely proud of his grandchildren's Jewish knowledge and fervor. André and his wife Claire meet the traditional benchmark for who may be called a Jew – one who has Jewish grandchildren. The two were married twice: in 1946 on their first visit to the US, when André's name was still Peulevey, and later in Paris with his name Scheinmann.

André's sister Mady shared his loyalty to family, passion for tennis, and generosity in friendship. 'Life before the war was just wonderful We had a wonderful childhood. We always got along well. He was just a terrific brother. Maybe because we shared so many common interests. We liked doing the same things. We were very much involved in all kinds of sports. Instead of going to movies we enjoyed going to theatre; we had season tickets to operas and concerts and did things together … He was very patient. In fact I remember while we were still kids he had the patience to teach me to play chess. If I think back now I don't think there are too many brothers would bother with their kid sisters to such an extent. I always appreciated that.'⁴⁹ The photographs she saved of her brother and their family during the years of darkness help recreate in these memoirs the world that is no more.

André's parents Max and Regina, Regina's sister-in law Madeleine (Mrs. Kuba) Thorn and André in Paris.

PART ONE:
I Am André

by André Joseph Scheinmann

Chapter I
My Story Begins

January 1933

Die Fahne hoch ... Horst Wessel Lied (Banners up ... Horst Wessel song).[50] I was tired of hearing the Nazi assault sections, the SA and SS, singing this song day and night while parading in the streets. It was written by a pimp who had joined the Nazi (National Socialist) movement in its early days and was later killed during a street brawl and made into a martyr by Hitler. I closed the window of my parents' apartment in Düsseldorf to shut out its words.

With a foreboding feeling about the Nazis taking over Germany, I was asking myself what changes this would provoke in my life and that of my family. My sister Mady and I had been brought up in the modern way: we played sports, attended public schools, and had mostly non-Jewish friends. At the same time, we observed tradition at home and my mother kept a kosher kitchen. She assisted my father not only in caring for our little family but also in his business.

Regina with Mady and Joseph.   Joseph as a small boy, with sled.

I was born Joseph Scheinmann on January 28, 1915, in – supreme irony – Munich, 'capital of the Nazi movement.' Brought up as a Jew, I felt myself to be very much a German national. I belonged to a German gymnastic club, and, to prove that a Jew could be just as good as any non-Jew, never hesitated to get into a fistfight if called names. I made myself respected by the other students.

I never knew my mother Regina Thorn's parents; they had died long before. She was born in Lvov. Her family had a strongly nationalistic Polish identity; her brothers had served in the Austrian army as officers, and when Poland became an independent state, they served in the new Polish army. One of them, named Uzek (Joseph) served on General Pilsudski's staff and reached the rank of colonel, which was otherwise unheard of for a Jew. Her brothers were all university-educated and very assimilated.

My father Max, born in Galicia, was a well-to-do merchant who owned a small chain of shoe stores, which he closed on the Jewish holidays. My father's father had come to America on a sailing ship in the 1880s. My grandmother did not want to go, because, she said, 'only thieves and hooligans go to America.' However, grandfather became an American citizen and was able to bring over four of his children.[51]

My father went to visit the USA in 1939, for my 21-year old sister Mady's wedding. War broke out and he caught the last boat back to Europe (a Dutch boat), back to my mother and his businesses.[52] Our parents were thus the only ones in my family who perished in the Holocaust.

Max, keeping a guard out, Regina proud and
Mady holding her uncle Kuba's hand.

Chapter II
Teen Leader

In the days and weeks which followed the arrival of Hitler to power, the atmosphere changed quite a lot at the school where I was a senior and my sister, three years younger, was in a lower grade. Some of the teachers became sarcastic with me; others – a minority – seemed to want to give me moral support. The students in my class started shunning me during recess. They always had things to do or someone to be with so that they could avoid talking to me or being seen with me.

Only one student never wavered from being my friend: Ewald Schmidt. His father was the director of an important paper, *Der Mittag*. Ewald did not join any of the Nazi organizations or take part in any of their activities. He kept in contact with me after our family emigrated and stopped writing only after his father was threatened by the Nazi authorities. He was a man of moral integrity; what he saw happening in Germany caused him much suffering.

André and Ewald playing chess

Ewald was made to pay for his convictions by being drafted into the German Army where he was constantly put into the most exposed and dangerous positions and was forced to meet his death on the Russian front. Despite terrific Russian artillery fire preparing a final assault on his position, he was forced to hold an artillery bunker and not allowed to fall back, and he was killed.

In 1933, things got worse very fast. Hitler had won the elections by a landslide, thanks to the votes of the small parties representing the right wing and some nationalistic splinter groups. Old and senile *Feldmarschall* von Hindenburg had named Hitler to be the new Chancellor of the German *Reich*. Hitler took over, passed laws dissolving all other political parties except his National Socialists. He declared the Communist and Socialist Parties to be illegal, incarcerated their leaders and many of their followers, and promulgated the Nuremberg laws that made second-class citizens of the Jews.

I had been involved in the Scout movement since I was six years old. I was an ardent camper, and enjoyed the company of non-Jewish scouts for war-games, singing competitions and other scout activities. The moment Hitler took over, things changed: hostility became the attitude of the day. I could have no more contact with other scouts. I realized that Jewish youth would need a movement of their own. We'd have to try to protect ourselves.

School started again as soon as the Easter holiday was over. By tradition, this was the beginning of a new school year. To my great surprise, some students who had failed and been told they would have to repeat the year had now been promoted to the next grade. At the first school assembly, the mystery was quickly explained. The headmaster of the school read decrees issued by the Hitler government promoting students who had been active in bringing Hitler to power, despite failing grades, on the basis that these students had given their time to work for the Nazi movement and did not have time to study.

It became evident that, from then on, there would be different standards used to measure students' work. Scholastic success would no longer be based only on hard work, intelligence and knowledge. Belonging to the Nazi party and being active in it would be enough to get through school. Jewish students, who were in the top 10%, would have to work harder to get passing grades.

Jews were no longer allowed to belong to organizations that were not 100% Jewish. They suddenly were isolated, deprived of friends and surrounded by hostility. A physical defense force would be immediately wiped out by the tremendous numerical superiority of the Nazi youth movements.

Jewish students, I was determined, should not fail. They should not become an easy target for the teachers who suddenly showed their true feelings, demonstrating an exaggerated nationalism and mechanically blaming Germany's loss in World War I on the Jews. They needed someone to guide them in this new situation and to help those who were falling behind so that they would not drop out of school. To overcome the new scholastic hurdles and bolster morale, an organization would have to be created to help and advise Jewish students attending all the city's high schools.

Düsseldorf had a strong Jewish sports club, featuring athletics, gymnastics, swimming, tennis, soccer, etc. This club saw its membership double as the Jews were excluded from other clubs and had no other choice. Despite my youth, I was running the children's gymnastic section and had over 150 youngsters from 6 to 16 under my direction. This is what gave me the idea of organizing all Jewish Junior High and High School kids to face their new world. I wanted them to know each other and to be able to help whenever there was a need.

Dr. Sindler, president of the Maccabi sports club, a very prominent pediatrician. was enthusiastic. He immediately offered his backing, and promised the use of his office, its staff, and money if needed.[53]

There needed to be a girl to head the female student corps. I asked a young girl whom I had known for years – and had been in love with – although I had never dared to declare myself. Ruth's father was one of the most respected businessmen in town, and one of the most active in the Jewish community. They lived in a beautiful home.[54]

Ruth was beautiful, intelligent and courageous. She gave her accord without hesitation after listening to what I had to say, and embraced me. (This was the first and only kiss I received from her. I never had a chance or the occasion to tell her how I felt about her.) She agreed without hesitation to run the girls' section of the organization.

We decided to call a meeting of all Jewish students at the Jewish community center, and over 90% showed up. I gave a speech explaining what I had in mind, and Ruth followed with another short speech along the same lines.

We told them that they would be facing a hostile world when the new school year started, that they could expect to be insulted verbally and maybe attacked physically. Their teachers would grade their work very harshly, and try to fail them or humiliate them.

The best students would have to give remedial help to the ones who needed it, both by helping them prepare for their exams and by pushing them to participate in sports programs so they could compete. This was no small undertaking, because many of the Jewish students spent very little time on sports; they had religious instruction every day if they were Orthodox or at least three times a week if less religious, and this didn't leave time for much else.

We set up a telephone tree to alert each other on short notice. I drew up a list of every student's name, address and phone number, and if there was something important to be communicated, every student could call another and within a few hours directions could be given to all. The last one on the list would report back to Ruth or me so we knew everyone had been duly informed.

We put our program to a vote and our ideas were overwhelmingly accepted. Study groups were organized as planned, with the best students helping the failing ones to overcome their deficiencies and get good grades. Three days later we decided to have a drill to see if the information network was functioning, and from then on, every three days some kind of message would go out on our network.

Soon our system was put to its first test. The Nazis were organizing victory parades all over the country, and Göring and other dignitaries were coming to our town. By agreement with Ruth, I went to see our school's headmaster and explained why I thought the Jewish students should be exempt from the parades.

The headmaster agreed to submit our request to the head of all the high schools. Within 24 hours the answer came back – negative. Jewish students would have to participate or be dismissed from school if they refused.

Ruth and I agreed we couldn't impose a decision with such grave consequences without consulting the parents. We passed the information through the network, emphasizing that the two of us, no matter what the consequences, would not attend the parades.

The results we received, during the next five hours that evening, were very disappointing: sixty percent of the parents were opposed to their children not attending the parades. It was their opinion that the government had been elected democratically and that it was the legal government of Germany; that as Jews they should not provoke the new masters of the *Reich*, who had plenty of other problems to take care of. They felt that, as Germans, they had to attend.

I went to see my headmaster again. I told him that I would not attend and neither would the majority of Jewish students. I would also inform the foreign press of the situation. At that time, Nazi Germany still wanted it to appear that liberty reigned within its borders, which were not yet hermetically sealed.

The next few days were heavy with tension and – why not admit it – full of apprehension. When I called the headmaster's office once again, I was told that the parades were official events of the Nazi organization for all high schools and that if any of us did attend, we would be severely punished!

I passed the news along immediately, taking the opportunity to tell the parents that they had been wrong to be willing to submit to such an indignity, and that it always pays to stand up for one's rights.

Intolerable situations frequently cropped up at the high schools. Name calling, beatings, exclusion from extracurricular sports and games were the rule. The Jewish students found that it boosted their morale to know they were not alone. The study groups worked out well, and we organized small parties to replace the social life we had lost.

Students whose parents had come from the Eastern countries (Poland, Russia, the Balkans) were less hurt by the social restrictions because they had always remained outside the German way of life and had not made many friends with native-born German students.

However, the students whose parents considered themselves to be Germans were deeply hurt to know that they were pariahs all of a sudden. Their parents were unhappy to see that their 'very best friends' no longer called on them or invited them to their houses, and were unwilling to visit with them anywhere.

During World War I, many Jews had fought in the German or Austrian Army, had been officers and were decorated. I too had wanted so much to be part of the new nationalistic movement. My father had served in the Austrian Army and been wounded in World War I, and I had been active in the sports club and participated in their patriotic meetings. I, too, hoped Germany would take revenge for its loss in the war and that it would regain its lost territories and former colonies.

I was exposed to different ideas when I joined the new Jewish scout movement, after being turned away from the German scouts because I was Jewish. During weekly excursions and trips during school vacations, I came to a deeper awakening to Zionism and to my place in Jewish history.[55]

Around the romantic campfires, I joined the nostalgic singing and I felt in my element, in my own milieu, a sense of belonging to my own people. Sure, there were divisions between the Eastern Jews and the assimilated German Jews, but just the same, we were *entre nous* (among intimates).

Discussions touched on many subjects of Jewish life and history, including the heroes the Jewish people had produced, going back to the dark years of the Spanish Inquisition, where Jews chose to be tortured to death rather than abjure their faith, and to Masada, where the Zealots fought the Roman legions to the very last man, killing their families and themselves rather than surrender, when arms and food and water had run out.

Our young people's discussions started to focus on a future outside of Germany. We all started to take an interest in going to Palestine, then a British Mandate, which eventually, according to the Balfour Declaration, was slated to be a homeland for the Jews.

André (center) visiting cousins in Palestine in the 1930's.

It was difficult to convince some of the parents that they should allow their children to join the Zionist organizations and let them go to farms where they would be taught how to work the land to prepare them for emigrating to Palestine. But as the Jews became more and more involved in activities among themselves, the idea of a Jewish State started to take shape in their minds. They read Herzl and Pinchas; they came to know about and admire Jabotinsky, the founder of the Irgun, a guerilla underground organization in Palestine.

The news coming back from Palestine was not always encouraging. Life was hard. People who had never done physical work became farmers, working fourteen hours a day, many of them earning just enough to feed themselves. They were living in one small room, after having been used to living in a large house with maids and service. We know now that they made it through, and they survived.

But the British were giving out very few visas to Palestine. Many Jews tried to emigrate to other countries. But no one wanted the Jews, fearing competition from some or that some might have to be supported – and because of a latent anti-Semitism, which always existed, and always will.

Still, most Jews living in Germany did not believe they would have to give up everything and leave. In a material sense, life was still very good; business went on despite the boycott propaganda by the Nazis, who told the German people not to buy from Jewish merchants or do business with them. It looked like the Nazis, with the exception of the most fanatical ones, like Streicher and Himmler, were not as mean as they had been made out to be. The Jews in Germany let themselves be lulled into a false sense of security which was to cost them dearly, as it did all the Jews living in Europe.

I found it difficult to keep the youth group going. Participation in activities of the group and attendance at its meetings dropped off. Many of its members had made some accommodation with their former friends. They did not want to be labeled as opposed to the new Reich, hoping and believing that there would still be a role for them in the community at large.

Chapter III
A New Homeland

Although he had served in the Austrian Army and been wounded during World War I, my father did not believe that that his decorations for bravery in the previous war would protect him. Many of his co-religionists felt they were Germans of the Jewish faith and that the Jews would still have a good future in Germany after Hitler became Chancellor of the Third *Reich*. But my dad, who was originally from Poland, had known pogroms, and was right about the hatred the Eastern European population had for the Jews.

Hitler had organized a *Putsch* – a lawless attempt to take over Germany in 1923, but had been arrested for high treason and sent to serve his prison term in the ancient fortress of Landsberg in Bavaria. This is where he wrote his book, *Mein Kampf*, the Bible of the National Socialist Party. Although nobody took the book seriously, Hitler was to realize almost 100% of its goals.

My father had started to denounce Hitler in 1924, going from meeting to meeting of veterans' organizations to label him a menace to democracy and the free world. He had instinctively felt the danger Hitler represented for the Jews in particular and the German people in general.

I had sad proof of this two days after Hitler came to power: my father came back with a black eye after a visit to one of his stores. A member of the local SA stormtroop had come to the store and asked to be given a pair of boots. My father usually gave him gifts for small services rendered, and had just given him a pair of boots a few weeks before. When my father refused him the boots, he started beating him up, and when he finally left the store, he promised he would soon be back.

The very next day, I accompanied my father to the railway station. He had a little suitcase in hand. Father knew there was no time to be lost. In another few days, he would not be able to leave the country. He was on the list to be arrested by Hitler's secret police and put away with other enemies of the Third *Reich* because he had publicly spoken out against Hitler.[56]

Max and Regina to his left with their staff at store in Munich.

Father had discussed future plans for the business with his loyal manager and right hand man, Max Loewy. He charged me to be careful and to prepare the departure of the rest of our family as soon as he would send news.

He cautioned me not to be taken in by the false impression that the Jews would be allowed to lead a separate life, a sort of apartheid, and be able to co-exist as an entity without being persecuted or harmed. No! My father insisted our family was to leave Germany as soon as he had prepared for our coming to France, a country where political asylum was still granted without too much formality. By sheer luck, my mother was able to fill a container with some of our furniture and, through a true friend, ship the container to France after she knew where my father was.

Even if we had to leave with nothing, my father was prepared to leave our stores, our money, our furniture behind. It was to be the start of a new life. We were to fight this new Reich, which would soon be on the warpath against the rest of the world. Six years later, these prophetic words of his became a reality.

I had planned to stay in Germany even after my family left, but when our French visas arrived, in June 1933, I decided to leave. I called what would be the last of our youth group meetings, a farewell for its most loyal supporters.

Ruth had already left for England. There were only a few of our original group willing to keep up the network and prepare for a hard and dangerous struggle. Many members of the Jewish community had been arrested and jailed by the Gestapo. Some were killed – official statements claimed while they were trying to flee, although it was obvious that they were not, because the gun wounds were to the front of their bodies.

Others were put into concentration camps, from which some were released and allowed to emigrate if they managed to get visas for another country. Some paid their way out of jail, having found officials in the Nazi Party who were not immune to bribes.

Unnoticed, my family and I left for France. My father was satisfied with the start he had made during the six months he had been away – he had opened a modest men's clothing store in a small mining town called Bruay, in Northern France. I clearly remember the train ride to Lille, followed by an hour ride on the bus.[57]

We didn't feel happy. Everything looked so dreary. Coal dust was hanging in the air and covered everything. The town looked depressing, just like small mining towns the world over. But being reunited made us fast forget our sadness. My father was waiting for us at the bus stop in the center of town, which happened to be right across from the store my father owned. Above the store, which was at street level, there was a little apartment consisting of two bedrooms, a living room, a dining room and a bathroom. Behind the store, across a small yard, were the kitchen and another bathroom.

We accommodated ourselves as best we could. It was quite a change from our beautiful six-room modern apartment in Germany, but at least we were away from the Nazi terror and the humiliation the Nazis had brought upon the Jews. We found friendly faces and soon made new friends.

Opposite the store was a war memorial honoring victims of World War I and a large social hall and headquarters for the Mining Engineers' Association. It was in a commercial district with other stores and small cafés. Although Bruay had a railway station, most commercial traffic came in by the bus which stopped opposite our store.

Over my father's store was a large sign advertising the name of the store, *Au Soldeur Americain*, The American Bargain Center. The name was chosen to recall his father, who had sought his fortune in America, and also to attract customers looking for bargains with flair.

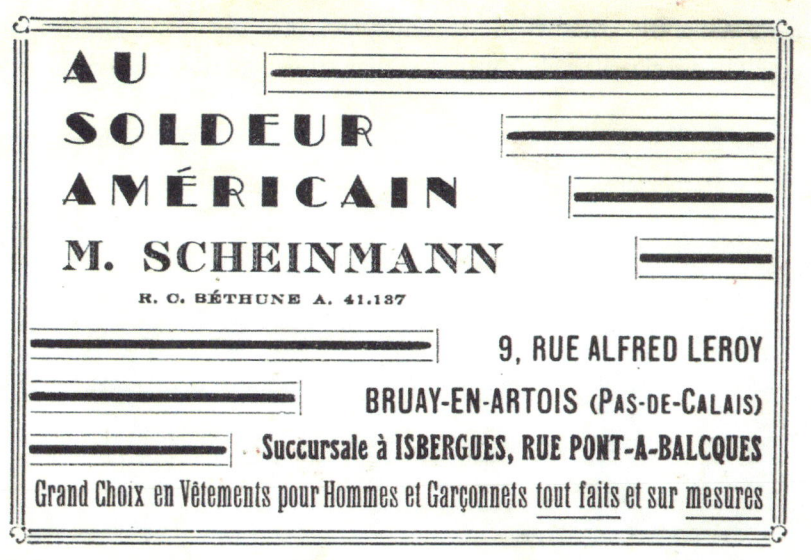

Scheinmann business card for the store in Bruay specializing in men's wear – the *succursale* is a branch store in another town. There was a Scheinmann store that specialized in racquet sports, and must have benefited from André's passion for those games.

Luckily, our exit visa had allowed us to ship out some of our furniture, paintings and other possessions, which arrived a few days after we did. Soon afterward, a little two-room apartment with a bathroom (still a rarity in those days) became available. My parents moved into that one, leaving me and my sister to occupy the apartment over the store.

One day, when I was in the store, a couple came in and asked me how I liked living in France and if I would be going back to Germany for a visit. If so, they asked me if I could deliver some documents to someone in Germany. They told me, frankly, that it was a dangerous assignment and that I would be shot if caught with the documents, which were inserted in a book. Without being given any further information, I delivered the book to an address I had to memorize.⁵⁸

I never again saw the couple who had asked me to make the delivery, but they gave the headmasters of two good high schools recommendations for me, which helped me continue my education in France.

Life continued peacefully. My father's store made good progress. The whole family helped build up the business. Eventually, I was sent to Paris on a buying trip, then made the manager of a second store my father opened in a town 30 miles away. The new store was an instant success.

André with his sister on his arm (third from right) at a tennis club dance.

I joined the Miners' Association Tennis Club and dated non-Jewish French girls. I found romance and acceptance wherever I went.⁵⁹

I read France's beautiful literature and believed that *La Belle France* would be a bulwark of defense against Nazi Germany. I was sure that if war came, the French would rise to the occasion as they did in 1914, and that France was strong enough to defeat Germany again.

Léon Blum, a Jew, had become Prime Minister; Jules Bloch, another Jew, Minister of the Interior. My heart was filled with gratitude to France. If it had not opened its borders to me and my family…

Chapter IV
War Approaches

The year 1936 saw the military reoccupation of the Rhineland, which was forbidden to Germany by the Treaty of Versailles as a result of their defeat in World War I. Had England and France intervened, the Hitler regime would have had to withdraw and probably would have fallen, because Hitler's forces were not yet ready to face the Allies. Hitler would have lost face and history would have been changed. But the Allies were scared and wanted to believe Hitler's reassurances that he did not want anything that did not belong to Germany originally.

The Treaty of Versailles had imposed an army limit of 100,000 Germans to serve for 12 years. This was a monumental mistake, as it allowed Germany to create a noncommissioned officer corps second-to-none. For years, German pilots trained in gliders and other motorless airplanes, since the construction of airplanes with military capabilities was prohibited. Germany had no tanks, but Hitler organized motorized units and conducted maneuvers with passenger cars and pickup trucks. In 1936, England and France allowed Germany to rebuild a naval force equal to theirs. The Germans clandestinely built the parts for far more warships and submarines, which were assembled in ports not controlled by the Allies. They built large torpedo speedboats, disguised as pleasure craft, which created havoc after the war started.

Germany was preparing a new kind of warfare, which later came to be known as *Blitzkrieg* – lightning war – based on massive air strikes, dive-bombing and tank attacks, followed by the infantry. The irony for the French was that a young French officer had tried to convince the French Army high command and the French government to create such a tank force; he had even written a book showing the advantages such a force would give to the French Army. The Germans also read the book, and they were the ones who took it seriously; the officer was none other than Charles de Gaulle, leader of the Free French and head of the French government after the War.

The next step was the *Anschluss*, the annexation of Austria, in March, 1938. In September, the Germans marched into the Sudetenland, despite formal alliance treaties that France and England had signed with Czechoslovakia, pledging they would come to its help in case of aggression by a foreign power. The Allies did nothing. After Munich, everyone was relieved.[60] War apparently had been avoided. This gave Hitler another year to build up his armed forces.

From our haven in France, we watched the situation for the Jews in Germany become more and more tragic. Arrests, beatings, internments and killings were daily events. Finally the Jews woke up and started to emigrate. The hunt for visas was not an easy one. Most countries did not accept Jewish immigrants. Little Holland, Columbia, Ecuador and Cuba sold some visas.

The constant call for violence in Germany culminated in the infamous *Kristallnacht*, in November 1938, during which synagogues were burned to the ground, the windows of many Jewish stores in Germany were smashed, and the stores looted and burned. Gravestones in Jewish cemeteries were overturned or besmeared, sullied and destroyed.

Each succeeding Socialist government of France did not believe in any danger. The warnings issued by the very talented journalists Henri de Kerillis and Geneviève Tabouis went unheeded. French xenophobia started to become manifest, but the existence of hate groups was taken to be a sign of democracy.

Even some of my friends questioned my loyalty to my host country, wondering what my father and I would do in case of a conflict with Germany. My father decided to show once and for all that he and his family really stood on the side of the French. He gave our German passports over to the French authorities and asked to be taken under the protection of France. We became *apatrides*, people without a country.

The day Germany marched into more of the Czech lands in March, 1939, my father and I went to volunteer for service in the French Army. My father, being too old and not in good health, was turned down for service. I was told I would be sent to Indochina for two years. This I did not want; I managed to be assigned to the Reserves instead. On August 28, 1939, I received my draft card. On September 2nd, France and England declared war after Germany ignored their ultimatum concerning Danzig and the Polish border.

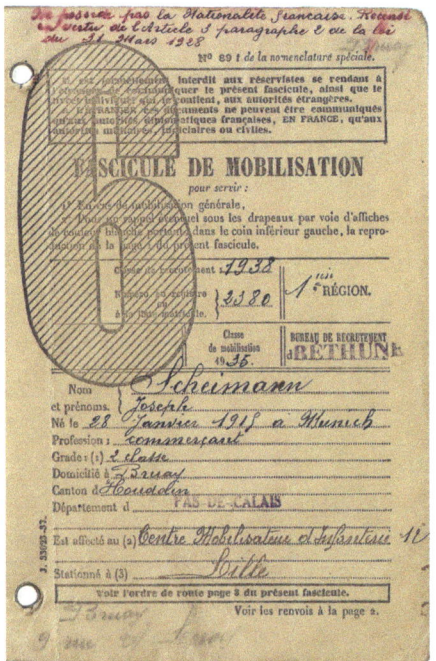

André's original French army registration booklet, 'Mobilisation Class of 1935, Recruitement Class of 1938' shows his true name, birth date and place and his parents' names. It shows he was called up for service at Béthune, assigned to the Infantry Mobilisation Centre at Lille.

In red ink at top is handwritten: 'Does not possess French nationality' and cites the relevant statute for that contingency.

Joseph Scheinmann Fascicule de Mobilisation/Draft card.

This war would not be as popular as the war of 1914. The German propaganda slogans (designed to discredit the mobilization) worked: 'Dying for Danzig', or 'for England', or 'for the Jews' was not something most Frenchmen wanted to do. The nation that had given the world Napoleon, Dugesclin, Surcouf, and many other brilliant warriors, no longer had the moral fiber to fight to the death if need be.

Across the Rhine, all 18 to 20-year-olds were seen parading with shovels on their shoulders but they were out exercising in military fashion and were organized like a real army. Germany had instituted two years of compulsory military service. Having unilaterally thrown off all the restrictions imposed on them by the victors of 1918, and having realized the Allies would not react in a military manner, the Germans now were ready to invade Poland.

The Germans faked border incidents. SS men, speaking Polish and in Polish uniforms, took over Gleiwitz, a small border town. To make it look more realistic, a group of political prisoners from the Dachau concentration camp, who looked like Poles, were put in Polish clothing and killed by poison injections before their bodies were left at the border, to 'prove' that Poland had invaded Germany.

Hitler had his pretext for invading Poland, which, like Czechoslovakia, had treaties with France and England, guaranteeing their assistance in case of foreign aggression. Just a short time before their invasion of Poland, Germany had outwitted the Allies and managed to sign a non-aggression pact with their arch-enemy, Russia. This treaty sealed Poland's fate: its eastern part would go to Russia and its western part to Germany. Poland, which had been divided twice already in its history and had regained its existence as a sovereign nation in 1918, once again disappeared from the map of Europe as a separate country.

Fascist Italy, which had been promised parts of France – Nice, Corsica and the North African colonies – stood by, thinking that Nazi Germany would be a fast winner in this war. Fascist Spain, ruled by Franco, was smarter than Italy, and stayed out of the war, despite the promises Hitler made to Franco.

In the meantime, the situation of the Jews remaining in Germany became desperate; very soon their fate would be shared by Jews in all the territories Germany had occupied or would occupy, from the Ural Mountains to the Atlantic Ocean and from Greece to Lithuania.

Chapter V
Fighting For France

I was incorporated into one of the 'élite' motorized infantry units. Twenty-five percent of my regiment was composed of draftees – untrained men – and 75% of reservists or men kept in the army beyond their legal time of service. The vehicles were an assortment of regular army trucks, armored carriers, and requisitioned private cars.

However, we were well armed. We were issued one light machine gun per every four men and one grenade thrower per group of twelve.

Inactivity did not improve the efficiency of our unit. Sure, every week we had to go on a 30-mile march with a full field pack, and once a month on a night march, and exercises were imposed. Only a few times did we go out to try our weapons. That was all. We did not even have a proper uniform. We were issued one khaki shirt, a khaki pullover, one pair of pants and one pair of shoes. We also received a greatcoat, a helmet and a gas mask, which, fortunately, we never had to use. Discipline was poor, and the *drôle de guerre* [strange kind of war, called the 'phoney war' in England, as the eight-month period between the declaration of war and the German spring offensive was called] was not used to train and prepare the French army for what was about to happen.

I thought I was 'pretty lucky' to be assigned at first as a driver for a provisioning officer. We were often billeted in private homes, and had no field or night exercises. Very shortly, I was put in charge of the company's officers' mess. When I took over buying their food and supervising the cook, I realized that this Polish man had been taking kick-backs on what he bought.

Not wanting to tell on the cook, and not wanting to be involved either, I resigned from this most sought-after assignment. This angered the company's commanding officer, who had me reassigned to an infantry group.

André, front row, right, with his French Army unit, possibly at the Camp de Sisonne. The eclectic uniforms and relaxed attitude in a time of war made him uneasy, but this photo is post-war, with André wearing his parachute wings, known as the "moustique."

Gone were the good life, the good food, and liberty, but I didn't mind. I made very good friends and was well liked by my commanding officer. There was only one problem: I had never learned how to manipulate a gun or present arms, so that during daily exercises my section was disciplined because I didn't know which way to turn or handle my gun.

I asked one of my new friends, a former officer candidate who had been demoted for insubordination, to give me lessons after hours on how to take a gun apart, how to march, and how to salute. This was how I learned about soldiering, and after a few lessons, I was fully part of my unit. I even wished that something would happen, because the inactivity became boring.

When my turn came up for home leave, I went home to see my parents. My father had made it back from the US, where my grandparents on his side had been living, along with all of his brothers. My sister, Mady, who accompanied our father, had stayed in the US and gotten married there.

My father, surprised by the declaration of war while in the US, had been able to make it back to France so that his wife would not be alone while I was in the army.

Soon after I got back to my unit from home leave, I developed internal bleeding and was sent to a nearby field hospital. While I was there, the Germans invaded Belgium, the start of their 1940 Spring offensive. I asked permission to leave the hospital, but was refused permission. I left anyway, without marching papers, to try to rejoin my unit.

The French armies were retreating on the whole front. There was no leadership and no will to fight. Most soldiers were just fleeing the advancing enemy and threw away their arms. The dive bombings demoralized the retreating armies. No air cover, no support from anywhere! Many French towns would be declared open towns to spare the civilians the bombings. The French government had fled Paris and was heading south.

Since the front had broken apart and no one in France knew where my unit, which had gone into Belgium, was located, I joined another group of soldiers who had also become separated from their unit. Very soon we found ourselves engaged in active combat.

During a bomb attack, I sought shelter under the overhang of a small hill and was buried when one of the bombs hit the hill. I was lucky: some of the other soldiers had seen me and dug me out. They put me on one of the last trains evacuating French soldiers back to France. Upon awaking, I found myself at the railroad station in Rennes, capital of the French province of Brittany.

I had a tremendous headache, but otherwise, I was all right. I asked the officer in charge if I could be returned to the front, wherever that was. Ironically, he refused to send me back, while others, who pretended to be seriously injured and did not want to rejoin their units, were sent back to fight.

I was sent to a hospital staffed by nuns. Located in a convent in Rennes, the hospital was run by a colonel who had volunteered for duty, despite having lost an arm in World War I.

After a few days, I was feeling pretty good. I asked the mother superior to intervene with the colonel, who was actually also her father, to send me back to the front. But first, they had me help with getting the mail and running errands for them in town, which broke the routine.

After a few days of this, the colonel agreed to hand me back my paybook and to sign official papers discharging me from the hospital to rejoin my unit, wherever it might be. I got my few belongings together and, the next morning, went to the railroad station.

It was crammed with trains full of refugees, soldiers, ammunition and other war material. I had hardly arrived at the station when an alert was sounded, announcing a German air raid.

Knowing from experience that the best place to survive a bombing attack was behind a wall or in a trench, I got out of the wagon I was in. I took cover behind the wall separating the railroad station from the town. A few minutes later, the bombs were falling, and by incredibly bad luck, one of the German bombers made a direct hit on an ammunition train carrying a load of dynamite.[61]

The result was terrifying. Entire wagons went into the air. Hundreds of wagons were blown apart. Six thousand civilians were to die that day, and thousands of casualties resulted from that hit. The munitions kept on exploding and added to the terror. The bombers were long gone but the explosions continued; people believed they were under fire from enemy troops. Seeing the wounded and the dead increased the panic which the survivors felt.[62]

I went back to the hospital I had just left and asked to see the colonel. I volunteered to help evacuate the dead and wounded. For this I needed a car, because all the ambulances were busy and there were not enough of them. The colonel signed an order allowing me to take possession of any car I would need wherever I found it and as much gas as I would need.

Starting at six in the morning, I worked 24 hours without sleep, picking up bodies of the dead and the wounded, trying to help the lost find their luggage and their families who had been put up in make-shift shelters.

On the third day, I decided I was no longer needed and drove toward the Loire River where the French army was supposed to be regrouping. Everywhere I encountered fleeing civilians and army units looking for their officers and wanting to know what to do. No one knew, of course, where my unit was. At the Loire River, I learned that all the bridges had been blown up and there was no way to cross. I decided to return to Rennes, to the hospital.

When I came to the outskirts of Rennes, I met a group of machine gunners who were fully equipped and willing to fight. I prevailed on the sergeant commanding the little troop to take up position on the main road leading into town. Hastily, trenches were dug and the machine guns put into position.

We had barely accomplished this when a delegation of the townspeople came and begged the sergeant to take up position further away from the town. That's when I realized that further resistance was useless, that morale was broken and the will to fight no longer existed.

I left the machine-gunners and went back to Rennes. The next day, the Germans took over the town and the hospital. A German officer presented himself and ordered the soldiers with light wounds, or who could be moved, to another hospital. When I arrived at the new hospital, which had been set up in one of the high schools of Rennes, I started to think seriously about escaping. I was afraid of being recognized and shot as a German-born Jew who had served in the French Army. I was also at risk of being recognized as a courier for the couple who had visited my father's shop a few years before and had asked me to take papers to Germany, which I had done.

I managed to get a letter to my parents through a soldier who lived near the town where I had lived. I told my parents that I was OK, and I gave them the address of the hospital. I asked them to send me civilian clothes with some money sewed into the lining of the jacket. They could give it to the driver of the trucks that the Germans were allowing to go from some of the occupied zones to other areas where the population was in need.

I was not sure the letter would reach my parents or that a package they would send would get to the hospital. But to my great surprise, hardly a week later I was called to the hospital office to receive a package. Everything had gone well – I had my civilian clothes and I found money inside the jacket lining.

At the hospital, I made friends among the medical personnel, who were all from the north of France and were inclined to help someone who came from the same area they did. I had only one thing in mind – to escape before being shipped to Germany, where all prisoners were to be transported. It would have been much more difficult to escape from inside

Germany than from inside France, where I could count on help from the civilian population.

It was July 1940, and things had been going rather well for Hitler's armies. Germany was convinced that the war would be over by Christmas that year. They started discharging prisoners of war from the hospitals. Every day prisoners were discharged, after a review of their medical records.

I asked my doctor friends if they could help me receive such a discharge. The Germans set one basic condition: the prisoner to be discharged had to have undergone an amputation or an operation of some kind. Of course, I wasn't going to have a hand or foot cut off, but my friends knew of my past history of intestinal bleeding, and suggested I have an operation for hemorrhoids. They said everybody had some, and that the staff included one of the most famous surgeons for internal medicine. So, in the name of liberty, I agreed to the operation. My friends prepared my file, and as soon as the operation was over, I was presented to the German officer in charge. I tendered him my medical form, which needed only his signature and the stamp of the German army, the eagle holding a swastika in his claws. To my horror, I was refused the discharge. Had I gone to all that trouble of being operated on, for nothing?

I started thinking. I had the form which needed only the signature and the stamp ... I had met, among the other hospital patients, a man who had served time in jail for forgery and who had been released when he had volunteered for service in the army.

I asked the man if he could forge the German's signature and the fellow assured me it would be no problem. But how to get the stamp with the eagle? My friend told me to get hold of someone who had just received a medical discharge, bring the discharge papers to him with a raw potato and he would then manage to reprint the eagle.

I went to the hospital kitchen and for a few francs negotiated a raw potato. Then I went to see a soldier who had received his discharge and asked him to let me borrow the papers for half an hour. My forger friend applied the still-wet stamp on the form to the inside of the raw potato, then applied the potato to the form, imitated the officer's signature, and my discharge was ready.

I prepared my affairs and went to the gate to see how the discharged prisoners were released. After a few days observation, I saw that the routine was for a German non-com to come to the gate and tell the guards how many prisoners were going to be released. These prisoners would then show their discharge papers and walk through the gate.

Three days went by, and then a large contingent was liberated. The guard that day was quite old and half asleep and did not count, so I got in the middle and walked out.

It was out of the question for me to go home. Everyone there knew me and the new identity I had been given in the army would be of no use.[63] I went to the home of a French non-com from Rennes, who, although he too was a prisoner of war, was an administrator in charge of the prisoners at the hospital and had been authorized to go home every day.

I changed my clothes there and then went to see a lady who had been part of the Red Cross organization visiting French prisoners, especially ones from other parts of France who weren't getting mail. I told her I had been discharged, showed her my papers and asked if she or any of her friends could rent me a room so I could stay in Rennes. She was a widow, she had a large apartment, and she readily agreed to rent me a room.

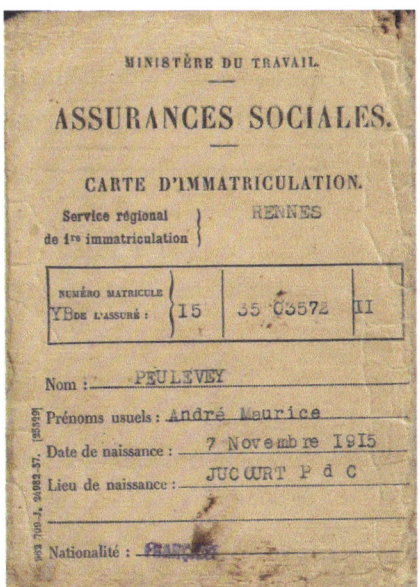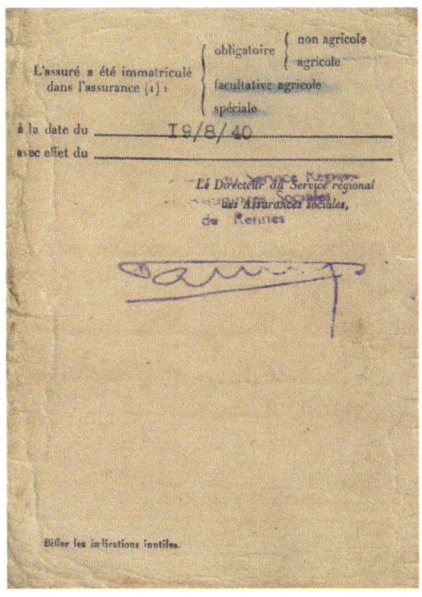

André's ID card for Social Security in Rennes, indicating
French nationality, left, and dated 19 August 1940,
after he escaped from prisoner of war hospital.

Chapter VI
Spy For The British

Having settled in Rennes, Brittany, I now had to find a job. I went to the town hall employment office and found that a few thousand former soldiers were all looking for jobs, too. But a few days later, the fellow in charge sent me a note and asked me to come in. I did, and the fellow asked me if, by chance, I knew German: the German occupying forces were looking for interpreters, and paying them tremendous salaries, extra food stamps, etc. I had no intention of working for them, and I turned it down.

But then came a request from the French National Railroads (Société Nationale des Chemins de Fer – SNCF) for someone who could serve as a German interpreter. They did not want naturalised Frenchmen, nor Poles, etc. But as I had been given a different name and identity in the French Army, I seemed to qualify.[64] After a brief exam at railroad headquarters and an interview with the head of the SNCF for Brittany, I got the job. It paid less than the Germans did, but that was fine with me.

I discovered that my new boss, Louis Turban, was married to an English woman. Turban had just been released from a prisoner-of-war camp because the Germans needed the French railroads, and orders had been given to release all SNCF personnel immediately after the surrender of France.

When we first met, Turban treated me correctly but was very cold. Apparently, he was afraid that his interpreter might have been planted by the Germans to keep them informed of what was going on. The Germans made some very harsh demands and were very arrogant. Mr. Turban could hardly keep his cool.

When the Germans left his office, Turban slammed his fist on his desk and said he would rather return to the prisoner-of-war camp than please the f.....g Germans in any way. Then he looked at me and said I could follow them and tell them, verbatim, what he thought of them and what he had said. I answered that I did not like them either, and that everything should be done to further French civilian interests and as little as possible to please the Germans.

The atmosphere changed immediately, and Turban became very open and friendly. He confided that he was married to an English woman – which I already knew. A few days later, I was invited to meet Mrs. Turban at dinner at their home, and we all got along very well.

Things were going to move very rapidly after that. A few days later, Turban called me into his office and asked me if I wanted to join the Free French.[65] Turban had been contacted by a former intelligence officer of the French army who had joined General de Gaulle's forces and had been sent to occupied France to organize an intelligence network. The networks that I was to work with were the 'Overcloud' and 'Jonny' networks.

The contact had come to Turban because the British had the membership lists of all Franco-British friendship organizations. One would only belong to them if one of the spouses was born British. They figured there was very little risk in contacting any member of these groups; at worst they would refuse to become active, but they certainly would not betray the contact to the Germans.

Turban was asked to organize a sabotage, escape and intelligence network – he was ideally placed at the SNCF.

I proposed to him that I would be the contact man and organizer of the network, that he was too valuable as head of the Railroads in Brittany, and could not be easily replaced if he were arrested. I was freer to move around, and Turban would cover me for any missions I would have to accomplish. If there was a slip-up, Turban would not be exposed.

Turban was in control of over 3,000 railroad employees. Brittany was one of the most important and sensitive areas in France, as far as the Germans were concerned. Along the Atlantic coast were several large naval stations formerly used by the French navy. For their submarines, the Germans were building up some of the ports as bases from which they attacked convoys trying to reach England. There was an important airbase in Rennes from which the German bombers left to bomb England.

I became the head of the military organization [*La Bête Noire*/The Black Beast] with Turban, my railroad boss, covering me when I was needed for clandestine work. I realized there was need to create an office that would take care of German needs, leaving Turban free to run his railroad without being bogged down in constant German demands, telephone calls, office visits etc.

I suggested that I be given an office with a secretary, a telephone and a title. I became 'SNCF delegate to the German occupying forces' and was to handle all of their demands. If something technical came up, of course, I would see my boss, but would otherwise be able to handle and organize things as I saw fit.

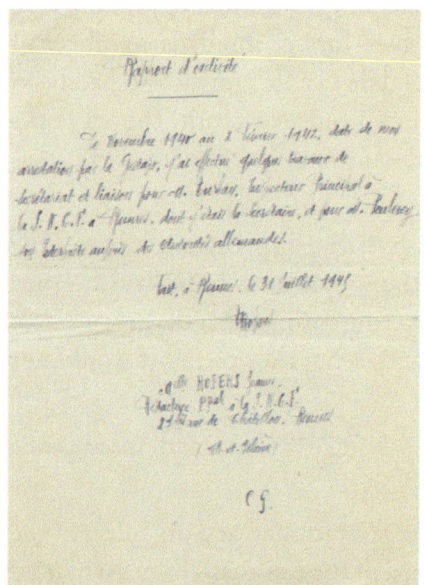

Report of Activity

From November 1940 to February 2, 1942, when I was arrested by the Gestapo, I did some secretarial and liaison work for Mr. Turban, Chief Inspector at the S.N.C.F. in Rennes, where I was his Secretary, and for Mr. Peulevey, his Interpreter with the German authorities.

Signed, in Rennes, July 31, 1945

Miss Ropers Jeanne

Chief Writer at the S.N.C.F.

24bis rue de Châtillon, Rennes

(Ile-et-Vilaine)

Statement by Jeanne Ropers in 1945 to explain her work in the Resistance as secretary for Turban and Peulevey.

I alerted the German services as to the creation of this liaison office, stressing that this would help to smooth out relations between the French and the occupiers, avoid any unpleasant situations, and guarantee the perfect execution of German needs and demands.

The Germans were delighted, of course, and from then on, every detail went through my office. If the Germans needed a compartment or a whole car or a train, it would go through me: at all times I knew what the Germans were up to, what materials they transported, what troop movements went on, where the units went and what armaments they had, etc. The Germans could not move a single soldier or civilian without the British knowing where that soldier was being sent, what he was supposed to do and when.

I also made it clear to the Germans that they would also have to cooperate with me, keeping me informed of any arrests or complaints they received about anyone who worked for the SNCF. I could often give the Germans a plausible explanation when an incident happened in which the Germans suspected sabotage and I could keep some of my people out of jail. I got along well with the German railroad officials, and became known by, and knew, the higher-ups running my area.

Turban informed the SNCF in Brittany that I was his personal representative and that they were to trust me. This made it possible for me to contact various station heads, inspectors, service department directors, and to recruit some of them to serve in the underground. I could use the telephone and the railroad dispatch system which connected me with every station, from the smallest to the largest. I had the use of Turban's personal car, and a generous gas allocation.

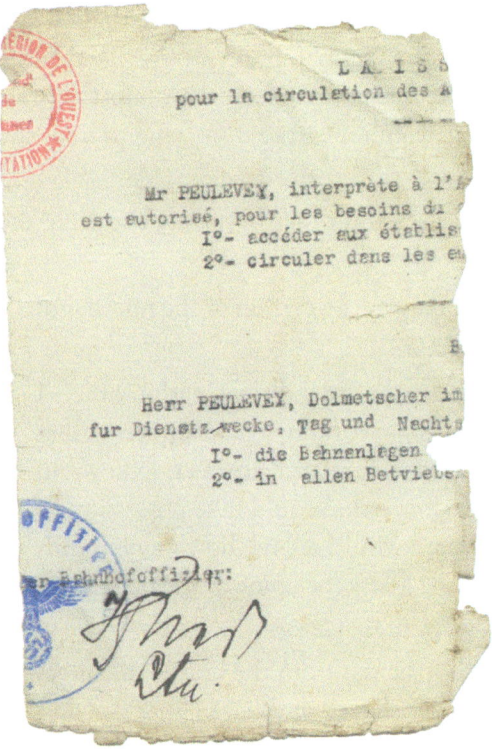

Half of André's *laissez-passer* – his interpreter/Dolmetscher pass -with stamps of the French Railroads and of the Third Reich, signed by its Bahnoffizier [railroad officer.] It authorizes him to enter buildings and move around, day and night, on the railway and all...

The author thinks he may have torn the pass in half when he was in England and met with Colonel Passy, (André Dewavrin) head of de Gaulle's Intelligence Service, who may have kept the other half to be matched as a proof of André's identity. Passy was a reference for André after the war and signed his travel orders to London in December 1945. Or the pass could just have been folded too many times when André hid it.

After a few weeks, I was officially second in command of the department for all of Brittany. The information the British received from me was invaluable. I told them what types of troops were moving – veterans, new recruits, specialists – and what type of armaments.

Next, I was able to place a cook at the German Air Force base at Rennes. The Germans had emptied all the civilian homes around the airport. When they needed a cook, they came to me. I found a fellow who had been released from a prisoner-of-war camp and needed work. He was of Polish origin and could speak German. I got him the job, which was extremely well paid and lucrative: he had access to a lot of food which he could give to his family or sell on the black market.

I put one condition on his getting the job. He was to stay up at night to check on the German bombers, from the hour they left until they returned from their raids over England. Knowing all the scheduled details of these bombers and their speeds, the British, after a few weeks, were able to figure out their flight patterns and knew exactly what to expect from the Rennes airport squadron.

The RAF nightfighters came out to meet them and the German losses became tremendous. The morale of the German pilots deteriorated badly and the Luftwaffe (German Air Force) tried to bolster their pilots' morale by sending in women to handle the telephones, radio, etc. and to be at the disposal of their pilots.

I had three ways to check the losses and other occurrences during the raids:

1. The cook, although he could not always be certain of the number of planes that did not return.
2. An informant at the hotel across from my railroad station office. I befriended a young woman who was working as a chambermaid at the hotel, and whenever a pilot failed to return after a raid, his room would be sealed until the provost marshal could take possession of all the pilot's belongings. The maid would tell me how many rooms had been sealed and very often she knew the name of the pilots, and their rank, as well.
3. The conversations at a barbershop across from the hotel. The pilots used to go there after a raid, to get shaved and have a massage and unwind. I went there every morning to have a shave and a massage,

and to listen to the pilots talking about what happened. I got a lot of details that way. One would say that he had had to get rid of his bombs over the water; another said he did not reach his assigned target because of the heavy and efficient anti-aircraft fire or because his plane had been hit.

But I got my best information straight from bomber headquarters in Germany. At the railroad station in Rennes, the telephone switchboard was used not only by the French SNCF people but by a few German railroad telephone operators who would process all the German calls. After a while, the German and French operators, mostly older people, became friends, and very often a German operator would ask a French colleague to take over for him while he was having a beer. The French operator knew how to connect to the various German command posts and I would have them call and connect me to bomber headquarters.

I would take a very domineering tone, and, giving a phony rank and name, ask for the results of the most recent raid. I would get the number of planes lost or hit, how many pilots had been shot down or wounded, and the evaluation of the raid. The German officers never suspected that the caller was not a Prussian officer, but an agent working for the British. Each week, this information was sent by courier to England. It was really very simple and it worked out just fine.[66]

I had also found out where the ammunition storage vaults were and how far underground they were. When the RAF (Royal Air Force) located these vaults on their maps, they could then direct their bombings accurately onto these targets and provide some nice fireworks.

In some parts of France resistance fighters would derail trains by tearing up some of the tracks or by putting sand in the wheel axles. But this type of sabotage would backfire, because the Gestapo would arrest people living or working in the area where a derailment took place, and shoot them.

Turban and I worked out another plan. When the Germans planned to enlarge existing ports, or construct submarine caches or new airfields on the coast of Brittany, we were notified at the French railroads about the need to get more personnel to handle the traffic.

Villages or towns with stations along the way served by one or two employees, and that used to see one or two trains coming through each day, would have to add another four to six employees each, to handle the

24 trains arriving full of construction materials and leaving again empty each day: this actually meant 48 trains to handle daily. The stations had to be staffed for three shifts to make sure the barriers closed and reopened. Railroad people were going to have to be brought in from other parts of France where they were not needed as urgently.

So when my boss received orders from Paris to get more personnel, he would start calling up railroad men from other regions that were seeing little activity. He would call the men and tell them to take ten days leave. (When the war had started, railroad people had been mobilized and had not been able to take any time off.) Then he gave them time to find a new place to live, which was very difficult and time-consuming, and required at least another week.

With typical German efficiency, in the meantime, building materials started rolling, as if we were able to handle it; and of course, after two weeks of rolling in day and night, every station garage and depot was packed with boxcars which could not be brought to their terminals and unloaded. Torpedoes and ammunition for the U-boots were stuck; containers with fuel for submarines were blocked. These gasoline tank cars remained in the open in the depots and became an easy target for the RAF.

Trains were blocked from the coast of Brittany – from Brest, Lorient or St. Malo – far down the line toward Hamburg and Berlin. Nothing moved, thousands of civilian workers were idle; they were being paid to do nothing, the German U-boats lacked torpedoes and their new construction projects fell behind or did not progress at all.

I prepared a report about this situation and went to see the head of the German surveillance office and complained about our inability to unload these freight trains. I held the German *Todt* organization responsible, talking about them sabotaging the war effort and I threatened the Germans by telling them I intended to send reports to Berlin. The Germans could not accuse the French of sabotage; we were accusing them of sabotaging our railroad work, and it was really comic to see us complaining about a lack of organization on the part of the Germans. Turban and I had many laughs when this happened, and the RAF did a good job destroying valuable transports.

The Germans developed new strategies and weapons to counter the British night bombings. They set up anti-aircraft positions on the tops of church towers and put Red Cross markings on buildings, which was against the rules of the Geneva Convention. Through my agents, the British would be informed of these phony Red Cross locations and they would be bombed out.

The Germans also had a new anti-aircraft gun, a double- and triple-barreled machine gun surmounted with a powerful searchlight. Once the attacking aircraft was caught in its searchlight, the machine gun would lock onto it as a target. The British pilots found a defense; as soon as the aircraft was caught in the searchlight, the pilot would fly into the beam and fire his own machine gun, destroying the German anti-aircraft gun and killing its gunners.

Days, weeks, months went by, and the French people became more and more unruly. More acts of sabotage were committed, more demonstrations against the occupiers took place. Reprisals also became harsher and harsher. But more and more German military and civilians were attacked and killed, despite the Germans' taking revenge by shooting hostages taken from among the French, usually well-born industrialists, former officers, political leaders, university professors, etc.

In order to protect their bombers, the Germans built dummy wooden aircraft and placed them around the field. As soon as I had the exact location of these decoy planes, maps would be sent to England. The RAF would send a plane over, and have it throw down paint brushes and paint cans.

I saw to it that this was known, and the Germans were made the laughingstock around town. This helped boost the morale of the population and brought more people to join the underground. It showed the French people that the Germans did not always come out on top, and made them prepare themselves for the day when the Allies would storm the French Coast and liberate the country.

What was at first individual, unorganized resistance quickly became well-organized and disciplined demonstrations. These started with attempts to ridicule the occupiers. Rennes was a large university town and the students were naturally inclined to demonstrate openly against the Germans.

Friday night was the night students would usually go to the movies: the price of the tickets was lower that night. Most people would come just for the two feature films, and in between, during the newsreels which were prepared by the Germans and showed their victories in Russia and in Africa, everybody would walk out for a lemonade or some fresh air.

So the Germans ordered that no one could leave the theater when the news was shown after the first feature film and before the main film. Spectators would hiss and boo and make all kinds of noises when the news came on. The Germans then ordered the lights remain on during the news so that their people could see who was demonstrating and then arrest them.

The following week, all the spectators came with a newspaper and when the lights went on for the news, one would see a sea of newspapers spreading all over. Then the Germans forbade newspaper reading in the movies.

What to do now? One could not leave the movie when the news came, one could not whistle or make other noises or gestures, so it was decided to applaud as loud as possible when the news showed big German victories, or the taking of prisoners or whatever. This caught the Germans by surprise, and they did not know what to do. People were applauding them; how could they not be proud and happy? At first the Germans were pleased, but when they realized that it was just another way of ridiculing them, applause was *VERBOTEN* (forbidden).

The Germans had the habit, when they went to a café or restaurant, of entering with the Hitler salute and then hanging up their belt with its sidearm in the cloakroom. To spoof them, the students took to carrying army belts with bicycle pumps attached, and they entered a café the same way, then did as the Germans did, they took off their belt with the bicycle pump and left it in the cloakroom. There was nothing the Germans could do about it. And so it went, on and on: each new restriction provoked a reaction and the Germans wit was no match for the Gallic wit.

Free French Radio called for demonstrations on Sunday morning.[67] This was the time when everybody would usually walk up and down the main street of Rennes. The students would meet their girlfriends there, or hope to meet one. Free French Radio asked the population to stay home on a given Sunday, so, on that particular Sunday, the streets were deserted – and the Germans naturally noticed it. The following Sunday, the Free French Radio asked the people to come out at a certain hour and walk in groups of three and four for an hour. That too would happen. Gradually, the French people realized that it was worth fighting; that the Germans were far from winning the war and that there would be no life worth living under German masters.

After an order came from Germany to release prisoners-of-war from custody if they were working for the railroad, I had a very funny adventure. I suggested to my boss that I visit some of the prisoner-of-war camps. I would show the camp administrator a copy of Hitler's order to release railroad people and ask the Germans for all railroad workers or employees.

In Rennes there was a camp with Senegalese prisoners and I found four prisoners there who, when the war started, had been working for the *SNCF*. The four black prisoners were overjoyed when I came to pick them up. First, I took them to a good restaurant to get them their first good meal in months, then I presented them to my boss in order to get them an assignment. It was agreed that they would be sent somewhere where they could stay together, so they would not be lonely.

Whenever they came to Rennes they would visit me, and we would march through town. It looked like I had bodyguards, and, as three of them were over six feet tall, it was impressive! If I had wanted to go to Senegal after the war was over, I could have run for any office and been elected. They could not thank me enough for liberating them, and getting them out of the misery of being German prisoners of war. The Germans had been treating them like animals, because they considered blacks to be lowlife creatures – *Untermenschen* (subhumans).

I had taken advantage of being in a university town and registered as a Master's student in German philosophy and literature as a cover for my excellent German. I also joined a class at the Beaux-Arts school in dramatic arts.

Among the other students, I met some very interesting, bright boys and girls. Everyone knew I was in a key position at the French railroad office, and students involved in the French underground soon approached me and asked me to give out vital information about the movements of the German military.

One of them was my girlfriend, a very beautiful Jewish girl deeply involved in the underground, and when she begged me, I told her: 'I am working for the *SNCF* and like all French Civil Service personnel, I had to swear an oath of allegiance to Marshal Pétain. I have only one head to lose and I don't want to engage in any unlawful activity.'

My girlfriend dropped me, and a lot of the other students no longer talked to me. Friends who listened to the Free French Radio for me were warned that I was a collaborator. All this, of course, was an extremely good cover.

The Germans never did suspect me, although I made it clear to the German railroad men that I did not enjoy being deprived of my liberties by the occupation, and I never accepted invitations to dinner or anywhere else with them. I kept my day-to-day relationship with them strictly business-like. I had to see that things went smoothly, but I didn't have to be in favor of a final German victory. No one, of course, had any idea that I was Jewish.

The French Army, when I first enlisted, had provided me with a fool-proof identity, and no one ever knew who I really was.[68] Even the British Secret Service never knew. I wonder, today, if they would have entrusted me with so much responsibility, if they had known I was Jewish. I could have even gone over to the other side. Seldom was such a real switch of identity so perfect. The fact that I was studying to be a professor of German at the university level made it credible that I spoke German so well.

Although it was a term not used at the time, I was doing simultaneous translation. When the Germans came to see my boss, I would translate while they talked, and when they had finished, each party knew exactly what had been said. I did the same when my boss answered in French.

And the head of the German office, the German department head of the railroad for Brittany, Turban's counterpart, liked me a lot also. And one fine day, he said to me: 'Listen, I have a big meeting coming and I would like you to be my interpreter.' But I said that – I was dying to go to that meeting – but I said to him, 'You know, you have to ask my boss – me I can not decide – I work for the railroads, I am a railroad employee.' Then he said: 'Good, I am going to ask him.'

So, obviously, my boss would let the Germans 'twist his arm' to let me go to help him during some meetings and inspections of crucially strategic construction sites such as new submarine caches, mine-sweeper bases or airfields, all of which needed the help of the French railroad to transport their materials and personnel. Turban said: 'Well, I need him, but nevertheless, for several weeks, I am willing to lend him to you!' And so, that went very well. No one thought that a German high-level official would bring a non-German interpreter along.[69]

I had a chance to inspect U-boat bases, mine-sweeper units, the port of Brest where the Germans kept their famous armored pocket battleships, the Scharnhorst and the Gneisenau and the famous Bismarck. I was aware of the progress of the refitting done on their ships, and I could pass on to England all pertinent information concerning the results of the night bombing the RAF made on the ships and defenses at the port of Brest in 1941.

The RAF bombed the 'grand hotel' of Brest using a percussion bomb, which exploded only after having gone through the roof and the different floors and gotten to the cellar. A few hundred high-ranking German naval officers and Army brass had all assembled there to celebrate the Führer's birthday. They were killed in that bombing. Göring was visiting too, but unfortunately, he arrived late and was only very slightly wounded. The information that made this possible had come to the English Secret Service from one of my trusted local agents.

The raid had very outstanding results, all in all, and made me and quite a few people happy.

At Christmas, 1941, the English made a drop. The container, for once, did not deliver explosives or weapons, but gifts for the members of the network: clothes for the women, chocolate for all, whiskey and cigarettes.

As time went by, I extended my activity beyond the railroad. My boss knew the head of the State Police and I got some State Troopers involved. At one drop, the Germans had heard the airplane and, suspecting a drop, sent out scout cars to see where the plane had gone. I had posted a State Trooper on a bridge which had to be crossed to pick up the container. The trooper stopped the Germans, telling them that the plane had missed its target and an unexploded bomb was lying in the field, very close to the road; he advised them to use a detour to avoid any danger. The Germans expressed their thanks, and turned back; the drop was received, and no one was caught.[70]

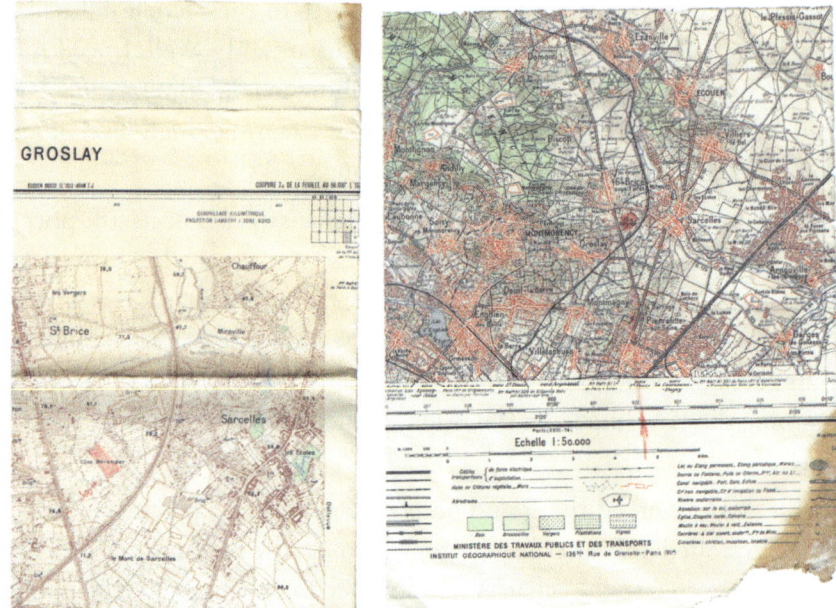

These maps of the Clos Béranger dropping zone from André's archive is not in Brittany but closer to Paris. Groslay shows a rectangular strip highlighted and marked by hand with a distance or dimension of 300 meters; smaller scale map of L'Lisle Adam, also in André's archive, with the same location highlighted by hand and with an arrow pointing to it also in red pencil, shows more traces in corner of an attempt to burn them.

At one point, I went on an unsuccessful mission to see if the Count Estienne d'Orves, Naval Ensign sent to France by de Gaulle, could be saved from execution.[71] I had been given the name of the Catholic priest who was allowed to see d'Orves, confess him and prepare him for his death.[72] If my memory is correct, the priest was attached either to the famous church of St. Sulpice (Manon Lescaut's church) or another large church in Montparnasse and took confession on certain days.

I went to find this priest at the confessional, told him I was an agent of the FFL (Free French) and trying to organize d'Orves' escape. The priest told me that the Count had been extremely well treated by the Germans, who respected his calm courage. A high-ranking German officer had authorized the Count to have more visitors, to get all the books he wanted, and food, and to write, if he would give his word as an officer and a gentleman that he would not try to escape. The Count swore to it and had accepted his fate – to die by German bullets. The priest told me that the Count would not cooperate in escaping as he had given his word.

Thus ended my first and only visit to a church confessional. I went back to my boss in Rennes to report what had happened. I was very disappointed because I had hoped to organize a coup, free the Count while he was on his way to his execution at Mont Valérien, near Paris, and fly him to England.

A few weeks later the famous posters on the walls of Paris announced that the Count had been shot, that he died with dignity, bravely shouting *Vive la France, Vive de Gaulle,* before falling under the German bullets. Another valiant, good officer gone!

One day, one of my contacts informed me of another resistance group, organized by a lady named Suzanne Wilborts, from the Isle de Bréhat. Mrs. Wilborts had organized a complete network which I was to take over and integrate into my own, giving her much-needed contact with England. This group soon spread all over Brittany.

Ledger established by Madame Louis for the French government of agents of the Georges-France/Group31 network state that Madame Wilborts 'was recruited by 31AQ' (André), that her agent code was 31.AQ/1. This page also lists her daughter Yvette, later known as Marie-José, who 'helped her parents in the network.'

Wilborts' oldest daughter was a nun who nursed French resistors in her surgical ward for men at Ploermal. Her second daughter took messages to

Nantes, which was a very 'hot' town, where incidents happened every day and hostages would be shot in reprisal every day. That daughter rejoined her husband, an escaped prisoner of war, in Marseilles and the couple got over to Africa, where he joined Le Clerc's army. The whole family was part of the network. Mr. Wilborts paid the price: he died in Buchenwald in 1944. Mrs. Wilborts lived to see her nine grandchildren, before she passed away in 1957.

[His youngest agent, Marie-Jo Chombart de Lauwe, wrote and spoke about André in films and published autobiographies and more intimately in her letter to him in 2000:]

> *'I used to roam the Channel coast to gather information. I brought Harry Pool to Bréhat from the farms where he was hiding with other Englishmen behind Tréguier.*
>
> *In the Spring of 1941, we received a visit from an envoy from London, who made the contact for us with Turban, the head of the network to which the small network directed by my mother, called "La bande à Sidonie," eventually became attached.*
>
> *We came to Rennes to meet him, and also discovered 'André' Peulevé [sic] – you – and Louis Le Deuf. Having passed my final high school baccalaureat exam, I was starting my studies in medical school.*
>
> *I used to fetch the documents and coastal maps assembled by my mother and bring them to Rennes. There, I passed them either to Louis Le Deuf (Place Saint Sauveur), or to you, at our appointed meeting places, the Café de l'Europe or at the Café de la Paix. I was eighteen. People also called you 'Le Neveu' (The Nephew). I also remember a dinner with Joël Le Tac, Andrée Conte, his wife, and Rina Louette. I met those two women again at Ravensbrück, along with their mother Yvonne Le Tac and Gaby Norman...*
>
> *I learned by your account the magnitude of your work as a secret agent of which I only knew a part. I congratulate you most heartily. Be assured of my esteem and of my very long-term friendship engaged during the year 1941-1942 in Rennes. Very cordially...'*[73]

> J'ai appris par votre récit l'ampleur de vos actions d'agent secret dont je ne connaissais q'une partie. Je vous en félicite vivement. Soyez assuré de mon estime et de ma très ancienne amitié nouée durant l'année 1941-1942, à Rennes. Très cordialement
>
> Antony, le 17 mai 2000
>
> Marie-José CHOMBART DE LAUWE
> (née WILBORTS)

The last paragraph of Marie-José Chombart de Lauwe's letter to André in 2000.

Both Marie-Jo and I remember a member of their network, Jean-Baptiste Legeay, a Christian brother who taught in a school in Nantes.[74] When the organization was infiltrated by a double agent, Jean was captured, and although he never talked, he was beheaded in Cologne with five other members of this network. The German barbarians did not hesitate to execute French patriots in this cruel manner, in order to frighten people and make these patriots' end more terrifying.[75]

What people would do something like this and call itself civilized? Cultured? We shudder when we read about beheadings in the Dark Ages, yet here in 1943, in the prison yards of Cologne and some other cities, like Berlin and Stuttgart, every day patriots were being beheaded! One of the members of this [Legeay] group who met that fate was the mother of 12 children, a simple farm woman. Her crime? She had given overnight shelter to an escaped POW. Nazi 'justice', Nazi 'culture'!

Although I realized that I would be very vulnerable if too many people knew about my activities, this was the first phase of the Resistance in France, when there was no way to specialize in one thing only. My network was used for intelligence gathering, sabotage and evasion, and the transport to England of pilots who had been shot down, volunteer French pilots, Navy personnel, radio operators and other specialists.

My group was responsible for getting one group of ten pilots out of Nantes. The British pilots were instructed not to open their mouths while they were being escorted through town to the railroad station. They were officially registered as deaf-mutes. The nurse, in uniform, was to escort them to a Red Cross van. The transportation had been arranged ahead of time: I had gotten traveling papers from the German Field Kommandant for these 'unfortunate persons' to be transported to a special hospital for deaf-mutes.

There came a point when I was cut off from England, because the courier, Madame Louis, who came every week had been caught, and with her, the whole Groupe 31 courier network.[76] This created the problem of how to get in contact with England again and keep the network going. There was no problem continuing the sabotage, for which we did not need contact with England. But how to pass on the intelligence gathered and brought in by over 150 agents?

I decided to look around and I soon noticed two young men who always ate at a restaurant not far from the railroad station. They always wore navy blue trench coats and, in their lapels, the insignia of radio operators for the former French Air Force. I observed them for a few days, and saw that they were contacted by young civilians who always seemed to be a little afraid of being seen: they always looked around carefully when they entered the Café and talked to one or the other of the young men in trench coats.

I asked them to make contact with England. Of course, the two men protested, and said I must be crazy to think that they would engage in such dangerous activities. They did admit to having been in the French Air Force, but said they had been demobilized in the unoccupied zone and had returned to their hometown. I said that of course I understood they could not trust me, but that all they had to do was radio my request to London for contact, materials, etc., and if the answer was positive they would know they had nothing to fear. I told them I would be back in touch in 48 hours.

Sure enough, the answer from London was to give me all the assistance I needed. The men asked how I had come to contact them. I told them they really should be more careful in order to avoid arrest: no more blue trench coats, and no more pins in their lapels indicating their activities and profession, and not to spend too much money too openly.

That was when Turban and I became involved with the Free French underground, headed by de Gaulle from London, and working in parallel and sometimes in competition with the British Secret Services.[77] Joël Le Tac was leader in Brittany [of the Overcloud network run by De Gaulle's BCRA with SOE/Special Operations Executive.[78]]

[Le Tac's biography describes how he came to contact André:]

'At that time, toward the end of 1941, I had innumerable contacts ... I understood that the figures allowed de Gaulle to assert himself with the English, who seemed to doubt the legitimacy of his claims ... (but) the orders given to me by those who were cozily ensconced in London – recruit, recruit and recruit some more – seemed to go against the interest of Mission Overcloud...'

As a precaution, he (Joël Le Tac) set a policy of meeting only the heads of the organizations working with him. That's how he got to know the 'boss' of the railroads at Rennes, André Peulevay (sic), the man in charge of FER 1.

'The third "DZ" (dropping zone) was named FER 1, simply because government railroad (Chemin de fer) agents were responsible for it. They were made available to me by André Peulevay (sic), my only contact from this network, who was put in place by the Intelligence Service. It was a very effective network centered in Rennes which provided invaluable information on train movements. This intense activity of course caught the attention of the British.'[79]

Turban had been contacted by a man who had just been parachuted in, and who knew of Turban from Mrs. Wilborts of Ile de Bréhat. Turban followed the procedure he and I had agreed on: Turban would deny any activity and would say that he could not help and did not want to, but that his personal interpreter would possibly be interested. Turban therefore told this visitor that he would set up a meeting with me, nothing more, and that he wanted no more contacts please, no visits, they should just ignore him.

1920s postcard shows the Rennes train station with the benches that André could see from his boss' window.

The meeting was set up on a bench in front of the railroad station. Turban called me into his office, where from the window we could see the bench and the person in question. I strolled down to meet this visitor. The man was Yves Le Tac and a little later his brother, Joël Le Tac, joined us.

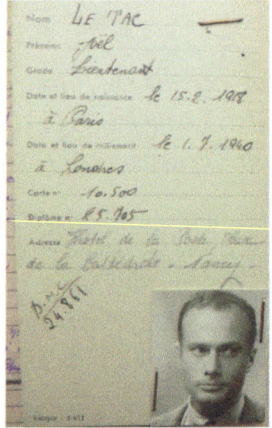

Post-war documents for Lieutenant Joël Le Tac, left, © Service historique de la Défense – 16 P 295515, courtesy Pierre De Jeagher, similar to the one for André, at right, where Capitaine Peulevey is id'd with the Overcloud network. Center, Yves Le Tac, from a photo taken about ten years before he met André, courtesy of his daughter Monique.

I was pretty sure these people were all right, and were really what they indicated they were, that is, Free French agents. I engaged the conversation and for about an hour talked about a lot of things but never anything serious. The two brothers started to wonder what I really stood for. They were just as cagey.

Finally Yves opened up and said that he had just come from London and had been entrusted with a mission by General de Gaulle himself: De Gaulle's special assignment for Yves Le Tac was to organize French students, to bring them the message that they must fight the enemy and tell them why they were fighting – in other words, to counter the German propaganda machine and the collaborationist press, all over France.[80]

[Yves, during the trip the three would make to London, on January 17, under the code name Granville, wrote a report about the Comité Rennais des Etudiants (Rennes Student Committee run by Max Eidem) and their clandestine paper 'La Bretagne Enchaînée' (Brittany in Chains.)[81]]

'This paper is now published twice a month, distribution limited mostly to the city of Rennes, but reaching some corners of [the 'département'/administrative area] Ile et Vilaine; it has a great influence among business people.

'This informant does not know its exact print run but can say it is undoubtedly more than 1,000. The Committee is headed by 4 leaders and has 200 to 300 young men and women recruited among the students, particularly of the Medical School, who write for the Committee.

'This informant is convinced that it will be among the young that real and effective actors can most easily be found. The young aspire to something new and something clean. Some of its members, although not at all influenced by communal ideas, joined the Communist Party because it is the only one with which they are in contact and because in any case, it gives them ideas for the future.

'The French are unarguably tired of the chaotic regimes that preceded the armistice. They acknowledge that it will be necessary to have a government capable of assuring its authority in the country. They are however, more and more enamored of individual freedom and suffering from the oppression they are now forced to endure.'[82]

Yves told me that his brother Joël, his mother and many others were running a sabotage organization; and that they had their own radio operator and other direct contacts, via Spain, with London. This is what I wanted to hear – to find a direct contact.

The thought came to me immediately: why not turn over all my saboteurs to Joël and, in exchange, get all his people who were gathering intelligence information? Joël could also take over the escape organization. That way, everything could be handled in an orderly way.

[More from Joël's biography about André:]

'At first, he had everything it could take to alarm me: he was the interpreter for the Germans of the Reichsbahn (German Rail system) and those in charge of railroad traffic in Rennes railroad station. He was a German Jew, blond with blue eyes, and he spoke

French with a melodious voice. He was known to the world as Peulevay [sic], but his name really was Schweiderman [sic]. He was a strange young man who surprised me by the carefree way he threw himself into the world of intelligence. After having met him in a bistro in Rennes, I invited him to come see me in Paris, Rue Gît-le-Coeur.'

Joël Le Tac was nursing uneasiness about André Peulevay. He wasn't quite able to get a handle on him, and wanted to find some relief for his anxiety. After meeting him at his home, Joël Le Tac put one of his former buddies from Mission Josephine B., chief-corporal Cabard who had just come back from the free zone, to shadow him.[83] Cabard followed through and dogged André Peulevay to the Gare Montparnasse, where he took the train for Rennes. *'I certainly was reassured. There was nothing that could create any suspicion whatsoever about Peulevay.'*

Furthermore, André Peulevay [sic] outdid himself. He asked Joël Le Tac if it would be possible to have his radio operator send a mass of information collected by his railroad network. 'In theory, the equipment under the control of Alain de Kergolay was exclusively to be used for "action" [special ops] messages. However, because at that time, we were only using the radio for routine communications, I agreed to put Joe X's radio at the disposal of the railroad group. I myself put the messages from Rennes into code.'[84]

The documentation from the London files of De Gaulle's Secret service outline the contributions Joël Le Tac was letting the BCRA know he was bringing in from André's networks:

28 December 1941: (date of report received in London on 1 January 1942, just ahead of his arrival with André, who had introduced him to the three named networks.)

```
'Joe'/Joël announced having just made contact
with 'organisations in the area of Rennes 'that
will be important in terms of "action": the Comité
Rennais des Etudiants [Rennes student committee],
whose system of propaganda is the underground
paper La Bretagne Enchaînée [Brittany in Chains],
La Bête Noire [The Black Beast] constituted by
```

agents of the S.N.C.F. who handle important means of liaison, transport, future action and current sabotage ... [and] the I.S. organisation of Sidonie Gibbons, that will be useful'...

December 29: 'Rapport JOE' (excerpts)

Rennes Region:
I) Comité Rennais des Etudiants
Contact address: Ménard

....students from all areas of study... originally worked on propaganda via publication of 'La Bretagne Enchaînée' ...their action was small scale activism such as the release of tear gas in theatres projecting German films, bludgeoning notorious collaborators. Since we've met with them, an action branch was created under the leadership of *Ménard*, directly under my orders, and a propaganda branch, led by *Normand*, under the orders of *Yves le Corre*. [Alias of Yves Le Tac]

The ideal form of association for young people is clubs. One club in particular, stimulated by Ménard, meets regularly. Under cover of dances and music, these clubs have three goals:

1) get the agents together and supervise them

2) orientation for propaganda, action and sabotage

3) identify individuals capable of acting for us.

To that end, these clubs include members who are neutral and ignore the clubs' true goal....

II) Organisation 'La Bête Noire'
....almost exclusively dedicated to action and sabotage. Contact address: Remault [sic]

(Source: Fabrice Bourrée/18P3 25 Overcloud file.)

Chapter VII
By Night To London

The deal was settled: the Le Tac brothers agreed to take me to London on their next trip, once they received the OK from their commanding officer. Joël Le Tac agreed to meet me in Paris three days later. They had received the OK from London.[85]

The British Intelligence Service very much wanted to meet agent 31AQ as I was known. My precise and detailed weekly reports had been found accurate and immensely valuable, and the information supplied by agents all over Brittany demonstrated that my organization was good.

In Paris, I paid a brief visit to my parents, who had fled their home in northern France and were hiding in a small hotel in the Rue de Rivoli.

As soon as I set foot in Paris at the Gare Montparnasse (one of the Paris railroad stations), I had the feeling I was being followed. I ducked into a hotel I knew and straight out the back door. Having shaken my follower, I went to see my parents.

But on my way to meet Le Tac again, I noticed the same man was following me, having found me again by sheer luck. I put my book knowledge of Sherlock Holmes to good use and shook him off again. In order to be sure to have lost him, I signaled Le Tac to follow me to the toilet and we agreed to change our meeting place to the Café de Flore, on the Boulevard St. Germain, an hour later. We couldn't be overheard there – it was always mobbed, and not just with students.

Le Tac gave me directions to their parents' home in the little village of St. Pabu on the Brittany coast, some 50 miles west of Brest. We agreed to meet there in two days. I returned to see my parents and told them I was going on an important mission for the railroad with my boss.

I told them I wouldn't be in contact with them for a month, but they shouldn't worry. My father was not fooled: he offered to help, then wished me luck. Little did I know I would never see my parents again: they were to be deported and murdered in Auschwitz.

After the Le Tacs confirmed the time and place from which they would leave for England, I went back to work at Rennes. I had two days to prepare. I informed my German railroad contacts that I would be using my upcoming vacation to have an operation.

At my favorite pastry shop, I placed orders for six weeks' worth of cookies and croissants to be delivered to my parents, with letters I prepared in advance. They must have received the last two letters after I got back from England and was already in the hands of the Gestapo.

The Le Tac home stood right on the beach, surrounded by other small cottages which had been taken over by German soldiers to watch the coastline. Radio contact had prepared the passage to England, and seven people assembled two days before the actual trip. They were a pilot, two journalists, Joël and Yves Le Tac, myself, and an English officer in the organization running the Le Tac sabotage network.

Joël's biographer wrote about the departure:

'During the first days of January, 1942, the villa at St. Pabu became a nest of spies. One after another, resistance operatives found their way to the Le Tac home.'

Photo of her grandmother Yvonne Le Tac, courtesy of Monique Le Tac, as seen in her book, *Yvonne Le Tac: Une femme dans la siècle (de Montmartre à Ravensbrück)*

[In her book about her grandmother, including her own memories of being there at the time, Monique writes about the start of that trip:]

'Despite the restrictions, Yvonne did all she could to prepare a generous dinner, a stew with vegetables from her garden. She watched them as they passed the bowl from hand to hand: they were all 20 to 30 years old, like her sons: André Peulevay [sic] head of the railroad group in Rennes, Jean Forman, Robert Simon [his real name: Bertrand Paulin] head of the Parisian Valmy network, Henry Chenal, Air Force officer, and Henri Labit, small and dark-haired, no doubt the youngest one, like her son Joël.[86] Yves commanded silence, to listen to the BBC, short nonsense phrases against background noise that sometimes made them difficult to take in. Tension lined faces, they'd been waiting for three days... "Aide-toi, le ciel t'aidera." [Help yourself and heaven will help you.]

```
29.12.41              à JOEN                    No.6.
                                              (OVERCLOUD)
. . . . . . . . . . . . . . . . . . . . . . . . . . . . .

Pour JOE.-

1.-     Etant donné votre 7 du 26, opération acceptée aux dates
proposées par vous. Si opération empêchée comme hier soir cause
mauvais temps, peut avoir lieu première nuit favorable aux heures
indiquées par vous jusqu'à nuit du 10 au 11 janvier, je dis 10 au
11 janvier. Vous préviendrons B.B.C. par phrase:

              "Aide-toi et le ciel t'aidera".

2.-     Recevrez par cette opération opérateur avec poste, cour-
rier, cristaux nouveaux, plan et fonds.

                                          f i n
```

Confirmation sent to Joël by wireless from London confirming the agents will know the trip is going through when they hear the code phrase on the BBC.

'Finally the message, twice repeated. They're all on their feet, expressing their enthusiasm with uncontrolled shouts, repressed brusquely by Yvonne, who uses her teacherly authority: "Will you be quiet! There *are lots of German soldiers a few feet away, and we are supposed to be only three people here!"* ' [87]

[In February, 1958, an obituary tribute by André for Yvonne Le Tac was published in a journal by and for veterans of the nighttime voyages between France and England.[88] In their introduction to 'Madame Yvonne Le Tac is Gone' the editors wrote: 'Now, to pay true homage to her memory, *Gens de La Lune* (*People of the Moon*) publishes an article that our camarade "Peulevey" kindly sent to us from the United States.']

'A considerate and attentive hostess, she provided comforting provisions when they were already scarce. Yvonne Le Tac participated in all our departures. She pulled out the canoe, hidden less than 20 yards from a house full of German soldiers, that was to take us 4 miles out to sea to meet the English speedboat. When several departures had to take place at once, she would lead us to a promontory, carrying a grenade in each hand, ready to do anything to ensure our departure, pacing along the cliffs with those of us who were to leave later or walking us around German sentries, and she would not go home until the last of us was finally embarked...

'She was arrested on February 7, 1942. She was 60 years old. Those who knew the camps know what ferocious energy and stubborn willpower were needed to endure for 40 months in prison and in the camps, Ravensbrück, Majdanek, Birkenau, where she broke her arm. With no care, she weighed only 25 kilos ... After the Liberation, the Russians kept her for some months more, then repatriated her via Odessa ... She found Yves, liberated at Dachau by the Americans, Joël, at Bergen-Belsen, by the British, her daughter-in-law Andrée at Mauthausen, by the Red Cross...

'This summer, when she kissed me as I was leaving for the U.S.A., she wished me good luck as she did when we left for England. I told her Au Revoir [Till we meet again] and she said: "No, not this time." A Lady has left us. But she will live on in the memory and hearts of those who had the privilege to know her.'

Mme Yvonne LE TAC n'est plus

*I*L y a deux mois à peine, nos amis Joël, Yves et ~~Marie~~ Roger Le Tac conduisaient leur maman à sa dernière demeure.
De nombreux camarades de l'Amicale assistaient à l'émouvante cérémonie.
Aujourd'hui, pour rendre un légitime hommage à sa mémoire, « Gens de la Lune » publie un article que notre camarade « Peulevy » a bien voulu nous adresser des Etats-Unis.
La rédaction du journal, se faisant l'interprète de l'Amicale Action, vient ainsi adresser à la famille Le Tac le témoignage de sa sympathie et de sa sincère affection.

New-Bedfort, Mass. 29-12-57

ELLE laisse un vide que rien ne pourra combler Sous son aspect frêle, elle fut une grande dame. Son courage indomptable, sa volonté de fer, son patriotisme ardent et pur devaient se dévoiler dès l'arrivée des premiers détachements allemands dans sa Bretagne. Distribution de tracts, manifestations en faveur d'aviateurs anglais tombés en mer et ramenés à la côte, rassemblant autour d'elle une population encore hésitante, dédain affiché lors des perquisitions par les soldats allemands devaient la conduire une première fois devant le tribunal militaire. Quinze jours de prison en furent le résultat. Loin de désarmer, elle recevait Joël et ses camarades parachutés d'Angleterre, et aidait Yves qui jetait en Bretagne, les bases d'un grand réseau.

Sa maison devait devenir rapidement et sans cesse le relais d'une route qui menait à Londres. Combien des nôtres sont passés par là : Scamaroni, Labit, Riquet, et d'autres qui ne sont plus là, hélas pour parler des longues heures passées dans ce hâvre de paix.

Hôtesse attentionnée et attentive, assurant un ravitaillement réconfortant à une époque déjà difficile, Yvonne le Tac participait à tous nos départs. Avec nous, elle tirait le canoë qui, caché à moins de vingt mètres d'une maison pleine de soldats allemands, devait nous amener à six kilomètres en mer, rejoindre la vedette anglaise.

Lorsque plusieurs voyages étaient nécessaires, elle conduisait à une pointe avancée, une grenade dans chaque main, prête à tout pour protéger notre départ, longeant les falaises où déambulaient les sentinelles allemandes, ceux de

Mme LE TAC

nous qui devaient embarquer aux tours suivants et elle ne rentrait que lorsque le dernier d'entre nous était enfin embarqué.
Sa maison était un constant arsenal où étaient entreposés : mitraillettes, revolvers, poignards postes émetteurs, que sais-je encore.
Elle fut arrêtée le 7 février 1942. Elle avait 60 ans. Ceux qui ont connu les camps savent ce qu'il fallut d'énergie farouche, de volonté opiniâtre pour supporter durant quarante mois, la vie des prisons et des camps, Ravensbruck, Maidenec, Birkenau où elle se fracture le bras. Laissée sans soins, elle ne pèse plus que 25 kilos. Une Polonaise qui s'attache à elle avec le plus pur dévouement, l'aide à se remonter.

Vient la Libération. Les Russes la gardent quelques mois encore, puis la rapatrie par Odessa. Elle retrouve à Marseille, sa famille au complet : son mari, libéré à Compiègne, Yves, libéré à Dachau par les Américains, Joël, libéré à Bergen-Belsen par les Anglais, Andrée, sa belle-fille, libérée à Mathausen par la Croix-Rouge Suisse. La « Famille miraculée » dira Maurice Schumann.
Las ! pour elle les difficultés ne devaient pas cesser. Elle reconstruit sa maison de Bretagne où elle se retire pendant plusieurs années. Une première chute : elle se fracture omoplate et clavicule Il y a trois ans, une seconde chute : elle se brise trois vertèbres. Elle ne devait plus se remettre. Elle revient à Paris, entourée de l'affection de ses anciennes élèves dont plusieurs remontent aux générations de 1901 et qui lui sont restées fidèlement attachées. Elle était leur « grande amie » et leur conseil.

Cet été, quand elle m'embrassa, au moment où je repartais aux U. S. A., elle me souhaita bonne chance, comme au temps de nos départs en Angleterre. Je lui dis « au revoir » et elle me répondit : « Non, pas cette fois-ci. »
Une lady nous a quittés. Mais elle continuera à vivre dans la mémoire et dans le cœur de ceux qui ont le privilège de la connaître.

Obituary by André with the headline 'Yvonne Le Tac is no more' in *Gens de la Lune*.

Le Tac *mère* was a remarkable woman, known all over the area for her anti-Nazism and pro-British sentiments. Even the Germans had given up on being billeted in her house. The former director of a Middle School, she gathered information and passed it along to her sons. She was taking care of her son Yves' daughter, educating her, teaching her English and music, and doing a remarkable job.

Her husband, a retired schoolteacher, was less visible but approved of his wife and sons' activities. They both knew the risks they were running by storing arms, explosives and intelligence materials in the house. A street in Paris carries her name and a plaque has been placed at 5 Rue Gît Le Coeur, their apartment which served as operation headquarters for the group when they were in Paris. Both brothers were sent, on the same transport that I was on, to Natzweiler, arriving in July, 1943. Both survived.

We were given a cordial reception aboard ship, but the weather was stormy. I got very sick; even the sailors were. To make matters worse, an alert was given and an air attack feared – all took up battle stations. Only an auxiliary motor, for the first 20 miles or so, was used, its sound muffled by its location in the middle of the boat. But further out, the MTB started the powerful main engine and three hours later the English coast was in sight.[89]

Nighttime impression of the MGB 314 created by the author as a negative.

After two hours sleep, we arrived in England and were processed in by a group of French and British officers who checked us out and helped us get to a restaurant and a hotel in London. ['Baths and breakfast were provided for the seven men, their papers collected and sealed for H.Q. inspection, transport arranged to Truro, where they were put aboard the 12:05 train in charge of Sergt. Peake and C.P.O. Pierre' – from the official report submitted the next day by their accompanying officer on the trip, Lt. RNVR Gerald Alfred Holdsworth.[90]]

Before getting into the kayak to ferry out to the MTB, I had fallen into the ocean and gotten wet up to my waist. A close call! I managed to keep my briefcase above water with all the intelligence reports gathered during the last ten days that I so keenly wanted to reach England in safety.[91]

I got up very early and left the sleepy hotel looking for a dry cleaner who might iron my pants and spruce up my jacket. I was going to meet the big boss of the French section of the Intelligence Service. [Wilfred 'Biffy' Dunderdale] When I found a cleaner, I told him I was a merchant marine whose ship had been torpedoed, as this was a common thing in those days, and many foreigners served on that sort of ship.

In a short time, this man helped me look presentable, having ironed my pants and cleaned my shirt and jacket. Suddenly, I realized I had no money to pay – I told the man I'd go to my hotel and be right back. The dry cleaner wouldn't hear of being paid – this was his small contribution to the war effort. He insisted. He offered me tea and toast, and wished me luck.

Mission accomplished, trained, and with the confidence of my superiors in the Intelligence Service, I returned to France with the Le Tacs. At first we planned to be parachuted in, but contact to ensure the drop could not be established, which should have forewarned the British that something was amiss.

[In his interview at his home with Mel and Cynthia Yoken, 25 years after writing this memoir for his son, his self-censoring lessened, André gave more details, and humorous ones, in French (translated by Cynthia Yoken)...[92]]

> *'And then, on arriving, I said: "Listen, I want to see so and so" – the English contact. And there was a French officer who had come who said: "Listen, what do you need to be with the English for, you can work with us!" I said: "No but listen, I began with them, I*

am going to finish properly with them!" And so they separated us; the Englishman came to get me. And it was very funny, he was an Irishman, he was six feet, six feet two, a civilian, a volunteer. He was paid a dollar per year. So yes, there were lots of Englishmen who had signed up for a dollar a year. And ... he was called Greene and his first name was Tom. And he had an office in the middle of London, and so that was Uncle Tom's cabin; and it was also the password, if one wanted to know if he was there, one spoke of Uncle Tom ... and that's where we went. There was a debriefing. There was all that. You started there ... And then there were instructors for the codes ... you had to learn code and I found out that I was one of the first agents who had worked for such a long time without being taken. That had been already since June-July '40...

Then they introduced me to a radio operator, who would be my radio operator.[93] And they gave me two codes, one for me personally and one for the radio operator. The radio operator didn't know my code: the English were wonderful for intelligence. The radio operator knew only his code but I knew the two codes. So, if I had information to give, in theory, if I didn't want the radio to know it, I put that in my code, that was the idea. And the radio [operator] that they gave me had been already one year on an English boat; he was very good, because the radios of the English navy were wonderful, the radios of the navy were the best. And so, as he had been on the boat Admiral Nelson, his nickname was Nelson. One didn't disrespect the name![94]

And yes, then ... One had to go to school for code, for demolition, all that ... It was necessary after all to know something about how to demolish a bridge, derail a train, weapons. There were specialists for [teaching] everything. And then, there was the parachute training. It was beside ... Blackpool. And there was a parachutist station there, and so one went to the training, and one jumped two times a day.

Because one didn't have a lot of time, for me it was necessary to do it in 8 days, 10 days. I had to get back. I couldn't be away for months on end. I had to get back after 15 days, because I had prepared my absence already with the Germans, saying that I had bleeding from the rectum, I had to go to a hospital, that I had vacation coming, *and I would be absent for 15 days, and so they weren't surprised that I was not there.*

And so one had the parachutist and demolition training ... And that was that ... And then once the training was finished and one had gotten it, one was in a hurry to leave again. I was a volunteer to leave again. And what's more, I had my parents who were in Paris and I wanted to get them out, because I thought to have them leave on the next convoy to England.

And so we left from London for the coast. And there was something then, the English knew something but they didn't tell us. And they said: 'No, there's a change, they can't be waiting for you on the [improvised air] field that they had prepared.' ... Me, I was very happy with that because me I preferred not to jump again.

So ... er ... We were transported, we went to Manchester in England somewhere, and then in a train, in a sleeping car ... So it was very funny. We left London, in a sleeping car, and the train had not still left, we were five ... three, four ... and we were there at the window, all of us with ranks of Lieutenant, of Captain. And there, there were several superior English officers and who wanted the sleeping car. So the commissary guard said: 'But I don't have a sleeping car!' Then there was a General who said: 'but – and those!? And the Captain there?' Then the commissary guard said that he knew who we were and he said: 'If you were going where they are going, you would have also the right to the sleeping car there, but for you, I have only a seat in a first class compartment.' Ah, for sure, the English were very good! We were left in the sleeping car, we were happy because they made him see, it was us! That's how we left in the sleeping car and then we embarked.

[February 1-2, 1942] We went back the way we had come. Five miles off the coast of Brittany at St. Pabu, a rubber kayak was lowered into stormy waves and we began our perilous journey back. The Germans were sleeping, and despite a beautiful full moon, all three of us made it back to Le Tacs parents' house. We used a flashlight to signal to the crew of the MTB that all was well.

I caught a ride back to Brest on an empty bus usually reserved for ferrying German Navy personnel from the battleships the Prinz Eugen, the Scharnhorst and the Gneisenau to their stations inland. This was how I learned that all personnel, ammunition and coal were now on board – all signs that the ships planned on leaving. I had already told the Intelligence Service that reports of severe damage to these ships were grossly exaggerated – now I had proof they were going to leave. I could hardly wait to get back to Rennes and get the message over to England.

As I talked with the driver, we realized that I had known his wife in Northern France before they were married, and that the driver, although he worked for the Germans, was not a Nazi fan. I asked him if he would be willing to meet with me or someone I would send on a regular basis, to inform me of what was happening in the German Navy and on board these ships. I took out a pack of Player cigarettes and offered it to the driver, who was taken aback. I told him there would be more to come if he performed – if not, he would not live to see France liberated.

The bus driver took me to the railroad station in Brest and agreed to work with me. Five hours later the Paris Express stopped in Rennes, and I slipped out of the station and got home without being seen.[95] By the next morning, I found out that most of my comrades had been arrested.

The radio operator was responsible for helping to identify me as an agent. The Germans had been confronting agents, as they arrested them, about me, but all denied knowing me, or ever having met me. Group 31 had been arrested in its totality, up to Turban and me. The Germans put two and two together, that Group 31 was 95% railroad people and figured out that my boss and I were the ones they had not been able to arrest or identify.

The mistake the radio operator had made was that, contrary to the most elementary instructions, he had not destroyed every message sent or received. The Germans found a message about me. They also showed the arrested radio operator a photograph of me.

The radio operator knew that I had gone to England and thought the British knew the network had been infiltrated. Thinking that I was safe in England, and that I would not come back to Rennes immediately, the radio operator decided, under torture, that there was really no reason to deny anything about me. He told the Gestapo that he did not know a 31'AP' [Turban], but that 31 'AQ' [Peulevey] had been called back to

England. There was no reason for him to suffer more torture, as long as I was safe. The radio operator did not know that I was on my way right back to Rennes, and I did not know the Gestapo had found me out.[96]

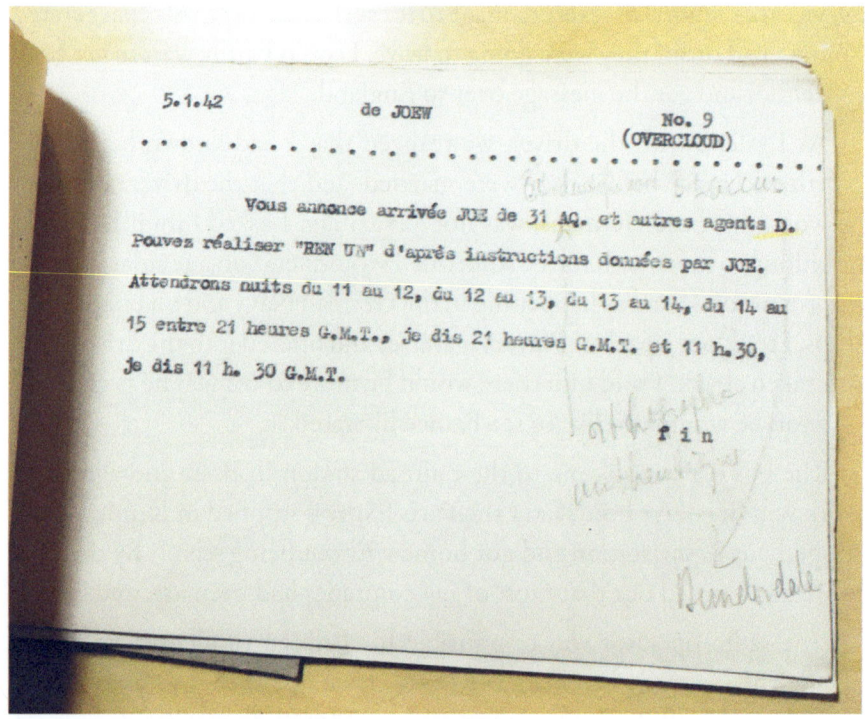

From Joël Le Tac (JOEW) Overcloud wireless message to France, annotated 'authentic spelling', announcing the arrival (in London) of 31 AQ (André) and other Dunderdale agents, also giving the go-ahead for a parachute drop code-named 'REN 1' and the times that the operator (in London) will be awaiting messages. From the Overcloud network file 28P3 25 at Vincennes.

Chapter VIII
Prisoner Of The Gestapo

[February 4, 1942] If I had had more experience, I would have followed my instincts and remained prudent. I would have contacted the British and disappeared. But I made a mistake. Overconfident, I decided to show up at the office as if nothing had happened. I had prepared a perfectly good alibi to establish my whereabouts during the last four weeks.

I figured that, even if I was arrested, temporarily, my position would be much stronger once the Gestapo released me. I would be able to do a better job than before, and could go to Jersey and Guernsey. I figured I would organize a second complete network and return to England. Overconfidence is the last thing a secret agent or a spy should have. Always follow your instinct and remain prudent. I had been working successfully for 18 months because I had been relatively careful.[97]

I went to my office, stopping by to pay a visit to the assistant to the German head of the railroad section. His eyes flew open as if he had seen a ghost. Of course, he asked me to sit down and have a cup of coffee, as usual. Then he excused himself for a minute. He made a telephone call from the office next door, to alert the Gestapo, who had been looking for me high and low! Fifteen minutes later the Feldgendarmes (German State Police) arrived, and I was under arrest.

I was taken to Gestapo headquarters, where the reception was rather cool. They were furious to see that they had been dealing with 'André' in railroad matters for over a year and had come to trust him, and now he turned out to be the super-spy they had been looking for, so long!

I was cuffed, hand and foot. All my personal belongings were taken away. In front of the small closet where they had put me, they posted a German soldier, armed with a machine gun and grenades. Houdini himself could not have escaped.

Twenty others, most of whom I knew from the Le Tac sabotage network, were transported to the local jail in Angers, where we spent the night. I tried to escape, but was caught outside my cell and put under special surveillance. Next morning, we were taken by train to Paris.

Because all the agents in the Intelligence Service group I belonged to were under the immediate supervision of (the Englishman) M.T. Greene, a.k.a. 'Uncle Tom,' I used the pseudonym 'Le Neveu,' which means 'the nephew.' When a German civilian passed through our train compartment asking for Le Neveu, of course I did not acknowledge. There was a commotion and the non-com in charge of guarding the prisoners was called in on the assumption that Le Neveu might have escaped. Then another civilian came into the compartment and asked for Le Neveu, to no response. He then smiled and asked for 'André' and pointed me out to the other German civilian.

Until I found out a few days later that the man who pointed me out was one of the top counter-intelligence agents of the Abwehr (German Military Intelligence) section run by Admiral Canaris, I had been confident that my identity was safe, and that only the English could know who 'Le Neveu' was.[98] I never expected my radio operator to keep the messages to England that I had signed 'Le Neveu.'

From the Gare Montparnasse our group was brought, cuffed hand and foot, to the Fresnes prison. Night had fallen, I had not eaten for two days and was starting to feel a little weak. I fell asleep on my cot. In the middle of the night, a strong, bright flashlight shining in my eyes woke me up, and I was asked my name, birthday, town and name of my parents. The Gestapo figured that a person who was half asleep, under horrendous pressure and maybe fear, and who had not eaten, would give his real name.

For months on end, however, I had trained myself to personify the identity I had been given by the Army, to the point where I practically believed I was really André Peulevey. I was ordered to stand up and brought to another cell for interrogation by the Abwehr officer in the presence of more uniformed Gestapo. Of course I denied knowledge of any activity. Claiming my innocence, I protested the way I was being treated.

It was midnight. My interrogator decided to increase the psychological pressure, and said, 'Of course if you don't talk, we have the means to make you.' He put me into a limo and drove to Paris. Around 1 a.m. we arrived at Avenue de l'Opera, and stopped in front of the Hotel Edouard VII, one of the Gestapo's infamous locales for interrogation. Nothing serious happened that night.

They just insisted that I wise up and come to terms and tell them everything – that I had until morning to tell the truth. Should I still refuse, they would use other methods. I knew perfectly well what these could be, but had decided not to talk, as I still thought there was no way to link me to any activity whatsoever. I always told my people I would never talk; even if the Germans later said I did, they should know I would never talk.

Next morning, things did not go so well. I was beaten and thrown back into my cell with promises of much, much worse to come. Two weeks went by like this, day in, day out, either at the Hotel Edouard VII or the Hotel Caulaincourt, Rue Caulaincourt. The Germans showed me depositions they were getting from other agent members of my group. They had decided that I was an important link in the organization, the probable head of over 300 agents.

Torture, more questioning. I knew that once I admitted something, I would be shot: in addition to not compromising other people, the best thing I could do for myself was to keep silent.

After holding out for six weeks, I found out the Gestapo could prove I had been in England. I do not wish to say who spilled the beans. Not all the people on my boat were arrested; some had stayed in England. But someone on the boat was responsible. Once I was sure the Gestapo knew of my passage to England, I decided to admit to it but to play down my role, in order not to reveal what I knew or who had been working with me.

I told my interrogator that I wanted to come clean, that I could not stand it any longer. Extremely pleased, the Germans returned me to my cell, gave me something to eat, and told me to rest for 24 hours, after which they came for me again.

Now came the interrogation which was to change everything – at least that was what the Gestapo thought. The next morning, I was, as usual, brought to the Paris office of the particular branch of the Gestapo which handled the A31 group and the Le Tacs.

I had decided on the line I wanted to follow to minimize my activities. I would lead them to believe that I was not really the big man they thought, but just a small cog in the organization, dealing only with economic issues.

Their first question was, why did I go to England? I told them they would not believe me if I told them the truth. 'Go on, try us,' they said. 'But you won't believe me! Do you still want the truth?' – 'Sure,' they answered.

I told them that in July 1939, one month before the war broke out, I had met a couple of English girls, twins, and had fallen in love with one of them and gotten engaged. My fiancée had returned to England and then one evening I was listening, as most people did (surreptitiously), to the BBC, and on the social news at the end of the broadcast, I heard that a wedding was to take place. The girl's name was the same as my fiancée's, but I didn't catch her first name, and from then on I had only one idea in my head – I had to find a way to get to England and find out if my girl had gotten married or not.

Out of the corner of my eye, I watched the Gestapo men standing next to me. They began hitting me over and over again until I fell unconscious. I came to in my cell, aching all over, bloody all over. My ears hurt, my ribs felt broken, some of my teeth were broken. But I had stuck to my story. I heard one non-com say that only a Frenchman could be so crazy as to risk his life for a girl.[99]

Feeling as hurt as I did, and having nothing to lose, I asked for the commanding officer of the regular German Army unit in charge of guarding all the prisoners.[100] I knew how much the Germans always wanted to appear to be doing things legally and properly, and I figured I might at least get some medical attention and maybe something to eat. I knew this was not over and I needed to get my strength back.

Sure enough, the prison Kommandant came. Still pleading innocence, I told him how I had been treated by the Gestapo, and that this was no way to treat a man who, being as knowledgeable as I was in German, could be a valuable link between the German and French people in the future new order and the great Reich to come, after the Germans won the war.

Apologies were made. The next day I received a visit in my cell from the head of the Gestapo himself, the infamous Colonel Knochen, who indicated that his forces did not always have trained interrogators available and that by no means should I have been treated as I had been.[101]

Knochen ordered medical treatment (bandage the ribs, stop the bleeding of the ear, give vitamins and restore feeding which had been suspended for three days) and expressed his hope that I would tell all I knew, and had done, and what my agents, if any, had done.

I was picked up again the next day for interrogation. This time I was treated very correctly – 'no more rough stuff.' I went on with my story, 'explaining' to the Gestapo that my fiancée's father was a high-ranking

English government employee in charge of economic intelligence for all the German-occupied territories. Of course the Gestapo wanted to know what the high-ranking person's name was, what he looked like, etc.

In order to remember what I said, should I be interrogated about it again, I adopted a very simple system. If the person had no hair, I said he had a lot; if he was short, I made him big, and so on, exactly the opposite of what he was.

Apparently, someone before me had used this same system to describe an imaginary Intelligence Service agent, because I heard the Germans talking next door and saying 'yes, this is him, the head of the service.' From then on it was easier going – the Gestapo had taken the bait and believed me, and from then on would believe almost anything I told them.

I caught a break. One of the interrogators was connected to the Propaganda Services and the press, and believed that I had told the truth. Knowing I had been to England, this interrogator figured he could get an eyewitness account of how England fared and looked after two years of bombing and constant submarine torpedo attacks on the merchant marine ships bringing supplies to England.

He asked me to write a report on what I had seen. Hoping that the war would end soon, I knew I had to gain time if I wanted to survive and see the end of the war. I accepted on one condition, that they would feed me so I could really sit down and write the story. Next morning, and for two weeks in a row, I was picked up in a private staff car, brought to the Hotel Edouard VII, and served a tremendous breakfast consisting of coffee and milk, white bread, butter, honey and jam in unlimited quantities.

After breakfast, I sat down and typed my report, starting this way: 'England can win the war. The railroads are functioning with practically no restrictions, one can eat at restaurants without ration cards, and almost everything, although rationed, is available in the stores, from shoes to socks, shirts, etc. Nothing seems scarce and prices are very low. With no cuts in electricity during the day or evening, clubs, theaters and movies are operating on regular schedules. Many young people have not been called up yet. Cigarettes, although rationed, are readily available and life is seemingly very close to normal..'.

This is the vein in which I wrote for two weeks. Then my report went to the Propaganda Service and the good times were over. The man in charge of me was called all kinds of names by his superiors, treated as an idiot and worse, because if German Propaganda were to reprint my description of daily life in England, it would go against what they were trying to convince the German people of – that the British were not far from giving up due to lack of food, coal, energy and what not, and that they'd suffered tremendous losses in the bombing.

For about a month I was left in my cell, wondering what the next step would be. One morning they came again, and informed me that I would be sent to a martial court. Sure enough, the next day I was driven to a military court in Rue Boissy d'Anglas, near the Place de la Concorde.

A young lieutenant introduced himself as my defender. He said that, after seeing the file, there was nothing he could do. I was guilty of going to England, listening to the radio, associating with all the wrong people: the only possible penalty was death. I would be shot.

Practically all of the members of my group, Network 31, had been shot by the Gestapo. They had all admitted to espionage, without denouncing anyone else. They were taken out and shot, except the woman who was gathering the information. Madame Louis had presented herself as head of the network to Turban and to me. She had told us she had come, as had most of her people, from Eastern France. She had seen mostly railroad people.

The Germans did not shoot me immediately, as they still had hopes I might tell them more, and I might be the big spy they had hoped I was, having in the meantime found messages all over bearing the '31AQ' signature and having heard more about Network 31. I had come back from England with two codes, one my personal code that only I, as head of the organization, knew; and one for the radio operator.

Under torture, the radio operator had apparently given up his code and the Gestapo were now able to decode some of the messages they found relating to me.

The new codes were quite complicated, and it would take many people a great deal of time to decode them. If they managed to crack the codes, the information would already be of only relative interest because of the time which had passed.

I finally got proof that the Gestapo had believed me, because one day my interrogator came to see me in my cell, in the company of another Gestapo man I had never seen. It turned out that this man was the chief investigator of Network 31. They hoped I would tell this fellow everything concerning my assignments, just as they thought I had started to do. The way I had taken the torture and beatings had convinced them.

I was again interrogated in a very professional police manner by another officer who took everything down in shorthand, read it over, and prepared his questioning for the next session. He was extremely good, and managed to drive me very close to coming up with information not given up to them until then.

The mental strain was worse than any torture I had previously endured. Throughout the interrogations, it gave me some peace of mind to know that if things got so bad that I would have to tell what I didn't want to tell, I could leave this world within half a minute. I considered swallowing the black pill given to me by my commanding officer in London, in case I could not take it anymore. I kept the pill until much later but always resisted using it.

I was going to be sent again to a court martial hearing. But I refused to leave my cell, saying that they would have to carry me out, that there was no use in going, that I would be sentenced to death for a second time, and, since I could not be shot twice, it would not make any difference.

A few days later, a clerk of the court came with a sheet detailing my identities, my refusal to appeal and my agreement to accept the court's verdict without being present. I signed it and was notified a few days later that I had been sentenced to death by shooting.

I was moved to another cell, on the 5th floor, where the prisoners who had already been sentenced were kept, three or four to a cell. Some were allowed to get packages and clothes from their families. I had managed to get a message to my friends in Rennes who knew where my parents were hiding, to ask them to see if they could get me some clean linen, socks, shirts, etc. – and if at all possible, some food.

I managed to get a few messages out, written on cigarette paper, rolled up inside the seam in the back of my long johns, where the elastic was. The Germans checked the dirty linen as it went out, manipulating shirts, underwear, etc. so that paper would reveal itself by a 'crissing' noise. So, on the night before the next anticipated change of laundry, I would very lightly wet the part of the underwear where the message was, just enough so that the paper would not make noise when the sergeant was feeling it over.

My friends had located my family in Paris and every two weeks they would get a nice parcel together, some chocolate, some fruit, some cake – all things not available on the market. The daughter of one of my friends, who had moved to Paris, volunteered to bring a suitcase containing changes of clothes and food to the prison every two weeks.

It was quite risky because the Germans could have tried to arrest her, believing that she too was a member of the group. She volunteered anyway. To my great surprise, one day the cell door opened, and I, too, had a suitcase. I had already been in the same cell for a few weeks with two other people who received packages regularly. Since everything was shared, hunger was no longer a problem. Only now I had my own food and could contribute to the others.

I suspected that there would be a message in one of the food items. Of course, the Germans checked the food very carefully and would cut the bread and cake in different directions to see if anything like a letter, a small saw or a knife had been sent in.

Sure enough, in a type of omelet, which my friends had cut into small slices, there was a message. The Germans, seeing that this omelet was all cut up, did not bother to check it further. Everyone started eating very carefully, and there in one of the slices was a message written on thin cigarette paper informing me that my friends had contacted a man who seemed to have close contacts with the Germans, and who, for a big sum of money, could save my life. My friends knew that I had come back from London with a large sum of money to be used to defray the expenses of the various agents bringing reports into Rennes and also to buy information.

Through a neighbor, I had gotten a small pack of cigarette paper and a pencil lead. While the others blocked the view of the little spy opening every cell door had, I sat down and wrote a message thanking my friends, consoling them, and telling them not to waste any money because there was no chance the Gestapo would ever release me, especially after I had turned down a deal.

The Abwehr captain had offered me a chance to 'turn' and work for the Abwehr. The captain had put forward one condition that made the offer impossible to accept: that I tell him about all the people arrested with me. The Abwehr officer was an old hand in this business and when I refused, he knew I would not be a turncoat, and gave up on me. He probably realized that, if he had allowed me to leave, I would have alerted the Intelligence Service and started the dangerous life of a double agent.

After being sentenced, I remained in prison for another five months, never knowing when I would be shot. Twice a week, on Tuesdays and Fridays, the Germans came to the prison, to take prisoners to be shot.

It was always an anxious moment when the soldiers came on the floor, and went from cell to cell, until they had passed my cell, and I knew I was good for a few days more. Some Germans liked to play jokes and stopped on purpose at various cells, including mine, putting the key in, turning it, opening the door halfway – and then closing it again, muttering 'No, not this time.' To live like this for five months is not very easy, and many prisoners would have preferred to get it over with.

I tried to escape twice while being interrogated but did not quite make it. Instead, I was put into 'the hole' for trying to escape, and for not talking. 'The hole' meant being cuffed hand and foot, in a dark cell below ground, with eight ounces of bread every three days and watery soup every day.

I was quite well known, having been in prison for over a year, so when I was put in 'the hole' the prisoners on the 5th floor gathered food from their packages, and gave it to the prisoner who helped the German guard bring toilet paper and coffee to the prisoners in the morning – the German thought the food was for his helper. It was left in the cell above mine, and after the guard changed, at 5 p.m. every day, the package would be put into the shaft and go straight down to my cell.

Each prisoner had been given a small shovel and broom to keep his cell clean – typical German *Ordnung und Sauberkeit* (order and cleanliness). I put the shovel in the opening so that, until I could pick up the food, if I was being watched through the spy hole, I wouldn't lose it. When all was clear I would climb up on the stool and pull out the small shovel which was like a drawer, then eat everything so that nothing would be found if there would be a cell inspection.

After a week, the Gestapo came to visit me in my hole and they were surprised to see me in such good shape: I had eaten a lot, slept a lot, and looked and felt tremendous. After three weeks of that, they gave up on me and put me back in my isolation cell on the top floor.

The prisoners in the various cells were not allowed to communicate with each other. Windows had to be kept closed and were often nailed –

always, in my case. I had managed to get the window open by applying a wet towel to the head of the nails and prying and prying from morning to night until the nails came loose and I could open the window. I cut the nails and put the heads back in the holes. When my jailers inspected my window they saw the nails in place, but they realized a few days later that I was talking out of my window. When they started opening the window with their key, the window came wide open and they saw what I had done.

Communications passed from cell to cell by Morse code, scratching on the wall, or using numbers of knocks according to the alphabet for those who did not know Morse. Newcomers brought the latest news from the Front and every allied victory was celebrated – usually around midnight – by singing patriotic songs.

Whenever rumor hit the prison that the Allies had been successful somewhere, at the last ring of midnight (a church bell nearby indicated the quarter hours, 24 hours a day) the prison inmates broke out in patriotic songs – the Marseillaise (the French national anthem), God Save the King, etc. A lot of noise went with it, banging the doors, all kinds of shouts. The German soldiers thought at first that a prison revolt was breaking out, and called for additional guards to quell it, but by the time they arrived, all was quiet and everybody seemed to be asleep. It drove the Germans crazy. Jail had its comic moments.

The German guards patrolled floor by floor. After 5 p.m. only a skeleton crew remained; the floor personnel were gone. The guards tried to walk without making noise, hoping to surprise prisoners talking or doing something that was *verboten*.

The prisoners found a very ingenious way to avoid that sort of surprise: at the end of each floor there was at least one cellmate who mounted guard. How? When the prisoners were brought shaving gear (for special occasions like a visit or a court appearance), they would break the mirror and keep a small piece, which they mounted on wire taken from the cot. Then the prisoner broke the little glass insert of the judas, the spy opening each door had so that the guards could look into the cell without having to open the cell door. The outside metal flap of the judas [peep-hole] could then be lifted, a piece of mirror pushed through, and like a U-boat periscope, the whole length of the floor could be seen. On each floor the prisoners even had a song to indicate that one of the guards was inspecting, and at every moment the whole prison population knew where the guards were.

Another favorite 'joke' was to play a trick on a guard who had been pestering the prisoners. In the cells there was a blind spot where a prisoner could be and not be seen by the guard: it was the toilet, in the corner, next to the door. When one of these particularly malicious men was on duty, the prisoner would open the window and disappear on the toilet. The guard, during his rounds, would see the open window. Although the windows still had bars on the outside, the guard would usually panic and spread the alert.

The guard was not allowed to open a cell door without the presence of the floor non-com or someone from the office. After 5 p.m. no one was at the jail office, so he had to call for outside assistance. By the time the non-com or Kommandant arrived, the window would be closed tight and the prisoner walking back and forth as usual.

The guard had to take all kinds of unpleasant remarks – 'idiot, imbecile, blind man, drunkard,' etc. from his fellow guards and from the Kommandant, who had been delayed on his way to a movie, dinner or meeting with a girlfriend. This was a little revenge taken by a prisoner for having been arrested or unjustly disciplined by having no soup or no bread, and lights on in the cell all night.

We knew not what the next hour would bring: death, however, was certain to come. Few people could sleep all night. Fear, pressure, the approach of execution, the thought of their beloved ones weighed heavily on the prisoners' minds. Many prisoners, like me, were in isolation. We had nothing to read, nobody to talk to, little or no food.

I walked for 12 to 14 hours: six steps in one direction, six steps in the other. In order to keep my mind occupied, I calculated the 'mileage' that I walked and figured it was at 9-10 miles a day. As other prisoners did, I would stare at the cracked ceiling or the wall, and imagine seeing figures, landscapes. We recited poems, tried to remember plays, just to keep the brain going in order to get away from 'tomorrow', which, whatever it would be, bore no good.

Hunger twisted stomachs and minds. The bread ration for 24 hours was about six ounces. The soup was watery, sometimes with two branches of a vegetable fighting a duel. Some prisoners made it a routine to divide their bread ration into four, six or eight parts, and rationed themselves to eat a tiny little piece every two hours. I tried, but realized that having a little piece of bread left over in my *napf* (bowl) tantalized my mind and required too much strength. I decided it was better to eat all my bread together with the soup, so that at least once a day I would have a feeling of not being hungry, to keep up my willpower to resist interrogation. For 11 months, I ate once every 24 hours. The only other times were when I was treated royally every morning, five days a week, while writing my famous report, and when I was fed by donations from other prisoners who were allowed to get parcels from home on a regular basis.

After my case was decided, I was put in with two other prisoners, and sometimes wished I was back in isolation. There is nothing worse than to be forced to live 24 hours a day with incompatible people. A timetable had to be established: who goes to the toilet, at what time? Who washes, when? When and how long does one walk? When can one rest and not be bothered by idle talk?

My cell companions and I started doing one hour of physical exercise every day, in order to be ready for any eventuality. I had not given up hope of escaping, and was more determined than ever to fight for my life, if and when they came to notify me that I would be shot.

I was fortunate to be with a very famous silversmith, whose family had already made silverware back in the reign of Louis XV, as a cell companion. He had been arrested on a preventive basis. He was a member of Colonel [François de] La Roque's party and the Germans, all of a sudden not trusting the Colonel anymore, had arrested all the members.[102] This was when Premier Pierre Laval was dismissed in a surprise move by Marshal Petain.

The Germans, being as indelicate as they are, always announced executions the day before so that prisoners would have 12 to 15 hours to agonize over what was finally going to happen.

On one floor, we had a man who had a beautiful voice, and many evenings he sang opera arias, to the delight of the entire prison population. Some of the prisoners, as they prepared to die the next day, asked him to sing Gounod's *Ave Maria*. One could not help but shiver and get goose bumps all over, hearing this beautiful voice rising into the calm of evening, sometimes along with the weeping of the condemned prisoner as he made his adieus to companions and family, confiding their address to other prisoners so that they would find out how their loved one had spent his last hours.

One day, I was transferred to one of the ground floor cells from which normally the prisoners were taken to be shot. I thought, 'this is it.' I started looking at the walls which had notes written all over them by other prisoners who had spent their last hours in this cell.[103] One 16-year-old wrote to his mother, asking for forgiveness and pardon for causing her so much pain, but ended by saying that it was better to die standing up than to live on one's knees. Most went to their death with dignity, reconciled with themselves, without regrets at seeing their young lives end so abruptly, before they even had known what life really meant.

After a few days, they came to put me back in my old cell, telling me only that it wasn't going to be right away.

Actually, my group and I owed our not being executed to two facts. At that time, 1942, the Germans were at Tobruk and thought the war had been won and would soon be over. Pierre Moureaux, a radio operator for Joël Le Tac, had parachuted into occupied France and had been arrested. During one of his interrogations he had met a young German Lieutenant named Kesselring with whom he had attended university in France. When the lieutenant found out Pierre was there, he visited him in prison and offered his assistance. Pierre thanked him, but said, 'Either my whole group, or no one.' This was impossible.

The young officer told Pierre that the best he could do was to get us all on the list of hostages to be shot in reprisal every time a German had been killed or whenever an act of sabotage, such as cutting a telephone cable, had been committed. Since the Germans were holding some 1,500 such hostages at Fort Romainville, outside of Paris, he figured that by the time they all had been shot, the war would be over.

Up to that time, the Germans still had not realized that the resistance was no longer some isolated individuals, but had started to be organized and directed from England. Incidents of sabotage and resistance became more frequent and more serious. My own organization was becoming more professional each day. After the Le Tac group and I were arrested, the Germans started realizing they were faced with a tremendous underground opposition.

We also had friends in Vichy (capital of the collaborationist French government) who were secret agents of the Allies, but who held influential positions with the Petain government. After [Pierre] Laval was called back to be Premier, they managed to prevail on Laval and some of his people, that if they really wanted the collaboration of the French, they should stop shooting 50 to 80 Frenchmen every week, because for each man or woman shot, they made 50 new enemies.

The Germans decided instead on a policy of making the resistance fighters disappear. Finally showing their true face, the Germans came up with a decree called *Nacht und Nebel* (Night and Fog) whereby those arrested would be shipped to unknown locations – supposedly to work camps – in Germany.[104] At least this way the French people would not be reading those famous posters that announced twice a week who had been shot for intelligence, propaganda, sabotage, and murder.

One day in July 1943, many cells were opened and the floor sergeant, who had taken a liking to me, told him that I would be shipped to a labor camp in Germany, with a large group to be interned there until the end of the war.[105] Needless to say, I did not believe him, but a few hours later, I found myself with 10 others in a cell, our personal belongings having been returned to us, along with a Red Cross food package.

It felt good to see some of the old friends again, to meet some new faces, and to know that for the time being, we had been spared. Of course, we immediately made plans to escape at the first possible moment and rejoin the FFL (Free French.)[106]

Chapter IX
'NN' At Natzweiler

[July 9, 1943] Early the next morning, 56 prisoners were ordered out of our cells, lined up and handcuffed two by two, loaded on closed buses and taken to Paris. We realized we were at the Gare de l'Est, from which most trains left for Germany, to the East.

A heavy guard of over 150 SS soldiers, machine guns at the ready, escorted our group of prisoners from the bus to the waiting train, to the astonishment of the few civilians who were already at the station.

I was chained to Dr. Lavoué, of Rennes.[107] I had heard of him and his patriotic activities, but had only recently met him during our interrogations. Dr. Lavoué, a physician, had the skin cancer typically suffered by radiologists, and, deprived of his usual medication, was in constant pain. He was a wonderful, cultured man of the highest caliber, absolutely firm in his convictions. He never admitted anything. The Germans tried hard, but to no avail.

During one of his interrogations of us, at the Hotel Edouard VII, the interrogating Abwehr (Intelligence) officer, Captain Walde, had ordered more food for Dr. Lavoué and me.[108] When the sergeant put the food in front of the Doctor, he told the sergeant to take it away, that he would not accept anything from the *Boches*.

We were destined to spend many hard times together. Many, many times Dr. Lavoué and I would talk about the future and pledge to each other that, if only two people came back, it would be us. We both returned at war's end. Our friendship ended only with the doctor's death, in 1981. He had been the oldest prisoner to survive Natzweiler – he was well over fifty when he went in. His courage and behavior inside the camp was exemplary and many comrades owed him their life, for helping them under very risky and trying circumstances. My God, the world could use men like him today!

The first *Nacht und Nebel* transport of French prisoners shipped from Fresnes prison in Paris by the Sichereitzpolitzei/SiPo (Security Police) included a dozen members of André's networks, including Barbe, Bidaux, Delauney, Le Deuff, and Lavoué on the first page of the list preserved at Arolsen Archives International Center on Nazi Persecution. On the second page of the alphabetical list, shown here, are the Le Tacs, Normand, Peulevey No.4368, and the death dates at Natzweiler for Etienne Maurel (died August 12 1943), Maurice Poge (died July 19,1943) and Louis Turban (died April 4, 1944).

https://collections.arolsen-archives.org/en/document/3128969

Partial list of the first French NN Prisoners arriving at Natzweiler on July 9, 1943.

Our hearts were filled with melancholy as the train left Paris and rolled toward Germany. Rumors that French prisoners were on the train flew ahead of us, and in many stations along the way we found that the French Red Cross had come to bring us sweets, food, clothes.[109]

The SS did not allow anyone near the wagons. Although they promised that the packages would be distributed among the prisoners, the SS, laughing and joking, kept the packages for themselves. German promises!

Chained to each other, we rode fourteen hours on the train. We were fed on bread with margarine and a cup of brown water, supposed to be coffee.

The train came to a halt, and we were ordered out. On the platform, we were met by guards shouting orders to get into formation. If a prisoner didn't move fast enough, the SS would set their dogs on him, to bite him; the SS would hit him on the head with the barrel of his gun; or kick him with his heavy, cleated boots wherever they could reach him – in the back, the genitals if they could, or the knees.

All the prisoners were finally loaded into closed trucks so no one could see them. I had seen the station sign when we had been unloaded: we were in Rothau, a small Alsatian town in the Vosges Mountains, in Eastern France, near the border with Germany (Actually Germany since the occupation of France in 1940).

Aerial reconnaissance photo of Natzweiler concentration camp made by the RAF (British Royal Air Force) in July 1944, with the main camp complex at top. Separate and below is the 'Struthof' farmstead, where the Kommandant's villa and gas chamber were located.

RAF aerial of Natzweiler. 19 July 1944. Courtesy of Eugène Marlot.

The trucks started climbing a very windy road, and after what seemed like an hour we came to a halt. The back of the trucks were flung open brutally. The prisoners got out, still chained together, under a hail of blows and constant yells. Then – silence – and a sinister-looking SS man, the infamous (Adjutant Chief of Camp) Wolfgang Seuss addressed us in his guttural Bavarian German.

I translated for the benefit of my comrades next to me, and an official interpreter in strange prison garb, with a red triangle and a number below it, on his left side, confirmed what I had understood: we were in a concentration camp.

We were told that we would all end up going out through 'the chimney.' None of us understood what this meant. Later we learned it was the chimney of the crematorium, where all the bodies were burned. [110]

Prisoner work crew processing corpses at the crematorium building. By Henri Gayot, a resistor and survivor of Natzweiler. Courtesy of the CERD and the family of Henri Gayot.

If anyone tried to escape, he would be punished with a whipping of 50 strokes and death by hanging. Suicides were not permitted; if a prisoner committed suicide, the others would be punished for it. We were told we were to be killed by the SS and not by our own hand.

From people I had known who had come out of the concentration camps and been allowed to emigrate between 1935 and 1938, I knew what was in store for us. I warned my companions that only the strictest self-discipline could save us and bring us home.

[André talked about more of the experience in his interview with the Yokens:]

I was lucky or unlucky. When we got to Struthof ... they only had Polish and Russian interpreters. And the guy who was doing the interpreting in Polish and Russian hardly knew any French. So the Germans – the SS said they knew, they had our files, everything else – and the camp commander [Josef] Kramer, the famous Kramer, came down, when we were first time at the showers there, and he said: 'Where is this interpreter?'

It was me but I didn't volunteer for anything! So he said: 'Look, it is very simple, unless he comes forward, we shoot 3 guys!' And we knew he would do it, I mean, he didn't hesitate for anything!

So my friends behind me pushed me in the back and said: 'André, go, go ... go,' and so I said, 'Here.' So 'OK, you are the French interpreter for the French block, the French barrack.' And so I had a position inside the camp which was better than just working there, because, somehow, being officially named the interpreter, they had to count on me and they wanted me to do things. And you know, the people who were running ... There was a hierarchy of prisoners, who were running our barracks. If they didn't do what they were supposed to do with the prisoners, they would go back to ordinary work without all the privileges. So they tried to put all chances on their side because they needed to talk to my friends! They couldn't talk to them otherwise! If these prisoners wouldn't do what they were supposed to do, the people who were in the barrack would be punished too.

So I had a position of responsibility which was not nice. Because there were things that had to be done. And I explained – we had a little committee among some of my friends in the office who were there – and I told them: 'Look, there are certain things we have to do. If we don't do them, that's suicide! We want to come back, we want to win the war. And there are certain things we have to do. You have to ... The rule is that the morning, you have to wash yourself in the washroom with ice-cold water, you have to strip! The water was ice-cold, and I have to translate, I have to tell you: 'Strip!' And it is not me who wants it but if you don't do it, you are going to be punished. When you are punished, you're either beaten to death or whatever it is so I explained to them, you have to bear with me, we'll make the best out of it,' and we did! And from then, I had responsibility and this would happen.

At the beginning, most of my companions did not believe me, and said: 'No human being can do what the SS said they would do if the prisoners did not submit to camp discipline!' In vain I tried to make them understand that they were facing animals, not human beings.[111]

It took only a few weeks until they came to agree, and followed my leadership, which became somewhat official due to the fact that I spoke German perfectly, while the Germans considered me to be French.[112] Little did they know who I really was...[113]

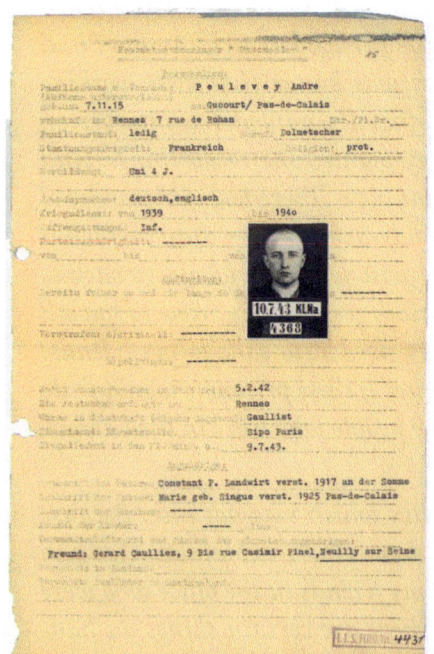

André's record upon arrival at Natzweiler, where all his records are for André Peulevey. His nationality: French, religion Protestant, his political affiliation Gaullist, his profession interpreter (Dolmetscher). and his languages: German, English. On one of the two following pages, he is said to have higher education in which his performance was *sehr gut*, excellent.

https://collections.arolsen-archives.org/en/document/3215794

André's arrival record at Natzweiler

From the Yoken interview:

When we arrived, we had to go through the political section. It means that they took down your ID ... And they asked you why were here and so on. So I told my friends, all my friends: 'Look, don't say you did nothing.' Because automatically, every French prisoner said: 'I am here for nothing. I shouldn't be here.' I said: 'Don't say that because they have your file. If you say that, they beat you half to death!' So some of them followed my advice and some didn't and got beaten up. And so, when my turn came, I said: 'I went to England, I had tracts, we did some sabotage work and so on ... and the camp commander ... [Kramer] It was just ... When he heard me talk, he said: 'Oh we have a guy who did something here! Who is not innocent! Oh that's fantastic! Here, come forward!' And that's how I got really closer to him. And somehow, he took a liking to me. It was stupid.

No, nobody knew my name, no. We had 5 Jewish prisoners. In this camp, there were not supposed to be any Jewish, [they were] strictly Aryan camps. And ... the Jews wouldn't have survived in that camp. Two of the five died in 3 days ... They couldn't make it. It was terrible the work. And the 3 others were transported to Auschwitz. And one of them, he lives! He was a tailor! And he got to Auschwitz, and at that time, the camp commander of Auschwitz was Kramer! Our first camp commander! Who was later in Bergen Belsen, and who was killed by the British, they hung him. But he was there, and then they took them out from the wagons in Auschwitz. They were immediately sending them to be gassed in the gas chambers!

And this guy ... What was his name ... Lemberger, I had helped him quite a lot ... He was in my Kommando. And I helped quite a lot and he couldn't understand it! Of course I helped him because he was Jewish. So I gave him a good job. In the silo [storehouse] where I worked. I helped him. He was surprised that I favored him with work. Because, usually, he was beaten up every time he went out! So when he jumped from the wagon [on arrival at Auschwitz] ... he stood out and told the camp commander he had been held at Struthof for 8 months. And it was funny, he [Kramer] said:

'Alright, you still stay with me.' Instead of sending him to the gas chambers. And he came back! Some things, you know, you never know!*[114]*

Our first group and the next two groups of French prisoners who arrived later that July 1943 went through the worst ordeal any national group experienced at Natzweiler, according to the old-timers, some of whom had been in camps for 8 or 10 years. The SS did their best to make the French understand that there would be no way out, except by death. [115]

French resistance fighters, classified NN (*Nacht und Nebel*) were placed under the whip of some of the worst camp inmates, specially picked to show 'these underworld animals, sub-standard French thugs' what camp life was like and what they had to expect. None of the other prisoners was even allowed to talk to the French NNs.

Looking uphill, US Signal Corps photograph #196997-5 of the barracks at Natzweiler, December, 1944. Courtesy Robert Abzug.

The whole set-up was sinister. Arrival time was at nightfall, after a long and grueling voyage with very little food. A narrow winding road brought us to the camp entrance, about 2,500 feet up the mountain. Called Natzweiler (after the nearby town) or Struthof (the name of a farm 200 feet below) the camp was built on a slope in such manner that the 12 barracks, in two rows of six on descending levels, were separated by wide platforms where the prisoners stood at roll call. The kitchen was located at the very top. At the very bottom was a building housing the disinfection room (which was also the laundry), the killing center and crematorium. The building opposite, at the bottom, was the jail barrack.

Steps on each side of the platforms led to the barracks. Looking down from the top of the camp, the odd-numbered barracks were on the left side and the even-numbered ones on the right. Barrack #1 housed the prisoner leadership, the so-called *proeminentem*: secretaries, labor chief, camp police chief, *Kapos*, etc. – almost all of them German prisoners. They all got food packages and mail from home. The rest of the barracks were mostly divided up by nationality.

Also at the bottom was the *Revier* or hospital barrack.[116] It contained a quite well-equipped operating room and a dormitory with some 40 beds for prisoners who were either privileged, very sick, or who had undergone operations. All the prisoners would eventually come to the *Revier* after work in the hope of getting some relief in the form of paper bandages and medicine when available (but that generally was very scarce) and *Schonung* (rest) – permission to remain inside the barracks for a few days and not to have to go to work, thereby escaping many forms of brutality, exposure, etc.

For three weeks in a row, including Sunday mornings, the [first] French [NN's] were made to pick up rocks outside the camp all the way at the bottom of the hill, carry them up through the camp gate and down the camp stairways to the lowest platform where they piled the rocks up. Then back up to the top of the camp (always on the run) and down the hill to pick up more rocks. When somebody could not run any longer, they would beat him and kick him until he got up again or passed out. In that case he had to be carried by the others, up and down, again and again.[117]

The extraordinary martyrdom of the first French NN transport, that included André, by Henri Gayot, a resistor and survivor of Natzweiler. Courtesy of the CERD and the family of Henri Gayot. Note: Gayot arrived in 1944, when the worst times (except for crowding and typhus) were over, and some of his renderings of earlier events were made from accounts of his comrades. This day's ordeal is recorded in many published narratives by survivors.

All day, 12 to 14 hours! At noon we had a half hour break to gulp down some boiling soup! I saw to it that the group of us would form close ranks, and decided who would carry, and when. I too carried the injured. Of course, some prisoners balked, because they felt their strength slipping away under the additional effort, and realized they would not last. I had to threaten them that if they would be incapacitated, I would not order anyone to carry them. We had to adopt the motto of the French Foreign Legion: *Marche ou Crève* (March or Croak).

It took some of my companions quite some time before they realized what was going on. I did what I could. I gave my orders in French. I picked some of my trustworthy comrades, the hard core of the lot, who had been to England during the war, as I had been, and who were convinced as I was that our side would win the war. They could assist and command the weaker or weakening prisoners. They had to make sure no one would commit suicide, because of the terrible reprisals we would all have to suffer.

When we noticed one of ours getting weak and ready to give up, I would talk to him, trying to give him hope and get him back to where he wanted to see his family again. If this failed, I would delegate one of the (prisoner) clergymen. If the prisoner was Catholic, the Catholic priest would talk to him for hours. If Protestant, the pastor would talk to him. If he did not belong to any church, a free thinker was delegated. If he was married, another married prisoner would talk to him; if he had children, the discussion centered on them.

My friends and I also did everything we could to prevent escape plots. It was practically impossible to escape, but when a prisoner was missing from roll call, the whole camp had to stand at attention until he was found. Once we stood for 10 hours, and more than 15 prisoners died as a result. I myself could have escaped, later on, and would have had a reasonable chance of success … But the reprisals would have cost the lives of at least half the French NN, and I could not face this tragedy, to leave them behind, just to benefit myself.

It was July, then August of 1943 and the sun at that altitude was hot, the air was thin and we got severely sunburned with nothing to soothe the pain. Very often gangrene set into the wounds and in a matter of days, the prisoner was gone.

After the rock-carrying ordeal, the French were formed into a work brigade, called a *Kommando*, to dig out a vault, supposedly for storing potatoes in the rocky hill surrounding the camp. This *Kartoffelkommando* was one of the harshest and most brutally worked-over groups. Increasing numbers of prisoners were wounded each day by blows and dog-bites.

There were always 20 to 30 inmates per barrack who had to be taken care of. Their wounds became infected and very little could be done for them, medically. For the first three months, the French had no infirmary privileges, no healthcare, no hospitalization, no permission to stay in for a day or two, to rest up and nurse our wounds. We had to manage whichever way we could inside our barracks.

We got some bandages and medicine, but basically, our three groups of French 'NN' were considered to be the scum of the earth, bandits, terrorists, subhuman, animals!

Return from the work Kommandos. By Henri Gayot, a resistor and survivor of Natzweiler. Courtesy of the CERD and the family of Henri Gayot.

Carrying our incapacitated comrades out to roll call as well as to work and back again meant to spend precious physical strength and then to eventually become a body that also had to be carried. Faced with refusals to carry, I had to convince some men that they might need to be carried in turn. This was a hard thing to say, but survival was at stake: lying on the roll-call platform meant special attention from the SS and the *Kapo*, who would beat the weakened prisoners into total disability. From that point on, only the crematory oven could bring an end to their pain.

Then came the first deaths. The corpses were thrown on the floor next to the toilets. People had to carry them to the crematorium. It was easy to find two men to carry a dead one: I made it a rule that they would get his soup. We tried to conceal the deaths for as long as we could, so that the soup or bread ration would be handed out to the weaker or sick inmates.

The first dead man in our transport was a highly decorated captain who had already served in both wars and came from good stock. I alerted some of my fellow officers and they lined up in a double row and stood at attention while the dead officer was carried through the barrack. At least he was given the military honors he deserved, and more than one tear was shed.

After a few weeks, I no longer found enough comrades to salute the dead. Indifference, the will to ignore reality, took over. It became harder and harder to make the others think that they once had been soldiers, soldiers without uniform, who had given their country all they had.

After a few months of being the dead men's only companion, I obtained permission to have them picked up from the roll-call platform instead. The dead were taken to the barrack which housed the showers, the disinfection cell and the cremating oven.

Before they were burned, a camp dentist had to take out the gold fillings in their teeth, to be delivered to the SS, who got tons of gold during those long years. The standing 'joke' was that when a new arrival had a mouth full of gold, he would not live long, because one of the routines for arriving prisoners was to have their teeth checked. The number of gold teeth or fillings was registered, so that no one could steal any of this gold and withhold it from the SS.

Terribly hungry, some prisoners resorted to drinking huge quantities of water or to eating grass. The doctors among them, and I, told them to resist these urges, because their worst enemy, diarrhea, would weaken them and hasten their end. The only treatment we had for diarrhea was to eat charcoal they made from burned pieces of wood, which absorbed water inside the body and firmed up our excrement.

Prisoners from other barracks, who could pass up the camp rations because they were living on the food in their packages from the outside world, sometimes gave their soup away.[118] But usually this was in the evening, when the soup had gotten cold. I again warned my group not to eat it because it would cause them diarrhea, but the sensation of hunger became such an obsession that it was difficult for any of them to resist. I had made many friends among the more fortunate prisoners and prevailed on them to give away a small piece of bread or whatever else they could afford, instead of the cold soup.

The NN's had a great and courageous German friend among the prisoners. He was the *Lagerkapo*, the most powerful, in fact all-powerful, *Kapo* inside the camp. He was the camp elder, who ran the camp police and oversaw the various *Kommandos*. His name deserves to be written in gold letters.

This man, Willi, was originally from Aachen (also known as Aix-la-Chapelle). In 1927, he had joined the German army of 100,000 men – the number was set by the Allies in the Treaty of Versailles after the German defeat in World War I. This army of professional soldiers served 12 years and provided Hitler with his cadres when he decided to defy the terms of the treaty and build up the Wehrmacht. Willi became a lieutenant in this new army. After being injured by explosives while training units of the Engineer Corps, he was transferred to the Frontier Customs Corps.

When Hitler came to power, Willi was called back, and asked to put on the black uniform of the SS and become a weapons instructor. Willi said he liked the army as such and the position of instructor, but that he did not like the 'black color' of the uniform. He was, at that time, at an SS training camp situated next to the infamous Buchenwald camp. He was marched right into Buchenwald and imprisoned there.

From 1933 on, every year, the camp Kommandant of whatever camp he happened to be in would ask him if had changed his mind and 'started to like the color black.' His answer was always 'NO.' He dared to talk back to the SS, which was unusual, and they accepted it.

Willi had a very sharp-cut face: hard blue eyes, an aquiline nose, a pronounced chin. He held himself ramrod-straight – every inch a professional soldier. The SS respected him because he had not come from a leftist background. He was somehow closer to them, but he was a convict, and he would not give in. What a man! Many Frenchmen, many NN of all nationalities owe Willi their lives!

Willi had talked to me when he first came to the NN barrack, and promised to give his assistance whenever possible. He came through, and was of tremendous help to my comrades when their rations were being stolen. *Kapos* punished prisoners unjustly by taking their rations, sometimes 3 or 4 rations, which they traded for cigarettes or other valuable considerations. One *Kommando* I belonged to had a *Kapo* who withheld 4 to 6 bread rations every day, under all kinds of pretexts.

I went to see Lagerkapo Willi about it and Willi 'unexpectedly dropped in' after the distribution of the mid-morning ration. He saw some of the prisoners sitting apart with nothing to eat. When he asked what was going on, I told him.

There and then, in front of the SS, Willi took his own ration out of his pocket and threw it on the ground in front of the *Kapo*, telling him:

'Here, you bastard of a fatso, your head is not big enough. Here is one more ration.' The *Kapo*'s face got red.

The SS in charge wondered what was happening. *Lagerkapo* Willi told him that in withholding bread rations, the *Kapo* had overstepped his authority; that, as a responsible German prisoner, that he could not condone that the *Kapo* was hampering the German war effort; and that even though he was in camp, he – Willi – wanted his country to win the war. Willi went on to say that he would have to report this to the camp *Kommandant* unless the SS saw to it that this practice was stopped. It was stopped.

Willi also handled himself differently than most at the higher echelons of the camp hierarchy. Most of them came from a Socialist or Communist political background and were very clannish. Willi looked at a prisoner in a different way: if he had been fighting the Nazi regime in any way, that was what counted. Because of his years of service as a customs agent on the Franco-German border, he was a Francophile and more flexible toward non-Germans. He and I became very good comrades![119]

I had a tantalizing problem. As the official interpreter for all the French NN prisoners, I had made a lot of contacts and everyone thought I didn't have a problem getting extra food. A lot of high-ranking camp inmates would come to me and ask me to recommend that they get an extra ration of bread or soup, or to recommend prisoners who deserved extra rations.

Everybody took it for granted that I had enough to eat. The truth was very different. I couldn't tell them that I too was hungry. For 23 months of imprisonment, with the six-week exception in Paris, I lived on the same rations as the other prisoners in my group.

But, as their assigned interpreter, I was in a way the leader of the French NNs; as such, I had an advantage. After the first eight weeks, I did very little hard physical work, which made it easier to survive on the starvation rations, and I was less likely to get injured in an accident, or to be beaten or killed by the SS while on the job. In fact, I even became a *Kapo*, although I never wore the *Kapo* armband, nor their special clothing, such as a tailored suit or leather boots.

It happened by accident. I had been designated to be the interpreter for a road gang, the *Strassenbaukommando* No. 2, and I accepted on one condition: that under no circumstances would the *Kapo* brutalize the prisoners in any way.

After a few days, this *Kommando* lost its *Kapo*, and the assistant *Kapo*, who had been sent to the camp for disciplinary reasons and who was crazy, really crazy, took the gang out. Of course, I had told him not to touch any of the prisoners, but it was to no avail: after hardly two hours at work, he lost his temper and started beating up some of my comrades. I took up a shovel and started to work – or pretend to – like the others.

The SS responsible for this *Kommando* arrived, and asked for me. During our terrible ordeal those first six weeks, I had somehow impressed him. SS Rottenführer (Corporal) Ehrmanntraut was known for his ferocity and nicknamed 'Fernandel' (the name of an ugly French comic actor) because of his protruding front teeth. Amazingly, this terror SS addressed me with the German form for respect, using *Sie* instead of *du* when he talked to me. I never showed any fear or cowering, but talked back and defended our prisoners whenever the case came up.

I was called over and I told Ehrmanntraut that our *Kapo* was not handling the *Kommando* in the best interest of the work to be done, and that I could not and would not share in the responsibility for the failure of this construction enterprise.

The SS man did not make any changes just then, but the next morning the *Kommando* had no *Kapo*, and orders came down that I was to take the group out to work. From then on I commanded that work gang. It became one of the most desirable *Kommandos*: there were no beatings, no stealing of bread rations.

When winter came, the cold, the lack of food and of medicine took their toll. Everyday, one or two prisoners died. A whole day out in the woods in the rain and no way of changing clothes caused a wave of pneumonia and similar illnesses.

A favorite sport of the SS was to disinfect the camp. No matter how cold it was, or how the wind and rain were blowing over the camp, the whole camp had to strip. The clothing was carried into the disinfection room, a room that was quite large, where temperatures could be raised to over 100 degrees to kill vermin, lice and other insects. The prisoners had to wait until their clothing was returned, which usually took half the night.

Next morning, at 4:30, up for work. Do not forget the usual morning routine, painstaking bed-making, washing up in the cold washroom with cool mountain spring water, all under the malicious eye of a 'stick-happy' chief of the barrack.

By the time NN prisoners and other foreigners were admitted to the *Revier*, the hospital barrack, the SS were allowing real doctors to run it. Why this humanitarian gesture? The SS had received orders from higher ups to see to it that the prisoners be kept alive. Prisoners had to be used to make up for the workforce shortage caused by the continuous call-up of Germans to replace those who had fallen or been imprisoned in Russia.

Dr. Lavoué was one of the doctors who helped many, many hundreds of prisoners to survive. He took it upon himself to bring in prisoners who were just weak but not sick enough to be admitted. He would have been hanged if the SS had suspected he was doing this. Whenever my little group noticed one of our comrades getting weaker and not being able to resist the bad climate, the work, the long roll-calls or the lack of food, I would ask Dr. Lavoué to take him in and see to it that he got extra food.

The rest, the warmth, the food and protection from beatings would restore the sick man in a few weeks. Then he would be dismissed from the hospital with a prescription for *Schonung*. He would receive preferential treatment, and would not have to leave his barrack for another 2 to 4 weeks. It worked great. Besides, many prisoners were actually sick and could then be diagnosed properly. Some medications could be administered to them, if stolen from the SS or traded for with the outside world.

Most NN prisoners had been issued shoes with a stiff wooden sole and a rough canvas upper. They had to exchange the shoes, which were too big or too small, among themselves to find the right size. Before they could 'organize' this exchange, the shoes often caused wounds to their feet, which became infected and which, if not treated, developed into larger wounds until gangrene set in and caused their death.

The SS did not allow any activities after work; there were no books, no newspapers, no music – yes, there was a band that played at executions – no contact with the outside world except through new arrivals.

Recently arrested members of the underground brought more hope to the prisoners, who were also encouraged by news from the various theaters of war. I got news from the prisoner who repaired radios for the SS. The repairman always kept a radio 'to be repaired' so that he could listen to the BBC from London, when he was alone for most of the day.

From 1943 on, by following the names of the rivers and cities carefully, we could tell that the Germans were retreating in Russia and Africa, every day. After their defeat at Stalingrad [February, 1943], everyone became convinced that the Germans had reached a turning point and had lost the war. Now, the prisoners knew that all they had to do was try to last until the end. Of course, it was extremely dangerous to spread the news – if I had been found out, the SS would have hanged me.

Kommandant Josef Kramer, far right, depicted smoking a cigar at a hanging at Natzweiler, by survivor Henri Gayot. André would have been among all the prisoners called to assemble that Christmas day. Kramer himself was hanged by the British two years after the scene depicted. Courtesy of the CERD and the family of Henri Gayot.

Every so often, when the *Kommandos* came back to camp, we would find that the gallows had been erected on the topmost platform and the whole camp would have to attend another roll call. Before the hanging, sometimes, a short official sentence was read out to the prisoners, but usually not. The condemned man received 50 or more lashes before being hung, as part of his punishment.

In my barrack there was a shower room, which was usually locked and where prisoners were kept. The chief of Barrack 10 was in charge of this informal prison, and the prisoner was kept in this small cubicle, which was also full of unused benches. Cuffed hand and foot, he had a blanket to cover himself with, which he had to do with his teeth. He received bread every three days and water once a day.

That is how some prisoners were treated before being hanged or shot, usually for having tried to escape. The punishment for escape was always death by hanging. Usually the SS displayed a grotesque sense of humor by having the would-be escapee wear a sandwich-board which read, 'I am so happy to be back.'

Besides the terror provoked by the ever-present SS, there was the intense terror created by the *Kapos* – prisoners who did the dirty work of the SS, in the hope of surviving the war. They did not work, they had more to eat, they were cared for at the hospital barrack.

The *Blockältester,* the *Kapo* chief of each barrack, was master over every other prisoner there. He could beat you to death, or hang you from the rafters. Just because he didn't like your nationality, or the way you talked or walked or he just wanted your bread ration, the *Kapo* could put you through exercises you couldn't endure, then make you stand outside or do 150 knee bends. If you passed out, the *Kapo* would revive you by throwing cold water on you, and when you broke down again this would put him in such a rage that he would just finish you off.

The dormitories in the barracks had bunk beds, arranged in rows. At the beginning, the prisoners had two blankets, one with stripes and one without. The striped ones had to be on top when the beds were made, with the stripes aligned from one end of the dormitory to the other. The so-called mattresses were sacks filled with straw, and had to be made square. Every day the SS came to inspect these details.

If a bed was found not to be made right, the prisoner had to exercise after work, run around the barrack, creep under the benches of the dining hall, jump over the tables, under and over the bunk bed until completely exhausted. In his weak condition, this signified his end. Some prisoners did not dare sleep in their bed out of fear of punishment; they slept on the cold floor and left their bed made up.

In this crazy unreal world of the concentration camp, these *Kapos* had completely lost self-control. They were carbon copies of the SS: whatever they had suffered at the hands of the SS, they handed down to their fellow inmates.

Some of the most painful episodes occurred at the morning and evening toilet. The Germans (both SS and prisoners) were absolutely 'cleanliness nuts,' so, no matter how cold it was, the prisoners had to strip and wash themselves from head to toe in icy water. If he was caught not stripping, a prisoner would be beaten unconscious.

The insistence on cleanliness was not for the prisoners' sake, but because the SS did not want to lose their workhorses to an epidemic. Large German firms paid wages to the SS for each prisoner working for them in their mines and factories.

After the camp routine became familiar to me and my group, and with reinforcements of weekly arrivals from resistance movements in Belgium, Holland, Norway and Luxemburg, the prisoners were able to convey a sort of ultimatum to the prisoner authorities in camp. After a few months we told these old-timers that we would no longer put up with brutalities.

We told them that, unless they started restraining the *Kapos* and *Blockältesters*, a situation would be created where the SS would have to intervene. This would mean that the high-level job-holders among the camp's prisoner hierarchy would lose their privileges. This ultimatum resulted in a practically all 'red' (Communist) camp command and things became much better, with the prisoners no longer being persecuted by other prisoners.

There was a very well-organized Communist cell operation inside the camp. Having been in camps for eight, and in some cases, ten years, the Communists very often held leadership positions in these German camps. News traveled from camp to camp with the reassigned prisoners, and of course the party hierarchy knew who the Communists of various nationalities were. They saw to it that they were taken care of in various ways, with more time in the hospital, better work details, and an organized bread collection and distribution system of their own.

Their behavior inside the camp was partisan. Only their people or prisoners willing to change their party, and who promised to become Communist after the war, would profit from their food collections or their influence with the camp administration in getting better jobs (kitchen, hospital or weaving duty.)

Although there was a high percentage of Communists among the French, I had a very powerful position because I was assigned to be the interpreter on their first *Kommandos*. I won the respect of most camp officials and even the SS, through those first terrible six weeks. And there were times when no one else spoke German so I had the ear of the *Blockältester* and wielded a lot of influence inside the barrack.

I would name those who could sweep the floor or clean the washbasin and toilets, and go over every detail of the dormitory. Whoever got a job like that was sure to get more soup after all the others had received their ration.

Of course I would also see to it that members of the various resistance organizations got these jobs and not the people imprisoned for black market activities, or volunteer workers in Germany who had committed some infraction against the work rules.

I made a deal with the Communist prisoners' leader: half of the positions which entitled someone to more food or better working conditions would go to their people, and the other half to the Free French underground fighters.

It was a bumpy partnership, just as it was after the war between the Western powers and the East Bloc nations. I could never trust them fully. I knew that if they could have killed me without penalty, they would have. They didn't hesitate to put all kinds of banana peels under my feet – one slip and I would have been gone. It was a constant fight, which I managed for a long time. It was nerve-wracking, but I did it because I wanted to see my comrades come home.

I saw to it that bread and soup were distributed evenly, and that there was no stealing. A small council of prisoners and I decided on a bread collection in addition to the one organized by the Communists. The rationale was that one mouthful of bread could not change much, but with 30 or 40 pieces redistributed to a chosen few, they could give a few men a new lease on life. It was sometimes hard to decide who would get these morsels of bread; it meant deciding who would live and who would die.

The Communists hated my guts, but for a long time they had no alternative. Sometimes there were a couple of other prisoners who spoke German, but they did not have the backing of the Free French groups, or they had to be bribed with extra bread rations, or they just weren't able to stand up to the Germans. I had shown leadership and determination, and even if I made some bitter enemies among my own people, it was recognized that I did what had to be done and said what had to be said.

I did not lie down when France signed the Armistice in 1940. I did not give in to the Gestapo and I would not flatten out before the SS. I decided that whatever was going to happen, short of being hanged, shot or beaten to death, I would see the victorious end of the war.

Prisoners who received food parcels, the Luxembourgers and the Germans, traded or tried to trade cigarettes for bread and margarine. I alerted the political leadership of the camp to get them to drop the practice. I was successful, but I attracted a lot of animosity from prisoners willing to give up their bread for a smoke. They came to hate me and told me I would have to account for all this when I got home. I would tell them that, since I was an officer, it would be easy for them to find me when I got back to France.

My friends and I established a very strict code of ethics. Knowing that their tiny fat ration could save a life, I was adamant that no one should accept half a cigarette in trade for a piece of margarine. Prisoners found guilty of making such deals would be put under strict surveillance and would never be given any jobs which would have garnered them a little more soup.

I imposed strict discipline in order not to give the prison command any reason to intervene, because once a prisoner was brutalized and injured, he had no chance of making it. The idea was to bring as many home as possible.

Many, many prisoners lost hope and once their morale was down, if their stronger comrades could not build them up again, they died in a few days. One could not live brooding about yesterday or today, one had to forget the past and the present, and believe in tomorrow – in victory.

I told myself, and believed that if only one man came home, it would be me – if only to be able to tell the world how inhuman human beings could be to other human beings; I would give my opinion of mankind in general, and the Germans in particular – and it wouldn't be very flattering.

In order to boost the others' morale, I would translate the communiqué from the German high command for the French prisoners every day. After consulting with some of the high-ranking military personnel among us, I would also interpret this news for them. For example, an announcement like, 'The German units were successful in occupying new defense lines prepared in advance...' would mean that the Germans had had to retreat and give up territory they previously controlled.

There were several generals and colonels in our midst. One was General Delestraint, who had been sent from England into occupied France by

General de Gaulle to head the secret army being formed in preparation for D-Day.

There were other remarkable men at Natzweiler. One was the *Abbé* (Abbot) Bidaux. If there is such a thing as a saint, he was one. From the start, he was the favorite target of Ehrmanntraut's fury. He would stoically suffer the beatings, the vexations, the constant brutalizing. He never surrendered. Even inside the barrack, the *Blockältester* went out of his way to punish the *Abbé*, but never a complaint came over his bruised lips. On the contrary, the *Abbé* consoled his other comrades and asked them to resist with all their mental energy and not to give in, but to believe in victory.

I was finally able to include the *Abbé* in my *Kommando*, and assigned him a very easy job, allowing him to be out of sight of the SS and able to sit down from time to time.

The *Abbé* Bidaux, who died in 1999, can hardly be described in these few lines nor can I do honor to the wonderful man of God and patriot this man was. Men like him can bring people back to a belief in God, to be good and to believe in high ideals. The memory of him and of the priest Jean Legeay, the teacher from Nantes who was decapitated by the Nazis, will always be alive in me. They were soldiers without the uniform. They did not lie down and submit to the feloniously collaborationist government of France and its Nazi monsters. These men and others were leaders, but little is known about them and unfortunately, few have ever heard of them. If we had more men like them among us, the world would be a better place.

Unwritten camp rules were strict. Taking bread away from another prisoner meant taking away his life, and a thief seldom survived if caught and proved to have stolen bread. The prisoners also had to protect themselves from traitors and renegades.

Captain X, for example, had been working for the Germans for over five years from inside the French government. He had been arrested because the Gestapo felt he had outlived his utility. Traitors never survive, even the enemy hates them! Napoleon himself said: 'I love treason, I hate traitors!'

When I discovered the high treason this man had perpetrated from inside France, I wanted him out of our midst, so he could not do his fellows harm. I reported him to the prison camp command, who decided to kill him.[120] Two weeks later, this former officer was found to have lice during one of the weekly inspections and disinfections. He was sent to the prison hospital where he was given an injection. Half an hour after being admitted, he was dead. Official cause of death? Heart trouble.

I spent my first few weeks as interpreter in the office where the prisoners were registered, interviewing new arrivals. I had a few very tense moments when a telex came from Gestapo headquarters for the concentration camps at Oranienburg; it was a message about a certain Peulevé held elsewhere who was an English spy.[121]

Looking at the SS man across from me, I said to him, 'What an incredible case, two people with the same identity!' The SS did not know what to think, but he telexed back that there was no doubt that the so-called André Peulevey was an inmate at Natzweiler; all his papers and Gestapo files proved it.

After working at the registration office when I first arrived in the summer of 1943 I worked as an interpreter at the *Kartoffelkeller* (ostensibly the 'potato vault', which many think was intended to be a missile silo) then as a *Kapo* on the *Strassenkommando* (road work detail) during the winter months.

Gradually the winter passed. Many had died, but many others had survived. Body and mind adjusted, the hope of victory finally took hold. We got word of the landings in Greece, in Sicily, of victory in North Africa.

It was 1944. Day after day, American bombers flew overhead, en route to targets in Germany, unopposed by the German air force.[122] The prisoners looked up at them, happy smiles on their faces. Their SS guards looked up also, full of hatred. Hundreds, thousands of planes passed over. There was a tranquility, a tremendous strength emanating from these seemingly slow-moving B-24's; they strengthened the prisoners' belief in a happy end, although they sometimes provoked more brutal beatings by the SS.

I had several chances to escape on my own.[123] Civilians passing through on their way to work in the camp's workshops not only left bread, but also offered me the opportunity to join the local underground group, which belonged to the resistance network '*Alliance*'. I had a good chance of making it to freedom, and was very tempted. I would have liked to be part of the armed struggle. I knew D-Day was near; there was so much to be done to help the Allied invasion.

But I had to think about the consequences my escape would have on the entire camp in general, and on the French NN's in particular. When a prisoner was missing, even just presumed to have escaped, the whole camp remained on roll-call without food, standing for hours in the cold of winter, the rain of autumn, the heat of summer; many collapsed and died. Prisoners of the same nationality as the escapee would be treated more harshly, with no extra rations and more hard tasks to perform. One escapee could cause hundreds of deaths.

Should I have escaped just the same? Leave my comrades exposed to the punitive measures of the SS? Cause the pain and death of many comrades? I decided not to do it; I told the underground I could not leave. It was a heartbreaking decision but it could be no other way. I gave up the idea of rejoining the invading forces or the active underground groups in the area.

I discussed his options with my closest friend, Dr. Lavoué, with General Delestraint and with General Frère, who was also a prisoner at Natzweiler (and who died there, of cancer.) They all endorsed my decision not to jeopardize the lives of so many French prisoners.

Then came the news of the landing on the Normandy beaches. The SS decided there would be no more foreigner *Kommandos* outside the camp. My road gang was disbanded. We wondered what our fate would be.

More than once, the SS who oversaw my detail had told me that rather than let the prisoners go, he and his SS colleagues would kill us all. I tried to get a small nucleus of prisoners together for self-defense, but very few responded, being either afraid or not believing these death threats to be serious.

Just before the camp was evacuated, during the last day of August and the first four days of September, 1944, the *Alliance* network, which had been planning to liberate Natzweiler, was caught in a trap and tragically decimated. More than 200 of their members were hanged inside the camp and then cremated.

Chapter X
Natzweiler – Four Episodes

A stay in the hospital

Natzweiler, 1943. I thought my hour had come. I could hardly walk, due to an egg-sized growth on the inside of my left leg, on the groin, probably from dirt constantly rubbing into the skin. Lack of medication and hygiene made it worse. Dr. Lavoué, who was not yet a camp doctor, advised me to have it surgically removed.

I did not want to leave my *Kommando*, knowing what would happen if the French prisoners did not stay organized within their barrack: the *Kapo* would be blamed, and lose privileges, such as cigarettes and more and better food, better clothing and leather shoes, and he would take it out on the prisoners.

Thus it was with a heavy heart that I asked for admission to the hospital.[124] Being recognized as a leading personality among the concentration camp 'mighty' of the day, I was able to move in and have the required operation. I had a few friends inside the hospital barrack – a Czech, a Dutchman and a Russian nurse – who promised they would see me through.

I was gaining my strength back rapidly but was not completely healed when the *Lagerkapo* (prisoner chief of camp) visited and told me that I should move out within the hour. Why? There was an SS inspection scheduled and all bedridden prisoners were to be sent on what the prisoners had nicknamed *Himmelfahrtskommando* – 'work detail ascending to heaven.' In other words, these prisoners would be killed.

The *Weberei*

I left the hospital and returned to my barrack. While I was away, the Communists had taken over. They had finally found another interpreter, who, for a few morsels of bread, became one of theirs. All the positions inside the barrack had been changed, so that only the Communists and their sympathizers were assigned to the better duties.

My friend, Lagerkapo Willi, had me sent to the *Weberei* – the weaving *Kommando* – one of the best work details in camp. It was indoor work, it was warm, there were no beatings, and one could sit down all day. I remained there for six weeks, enough time to see my wounds heal. And I took advantage of my second-in-command position to drastically reduce the production rate.

The *Weberei* was divided into two sections: one group cut the material, all kinds of textile remnants, into one-and-a-half-inch strips; the other group wove these together to make bumpers to cushion the shock of speedboats when mooring and to protect the ships' hulls at the dock.

This was clearly against the Geneva Convention – having prisoners work for the war effort.

The SS had assigned to the German, Dutch, and prisoners from some other friendlier nations that task of preparing the materials for the weavers, who had a quota. For extra-speedy production, the preparers received extra bread rations. Of course, they performed.

The French did not want to work hard, but had to weave the avalanche of prepared material. I changed the work around so that the French became the preparers and the others the weavers. Production dropped by 40%. The SS started to wonder what had happened. The foreman, questioned by the labor service, made it his business to find out. Threatened with being accused of sabotage, punishable by death, he demoted me and sent me back to my barrack.

A theatrical performance

In the meantime, my incision from the operation had healed. I could walk properly and was not afflicted in any way. Being available once again for work, I talked the camp office into giving me a wheelbarrow *Kommando*, which consisted of 12 to 21 inmates pushing material in wheelbarrows.

I had noticed that some repair work was being done on the structures of the SS barracks outside the inner camp, and that no one had thought of what to do with the material being pulled off the defective walls. There seemed to be demolition being done. Not having the slightest idea of how to demolish buildings, I indicated that this had been my specialty in the French Army. I was sure I could find some comrades I could rely on who really knew the business.

Sure enough, I was chosen, and selected my detail. We started wheeling anything in and out of camp at a very leisurely pace. Standing still between every trip, or even sitting down when no one was watching, made a good and easy detail for me and 15 comrades.

That is when I decided to organize a show to boost my friends' morale. I talked it over with some of my friends. They decided to produce a play written by Courteline, whose works were very popular. One prisoner remembered he had a collection of the plays which were in the *Effektenkammer*, the depot where the prisoners' clothing and personal belongings were kept in paper bags.

Immediately a call went out for would-be actors. They were selected the next day and they started learning their parts and rehearsing. A very gifted artist in our barrack offered to make the scenery, with the help of two other inmates. He painted designs on the panels which we brought in from the SS barracks that we were dismantling.

There were no orders to transport these panels back inside the camp, of course, but no one challenged the 'wheelbarrow brigade' as we openly wheeled these panels and moldings and some 1x4's into the camp. A very good cabinet-maker designed the scenery so the panels could be folded up in five minutes, and made to disappear under the roof of the barrack.

Four weeks later, on a Sunday, the first matinee was held. It was a tremendous success! There were three repeat performances, by popular demand. The risk was high – I could have been hanged and the participants beaten and jailed, but it had to be done.

A well-engineered, never-completed road project

Finally, the SS barracks were dismantled and rebuilt and my *Kommando* had to be disbanded. What next? A new project came up. The road leading to the camp was very winding. It had a difficult hairpin turn that some vehicles had not been able to negotiate successfully and where they had overturned. The call came to build this curb properly.

I came forward immediately. The detail was formed with members of another barrack of Frenchmen and the only thing holding it back was the selection of a *Kapo*. No one wanted to take on being *Kapo* of a French detail, for fear of being demoted and returned to heavy duty work if they couldn't make the men perform. So the detail, for lack of a *Kapo*, remained on roll call.

Finally, the SS gave instructions that its interpreter, that is I, should move the detail out until a suitable *Kapo* could be found. That is how I became the first and only NN *Kapo* at Natzweiler.

I had immediately gotten hold of another prisoner, a former officer in the French Army's Affaires Indigènes (Native Affairs) section. These were specialists of all professions who were stationed in the French colonies. They constituted an elite corps of volunteers, true idealists, very devoted and all absorbed in their task of training the natives for self-sufficiency. This officer, Jim Pelletier, knew how to build roads, how to figure out the declivity of a curve so that a vehicle would not turn over, even if taking it too fast or too close.

I asked Jim Pelletier to join the *Kommando* and he was delighted to be made head of planning the improvements. By entrusting him with calculating the elevations and grade, I spared him physical work, beatings and other forms of punishments which were often meted out to the most highly educated or professional prisoners.

Every day, I took out on my work crew a certain number of my comrades. Half dead, they needed the quiet of my detail and the ration which was given in mid-morning only to those on *Kommandos*. Quite a few were thus able to recuperate, and last longer.

As *Kapo*, I asked my comrades only that they listen to me and that they observe two rules. The first of these was not to scrounge for food. When we passed the SS lodgings, some prisoners were tempted to make a dash for scraps which might have been discarded in their trash bins. I made sure those prisoners were placed in the center of the rows, so that those on the outside of their formation, who had more discipline, would keep order and dignity for the group. Some hated me for this, but I believed that their morale was more important than eating SS garbage. The other rule I imposed was to march out and back in strict formation with their heads held high and proud.

The prisoners had to keep their hands on the seams of their pants, stiff and completely erect, and to march like dummies out through the gate, in front of the SS passing them in review. They had to turn their heads on command from the *Kapo* toward the SS controller who was reviewing the whole operation.

The *Kapo* would walk in the front row with the other prisoners and announce to the SS controller which *Kommando* they were leading and how many prisoners there were; the same procedure was followed on their return. On both sides of the camp road leading through the gate, the whole SS garrison not involved in guard duty or supervising the work details would be massed.

If G-d forbid a detail did not march out like soldiers on parade, the camp commander seldom missed the opportunity to order the SS to hit them with pick handles and rifle butts and have their dogs jump and bite them. Every march out and in was a critical juncture for the men's safety.

I trained my men to make sure they observed this ritual very strictly; my *Kommando* was a model of discipline. It was not only a question of their safety but a matter of pride, to show the SS that nothing could destroy their morale. My group reclaimed their dignity, which the SS tried so hard to take away from their prisoners.

Morale also soared due to the fact that my assistants and I gave our orders as French army commands – which was strictly forbidden. And as soon as we were outside the camp on our way to the workplace, our *Kommando* would start singing French army songs.

The SS thought this was great. They never realized it was a form of moral resistance and a sign of defiance. It impressed and pleased the SS to see the men going to work seemingly so serious and well-disciplined. I felt deep down inside that this helped my men to become men again, knowing their leaders were French officers, and that they were soldiers, men in the true sense of the word. Although they were obliged to live like slaves, they had not forgotten their ideals. It lifted their morale and gave some of them the spark they needed to live.

The SS guards moving the prisoners out and back to camp were generally from countries the Germans had overrun. They were ethnic Germans, part of the German cultural minority which existed in the Sudetenland region of Czechoslovakia, the Banat region of Hungary or those parts of Poland and Russia which at one time belonged to the Austro-Hungarian Empire. These men had been pressed into service with the SS to be used as cannon fodder on every front. When they were wounded, they were sent back to Germany or the occupied countries to do guard duty.

Most of these SS guards had eighteen- to twenty-hour tours of duty, and craved sleep. In order for them not to be surprised by SS inspectors popping up from nowhere, I would post prisoners to be on the lookout around the sleeping SS guard, to warn him if an SS inspector came into sight. These prisoners did not have to move a foot or raise an arm and saved what little strength they had in their weakened bodies, which weighed only 50 to 60 pounds. The guard would sleep, warmed by a fire on which twigs were also being carbonized for charcoal to treat the prisoners' diarrhea.

I set all this up for the guards on condition that they would leave the prisoners alone, with no beatings and no forced work. Ninety-five percent of the time, it worked. When I struck an agreement with the guards, it was because they knew me and they let me run the show.

I would guarantee that no prisoners would escape – this was the guards' main concern. They were afraid that if anyone escaped they would be punished by being sent back to the Russian front. I pointed out to them that most of the prisoners were in critical condition anyway, spoke no German, and had no chance to make it to liberty.

The group performed well; that is, they looked like they were working well. They were disciplined and orderly. I would walk from one end of the detail to the other, showing the others how to do things with little effort while making it look as if they were actually doing a lot.

I would prepare for inspection by having some of the stronger prisoners, the more recent arrivals, fill wheelbarrows with stones and sand. Then if they had just filled them up, half the wheelbarrow column would stand at ease next to their full wheelbarrows. The other half stood next to their empty wheelbarrows. They prepared the trees to be felled so that they were just about ready to fall over. The minute the SS inspector came into sight, the wheelbarrows would move, the trees would come down, and I would yell 'Move, Move!'

The SS were really impressed by this unusually hard-working French detail and left us very much alone. The inspectors would come and then leave again, very satisfied. Our main effort was to walk out and walk back like an elite guard regiment.

More than one prisoner owed his life to having been a member of my *Strassenkommando* (road work detail.) As long as it lasted, these were among the best moments we had lived through in camp. There was only very light work, no beatings, no harassment, equal distribution of bread, and a general atmosphere of release. There was no yelling or shouting except when the inspectors approached.

One day, the infamous Ehrmanntraut came to observe. Seeing the feverish activity, this brutal and infamous Rottenführer asked me, 'Do they also work like this when I am not around?' I looked him straight in the eye and snapped, 'Of course not!' SS Ehrmanntraut liked my answer, and let it go.

I added that he could not expect a *Kommando* to go on working like this with the little food that they had. I had a faint hope that *Kommandos* like this might get a little more to eat. It was in vain – but he left the *Kommando* alone.

Another time, Ehrmanntraut came with a newcomer, the SS groomed to be camp Kommandant, who took over the command after Kramer was reassigned to Bergen Belsen. He showed more humanity than his peers, and was also more intelligent than most.[125] He had heard of me and wanted to talk. He asked me if my comrades and I thought we could win the war. I decided to take a chance, and I asked back, did he think I would be there if I had not been convinced the Allies would eventually win the war?

The Kommandant did not react, but Ehrmanntraut said that, if it came to that, he would single-handedly kill each prisoner – and he meant it!

For seven months, I took my work detail out; the curve in the road was never finished. A stone engraved with the date and name of the detail and my initials stands at the curve we were supposed to fix.

Chapter XI
Dachau, Allach, Dachau

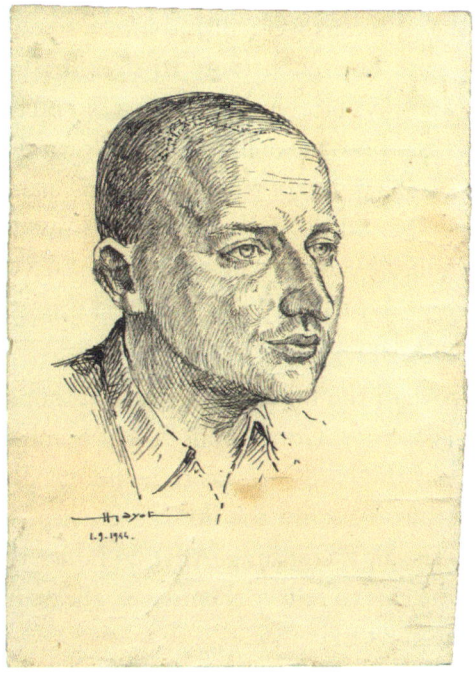

André drawn in pen and ink, gift of the artist – fellow prisoner Henri Gayot – dated September 1, 1944, a day or two before their move from Natzweiler to Dachau.

In September 1944, we received the big news: Natzweiler was going to be evacuated, the prisoners were going to be sent to Southern Germany, to 'safer' locations because the Allied troops were expected to be in Alsace soon.

I again had high hopes of being able to escape, but then I was selected to be the leader of one of the columns of 100 prisoners to be moved from the camp to the railroad down in the valley. The group leaders were advised that any defection on their part, or any attempt to overpower their guards would cause the execution of the remaining prisoners.

I prepared myself just in case there would be a general uprising, but the prisoner camp commanders were dead set against any uprising or rebellion: most of them had survived in camps ten years or more and did not want to take any chances with the end in sight. They saw to it that the guards were of mixed mind and nationality so that it would be practically impossible for any one column to have the cohesiveness necessary to rebel.

I took the lead of my group, and after a long march down to the railroad station, the prisoners were chased into the waiting boxcars – 50 to 60 per wagon, with not much room to stretch. The rations had not been distributed carefully and some groups lost out on theirs. Once inside the boxcar, I organized how the men would sit down; I then collected all the food and had a small group of trustworthy prisoners guard it, because I knew what hunger could do. I also convinced my comrades that the available rations should be divided up to last eight days, although the SS had announced a four-day trip. As it happened, I was right. The train trip to Dachau took eight days.

The long trek toward the inner *Reich* started. Trains were rolling day and night, at a snail's pace. Continuous Allied bombings caused delays along the tracks, and the hardship was tremendous. There was no fresh water or food for four days and the doors were kept locked almost 24 hours at a stretch. The air was stifling. After 24 hours, the SS allowed the prisoners to leave the cars to relieve themselves, always under the muzzles of their submachine guns, of course.

I was not allowed to join the men when they were let out. I had to wait for a double escort, because the Germans knew I spoke the language of the land perfectly and they didn't trust me. But at most stops, from the train, I was able to convince the German population that we were their countrymen and to give us water and sometimes food.

After about four days (normally a four-hour trip from Strasbourg) we arrived in the city of Karlsruhe, where the train stopped for over six hours. The Allies were bombing the station; the SS locked the doors of all the boxcars and went into hiding, leaving the train with its prisoners in the open. Bombs fell as close as fifty feet to the train, and it was sheer luck that nobody was hit – or, very possibly, the Allied Air Force was informed that some trains might be carrying prisoners.

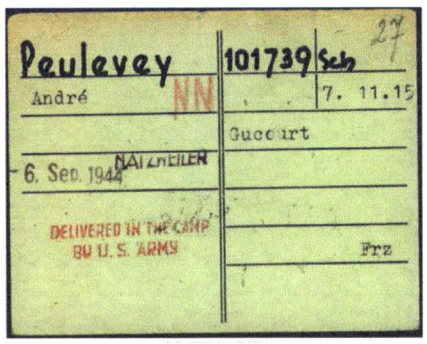

André' file card (top) with his prisoner number at Dachau #101739, arrival date 6 September, 1944 and status – NN

https://collections.arolsen-archives.org/en/document/10725079

and his 'list of valuables' confiscated when he arrived at Natzweiler July 9, 1943 and was given prisoner number 4368 that were reregistered at Dachau: blazer, vest, undershirt, trousers, underpants, pair of socks, pair of shoes, 2 pairs of house shoes.

Signed in acknowledgment by André.

https://collections.arolsen-archives.org/en/document/3215795

André's Dachau registration and personal effects transferred from Natzweiler.

Finally, the train reached its destination at Munich, whose railroad station was 90% destroyed. From there we were marched to the infamous Dachau concentration camp, one of the first and oldest built by the Nazis. It had everything; gas chambers, cremation facilities, a special place for executions. The large shower rooms could be used for torturing prisoners. A favorite sport was to hang a prisoner either by his feet, head down, or by his arms tied in back of him. The SS would keep the prisoner dangling from the ceiling, beat him, make him swing for hours until his arms came out of his shoulders.

Since 1933, Dachau had seen huge numbers of prisoners: first only Germans and Jews, then Austrians, Czechs, Poles, Dutchmen, Frenchmen, Norwegians, Swedes, Finns and some 35 other nationalities. On the roofs of the big barracks one could read '*Ordnung, Sauberkeit, Disziplin sind der Weg zur Freiheit*' (Order, cleanliness and discipline are the way to freedom) or '*Arbeit macht frei!*' (Work makes you free). Needless to say, very few people had ever gained their freedom.

Dachau in autumn, 1944, was filled beyond capacity. Transports fleeing the invading Allied troops flooded the camp. Hygiene broke down, there were not enough changes of clothing, and typhus started to develop as a result. Lice – lice carried the infection, and despite strict and continuous lice control and search, barrack after barrack became contaminated. The prisoners spent the major part of the day checking their shirts, underpants and other clothing for lice. In January and February, the epidemic was at its highest peak. More than 15,000 Frenchmen died from it. The only advantage the epidemic brought was that the SS hardly entered the camp anymore, for fear of becoming infected. Executions were still carried out, but little by little the SS lost control of the camp.

The hospital barracks remained heavily guarded. In them, experiments were performed including organ transplants, revival experiments on prisoners who had been immersed in freezing water to see how long they could stay alive, malaria innoculations, cancer implants, etc.

Prisoners were injected with bubonic plague and other gruesome diseases. A jovial prisoner in charge of one of the experimental barracks was called 'Typhus Uncle.' He promised injections that would cure the illness. Most prisoners died of course, but the offer of unlimited food, milk, soups, chocolate and fruit tempted many to volunteer, especially the Germans. The French and their allies were never volunteers. And many Jews were forced to submit to these procedures. 'Typhus Uncle' was arrested after the liberation and hanged after being duly sentenced.

The camp also had a bordello for the *Kapos*, who were given passes to go there as enticements to work harder. As a rule, political prisoners never used those facilities.

After I had been in Dachau a few months, I heard of a *Kommando* to be sent to Allach, a smaller labor camp about 10 miles away. Prisoners there worked for the Holzmann company, building missiles and other war materiel. I managed to be chosen to go, not that I would agree to work for the war industry as a slave laborer, which I never did, but because I thought it would be easier to escape from there without having the remainder of my comrades punished. But when I arrived at Allach, I realized the situation there was 'catastrophic' for the French prisoners.

The camp was led by former members of the Condor Legion, the group which had contributed to Franco's victory in Spain. These former German

Air Force officers were very patriotic – they just were anti-Gestapo and anti-SS, and had staged a revolt, for which they ended up in concentration camp.

This prisoner camp command were true-blue Nazis, and much as they hated the SS and the Gestapo, they also hated the French. I introduced myself and some of my comrades to them as having been paratroop officers of the underground Free French, which created more respect.

When I asked them why the French were so miserably treated in Allach, they told me they despised the French because of the way the French had treated the Spanish Communists who had fled to France after Franco's victory. The Labor *Kapo* had been Hitler's personal interpreter during his meeting with Franco, when Franco refused to allow passage for German ground forces to take Gibraltar and get to Malta through Spain. This officer had seen the end of the Spanish Civil War and the internment camps in France where the Spanish Communists were treated like animals.

I knew about the terrible conditions in these camps and did not deny it, but I also got him to agree that, no matter how badly the Spaniards were treated, they were not systematically driven into death. They had little to eat, but they did not have to work; they had the right of assembly; they could stay indoors when the weather was bad; and they were treated for illness and wounds – not as well as they should have been, it's true. They were left alone by the French State troopers. The SS, on the other hand, tried to surprise prisoners when they were in the latrines, and if they could not get away, they would beat them and drive them into the latrine hole and keep them there until they drowned.

I worked to convince the prisoner camp command that most of the French prisoners were NN's who had been soldiers – officers – like them, fighting under difficult circumstances against seemingly terrible odds.

Anyone who had joined the European underground in 1940, 1941 and early 1942 had to be an overly optimistic idealist – a believer in miracles, really. The German war machine controlled Europe from the Spanish border to the Ural Mountains; they stood at El Alamein, a short distance from Cairo.

But by the end of 1944, when we were in Allach, it had become obvious that Germany would never take Cairo or Moscow and was going to see its towns laid to rubble, its armies destroyed, and its younger generation annihilated. I told them what deep down they knew, that unless Hitler lost the war they would remain in camps forever. But they were Germans before all else, and thought themselves superior, no matter what.

However, I asked them to play fair, and not assign the French to all the worst work details. Since I was able to get the German *Kapos* at Allach to look upon the French more as political prisoners and less as pariahs, this perception translated into better work details for my comrades, the end of cement mixer night shifts, more 'soft' jobs, more of our men in the kitchen, more in the hospital, and inside rest and reprieve from work for some weak or sick prisoners.

I had found a prisoner in my barrack, Briquet, who had been a very well-known radio sportscaster. This gave me the idea of organizing another matinee such as we held at Natzweiler, to boost my comrades' morale. This one would be along the theme of 'France and its Provinces in Song.' Briquet would be Master of Ceremonies and would tell some funny stories to get things going. We agreed and the talent search was on. Within ten days, it was all set: 15 prisoners were willing to sing and talk, to bring their comrades a piece of France back into their misery.[126]

A month later, all French, Belgian and other French-speaking prisoners were invited to attend the matinee performance. I also invited the prisoner camp command, knowing that, if this spectacle went off well, the French position in camp would improve dramatically.

The whole operation, however, nearly never came off. The famous Sunday arrived, and prisoners from other barracks came to watch the spectacle. The curtain was to rise (symbolically) at 2 p.m. Everyone was ready, the first row of benches that had been reserved for them was already occupied by the prisoner administration chiefs. All the 'performers' were ready, but no M.C. – no Briquet. I went to look for him and found him in his barrack, sick in bed. He just moaned and groaned and said he could not go, that he had stomach aches, dysentery, and what not.

I knew that if such a highly publicized matinee did not take place as planned, the French prisoners would be the laughing-stock of the camp and would be even more persecuted than before.

I pleaded with Briquet, finally asking him what would put him in shape. The answer was stupefying: 'Some brandy with real coffee.' Where in heaven, short of robbing the SS PX, could I get these priceless items!

I went to see some old camp inmates, who told me that the kitchen people, who were stealing rations, had been doing a lot of trading with the SS guards. Although the kitchen staff was all Polish and bitter enemies of the other inmates, I decided to try. I had the reputation for being influential – I might get what I needed.

I went and pleaded my cause. And what did I have in trade? I knew they all wanted to go to France after the liberation. They knew I had been in London and figured I was high up in military circles, close to de Gaulle.

I promised that I would recommend them all for jobs in France after the war, that I would see to it that they would be able to immigrate and not have to go back to Poland.

I would have promised to make them Secretary of State, War, Interior ... They came up with two large cups of real coffee and two small glasses of French brandy. Briquet drank both, felt better and could not refuse to do as he had promised. Besides, I told him I would strangle him myself and throw him in the latrine if he did not perform, and I meant it!

The performance was a huge success. The prisoners forgot their misery for a few hours. The prisoner camp command admired the performance and had a good time. From then on, the French prisoners were like everyone else. Work assignments improved.

Many of my comrades owed me their lives. I also had a small group of friends who were all very close. We met in the evenings for discussions and brought bread and other food to share.

New Year's eve 1944/45 would be a memorable one. One of the barrack chiefs was an Austrian from Vienna. For committing petty larceny, he was thrown into the camps and wore the green badge of the criminal prisoners. This Karl Leber was a very warmhearted man. He became our group's protector and friend. In exchange, we shared with him whatever came in from the outside, and promised him that, once the war was over, we would testify in his favor as to his behavior in camp.

My group decided to celebrate New Year's eve in Karl Leber's barrack, after all the prisoners were asleep. We sat in his private room, ate the cake one prisoner had baked, drank some wine, sang long-forgotten popular French songs and when midnight came we all joined hands and sang 'Auld

Lang Syne' and 'It's a long way to Tipperary.' A rousing *Marseillaise* (the French national anthem) closed the evening, and we all went to dream of a better tomorrow.[127]

January 1945: Things looked brighter and brighter; since Stalingrad, the Germans were retreating. They had lost practically all of North Africa. The Allies were the masters of the sky. German cities and factories were bombed day and night, their submarines were sunk, thanks to the new radar system. The end was in sight.

German thoroughness finally caught up with me. Despite the fact that Oranienburg had been abandoned as the administrative center for the concentration camps, the Gestapo had been advised of the exact status of some of Dachau's inmates. The files for me and three of my comrades were forwarded to Dachau with official warning that we were NN category prisoners, and should never be allowed out of the mother camp.

A few days after New Year's, word came down for the four NNs to meet at the camp office, which was never good news: very often such a call was the prelude to execution. I said goodbye to my close friends and prepared for the worst. The four of us remained waiting for five hours outside the camp office, until finally the secretary came out and told us that we were going to be returned to Dachau.

I thought this would be the end, and that the SS were going to take us to the facilities for executions next to the crematorium there. I decided to get away during this short journey from Allach to Dachau.

It was as if the SS had read my mind. I was put in handcuffs and foot shackles. There was no way any of us could even dream of trying to escape. Besides, we were chained to the automobile in which we were being driven, and there was a barrier inside of the car so we could not get to the SS who was driving the car or to the one sitting next to him.

When I arrived in Dachau, my handcuffs and shackles were removed and I was relieved to find I was being sent back to my old barrack.

Thanks to my previous camp experience, I managed to be left off the list of available workers, so I remained inside the barrack and took over as *Stubendienst* (room orderly.) For the Nazis, this meant seeing that the barrack was neat and clean as well as the closets containing each prisoner's food, canteen, cup, spoon and some of the goods each prisoner might have been able to acquire (an extra rag, another pair of socks). For me personally, it meant being able to rest. For my comrades, I was able to organize regular and equal distribution of food and to halt the stealing epidemic which had befallen this section of the barrack.

Discipline in my barrack was good because there were no beatings and no favoritism when it came to distribution of food or clean shirts and pants. It was most important to keep discipline so that the SS would have no reason to come in shooting. I saw to it that the dead were kept on the lists as long as possible so that I could allocate their rations to the weak and sick prisoners.

Typhus was spreading inside the camp; life became quiet. In the morning, the dead would be thrown out the windows into the street between the barracks. Two hours later, a special work detail, which the French called *Mort Express*, the corpse transport *Kommando*, would throw the dead men on a cart to transport them to the crematoria.

As the numbers of the dead grew, cremation could not take place immediately and piles of corpses lay around waiting to be burned. One day I passed by a pile of bodies and saw that one prisoner was not completely dead. I looked around to see that no one was watching, then pulled him out and helped him back to his barrack. Later, this man wrote a book and one of the photographs showed him sticking out of the heap. And then, many years later, this fellow came up to me during a French concentration camp inmates' reunion. He asked me if I remembered him, but I didn't recognize him. He thanked me for saving his life. Just another episode.[128]

Then I came down with typhus.

Luckily, I had friends. A doctor Sternenfeld, who later after the war killed himself in Paris, watched over me. He gave me injections of strophantin with raisin glucose, which friends who were working during the day at clean-up details after the bombing raids had found and brought back, or traded with the SS for valuable objects they had dug out during the day.

I received about five injections of this substance. It kept my heart going and the glucose gave me some nourishment. A few aspirins stolen by other friends for me from the camp infirmary brought the fever down and after two weeks, I was out of danger. I lost thirty-five pounds and weighed 40 kilos [88 pounds], a walking skeleton like most of the others. A few extra rations nursed me back to some strength until the big day arrived.

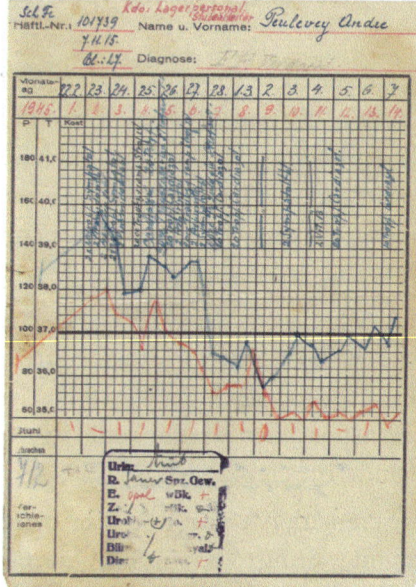

André's infirmary records at Block 27, the typhus ward at Dachau. Top: February 22-March 7, 1945. Bottom: his temperature stops being charted on April 28, the day before the liberation.

(From his personal archive.)

His 66-day hospital record, originally for 'suspicion' (of typhus) ending up with 'status: post typhus exanthematicus,' was probably kept up to date so he could check in with the International Prisoner Committee, for which the Typhus Block was a control headquarters. 'Since last December they tried to keep certain key inmates as "patients" in the camp hospital which they enjoyed a certain protection. They likewise enlisted the help of a great number of block and cell seniors to control criminal activities among the prisoners and to nip in the bud any provocative action which the SS might use to unloose mass massacres.' (Perry, pp. 14-15.)

André is listed on the forms as *K(omman) do: Lagerpersonal* (camp staff) and *Stubenältester* (Senior Barracks prisoner.)

First and last records of Dachau sixty-six day infirmary record for André from February 22 to April 28, 1945. From his private archive.

I kept in contact with former Free French and other underground leaders. The prisoner administration was preparing for liberation. They feared that when discipline broke down, some prisoners might get out of hand and kill some of their comrades, for real or imagined cruelty against them. The prisoner emergency council was trying to put responsible prisoners, like me, in charge everywhere inside Dachau.

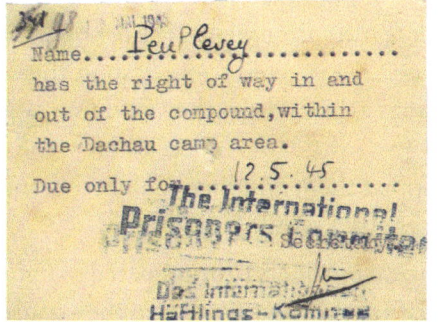

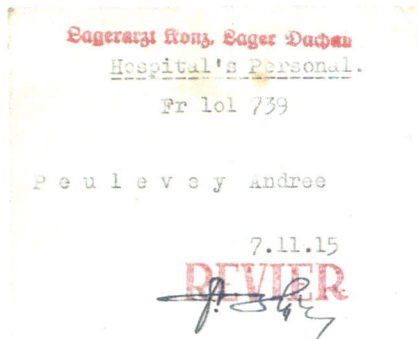

From his private archive, André's International Prisoners Committee pass and Hospital Personnel ID at Dachau. A report by the PWB/Psychological Warfare Branch of the US Seventh Army includes two pages about the International Prisoners' Committee. 'The aims of this group were simple. They wished to prepare for the advance of the Americans, save as many lives as possible in the last critical phase before liberation, and keep a record of criminal SS activities and personalities. The IPC is now the highest prisoner authority in the camp.' (Perry, pp. 14-15.)

International Prisoner Committee and Hospital Personnel cards for André at Dachau.

Actually, I owed my responsibilities to the fact that by never giving up hope for victory and liberation, I kept my sanity at all times and was able to survive the worst crises.

General Delestraint, De Gaulle's deputy assigned to occupied France, was executed a few days before Dachau was liberated. General Delestraint actually could have saved himself. The then acting camp *Kommandant*, the infamous Weiss, a notorious torturer and killer with over 10 years of concentration camp experience, had offered him shelter. But no matter how much Weiss insisted, General Delestraint refused and said he wanted to share his companions' fate. It wasn't, of course, that Weiss was plagued by conscience, but that he wanted to create a good alibi for himself, before sending this important prisoner to his death.

Besides General Delestraint, a series of well-known underground fighters were called to the office and found shot two hours later. This was consistent with the information I had received, that the camp administration had been ordered to execute prominent NN prisoners if the camp were evacuated or abandoned. I expected to be among them. My friends at the hospital barrack always kept a corpse they could say was André, should a call come for me to go to the camp office, where the SS usually picked up their prisoners, stripped them and then marched them, cuffed hand and foot, to the place where they would shoot them.

Word circulated among all the political prisoners to be prepared to fight once outside the camp, and not to take anything with them so they could move quickly. With the help of a Spanish doctor, Y. (Joseph) Capello, I managed to keep a few prisoners of my choosing in my dormitory. [129]

The sick lists were falsified: by showing high temperatures or some such, we were able to keep a few of the younger Jewish prisoners and their fathers. This is how Pierre Schillio and his father were saved. This was a highly dangerous undertaking, but so was any form of obstruction of SS rules.

During the last weeks before the liberation, the camp was very tense; no one knew what the SS had in store for their prisoners. Escaped prisoners who had left and returned told of massacres in the surrounding woods. The American Army found a train with thousands of Jewish prisoners who had been gassed in the railroad cars.

Chapter XII
Freedom and Loss

April 29, 1945 arrived. A rumor spread through the camp: 'The Americans are here!' I left my barrack to go to the camp gate, to greet our liberators. A few shots were heard, the SS guards surrendered and opened the gates, and the first Americans came through. I ran to the gate and threw my arms around the first GI; this one took 'his' helmet off and beautiful long blond hair fell onto 'his' shoulders. The first 'man' in was a woman photojournalist. The surprise passed. I hugged her again.[130]

But I could hardly believe that the nightmare was over. The prisoners immediately took over the camp command, repatriation procedures were set up, food was brought in. DDT spraying of all the prisoners, their beds, clothes, etc. began to stop the typhus epidemic caused by lice which had taken a toll of 18,000 prisoners in less than three weeks.

The hardest thing was to limit food intake. Prisoners would not listen to being told that they had to get used to eating again; they just tried to fill their stomachs, and during the first four days a lot of people died from overeating.

Before being repatriated, two fellow prisoners and I decided to pay a visit to the little town near the camp. Dachau, the town, looked devastated. The stores were closed, their windows were boarded up; the population kept themselves locked up in their homes. They were afraid of the prisoners and ran whenever they saw someone in striped camp garb. My friends and I went looking, but found nothing in the town we could use.

Glad to be going home, my friends and I climbed aboard the trucks which the 6th American Army put at our disposal. The drivers were all black and drove as if they were competing at a racetrack. In vain did we ask them to slow down: we feared for our lives.

Finally we arrived in Strasbourg and were put up in a camp for returning prisoners. There, I met some old friends I had thought long dead. They had been sent to other camps and *Kommandos* and here they were, alive and happy. We were sent by train from Strasbourg to Paris.

I had often thought of what might have happened to my parents back in Paris. I had little hope of finding them alive, knowing they had surely been deported and that they could not endure camp life for long. I had braced myself to not see them ever again.

After I arrived in Paris, I re-registered with the French army. They reluctantly gave me part of my back officer's pay, after telling me first that they felt I was not entitled to any pay, because I had been fed and clothed by the Germans.

The paymaster in charge, who was involved in some shady deals, kept some money for himself, and finally paid out $1,600 for four years from money the British had remitted to the French. It was a scandal, but what could I do about it?

André's Carte de Rapatrié issued May 1945 mentions the Lutetia, the Paris hotel that was the first stop for returning deportees from the camps, and records that he was given a welcome package, a beret, a suit, underwear, socks and shoes, a food card and a card for clothing, as well as a bonus of 1,000 francs that was later deducted from his back pay.

I got in touch with my very best friends. Sure enough, Janine Caulliez came to pick me up at the Hotel Lutetia and took me to have my first lunch at her relatives'. Her daughter had enlisted in the Women's Auxiliary Corps during the war, and all were overwhelmed with joy at seeing me again, alive.

I heard that my aunt and her husband had been saved by friends who had hidden them in their villa near Paris. I got the address of where they were living, in Le Vesinet. I had a faint hope that my parents might be with them because they had been hiding together in the same hotel in Paris when I was taken by the Nazis.

Taking care of business first, I reported to my commanding officer, the gentleman called 'Uncle' Tom Greene, who had taken possession of the same apartment he had before the war, at 69 Avenue Victor Hugo, and who was still working for British Intelligence. He gave me clothing and shoes.

He was happy to see me, and after a debriefing session, offered to have me driven to the outskirts of Paris to rejoin my family. A pretty English lady chauffeur who was a member of the British Auxiliary Territorial Service brought me to my Aunt Madeleine's and Uncle Kuba's home.

They had no idea that I was already back in Paris, although they had learned from the Red Cross lists that I was alive. It was a tearful reunion, then an awful silence. They did not know how to start. I made it very easy on them, telling them there was no need to talk about my parents. I knew what fate had met them, when they gave up hope of my return: they refused to go to another hiding place with my aunt and uncle, and had died in Auschwitz. There was never one mention made of my father and mother after that. When I was alone, I shed hot and silent tears; I had hoped against all hope that they would be alive.

The next two days were busy ones. I had to find clothes, show up for army debriefings, get ID cards from the police, etc. I still could not believe that I was free and alive. But there was also a big vacuum now. I had no aim, no duties. For the first time in years, I had to decide when and what to eat, where to go, when to go to bed and when to get up.

I told my former British CO [Commanding Officer] about the money I had been given to run my resistance network when I came back from England, and that it had not been taken by the Germans. I had entrusted it to friends prior to my arrest, and they had kept it – about $50,000. Mr. Greene went to Rennes with me to retrieve the money and thanked me for being so honest. That was all.[131]

Brooding about my parents, I set about to recover the store that had belonged to them in Northern France. By law, I could repossess from the occupier or receive compensation if they did not want to return the property.[132]

My uncle went with me to that little mining town, Bruay-en-Artois.[133] The store, *Au Soldeur Americain* ('The American Discounter's Place) had been bought by a Belgian who agreed right away to pay me something – not very much – but since I didn't want to go back and live there with the memories of my parents, I accepted his offer.

I also tracked down the person who worked as an interpreter for the Germans and had stolen the furniture and other possessions of the Scheinmann family. I intended to repossess my parents' belongings.[134] But by the time the court ruled that I could do so, a few weeks later, the fellow had moved out and disappeared.[135] I was too tired to chase him and lost out on it all.

Life in postwar France was not easy for anyone. It was a most difficult thing to do – to reintegrate and start back to work, forgetting the past. For most ex-prisoners this was nearly impossible either because they were too sick, or because they were used to abnormal human relations and unable to submit to normal work discipline. It took five years or more for the survivors to get pensions and good medical care, and many died before they could get help. And then, not having an ideal to live for any longer, they let go and disappeared in large numbers.

Having grown accustomed to dealing with situations according to my own judgment, I could not see myself staying on in the peacetime Army where I had to sign a form to ask for a pencil. Before resigning my position, I helped my people get everything they needed for medical purposes, recommendations for decorations, promotions, etc.

In order to process it all efficiently, I had a rubber stamp made with the Commanding Officer's name, then I would write under it 'per order of' and that cut through a lot of red tape. Having taken care of all the paperwork concerning former members of my group, I decided to demobilize myself, and used this rubber stamp I had designed to sign my own demobilization papers in September of 1945.

I started to look around for something to do, when I met a marvelous woman. During the war she had been in England, serving in the RAF. Claire Dyment was engaged in special intelligence, due to her brilliance and her knowledge of several languages, and worked for the signal corps. She listened to enemy pilots and deciphered their codes, then relayed their messages to the British pilots. She alerted the Navy about the German E-boats spying along the coast of England.[136] They caught the first one thanks to her efforts. Claire was decorated by the Queen.[137]

André and Claire were married under the name Peulevey when they traveled to the US in 1946, and then again in Paris as Scheinmann, before the birth there of their son, Michel in 1948. Claire at the Eiffel Tower (left); André and Claire later in life (right).

Great was my surprise and joy to meet her in Paris. The happiest years of my life were about to begin.

Now, what to do for work? I had to start a business or accept new work. I worked with my uncle at first, then went into business with my future brother-in-law, who produced fine-bristle paint brushes and shaving brushes.

My sister, Madeleine, who had been living in the US since before the war, and Claire's family and friends who were also in the US, all urged us to emigrate. After a visit to the US in 1946, we decided to apply for immigration papers. The procedure dragged on; there was always yet another document needed, and we still weren't really decided on going anyway.

Then one day, a friend of mine, who worked in the personnel section of the War Ministry, called to give me some news. Not only was he leaving for Vietnam, but the man replacing my friend was a former officer of the Vichy [French government which had cooperated with the Germans during the occupation] Armed Forces. He hated Jews and Free French officers; my friend predicted that in less than three months I would be re-mobilized and sent to Vietnam. I had no intention of going to Vietnam, so when the US Embassy called the next day and told us our immigration visas had come in, we decided to leave for the US.

For forty years, we enjoyed life together, until Claire died in 1986. Now there is not a day I do not shed tears for her. We had a son, Michel, who with his wife Brigitte gave us the joy of a grandson named Gabriel, a granddaughter named Clara after my wife Claire, and another granddaughter, Emma.

Chapter XIII
The Concentration Camp Universe

In order to understand why so many people could be kept under control by so relatively few, you must understand the organization of these camps. There existed a double terror, one exercised by the SS guard and the other by the *Kapos* who had been chosen to command the other prisoners.

These camps were experimental communities for a new type of state, which had its own rules, without any rights. Men were thrown into them and proceeded to fight to survive, with all their virtues and all their vices. They had more vices than virtues, and they fought just as much, if not more, against their fellow inmates than against the SS!

The SS managed to run the camp with relatively few personnel, thanks to their system of playing the prisoners against each other. Many of the *Kapos* wore green triangles, which meant they had come in as common criminals, often murderers. They were put in charge of the 'reds'. (The red triangle was worn by Communist, Socialist and other political prisoners.)

Many prisoners suffered more under the arrogance and intolerance of these brutal, power-minded and power-possessing prisoners than from the debasing acts of the SS. The SS were the visible enemy, in uniform, whip in hand and dog at the ready to bite. But a fellow prisoner's abuse hurt more because he was one of us. The most difficult thing was not to sink as low as the people who were henchmen.

My upbringing, traditional Judaism and bourgeois habits, had steeped me in a certain philosophy of how to behave in front of other human beings. Even when, due to the circumstances at Natzweiler, I became a *Kapo* – one of 'them' – I was able to resist the loss of dignity, which was a normal process in the camps, and maintain a firm conviction about what was right and what was wrong.

I was able to maintain my critical faculties about certain behaviors, because of my ability to form a meaningful picture and recognize the organizational structure of camp existence. I had an understanding of the people there who had been raped and become sick and perverse, and an ability to recognize what was typical of the individual.

Part of this account is full of a somber problematic of cause and circumstance. I do not want to put the German people *per se* on trial here. But one who has escaped with his life should not pass over in silence the horrible scenes he witnessed, or withdraw from the facts by maintaining silence.

I feel that I must, and I want to show the world how deep humanity can fall; this should be the main reason for writing this memoir. This deep fall is human, even if it seems inhuman. The world must be helped to avoid a similar venture into infamy. Most people in our western world are not hungry; they do not desire to be reminded or to be shown what can happen. The graves of the dead provoke outcries of justification of these acts of terror; those who try to justify evil accept more evil, in order to keep their consciences free.

Nazi Germany did what it did because of its *Führer*, Hitler; because of idolatry, nationalism, racist folly and, last but not least, militarism. Black uniforms were everywhere, smashing under their black jackboots the fate of the rest of the nation.

How many of these men are heroes in today's world, but only until someone who had been in a camp meets them and starts asking questions. Was he wearing a red, green or black triangle? Which camp was he in? Which barrack? Which *Kommando*? The SS were able to dehumanize their prisoners to such a degree that they themselves did not have to do any more of their dirty work.

All prisoners had their individual number below a triangle. Political prisoners had red triangles with the letter of their country of origin stamped in black ink in the middle of the triangle. With the weekly arrivals of foreigners – almost all of them 'reds' – the political prisoner faction became more and more influential.

There were also black triangles, for the so-called 'asocial' elements, such as a sales rep who had refused to go to work in a factory, a pimp, etc. The blacks were usually nice to their comrades.

Beside the separations between those wearing different colored triangles, there was hatred stemming from being of different nationalities. The German prisoners despised the French and the Poles were detested by everyone, but mostly by the Russians. In general, the behavior of the Poles, who managed to hold key positions, such as kitchen duty, was absolutely distasteful. They and the 'greens' were the most docile henchmen for the SS.

The so-called *Proeminentem*, prominent prisoners among the ranks of all these slaves and pariahs, had more to eat, less work to do, more protection from the SS because they were willing to mistreat their fellow inmates.[138] The *Proeminentem* dealt more harshly with the other prisoners than the SS did, because they were with them 24 hours a day. For 24 hours a day they exercised threats and control. Moral norms changed or were bent to a point of no return; love and hate were pushed to the extreme.

This world lived behind iron bars or barbed wire fences, under terrorist discipline, in a jungle of wildness into which shots were fired or people pulled out to be hanged. People gassed, poisoned, tortured and beat others to death, just to win material advantage. To gain or hold onto power, they would lie and intrigue so that they could become the new power classes.

One cannot really blame these men because we ourselves became hardened – we had to – in order to be able to live through the next day. For example, new arrivals had to undergo special treatment, beatings, etc. My comrades and I would just shrug our shoulders and turn away. We had changed: the first few weeks we would have seen red. We political prisoners would never volunteer to serve as executioners' aides, though.

One would hardly find a Dutchman, a Norwegian, a Frenchman or a Belgian who would become the easy tool of the SS – not that the SS wanted to see any foreign political prisoners holding down important jobs in the camps, anyway.

Terror – what does it mean? How many idealists became devils, butchers, torturers, who believed that their aims could allow the suppression of human rights, could allow them to torture, maim and kill other human beings for the sole reason that they did not agree.

Terror – Why does it work? Men, as a rule, can seldom resist when they find themselves suddenly in a terrifying situation. Their reactions become slower, uncertain: they are so afraid they very often become servile tools of their oppressor. Each human being has a certain resistance within himself, but he is paralyzed by the terror inflicted on him and no longer able to develop defenses. Loss of self esteem, or fear of physical pain provoke panic in us. Even men of normally strong character give in under the provoked illusion that they can save themselves.

Panic creates physical phenomena. Sudden heavy blood flow to the heart can, in some cases, cause a heart attack, while the brain loses practically all its blood. Lack of oxygen causes a diminishment of the thinking capacity and strong people feel themselves in a position of inferiority, much greater than it really is. This illusion gives the torturer a much greater superiority in his own tormented mind than he deserves.

Terror also works because the mass of people do not react uniformly. A few rebel, some duck and let the storm pass, others gradually join the ranks of their guards and lower themselves to the same level of brutality.

How could one survive a camp? Several ways.

Remaining a loner was one way, but that could be dangerous, because, as in the army, one needs friends and moral and physical assistance in difficult situations. However, the loner does not let himself be dragged down from his intellectual level, he is able to marshal a certain unreal strength acquired by his education, class or background.

Joining a group, or belonging to one, was a natural way to try to survive. Members of the same resistance groups practically automatically flocked together to help one another. The Free French and other patriots were soldered together by a common ideal, a common fight against the occupier, the enemy.

Then again, there was membership in a political party. I must say the members of the Communist Party generally showed a tremendous *esprit de corps*. As many as 90% of the prisoners who ran the camps were German Communists. They had reached that position by protecting each other, and because of that, they survived many trying years, indescribable brutality, and often torture.

The most important condition for surviving was to be able to adjust to the abnormality of camp life, to endure it as if it were normal. One could not even live the following day unless one forgot what happened the day before, and the day one was living through. This does not mean the prisoner had to forget his philosophy or religious principles that he had acquired long ago.

The reaction of the prisoner when he first arrived in camp was crucial. Having been debased and diminished through brutal acts against his soul and body in this unreal world, this living hell on earth, he had to react. If within the first three months his mental and physical system kept deteriorating, he was doomed and died fast. His body gradually lost the physical strength to resist, to exist: he looked to suicide as a way out. Unless his will to live, his mental constitution, was tremendously strong, he just let go and died. If he could not face the conditions as they were, the climate, the work, he was doomed. His soul, his brain, could no longer justify his existence.

The prisoner who had become a physical and mental wreck, but had survived the critical three months, would find himself sooner or later to be an obstacle to other scheming prisoners, and would systematically be eradicated. When the loss of dignity and the humiliation he had suffered smothered all that was good in him and freed deep-rooted evil instincts, which until then had been under control, the prisoner became a 'bum,' and rotten to his comrades.

Strength of character had little to do with social origin, and adjustment had less to do with social origin than with character. It was important to overcome the memory of one's former social standing and let one's real human qualities – sometimes ignored or untapped until then – come to the surface in order to master one's new situation. This was by no means a small feat.

Anyone who tried to transfer his social standing or rank from the outside world to the concentration camp milieu, the most contradictory social order – one without order – was never successful. He would be utterly destroyed from the start and become convinced of his total lack of importance and value.

When a general, a judge, a professor had, on arrival, to stand up on a stool, naked, and be shorn front and back by a criminal, then disinfected in front of all equally mistreated miserable human beings – if he tried to pull rank, he was lost for good. If one had no genuine identity in oneself and identified only with professional and social rank, to a caste or special group, he was lost – not only because of physical degeneration but because of mental destruction. Whatever stiffened his back got broken the moment he stood naked with no visible marks of rank or status before all the other miserable creatures.

This humiliation was suffered by all nationalities, but was harder to bear by people of higher social standing. They felt more downtrodden than simpler, more primitive beings. A laborer who had never tasted some of the finer things of life could not possibly miss them.

This is not to say that the normal world could be equated with this jungle, either. The criminals had an impulse for criminal artistry in finding a way to harm other people. The common criminals had little or no trouble getting close to the SS. The criminal found it relatively easy to make contact with his SS guard: like the SS, his inborn instinct or acquired nature made him willing to mistreat his fellow inmates to obtain advantages.

The criminal, like the SS, had an 'honor code.' A professional criminal, who had been active and consistent in his criminal behavior, had a sense of belonging to a special social class. In becoming an outcast from society, he acquired a certain professional pride in being excluded. Yet inside the group he belonged to, he developed a certain camaraderie and loyalty; like the SS, he had no reservations about what was right or wrong as long as it suited his group.

On the other hand, the 'asocial elements' had in them the will to be apart from society, they looked for contacts only to survive but not to make friends. The so-called asocial element did not get close to the SS, but would not hesitate to step on his fellow inmates for material advantage. The asocial element found a common interest with the materialism that governed the SS and the criminals.

Outside the law, another society, without humanity or principles other than common interest, was created between the SS and their criminal prisoners. These prisoners could let their bad instincts go, and satisfy their lust for domination over other men the way they had been dominated by the police, prison guards, and the SS themselves.

The soul of concentration camp prisoners had been squashed like grain between millstones. No one came out of it the way he had gone in. But generally people came out with the same convictions they possessed before entering. It would be a mistake to think of the camps as a melting pot. The camp unified reactions but not the men who went in. Whoever related to the SS must have had similar or equal characteristics to begin with.

One difference between the criminals and the asocials as compared to the SS: they would sometimes acquire new feelings, closer to those of the normal world, while the SS, believing they belonged to a special caste of men and were a race apart, never permitted the slightest individual variation.

An SS hardened more and more, and could not develop himself; on the contrary, he became more and more primitive. He was proud to belong to a world order which he was told he would dominate; he would be the master over the rest of the universe. He assumed that the rigidity of his actions would guarantee him a life of relative luxury, luxury he never would have acquired if he had had to work for it, because he had neither the intellectual means nor the will to do so.

Prisoners classified as criminals or asocials, but who didn't really belong to these categories, had to go along with the rest, because otherwise their hatred of the real criminals and asocials would have made their existence impossible and would have caused an early death. These prisoners still had the desire to find their way back to normal society, but they had to remain with their group in order to keep the group's protection against the SS. All they could do was to try to subsist, without attracting too much attention to themselves. They had to comply and carry the burden of their fate. They showed no opposition. They tried to keep soft jobs without hurting other prisoners and without attracting attention.

Others had no real reason to be in camp; they were just Frenchmen who were probably misguided by propaganda or greed. They were black marketeers, volunteer workers in Germany who infringed some rule while working there. Their punishment was not in proportion with their crime. But who was there to judge others?

It was important and difficult to make the decision that no extra food was to go to them, even when it was available. They got only the regular rations and treatment at work that was set out for all prisoners. They were left outside the circle of resistance fighters, who felt they had forfeited the right to be helped when in need. Of course this was a hard law, but it was observed. These particular prisoners had a hard time because they were excluded: being without friends in camp was the worst situation one could possibly face.

Beside the French resistance fighters, there were many prisoners of other nationalities at Natzweiler who were also NN's, (*Nacht und Nebel*) prisoners, who had been sent to camps under the Night and Fog decree of the *Wehrmacht* for the death punishment of political prisoners. Although many disappeared in the nightmare of concentration camp life, they usually had good morale and believed that the eventual outcome of the war would be an Allied victory. This kept them morally strong and helped them overcome terrible physical conditions.

Differences showed up occasionally between the different nationalities, but generally the foreign political prisoners demonstrated a common front and a cohesion which didn't exist among the German prisoners.

Some of these political prisoners, if they survived the critical first six months, became old hands at passing up hard or difficult work. They would disappear or just give the impression of motion without doing much. It was most important to conserve one's strength and any small physical reserves at one's disposal. Each motion could weaken the prisoners, most of whom weighed below 100 pounds and were very feeble. One had to avoid unnecessary motion or effort, while giving the SS guards the impression that one was really working. It was an art in itself. One had to give the impression, from a distance, of being a hard-working prisoner.

It took most prisoners a long time to realize that the SS would do everything they could to make them die, slowly but surely. Many, many inmates could not bring themselves to submit to the least discipline. When observed, they attracted the attention of the SS. From then on, instead of leaving them alone, the SS stayed with them constantly, making them work really hard and beating them endlessly, always wounding them in ways that could not be healed.

Once in a while a few aspirins became available, and some sulfur powder to disinfect the wounds and close up the scars, but most of the time these undernourished, exhausted prisoners had very little built-in resistance. Sepsis and gangrene announced their painful death.

While the prisoner's body was deteriorating under the regimen they were made to follow, the SS and the Gestapo were doing their utmost to destroy the prisoner's soul .With daily life so hard, so inhuman, death seemed the best way out to many. In order to survive, prisoners had to be proud of their past, convinced that what had brought them there was well worth it. They had to believe that victory was theirs.

Chapter XIV
Conclusion

After the war, André posing bemusedly in his Dachau stripes.

The world is still in turmoil. I have had no political ambitions and no longer take on noble causes, but I am happy to live in a country where men are free and can live according to their own convictions.

What do I have to say to the young people today? Fight for whatever you think is right, stand up for your rights. Never give up, even against all odds. Never give in to naked power and oppression. Live and help as much as you want others to.

Our memory has to remain alive. This memory has become a collective memory, because what we have lived through has meaning greater than ourselves. Beyond the events themselves, our experience can light a way to clarity in the future.

I still meet some of my former comrades from time to time; they still have not gotten over the treatment they received from the Germans; they can accept that so many had been shot, but not the Germans' dehumanizing acts or the way they kept their prisoners like animals.

This should never happen again. Germany must remain powerless and divided because, basically, the German people have not changed. They are still the same. Never forget that the guards, the members of the Gestapo and the SS were composed of normal people like us all; we must think of the consequences when we recognize that normal people – teachers, postmen, workers, doctors – could be turned into torturers and murderers.

What happened to us happened in an ordinary time. The Nazis could only accomplish what they did, first in Germany and later in all the occupied territories, thanks to a lot of complicity in high-ranking places, and also thanks to the indifference, lack of courage, ignorance, and will not to believe what seemed to be the incredible acts of the Germans.

Had the then-free world gone into active opposition to the Nazi executioners, they could not and would not have done what they did later on.

Being in the underground was rich in itself. It was a great feeling to be doing something, to have a goal.[139] With a target to reach, it was worth living even in dire circumstances – danger did not count.

Freedom of mind and physical freedom are a must, yet only when we lose them do we value them. No matter what the odds, these are worth fighting for. Even if the fight seems impossible to win, one must never, never give up. This is why so many women and men went to the ends of the earth, never to come back. And we few survivors must make sure their sacrifice was not in vain.

We must feel responsible for the destiny of everybody. This is what will inform us and help us become immune in the future; it will immunize us against all negations of the values on which our civilization is based. That is why we must not leave anything untold about this terrible past. That is why this book had to be written.

André in Rennes after the war. Andre is wearing his Forces Françaises Libres (FFL) wartime 'moustique' parachute wings on his right chest showing that Andre was jump-qualified and, pinned on his left chest pocket, an FFL version of the badge of Britain's Parachute Regiment Regiment badge, which he was also entitled to wear having undertaken his training in England. FFL version (with the Cross of Lorraine) was more coveted – showing as it did that he continued the fight from outside France. (See closeup of his medals and parachute badges further on.)

[End of the memoir.]

André's Official Reports
to the French Government

Report of Captain André Peulevey

Prisoner of war until the end of August 1940 I found myself facing the choice of going to England to continue the war or of staying in France in order to do so. Thinking I would be more useful here, I stayed.

Entering into the Railroads (Management District of Rennes) as secretary-interpreter I was after 4 weeks assigned to the SNCF [to deal] with the occupying forces. Being able to travel freely, having great technical resources (telephone, telegraph, car trains) at my disposal with the help of the Head of the District L. Turban (arrested and died in Germany) a network of sabotage groups spread throughout Brittany. The entire management personnel of the SNCF (Chief of PC, Division Inspector and others; station chiefs of the District all participated. Important centers in Rennes (PC) St. Brieux, Morlaix, Auray, Plechatel, Pouancé, Lannion, Chateaubriant, Mordelles, Montfort s/Meu, Rosporden, Paimpol, Landerneau, Lorient, Brest, Vannes, Quimper, Quimperlé and Quiberon. In almost all the other stations were members of the organization who were in direct link with the PC of Rennes via the dispatching of the [traffic] controller of Rennes. (Operators: Mevel, Jaffré, Bernon, active members of the group and recognized by the F[rance] C[ombattante]. The heads of other centers are all known to the France Combattante.

Starting in the month of October my first sabotage groups started to operate. I'll describe that further on. Our first goal was sabotage. The second was the parachute group; I put Lt. A. Leroux in charge of recruiting volunteers outside of the SNCF and he acquitted himself very well. I had many parachute terrains identified that could serve at the opportune time. At that stage it was about working in silence and without making any noise; the moment for a military intervention by the Allies could not be counted on for several years. I therefore dedicated myself to knowing as far in advance as possible the intentions and plans of the Germans (creation of new airfields, speeding up of the movement of trainloads of raw materials for the construction of submarine bases, construction of new bases for troops,etc.) so as to delay the execution of these projects or simply torpedo them, while imputing the fault to the German authorities themselves.

I was perfectly assisted by my hierarchical chiefs at the SNCF and we succeeded in blocking the rails at certain moments that were considered critical by the Germans; from Brest to Hamburg and from Lorient to Upper Silesia. Along those tracks not a single garage was free and some of their trains sometimes took 2 or more months en route. The result was a considerable slowdown in the construction of their projects, thousands of Todt workers were paid to do nothing, the rolling stock was immobilized for much longer that the German chiefs of staff foresaw it would take, etc. ...That's an example among many others, I am not mentioning all the accidental 'hot boxes', frequent machinery breakdowns; it would take too long to describe all the measures taken that were the basis of systematic and absolute sabotage and that for a stretch of 15 months, without the Germans noticing a single thing, this thanks to the close and discreet collaboration of all members of the network. I will no longer give the names of my collaborators, they having been already all recognized by la France Combattante. The orders were generally given directly by me or my seconds in command, either Mr. Remaud (since shot) Mr. Leroux, Mr. Lignel, Mr. Le Deuff. I myself conducted the necessary communications and which were weekly, for some centers.

Starting in the month of November 1940 I conducted intelligence gathering in a continuous way. Contacted by Captain Michelet (Michel probably) I made detailed weekly reports on everything having to do from close up or a distance with German military and civilian activities, railroad or not. Helped by my perfect knowledge of German and the trust that all the German services had in me, disposing of all the passes and wirecutters possible, I was able to penetrate all the military and forbidden zones in Brittany. So I visited all the coastal defense zones, naval and submarine bases (Lorient, Brest, St. Malo, etc.) all the airfields served by the Railroads (St. Jacques, Lannion, St. Bri.., Vannes, Dinard, etc...) I went on board German submarines in Lorient; I visited a new model of minesweepers at St. Malo; I was able to see everything for myself, I took photos, drew the installations to illustrate my reports. This took place usually in the presence of German high-ranking military functionaries and German civilians.

Being the Delegate of the SNCF and the Secretary Interpreter for the District Director I had to participate in all the military and economic conferences in which we were concerned. In this way, I set up a small intelligence network which kept growing. In March 1941 I was led to join up with FFC Network 31 where I worked under the registration 31AQ (Alias Martin). Le Neveu or André (my first name) was the alias used with my agents.[140] Starting from that time I regularly liaised between Rennes and Nantes or Rennes and Paris to receive orders from my boss and communicate them to others.

When my boss was arrested in October 1941 I found myself at the head of a large organization of sabotage on the one hand and of intelligence on the other with centers identified above, plus new centers like Bréhat and Carantec. One of my agents, member of a collateral group of the SNCF, had infiltrated the Gestapo in Rennes and we were able to pick up precious information from the point of view of CE [Counter-Espionage]. I won't give you more ample details on my activity as an agent, which is not possible given the multiplicity of little facts forming a whole (for example emptying a German gas mask during a visit to the *Feldkommandantur* while the guy was out, so as to verify if the Germans had found a new antidote for a new English gas that was thought to have been known to the Germans).

Having lost contact with London, but finding myself in charge of a radio that worked well I searched for a contact. That's when I met Commander Yves Le Tac who introduced me to his brother Joël. I then offered to put myself and my sabotage groups under his orders and to join his 'Overcloud' network – he for his part would share some elements with me who could obtain good information. During our trip to London this undertaking was ratified by the corresponding services.

I will go back in time to explain my activity preceding my arrest. After the disappearance of my Boss I tried to retrieve the elements that I knew to have been part of the 31 line. Partial success, but it almost got me arrested in Paris when I wanted to fish out one of our best agents who was working in the high command of the German army air corps, and I was followed, but succeeded in getting away. At the same time I took charge of a large group in Northern France, (Déan, of Chaumont, from Lille) having regained contact thanks to the Overcloud network and to the Jonny intelligence network (that I also found) I extended the reach of my organizations. I started by training true intelligence agents by teaching how to operate, produce reports, etc…

On January 2 1942 I accepted the offer of Commandant Le Tac to leave with him for England. There, I got my parachute certificate at Ringway, I followed all the courses of ciphers, codes, pick-up and others. On leaving England, I was put in charge of two important missions for which I had been designated Director, one for intelligence and the other for the evacuation of fallen aviators and parachutists to be repatriated – the organization of a new network with radio operators etc. For my first assignment, regular communications by sea (and by air) were planned, I myself had chosen two radio operators who were to follow me 8 days later. I carried very detailed instructions of great military import as well as a rather considerable sum. This was returned by me as soon as I returned to France [after the end of the war] because I was able to [hide] this money at the house of friends before my arrest...

On the day after my return from England, that is on February 5, I was arrested in my office in Rennes. Nothing was found on me I was even able to make the two films containing my instructions disappear. The search conducted at my place yielded nothing, my precautions having been taken before my departure for England. I was transferred to Fresnes via Angers. Very harsh interrogations (blows and torture) without results. In July 1942 I was identified as Agent 31AQ after a confrontation with a radio operator for the group who had received telegrams for me.

The 31 affair was judged in November 42, 15 agents were shot. My dossier was separated and I did not appear in court. I was cited in January 1943 Rue de Saussaies where Captain Lindemann and Chief Adjutant Sommer notified me of my death sentence for intelligence with the enemy, sentence that appeared in my file.[141] They told me that I was being held now to determine my other activities.

I was deported to Germany in July 1943 to the extermination camp of Natzweiler (Struthof) where I stayed until September 1944 – evacuated at the time of the Allied advance, I was sent to Dachau from where I was sent to Allach. Brought back to Dachau because NN in January 1945 I was liberated on April 29th by the American army. For two years I managed to avoid any *Kommando* working for German Arms production. I spent a year in solitary confinement at Fresnes and I came back to France after 40 months of imprisonment and deportation on May 18 1945. (Typescript copy in André's archive.)

Report of 'Joseph dit [called] André Scheinmann' to the French government

In the mid 1950's, André submitted this second report when his records were updated to his birth name. He gives his 'pseudonyme' as 'André M. Peulevey alias LE NEVEU', updates with his true birth date and location in Munich, his nationality as French and his rank as Captain in the (French) Reserves, and adds some important details. The name spellings are his.

I) Service in the Resistance from November 1940 to 29 April 1945: 'Prisoner of war on June 20 1940 – escaped July 26, 1940. Became interpreter in the SNCF – Rennes district (I&V) . Named Delegate of the SNCF to the German authorities. Professional and military activity ran conjointly. Monitored all movement on the extent of the SNCF network from Rennes. As Delegate, I represented the SNCF at all meetings with the Germans, whether about shipping of raw materials to Germany, troop transports, construction materials for their bases, etc. ... economic program ... for 15 months I slept an average of 4 hours, having to assume my professional activities and my covert activity at the same time. You have my complete dossier and I have nothing to add. [page 1]

II) Account of Activity and its Importance: Member of the George-France (groupe 31) network; head of the group 'Bête Noire' – sabotage group of the SNCF – Member of 'Overcloud'. Sabotage carried out from October 1940 to January 1942. Intelligence regularly transmitted during that same time. Recruiting of agents and creation of sabotage and intelligence network. Liaison assured to send messages to Nantes, Paris, Le Man, Bordeaux, etc. All these activities have been verified and are related in my dossier – proof of which is the receipt of this card of Deportee of the Resistance. Maritime operation and debarking and embarking of agents. Traveled to London and back.

[III) left blank]

IV.) Arrest: February 4 on return from London. During my absence a large part of the organization had been discovered (betrayed by Alain de Kergolec, Sub-Lieutenant, radio operator of the FFL arrested and went over to Service to the Gestapo, source of the sentencing and execution by shooting of 15 agents of my group, 'Bête Noire.')

V.) Decorations received: Order of the Army Corps 15 February, 1946; Knight of the Legion of Honor, decree of 12 March, 1946 [reissued 11 April 1952 to Scheinmann]; Officer/Medal of the Resistance, decree of 24 April 1946, awarded 17 May 1946

PART TWO:
Cher Camarade

Cher Camarade ... mon capitaine ... mon lieutenant ...
Monsieur Le Neveu ... 31AQ ... MI6 #99421 ... #4368 at
Natzweiler and #101739 at Dachau ... Martin ... Turquoise ...
interprète ... Herr Dolmetscher ... 0419064, French Liaison
Officer ... Agent from C ... A.N. Other ... Mon cher ami ...
Mon cher André ... Mon chef ...
Who was André Peulevey, really?

'Falsity only has the power to deceive others, but it
changes nothing with regard to one's identity...'[142]

Introduction:
The rest of the story

We could never know the camps as André knew them, or his life and times as he lived them, if he had not written his story. In this part of the book, we draw on both the public and private archives to illuminate how André managed his war, in ways his memoir sometimes only alludes to or does not tell at all. Besides pulling back the curtain on his comrades, André's personal collection reveals more than told in his memoir or admitted to in life about his own struggles and accomplishments.

Now his story, like much of the story of the French resistance, moves into another dimension with the opening of the National Archives of Great Britain and France.[143] New insights and perspectives from the archives continue to unfold the history that for more than 50 years was written only with the help of first person accounts.[144] Even with these government sources, the caveat of Vera Atkins, still applies: "No one can write a book about resistance and get it straight; the reality is always more complex than what any author can express."[145]

Even more significant, André's private archive, revealed by his son a few years ago, is a vast and valuable addition to the institutional resources. The first chapter of this part of the book tells how and why André and the SIS worked together, then how they negotiated with the French in London to reassign his saboteurs to the SOE and the BCRA while preparing him with funds and radio operators to set up two new SIS-funded missions.

André begged me at our last meeting to tell his story 'for my comrades.' Who were his comrades? His memoir mentions a dozen – his private archive reveals hundreds more, and paints a portrait of each one. The second chapter of this part of the book conveys some of their story, as he discovered more about them, and they discovered more about him – the man his agents wrote to after the war as 'Cher Camarade.' Writing their history into the ledgers, he worked for them longer than they worked together in the Resistance. His special friendships with some of them come to light.

Leafing through his personal papers we discover how he morphed and maintained body and soul, and the very much needed caring and protection that he gave and sometimes received. In the third chapter this focus becomes more personal to him. The precarious and vulnerable positions he found himself in did not end with the end of the war, nor did his strategies for navigating them.

We see he parlayed his illness and stay at the typhus ward in Dachau into being listed as 'camp staff' and taking on yet another *sub rosa* leadership and rescue role with the International Prisoners' Committee. We discover that – and why – he joined a half-dozen 'Officer Clubs' in Paris – while being tracked by the French police as an 'alien' non-citizen. We glimpse his attempts to continue in intelligence and to work in the European community.

More intimate details emerge as to the toll taken by his personal struggles coping with the loss of his parents and the expropriation and thievery that robbed him of his cherished possessions. There were sequels of his concentration-camp experiences that he never shared, from chronic, life-long illnesses to an attack-dog bite at Natzweiler. He finally comes to a resolution with his return to a pre-war identity as he left Europe behind.

Chapter 1
André's War:
Resistance and the SIS

We see him working his way through nations at war, the influence of his male relatives in uniform and in resistance to Germany, and his mission with the Secret Services of two other countries, though not a citizen of either.

> 'Clashes on the battlefield could be fought by men of relatively limited gifts, the virtues of the sports field: physical fitness, grit, a little initiative and common sense. But intelligence services suddenly needed brilliance.'[146][147]

On his torturous and exciting journey, André, born in one country, became a fighter for freedom in another, and, cloaked in a false identity, managed to spy for a third. What, beside personal survival, fueled this compulsion? He always said that he had wanted to rise so far in the networks – to go to England especially – so that the next time he went he could take his parents to safety.

Although his parents were immigrants, André felt at home in Germany, and even wanted to stay on when they left in 1933. He felt all the more keenly the dislocations of the society to which his family had been contributing members (socially, militarily, and economically) when their home and their livelihood were threatened. André's individualistic vision and insights – very different from the start than the common wisdom that all would be well – had been imparted to him by his parents. They did not accept the status quo in Poland nor in Germany, their first country of refuge.

'My father was a militant,' André described him in his 1997 Survivors of the Shoah interview.[148] His father was Max, an immigrant to Germany, was born Mendel in Galicia, Poland, under the rule of the Austro-Hungarian Empire. 'He had been in the Austrian Army and he was wounded in the

[First World] War. He was very active in the Austrian-German association because he thought it was important for a Jewish man to be a veteran, and so on.'

André's father Max Scheinmann, near time of the beginning of this story. At right, Regina with her brother Kuba and his dog Jeakky, near the end of her story.

Immediately after Hitler's *putsch* (attempt to topple the German government by armed force) in 1923, and continuously from then on, Max spoke publicly about the Nazi threat at German veteran organization meetings. 'He didn't believe it was any good and he tried to warn people what was coming, to no avail. He made those speeches to open meetings, to organisations, to the general public. When we lived in Düsseldorff, before we left, he had a license to carry a gun; the Gestapo came, picked up the gun and his license in 1933.'[149] Max was thus a fighter, an early German resistor, an outspoken enemy of Fascism and a powerful example for his son.[150]

After the German occupation of France, André was resisting the nation of his birth from outside Germany. Like his father, he may be considered part of the German resistance to Hitler. Taking pride in military accomplishment came to André also from his mother's brothers, who served in the Polish Army.

André's War: Resistance and the SIS

André's Polish uncles in military uniform, and his uncle Joseph Torn who, as André comments in his memoir, 'served on General Pilsudski's staff and reached the rank of colonel, which was otherwise unheard of for a Jew.'

Some compare relative intelligence skills by nationality, others by culture.[151] Are resistance and espionage more likely to be chosen by people who, like André, have an early awareness of being out of kilter with their environment? Are such people more likely to be successful in a variety of languages, cultures, and mores?[152]

Repeated separations from each community, starting from when his family left Germany, not only protected him from outside threats but also gave André the power to realize his individual strengths apart from group identity.[153] The separation from his parents and not knowing their fate may have been the circumstance that liberated him to save himself and others. Andre's analysis of survival in the concentration camps, couched in general terms, would apply to himself as well:

'It was important to overcome the memory of one's former social standing and let one's real human qualities – sometimes ignored or untapped until then-come to the surface in order to master one's new situation. If one had no genuine identity in oneself and identified only with professional and social rank, with a caste or special group, he was lost – not only because of physical degeneration but because of mental destruction.'

André's truth, that freedom is a right, drove him to continue to engage in the fight after the Army, the government leadership, and the citizens of France, the country he was fighting for, asked him to accept defeat. One of the women in André's networks, Simone Alizon, later wrote: 'It is true that one had to be a bit crazy and have faith enough to move mountains to fight against an adversary who was winning on all fronts, occupying all of Europe.'[154]

Many of the early resistors did not even know that they were working for the British. Their hope and ambition was to work 'with London' – a bastion of freedom just across the channel from their shore. Resistance, espionage and counter-espionage were thus bedfellows in the war for liberation from the Nazis, and not just in France, and not just by Britain.'[155] Few of the lower-echelon French resistors, delighted to be in touch 'with London', knew where their reports were going, and many would have been surprised to know that it was to the SIS... [156]

Britain reciprocated by cultivating the resistance in Brittany.[157] The British supported its nefarious and heroic deeds because 'the enemy [German] forces in France constituted the most direct and immediate threat to Britain, and the most decisive actions of the war would have to be fought on French soil.'[158]

It was fortunate indeed that André had ended up in Brittany, the region of France most engaged in the Resistance. Not only congenial to his fighting spirit, but to his (secret) identity as a 'stranger,' Resistance was mixed-class as well as mixed-nationality, although it's been recently claimed that the Resistance in Brittany was composed in greater part of 'indigenous' French than in the rest of France, occupied or unoccupied.[159]

André had been officially assigned a new identity after he enlisted, complete with a different real name, parents, residence, and date of birth.[160] This was a typical practice in the French army as well as in their Foreign Legion. It was feared that soldiers with a German name would be shot as traitors rather than be treated as prisoners of war. And so Joseph Scheinmann for twelve years lived with the 'strange bedfellow and unexpected ally' of a *pseudo,* an alias. 'André Maurice Peulevey' became so familiar to him that he wouldn't even blink if he heard the name Joseph ... and in fact, he kept the name André even when he legally went back to his birth name in 1951.

Andre first manifested his shape-shifting strategy when he liberated himself – escaped – from being held at a prisoner of war facility in Brittany when he learned that all prisoners were to be removed to Germany. The ID card he obtained at that point from the French Social Security office showed him to be a French citizen.

Engagement in active resistance 'is based on voluntarism and the desire to go beyond the status quo, at the risk of losing one's bearing in reality.' André's desire to go beyond the status quo, the reason why he and so many found their struggle so exalting, was that he was going beyond one reality to meet himself in another, as many do in their mid-twenties, even in less troubled times.

When André showed up for his interview the office of Louis Turban, *Chef d'Exploitation* (Chief of Operations) for the French National Railroads/SNCF headquarters in Rennes, he was already armed with the 'imagination, the audacity and tenacity' which Rod Kedward attributes to most early Resistance.

He accepted the position as a German-French interpreter after confirming that he would be working for Turban, not for the Germans. When he walked into his future boss's office he already had done his research and knew that Louis Turban was married to an Englishwoman. So his 'strategic opportunism' as Olivier Wieviorka terms it, already had him pegging Turban as a good bet for hating the Nazis.

Turban's wife, Agnes Ingham, a graduate of the University of London and a teacher of English, became leader of the South Brittany sector of Turban and André's territory for 'Groupe 31' (known as Georges-France after the war). She was arrested at the very beginning of February 1942, at the same time as her husband and André.[161] Condemned to be 'deported to die in captivity', she was sent to be a hostage (held to be shot in future reprisals by the German occupiers) at the prison of Romainville but was released on 10 March 1943.[162]

Louis Turban was a highly educated engineer from one of the *grandes écoles* (elite French graduate schools) – the ENSAM, École nationale supérieure d'arts et métiers.[163] André, a high-school grad (possibly) and an immigrant *apatride* (with no nationality) would now be working with a member of the French élite old boy network.[164]

André brought a brilliant scheme, fully-fledged, to his boss in order to damage the German command of the railroads under the guise of assisting them. Using his native knowledge of German personality and culture, he chose the vocabulary and attitude that would lead the enemy to trust him: words like 'demands, perfect, organize, perfect execution, detail' lulled the German higher-ups, catering to their vanity, arrogance, and obsessions. 'Intelligence is about people and the study of people.'[165]

Along with physical sabotage conducted by their first network, *La Bête Noire*/the Black Beast, André and Turban worked out a more subtle, long-lasting and far-reaching form of sabotage, scheduling employee leaves at just the time that the Germans were gearing up for shipments for their various construction projects. [166]

Taking the initiative and preemptively playing the aggressive victim in a partnership that was literally 'going off the rails,' André guided the blame onto the Germans for their 'lack of organization.' [167] André would continue to use this ploy of his supposed shared interests with the Germans when he ended up in Gestapo prison, under interrogation, and in the camps. His command of the oppressor's language, mindset and attitude worked 'within the major language system to undermine [the] oppressor's regime of signs and values.'[168]

Although agents were not supposed to join multiple networks, the network leaders inevitably knew of others. Because André had access to London, in 1941 smaller networks gravitated toward him to gain a pathway for their information. These included the groups of Christian father Jean-Baptiste Legeay and the groups of Jean Le Dantec, Georges Lehmann, and La Bande à Sidonie, headed by Suzanne Wilborts. '[169]

'It was only from July 1941 that we joined up to Group 31 of the Intelligence Service. at the request of engineer Turban of Rennes, who directed that group for Brittany,' according to Wilborts. 'His secretary André PEULEVEY P2 came to my house to ask me to only do intelligence for them, with my whole group, which I accepted. Jean LEGEAY did the same when I asked him to. Therefore, from that time on, I would give all my papers to TURBAN, bringing them to him myself when I would go to lunch with him in Rennes, or sending them via my daughter, YVETTE who was weekly liaison agent. It is certain that he transmitted them to England under his name...'[170]

That youngest daughter of Suzanne Wilborts, Yvette, later known as Marie-Jose (Mari-Jo) Chombart de Lauwe, tells in her autobiography, *Resister toujours (Always Resist)*: 'I regularly shuttled between the coast and Rennes. My *Aussweiss* [permission to pass] had been renewed. I could move between the shoreline and the interior of Brittany. Great luck. Bicycle, train, bicycle. I hid the documents that I carried in my physics and anatomy course materials. I handed them over in Rennes to a man that I knew sometimes under the name of André Le Neveu and at others as André Peulevey.

'He was in his twenties, with light-colored eyes, fine features ... I knew almost nothing of this man on whom my life depended. I was to learn more after the Liberation, when I was to see him again in Brittany. His real name was Joseph Scheinmann. His life was out of the ordinary. He was a German Jew, born in 1915 in Munich. His family emigrated to France, fleeing the Nazi tide. He volunteered for service in the French Army in 1939 under the name André Peulevey. After the defeat, he became the German interpreter at the SNCF. Perfect cover for his clandestine activity. He used to go to London occasionally to report in or receive instructions. He was the second in command to Turban. Arrested at the same time, he was deported to the Alsatian camp of Natzweiler-Struthof, then to Dachau. Under the name of Peulevey, fortunately: the SS never knew his true identity. After the war, he went off to live in the United States. From there, he sent me a manuscript of his own story, that I kept...'[171]

Writing to André in January 2000, Marie-José, on her letterhead as President of the Paris-based Fondation pour la Mémoire de la Déportation, gave André feedback and encouragement to publish his story, and reminisced with other details of his account and hers:

'In the Spring of 1941, we received a visit from an envoy from London, who made the contact for us with Turban, the head of the network to which the small network directed by my mother, called 'La bande à Sidonie,' eventually became attached...'[172] I used to fetch the documents and coastal maps assembled by my mother and bring them to Rennes. There, I passed them either to Louis Le Deuf (Place Saint Sauveur), or to you, at our appointed meeting places, the Café de l'Europe or at the Café de la Paix. I was eighteen. You (André) were also called 'Le Neveu' [The Nephew]. I also remember a dinner with Joël Le Tac.'

And so we come to Joël Le Tac, a well-known member of the Free French resistance and his brother Yves, who is much less celebrated today for his role in intelligence and propaganda and building the network in Paris than Joël is for sabotage. Reading both sides of the story of the meeting of Joël and André, one realizes that in this most dangerous game, suspicion was used as a precious ally in choosing a teammate. People looking into the history of these secret enterprises have remarked on how decisions to join or avoid often were made in a split second, based on a look, a first impression.

The challenge was compounded in the case of the Le Tac/Peulevey alliance by the fact that they worked for different intelligence services, and different nations. Through them, Resistance and Espionage were mated in the collaboration of the Free French/BCRA and the British Special Operations Executive/SOE-RF, that Joël belonged to, with the British Secret Intelligence Service/SIS/MI6 for which André and his networks were operating.

Until November 1941 when they joined up with Le Tacs, André and Turban had been supported by the SIS. This was also the case for most of the smaller networks they directed or worked with (Aigle, La Bête Noire, La Bande à Sidonie,) and many of the agents they recouped from networks broken by betrayal including their main network, Georges-France/Groupe 31 and those of Father Legeay, Lehmann, Le Dantec and Johnny. André was SIS agent # 99421, and his official nickname 'The Nephew' reflected his relationship with his SIS/MI6 handler Thomas Greene ('Uncle Tom.')

The rivalry between the various services for agents mirrored the jockeying between the heads of governments of France and Britain.[173] Among French agents, wrote Jean Pierre-Bloch, 'At one time it was an unpardonable crime to have worked with the British.'[174] André, a self-guided outsider with mostly professional, rather than personal and family ties to the community, would not let opprobrium get in his way. His determination to only 'work with the British' was unshakeable.

Even within the British services, the SIS ('Hush Hush') clashed with the SOE ('Bang Bang!'), the organization hatched out of the bosom of the SIS at the beginning of WWII to 'set Europe ablaze!' 'Whereas they [SIS] naturally desire quiet waters in which to fish for Intelligence, the activities of S.O.E. in the same regions ... inevitable stir up trouble. Consequently there is a fundamental clash of interests in whichever part of the world the two organisations are working.'[175] And SOE was the organisation most visibly supporting De Gaulle's BCRA, that the Le Tacs worked with, while André served the SIS.

These differences were resolved during their trip to London in January-February 1942 . The collaboration was underway even before their trip to England, as seen in both Joël's biography and André's memoir of their first meeting six weeks before they left. The negotiations that André and Joël Le Tac began before they arrived in London – the switching, melding and disentangling of their sabotage, intelligence and evasion missions and networks – was ratified while they were there, in agreements that represent an early and as-yet-rare cooperative endeavor of the BCRA, the S.O.E. and S.I.S.

On the trip to London, André was the only SIS agent in a BCRA and SOE crowd.' When André got off the boat in England, De Gaulle's BCRA for whom the Le Tacs were working in liaison with the SOE RF (Free French section) did their best to whisk him away with the others, but he insisted he wanted to work with the British, 'because the English were the only ones who had something going on – nobody else...'[176]

Although no records are ever made available by the SIS, the [re]assignment of their networks, agents and direction are documented in the SOE reports about Joël Le Tac at the National Archives of Great Britain located at Kew. They record his association with 'André Maurice [... blank space] AKA Le Neveu. Where photos are said to be attached thereto for Joël and for Yves Le Tac and Andre Maurice [...], Le Tac headshots are still there while there is none for André.[177]

The reassignment of duties that was to both men's preference was endorsed by the British based on the divergent abilities of Joël Le Tac and André. SOE portrays them in a tactful but ruthless comparison dated January 16, 1942 at the mid-point of their stay and after their debriefings: 'Overcloud [Joël] has been unable to supply us with the information required by you, his work being action and not intelligence. Some information, however, has been obtained through an agent of Commander Dunderdale's who returned to this country at the same time as Overcloud. For such items of intelligence I suggest you would be better served by dealing with the Intelligence Sections...'[178]

At their initial meeting, as André recounts it in his memoir, one can see that within an hour he had not only decided to work with the Joël and his brother Yves (who was the one with whom he remained lifelong friends) but worked out in his mind the strategy that would take them through their meetings in London with their agencies and the future of their networks: *'The thought came to me immediately: why not turn over all my saboteurs to Joël and, in exchange, get all his people who were gathering intelligence information? Joël could also take over the escape organization. That way, everything could be handled in an orderly way.'*

André was writing the script carried out in London by the agencies: his disentanglement from sabotage, that was more 'up the alley' of the S.O.E. and Joël Le Tac, even though sabotage had been the heart of André's first networks operating from the railroads, Bête Noire and Aigle. André showed no vanity or personal stake in holding on to them, given the expediency and efficiency of organizing the talent and resources at hand. It seems André had carte blanche from Turban, as always, to do whatever he thought best. Turban's name or person does not appear in any of the SOE documents about the trip.[179]

This was a novel restructuring of networks between three secret services of two countries: the BCRA and SOE-RF took the sabotage branches of Georges-France into Overcloud, and the SIS would have André work with his intelligence and escape assets of Georges-France as part of developing his new Turquoise mission/network.[180] Yves might have kept his propaganda interests in Overcloud or been tasked to work with André. The lack of detail in the SOE files about Yves's work and his time in England leads to the supposition that he too was working with SIS.

It was André who brought the larger network and more established service to the negotiations. Describing the new assets he had acquired from André, a 'Special Report on "The Black Beast"' to his SOE RF overseers 'From JOE' on 22 December was received just before André and he arrived in England. Joël describes André's sabotage network *La Bête Noire*, that had been running for over a year, as 'an important organization with a great number of agents of the SNCF [French National Railroads.] At its head are people occupying important positions in the C. de F. [Chemins de Fer/railroads]. After several discussions with the person in charge of the organisation, I decided to give this organisation the same importance as a region. This organisation from now on will have its dropping zone and its provisional depot under the name FER 1 ... This organisation needs a radio transmitter ... At their suggestion, that radio could function by dynamo powered in a moving train, and thus could rapidly send news from different places."[181] This ingenious suggestion from 'the person in charge of the organisation' has André's Cheshire cat grin all over it.

How much of André's networks became a substantial portion of Overcloud is depicted in Joël's post-war report 'Historique du Réseau des F.F.C. "Overcloud"' where he says it was composed of : '1 intelligence service, called 31; 1 action service (connected the B.C.R.A.); 1 evasion service (connected to Slocum and Holsworth [sic]); 1 sabotage service (in liaison with SOE "Bretagne Enchaînée"); 1 propaganda service (Captain Bozel) and two sub-networks: "Bête Noire" in Brittany and "Valmy" in Paris.' [182]

The memos from the SOE show divergent numbers of 'agents' ready to work with Joël, but they all show that, as André and Joël anticipated before they arrived in London, that mass would come from the transfer of Bête Noire to Overcloud. A memo from Piquet-Wicks to Gubbins on 28 January 1942 as André and the Le Tacs were wrapping up their trip to London 'gives OVERCLOUD [under Le Tac] an approximate number of 2000 persons ... ready for active work in Brittany.'[183]

How did Le Tac and his handlers come to this figure? The memo quoted above, 'Numbers and Dispositions for Overcloud' states: 'Overcloud's main contact in Brittany is with an organisation of the SNCF (Société Nationale des Chemins-de-Fer) involving a minimum of 500 employees who are prepared for passive sabotage, i.e. the slowing up of time tables, diversion of merchandise and supplies, etc., but who are at present not trained in active sabotage: in any case, they lack the necessary material. At Rennes, Overcloud can depend on approximately 300 potential active agents, mainly drawn from the student class ... At Vannes ... 400/500, at St. Malo ... 500 persons, at Paimpol ... 100 ... The above gives Overcloud an approximate number of 2000 persons in whom he has confidence, and who are ready for active work in Brittany.'[184] The estimate of 300 agents from Rennes is the figure André always mentioned to be the number of his agents.

André went over to London as Le Neveu and came back as Turquoise with 'two new important missions' to head, for intelligence and evasion.[185] His new network would be named Turquoise, as some SIS networks were known by the names of colors. André as its leader would be known by the name of his network, just as Joël was named 'Overcloud.' Since André's were SIS missions, they are still invisible to history, except for the letter of reference in André's archive from Thomas Greene and the receipt for funding of his mission from J.E. Gentry. There are also the documents provided for registering his activities with the French government including from Joël Le Tac, who also mentions André's 'two very important' new missions.[186]

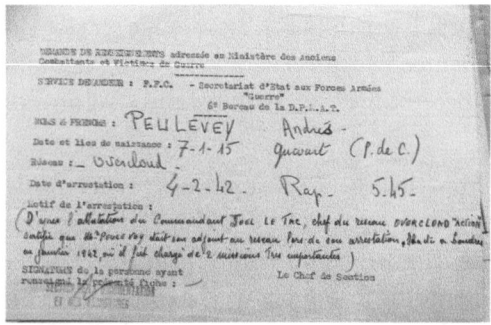

Joël Le Tac signed these information cards documenting for André's 'coming back from London in charge of two very important missions' (top) and 'belonging to network "Action" as part of, in succession, "Aigle" "Georges-France" "Bête Noire".' (bottom.)

Thank you to Pierre de Jaegher and Pierre Tillet for Service Historique de La Défense at Vincennes records GR 16P539178.

Reference cards sworn to by Joël Le Tac for André.

It is likely André got his MI6 agent number 99421 while he was in London. For (SIS) Group 31 (renamed Georges-France after the war) he had been Agent 31AQ.

In the Spanish trial of the Georges-France (Groupe 31 as it was known during the war) network, the network is identified as a Deuxième Bureau – French Secret Service network – relating to the pre-war work of Madame Louis, its head, and others that she brought in to the organization. In the lists presented at that trial of what its agents were paid, André is listed as

'Martin' with his code '31AQ' and Turban, by his alias Tutenglair, with code '31AP' – both receiving 3,000 francs (per month). Another page, also in Madame Louis' hand, lists payments by location, for Rennes: 31AP is listed as receiving 3,000 and 31AQ as receiving 5,000 francs.[187]

The name switch of Groupe 31 to Georges-France, with its heavily patriotic flavor, a change that was made after the war, leads back to the question: these individuals/agents – most receiving a stipend from the British – were they Resistors or spies? Should their missions/networks be considered Resistance or espionage? Olivier Wieviorka settles the question thus: 'If you situate the question from the point of view of London, they were spy networks ... if you situate it from the point of view of French members of those networks, they were resistors. They were not professionals, even if they were paid; they wanted to contribute to the defeat of the Axis and acted accordingly...'[188]

One of the results of the opening of the French Archives is to allow researchers, for the first time, to go through its documents analytically, as Guillaume Pollack, has done. Sponsored by the French Department of the Army, DMCA (executive branch for memory, culture and archives), his 2022 book, *L'armée du silence* quantifies the number of agents and networks 'reporting to/financially dependent on Allied Secret Services.' Pollack notes that even with the handicap of almost 50% of SOE networks not having been allowed to be registered, between 1940 and 1942 the preponderance of networks of Resistance in France were those of MI6 and MI9. He states that in 1940, there were 10 for the Free French and 12 for the British. In 1941, when SOE deployed its first networks in France, eight were registered to the SOE, ten were added for the BCRA and ten for the IS. It was only in 1942 that he finds the numbers reversed, with seventeen networks added for the British and 41 for the Free French.[189]

The jockeying for control of the French resistance of which André was a part was high drama of truly historic import. De Gaulle, who had opened his unofficial government-in-exile outpost in London in late June 1940, was adamant to head France resurrected as an independent nation free from Allied control and administration. He continued to struggle with Churchill and Roosevelt up to the moment of D-Day, about which he was kept in the dark.

During the first two years of the war when André chose to serve Churchill, de Gaulle in any case lacked financial and technical means to nurture the amorphic and un-hierarchical interior resistance. And the flavors of Resistance were as numerous and varied as the networks themselves, with sympathies ranging from monarchical to anarchical, Catholic to Communist, and everything conceivable in between. Even when the Resistance validated his leadership, De Gaulle was ambivalent about its lack of military structure and control.[190]

De Gaulle's Director of Intelligence, Colonel Passy, at the end of his first volume of memoirs about their London operations, after describing their efforts through the end of 1941, candidly assesses their lack of progress (and their agents) in a way that does charmingly little credit to the Free French operation. It also demonstrates in contrast how effective and momentous the SIS-supported networks in France, especially in Brittany, had been during the first 18 months of the occupation, when André was operating, and how valuable were the resources of manpower and organization that he brought to the BCRA/S.O.E network, Overcloud, in December 1941 and January 1942.

'In truth,' wrote Passy, 'the practical results that we achieved from all these [French-run] missions were almost nil; first, because our agents, although full of good will, mostly lacked class or seriousness (but since we had no others we had to use the same ones several times) and also because the French resistance was still at the baby-talk phase.[191] At the end of 1941, we could detect so to speak nothing coherent or solid among all the vague hopes that we had been able to discern. In the occupied zone, apart from some groups of officers brought to our attention by our intelligence agents, we had been able to uncover no organized resistance movement.' [192]

Henry Noguères, a resistor throughout the war, agrees that in the first year, 'In truth, of all the French, active resistors do not even constitute an appreciable minority. Even more serious, "sympathizers," even passive ones, were no more numerous.' He looks to the second year as the time when 'fumbling and mumbling would progress to growth spurts. And after the pioneers would come the organisers. As time went on, the Resistance, little by little, would take on a new persona. But it will always recognize itself in the few women and the few men sketched in these pages. By whose light, from the first night, would never cease to "shine and burn the flame of the French Resistance." ' [193]

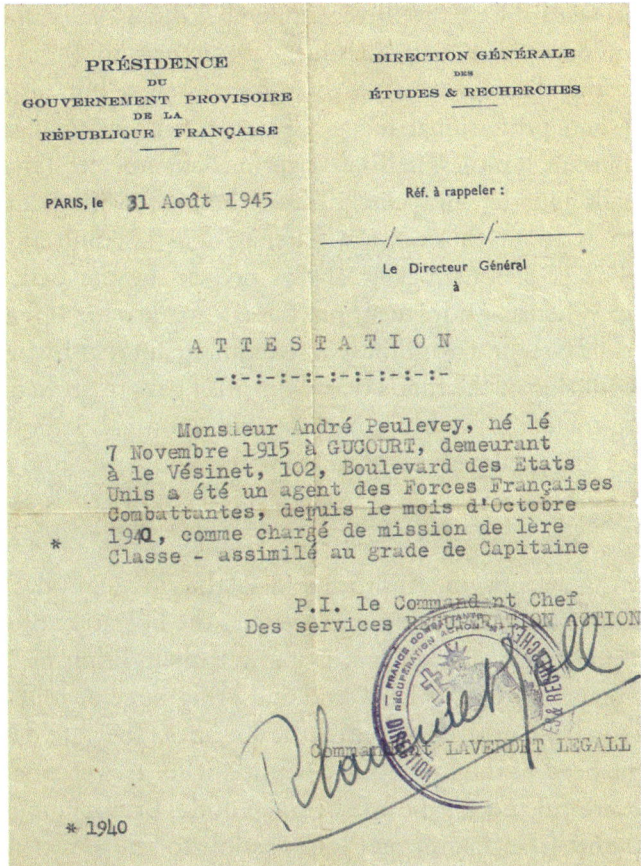

Attestation that André served as an agent of the Forces Françaises Combattantes from the month of October, 1940 on. Signed by Laverdet LEGALL, Commandant Chef des services Récuperation Action. From André's personal archive.

Those pioneers included André and his SIS-related groups and networks in Brittany working for evasion, sabotage, and intelligence. The British exploited and encouraged that region's effervescent reaction to the German occupation. Brittany is acknowledged to have been in the forefront of rejection of the Germans and preeminent of all the regions of France in Gaullist and pro-British sentiment, first to step up to resistance and in greater proportion to all others.[194] André's humorous accounts of the stalwart and witty gestures of mockery across Brittany, its movie theaters, bars, and in its streets, vividly depict its public resistance to German occupation.[195]

Comparing André to a well-placed member of an 'old' French family, Victor Chatenay, whose memoir is full of references to Thomas Greene, illuminates the discrepancies of their social status but also of their personality and professional focus. Chatenay, who worked in the SIS offices in London, is pitiless in his descriptions of his bosses, (and André's) whom he calls 'Dunder' and 'Uncle Tom.' Compared with André's silence and discretion about those two, Chatenay does not pull any punches about Greene, a debonair giant always dressed by the best tailors of Saville Row. Whereas André mentions Greene worked for 1 pound a year, Chatenay calls Greene a skinflint whose requirement that his agents keep minute accounting of the funds that the British gave them was the 'cause of immense tragedies.' [196] More harshly still: 'As usual, I find myself in the presence of a total cretin. I don't think one could ever find a man less suited to the office he holds. He's an elephant making lace. He's stupid and mean...'[197]

Neither can one imagine André in some of the glitzy episodes Chatenay recounts about himself, one for instance after the liberation of Paris: 'My friend Greene, called Uncle Tom, is going to help bring me to Great-Britain by plane. He asks if I can find and bring three or four bottles of Veuve-Cliquot of a great vintage that he specifies. They are destined for the supreme head of the Intelligence Service, who, as everyone knows, is the most powerful and the most secret man of the British empire. Greene well knows that [the champagne] is impossible to find and that it would be fantastic luck if I were able to do so. I ask Raymond Chatelain who, right off, at Fouquet's or Maxim's, or elsewhere, finds them, and gifts them to me. Greene is staggered, and what's more, since I didn't pay for them, I make them my gift. Not having to pay anything, the penny-pinching billionaire is overwhelmed by my munificence.'[198]

The names Chatenay and Chatelain relate to castles. André's names hardly do. He and his agents frequented the Café de la Gare or the Café de la Paix across from the train station, not Maxim's and Fouquet's, the haute cuisine emporia that had been patronized by the Nazis and black marketeers and collaborators during the occupation. Even Peulevey, André's alias, approximates a meaning of 'brought up little.'

Indeed, the resistance cut across many strata of society, as can be discerned by the testimonial letters that fill André's personal archive, written by car repair garage owners, photographers, chemists and secretaries, as well as by members of the aristocracy.[199] 'The small bourgeoisie, craftsmen, laborers, farmers, were proportionally, and on the whole, more likely to be resistors,' according to Colonel Passy.[200]

Now why, when he got off the boat, when all the other agents went with the French, did André say 'I want to work with the British'?[201] Even under pressure of the multiple cultural forces at work in his new social environment in Brittany, the politics of German occupation, and continual sleep deprivation of managing two full-time jobs, one official (for the railroads) and another occult, André managed his career very strategically. When I knew André, and he was asked to what one factor could be attributed the allied victory in World War II, André answered the boy's question before the breath had left his lips: 'Churchill!' [202]

André fully grasped the stature of de Gaulle, both as leader of the Free French in exile in London and in his future role as leader of France after Liberation. He identifies himself as 'Free French' in his memoir in connection with his mission to d'Orves and on departure from Fresnes to Natzweiler, and as a 'Gaullist' under interrogation, and in the concentration camps. After the war he gave de Gaulle's Secret Service head's name, Passy, as a reference for his own status and other honors, and to facilitate registering his agents.

His work in the resistance, however, must have given him a first-hand view that the Brits' was a superior intelligence operation. It didn't take being a rocket scientist to know that the British had every advantage that the French in exile did not; André's finer understanding may have been that de Gaulle was harnessing the efforts of the Free French, and to some extent limited the role of the BCRA, to nation-building in the long-term rather than defeating the Germans by any and all means, which was André's goal.

He had seen the British stay in the war when all Europe had caved to the Germans and the Americans stayed away. He was indebted and loyal to the British who made possible his trip to England that he hoped would be the forerunner to bringing his parents over. More tactically, had André joined the French on arrival in Britain, he would have had to put himself, as well as his operations, under the leadership of Joël Le Tac, whose measure as a loose cannon he must have immediately detected.

Joël's unpredictability was confirmed upon their departure from Brittany, as Lt. Holdsworth reported with understated vehemence to

Captain Picquet-Wicks, in his 'SECRET' report of January 6th/January 7th,1942. 'Overcloud [Joël] whom we rather expected would be returning to the mainland in his canoe, was insistent that he needed to accompany the others to H.Q. [London.] It was pointed out to him that as far as we knew he was not expected ... but he still thought it urgent ... please provide us the opportunity to have the fullest conversations with Overcloud on this subject.' [203]

Not only the British, but also the French noted the erratic indiscretions of Joël. Addressing some of the many ways in which they judged his work to be inadequate, undisciplined, and off target, his BCRA boss had sent two scathing and very lengthy messages to Joël on December 5th. Highlights of 'Courrier 1' include: 'you seem to be wanting to do too many things at one time. You have a well-defined mission; accomplish it, and report on your progress in detail...' Courrier 2: 'We are obliged to observe with regret that your work does not at all correspond to what we expected of you when you left [in October] ...1) You announced in your No.1 [message] "from now on, regular transmissions." That's false, because you gave us no news between October 30 and November 17. We remind you that we can only help you when you will decide to work seriously. 2) Contrary to what you seem to suppose, we are not simply providers of merchandise. ...3) You take initiatives that do not pertain to you and only complicate your task ...Who told you to contact Renault and Cartigny...? Who authorized you to bring over Kopernic and pilots...? Who charged you with mixing into the technical organization of the Paris region...? Who authorized you to cancel everything that involved Baudoin? We ask you not to make decisions that are beyond you. Occupy yourself with your own work, that's enough and will be more useful. By sticking your nose into everything you will get caught...'

It may be that these reprimands were the reason Joël inserted himself into the trip to London when he 'was not expected.' He was on precarious footing with the Free French, but wanted to remain Chef de Réseau (network leader). Whereas he previously had been sent to France by the BCRA on sabotage missions with one or two other men only, he now wanted to assert leadership over the vast network he planned to acquire from André and the SIS. And Joël's older brother Yves, who was listed as being on de Gaulle's 'General Staff' for intelligence, although he had not yet been to London, was going over with André.²⁰⁴ It is no secret that the brothers' relationship always was competitive as well as collaborative.

Yves Le Tac had started a group in Paris in 1941 while his brother was off doing sabotage and returned from this, his first trip to London with a detailed and elaborate mission for intelligence for the BCRA. Yves and André, who got along better, may have planned to work together on Intelligence, which was to be one of André's new missions for the SIS. André and Yves remained lifelong good friends. And Yves receives far less acknowledgement, let alone acclaim, for his Resistance work, up to today.²⁰⁵

Honoring his unerring instincts about Joël and his determination and focus to work with the SIS, André was able to use his time in England to separate his operations from Joël's and be given a leadership position of his own and a lot of funding (two times as much as given to Joël) to run his two new missions for the British under his new codename, Turquoise.²⁰⁶

Not to be minimized in his choice to continue with the British was also the bond with his handler, 'Uncle Tom'. Greene had great respect for André in return, even insisting on taking a few more hours together by going with him on departure from England, although an accompanying officer had been assigned to do that. (Details further on about the trip to England.)

André's alter-ego Chatenay, who worked in the SIS offices of Dunderdale and Greene for eight months when his return to France for them was considered too dangerous, even criticizes the conducting officer assigned to André by SIS, code-named Goodfellow, who was actually Robert de Lesseps. Chatenay describes him as 'a young gentleman [as in: member of the nobility] ... I resent that he hasn't realized that de Gaulle's mission is providential, that his value is exceptional, and that he didn't add his handsome name to the Free French, jilting the English.'²⁰⁷ André never said anything negative about any of his team even in conversation.

André is documented in the photographs made in England of him in disguise. Such disguises were created by theatrical production professionals in the employ of the British government, including James Ernest Elder Wills, the head of SOE's Camouflage Section, and camouflage officer Lawrence P. Williams.²⁰⁸

He mailed these photographs of himself in disguise to his sister Mady in Massachusetts while he was in London. 'I got a letter from André, from England, and in the letter he mentioned he might be able to write to me again and even send pictures. I was thrilled because I even received another letter with some pictures. But I began to worry because I figured out something was not just right because there was no way of traveling between France and England at that time. How could he have gotten to England and communicated from there unless he was involved in some kind of underground activity?'[209] She did not hear from him again until the end of the war.

Photographs of André in disguises created for him in England.

The naval disguise (HMS/His Majesty's Service) originated with R.N.V.R. Holdsworth, who accompanied André on the boat to and from England. In a memo to Picquet-Wicks, 28 January 1942, Holdsworth requested to borrow a sailor's outfit for the purpose, as he puts it, of 'faking-up the naval paybook. Why not provide the agents with bogus Naval pay-books and identification discs so that if we all come unstuck together we all stand a chance of being treated as prisoners of war. Once up on the beach the agents could immediately destroy this valuable short-term cover.'[210] Picquet-Wicks wrote back: 'Your suggestion is an extremely good one. Unfortunately, however, the Naval Liaison Officer has no naval uniforms at his disposal. As photographs need only be of the agent's head and shoulders, would it not be possible to have the necessary photographs taken at your place, where a seaman's jacket and cap can be borrowed for the purpose?'

 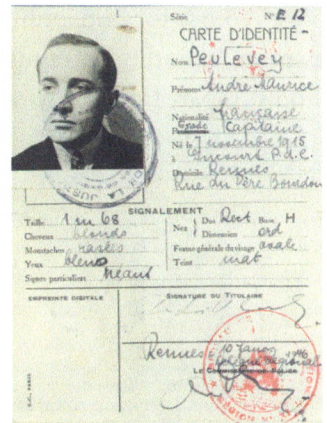 

Not all the photos taken of André in London show him smiling. He used another of four SIS portraits of him in a business suit and striped tie for his 1946 French id, so he must have successfully hidden it, as well as his British bankroll, and possibly more documents, on his return from England before his arrest. He spoke of having chosen the storeroom of a furniture store for that purpose.

For their foreign secret agents, or their citizens destined to return to occupied Europe, the SIS used SOE training schools where the SOE developed characters and scripts, casting and coaching acting, costume and prop design. Agents – the actors – put on the performance of their lives.[211] Some of the acting instruction took place in interrogation scenarios and '96-hour schemes' that agents were tasked to create – to incorporate skills such as passing secret messages, doing reconnaissance, and escaping a pursuer. The instructor who devised and supervised these performances was Paul Dehn, who went on to be a scriptwriter for films like *Goldfinger* and *The Spy who Came in from the Cold*.[212]

Given André's demonstrated record of successful intelligence work for over 15 months in enemy-controlled territory and his scant month in England – which was booked up with meetings between the SIS and BCRA and SOE, and his planning for his new mission with Thomas Greene and Wilfred Dunderdale – it is doubtful the André underwent a full training conducted for SOE's 'amateur' agents at Beaulieu, 'Finishing School for Secret Agents' or at any of their other Special Training Schools.[213,214,215] 'It may well be that, because André had such a short time in England, the

SIS put together a "bespoke" course for him, pulling in instructors to one location to give him classroom/theoretical training, rather than sending him out to the usual "schools" (apart from his parachute training).' [216,217]

Major Paul Dehn, second from left, Political Warfare Instructor, training instructor and costume designer and Captain Art Bushell, fourth from left, who corresponded with Andre in 1946 as part of SIS mop-up operations about founders of Resistance groups in Brittany. Photo and caption with signatures of Personnel later stationed at Camp-X Training Camp in Canada 1943-1944. Courtesy of Lynn Philip Hodgson, http://www.camp-x.com

Wouldn't it be interesting to see comments on André's performance, as Joël Le Tac's radio operator, ('Trained here. Loaned by Free French') Alain Raymond Marie De Kergolay (who later betrayed André) received, for the following courses, among others: 'Fieldcraft: Good – Close combat: Very good – Weapon training: Pistol fair. Tommygun good. Rifle good. Bren good. Grenade Fair – Explosives, etc.: Good knowledge – Map reading etc.: Good – Commandant's remarks: A well-educated man, intelligent but, I think, a little lacking in drive. I did not consider him quite up to the standard of the others.' Another document, in French, from the Overcloud file at Kew, twice says De Kergolay 'could become dangerous' and also reports that he is of 'weak character, very influenceable (especially by money.)'[218]

For André as well as for other agents, a good performance could lead to encores. Agents in enemy territory had to play their part to perfection, every day. Although he would have few playacting 'encores' as a free man, his new training may have contributed to his successfully hiding his documents and British bankroll and dealing with interrogations. André had many dire occasions to use these skills after his arrest to save his life, the life of his comrades, and to hide the role and funding of the SIS, through to and even after the end of the war, and for the rest of his life.

Parachute training is the only part of the course for secret agents for which we have his completion certificate from his instructor, issued to him when he was in London in December 1945-January 1946. André's back was injured in the parachute training, which may be why he made only three instead of the usually required six jumps from a plane.[219] To the end of his life he suffered from the injury, and typically, he mentions nothing about that in his writing, nor does he give details of the training.

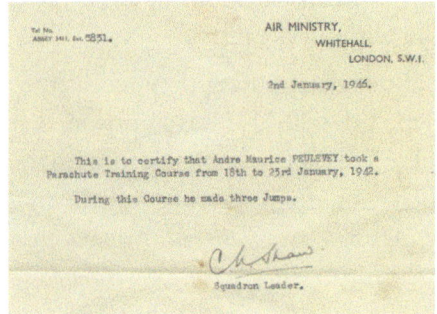

Squadron Leader Cautley Nasmyth Shaw signed parachute training course, lasting from 18 to 23 January 1942, certification from the Air Ministry, London. 'During this Course he made three Jumps.'

'Wg Cdr Cautley Nasmyth-Shaw, [was] an RAF officer seconded to SIS.' —Nick Fox.

Parachute training course certification from the Air Ministry, London.

Parachuting was in its infancy, and there are several agents who record how the training was done at Ringway air base, where André's instruction took place. Colonel Passy felt he should undergo the same training he demanded of his Free French officers who might be required to jump into France and offers a vivid description.

'It was, at the time, the debut of that sport, and we were not very reassured, because the percentage of accidents, approximately five per thousand, seemed relatively worrisome to us. I went to Ringway in the company of Lagier. As soon as we arrived, we were brought to the field to be put in the mood. We witnessed the drop of bags of earth being parachuted; at least half of the parachutes didn't open and the bags crashed to the ground with a dull thud that was hardly reassuring. We exchanged looks, a bit pale ... but after all, a few of the parachutes had in fact opened; so we had a chance! ... After a few hours [of high bar gymnastics] we were a mass of cuts and bruises, we moved with difficulty, our legs akimbo, taking on stairs like senile old folks. As soon as we were in that pre-comatose state, we were declared "fit" for trial jumps. We were stuffed into old Whitley bombers, ten to a plane ... we had already practiced in a similitude of the hatchway, over a thick mattress ... We repeated the exercise six more times, at lower and lower altitudes, down to 500 meters ... and were thereupon declared to be parachutists...'[220]

In his 'Report from Captain Peulevey' destined for the French government, André wrote only: 'I got my parachute certificate at Ringway, I followed all the courses of ciphers, codes, pick-up and others.'[221] Interviewed by Helen Sendyk for his oral history interview, he summed up differently, but just as briefly: 'I went to England, became a commando, martial training, sabotage and so on.'[222] In his memoir, he even more discreetly wraps up his time in London, without details.

Other agents have written books about the training they received[223]. British Second Lieutenant Robert Sheppard, who also was imprisoned at Natzweiler for his efforts with the S.O.E.: 'We were to be gangsters with the knowledge of gangsters but with the behavior, if possible, of gentlemen.'[224] André, as a gentleman, wrote simply: *'Mission accomplished, trained, and with the confidence of my superiors in the Intelligence Service, I returned to France with the Le Tacs...'*

The fateful return from England of André and the Overcloud mission is told in Joël Le Tac's biography: 'On the first of February, Joël and Yves Le Tac board the MGB submarine-chasing vessel. André Peulevay [sic], the head of the railroad network in Rennes, the Intelligence Service network which Joël was collaborating with, accompanied them in the crossing that returned them to the coast of Brittany. He's got a brand new radio. Each has a great deal to do in the weeks to come. André Peulevay of course heads straight back to Rennes.'[225]

André, in his memoir, professionally analyses how he fell 'into the mousetrap' on return from London. We can offer other speculations. Was his 'overconfidence' brought about by almost four weeks in a free country, out of the pressure-cooker of living under threat of exposure 24/7? Had his important and interesting meetings offered him surcease from the torment? Did he slip back into the expectation of decency that had been his for most of his life? Was he too hopeful? Too professionally conscientious and ambitious? 'They [the British] didn't ask me to go back [to France.] I was a volunteer. My parents were in Paris, I wanted to send my parents back to England. And I had to go back. I had an organisation.'[226]

Attachment to one's family, such as André's to his parents, was a consideration foreseen by people who recruited Secret Agents. 'One wanted normal, natural people with the qualifications and the courage and the motivation ... people who were without strong family ties would be at an advantage, not somebody who was wondering about what was happening with their wife or their husband or children. They had to be individuals on their own and prepared to work on their own, or with whosoever it was necessary to have an association,' according to Captain Selwyn Jepson, Recruiting officer, French Section, SOE headquarters, London. [227]

André identified the capture of their network at the beginning of February 1942 as an inflection point when the German understanding of the Resistance changed: 'The Germans didn't know that England had a big organization everywhere, that the underground existed. Because until then they had been shooting people for putting up posters that said "We are going to win the war," sabotage, things like that, but they didn't know that there was really an existing underground.'[228]

André's Legion of Honor citation[229] mentions specifically that he was in no way responsible for the knowledge of the extent of his organization: 'Was arrested February 5 1942 at RENNES, succeeded in making all the documents in his possession disappear, thus depriving the Germans of them.' [230] He endured torture and interrogation at the Hotel Edouard VII and at the Hotel Caulaincourt, without admitting to anything (as he had promised his agents) and not only for their sake, but for his own: 'I knew that once I admitted something, I would be shot: in addition to not compromising other people, the best thing I could do for myself was to keep silent.'

Chapter 2
From SIS to a place in French history: André's post-war service to the Resistance

We watch him strive and maneuver for the memory and honour of his comrades through competing alliances in peace.

> 'No twenty-first century perspective on the personalities and events, successes and failures of those days should diminish our respect, even reverence, for the memory of those who paid the price for waging secret war.'[231]

If working for the British during the war was complicated for Frenchmen like Lesseps and Chatenay and many others, including André, who was thought to be French, it was just as complicated or more so afterward when they were wrangling their way and their agents into the French government Resistance files.

The rivalry between the French and British governments for agents during the war is mirrored by the rivalry for memory up to today. French historians are only starting to speak the complex truth that their earliest Resistance networks were supported by and relied on the British.[232] Because both countries kept their records closed for more than 60 years, most agents died unknown.

However, André had the insight and perspective to keep his personal records, and an archive of his networks. His voluminous archives, that his family partially kept, and kept secret for almost 20 years after his death, record much about his sustained commitment and process for getting paid and winning awards and helping others to do so.[233]

We do not know exactly why André kept this archive. Its existence perhaps indicates his wariness about the fluctuations of fate, fortune and reputation in a changing world. It lets us know him beyond the structures and physical limitations of his lifetime. His personal documents about his own career let us glimpse his own harrowing struggles to live a life of civic dignity.

His long-hidden archive also contributes to the evolving history of the Resistance in France.[234]

Formally assigned to be *Liquidateur de Réseau*/Registrar for the Overcloud network from summer 1945 on, André began to write hundreds of his agents into the history of the time they had just lived through or perished in creating. André's papers establish, confirm and extend detailed knowledge of the very first Breton networks of resistance, espionage, and escape of Frenchmen, downed British flyers and soldiers escaping the debacle of Dunkirk. His archive paints their portraits, as well as identifying names, nature and dates of service from the very first weeks of the occupation of France in the summer of 1940 through the first half of 1942.

Other *liquidateurs de réseau* – network registrars like André – must have received similar documentation; but it is not known how many similar archives of background material, if any, were preserved by their registrars. The *liquidateur's* contribution was to enter the agents' information into a ledger for their network. Once that agent's listing was certified, as André's collection of so many original source documents indicates, it is possible that they were not required to be turned over or preserved.

His keeping his archive demonstrates his dedication to the history and to the honor of his comrades, and gives a poignant reference to all his cohort had lost. How painful it must have been, to do the work of a *Liquidateur de Réseau*, after years in the Resistance when he would have had to (pretend to) ignore the fate of those who fell into the hands of the enemy. Then after the war he had to pore over the records and testimonials of those who had disappeared and think of all those in his networks whose names would never be known.[235]

André wrote to the head of registration for agents of the internal resistance (FFC) that 'due to the great decentralization of our network, it has not been possible to find all the agents again … some of the seconds-in-command of the group not having returned from the camps, only chance will allow me to give recognition to those who are entitled to it. I knew their activity, but not their identity.'[236]

Rémy (Gilbert Renault) leader of the CND Castille Network writes in his memoir about his similar challenges: '…the faces, the images, the facts came rushing back. And I found friends who were living, we spoke of our dead, of our prisoners. Some wrote a report, at my request. I was able to verify dates, retrieve an episode I had forgotten ... I have not been able to reveal [and] those who might have been able to have disappeared. Dead? Deported to Germany? For many we would never know ... In our network, we were several hundred. How many? I will never know. Of all of you, my friends, I only knew those it was essential to know ... Your body perhaps lies at the bottom of the rot of a mass grave ... Your mother, your wife, your children may be in distress. I can't help them, I can do nothing for you because I never knew your real name.'

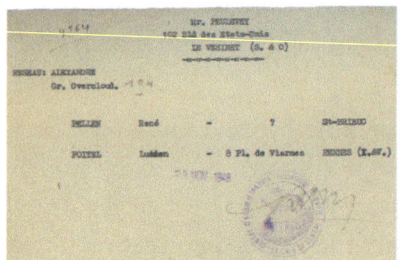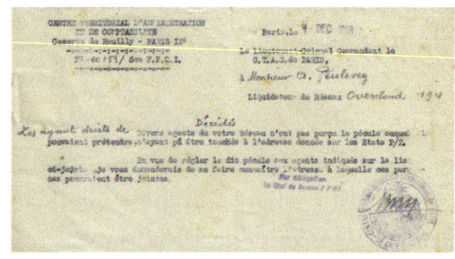

Documents dated November and December 1948 addressed to Mr. Peulevey, Liquidateur du Reseau Alexandre/Overcloud asking André do search for its agents. From André's archive.

Marie-José Chombart de Lauwe, André's youngest agent, wrote her impressions this way: 'I would only know the names of many other members of our network at the moment of our arrest or at Ravensbrück. And, for some like Peulevey-Scheinmann, only after the war.'[237] Those who had actually been in the camps, like André and Marie-José had a different way of expressing themselves. than Rémy, who supplements with his eloquence. Perhaps the actual survivors were avoiding PTSD, or perhaps they were under the impression that no one would understand who had not been there.

André's collection of testimony from and about his agents forms a broad and democratic portrait of the members of a half dozen of the earliest networks, not just their most famous members, although some of those too are included, such as Madame la Comtesse de Lorgeril. Sister-in law of Count Honoré Estienne d'Orves, she hid many in a tower at the edge of the woods on her castle's estate.[238] 'There anyone could hide out, while the Germans were quartered in the main castle and could access her private quarters at any time. Despite that, she housed, sheltered, dressed in civilian clothing and obtained fake id's for Poles and Frenchmen.' M. Devaux wrote this dignified plea in his letter to André, asking him to see that she receives honours.[239]

Pleugueneuc [Brittany] March 26, 1945

Sir,

As you are so kind as to take care of the dossier of Madame the Comtesse de Lorgeril, I rush to send you an important 'document', it's a fake ID card she established and that was returned to her by the Police.

She established others, she didn't keep [to next page] the names for fear of compromising these young people…

You have there, Monsieur, a great cause to defend, or rather, to uphold, and I do not doubt that with your savoir-faire you will succeed.

With my thanks, I pray, Sir, you will believe my best regards.

Letter to André asking for recognition for Madame La Comtesse de l'Orgeril.

As was done for the countess, the contributions of car mechanics, opticians, photographers, housewives, students and farmers are devotedly delineated in correspondence André saved. Many wrote for each other, especially for the ones who fell in front of a German firing squad or who never came back from the camps.

Marie-Christianne Seidel wrote in her application for Déporté Interné Résistant/DIR certification that she 'was contacted by Mr. Legeay, agent of Capt. Peulevey head of the section for Nantes and Brittany. I was Chef de Groupe in charge of centralising intelligence, maritime activity, sheltering Allied aviators (in my own home) three of whom (Canadian-English-Scottish) were arrested at the same time as I.'[240]

Seidel was a devoted correspondent and helpmeet for André in collecting and presenting the relevant information for him to enter into the official network files and submit their agent names for honors.[241] She contributed dozens of lists and synopses under various rubrics: 'Imprisoned', 'deported and returned'; 'died in deportation'; those who spent a few months in prison, and the ambiguous 'never imprisoned' as well as a half dozen people who broke under interrogation and gave up others.

Although traitors could have suffered fatal reprisals in the immediate post-war period, Seidel never called for punishments that would make the families suffer; to the contrary. In the most severe case, she called for no other retribution than withholding honors and pensions for a woman who was active from summer, 1940 to October 41 (when the Georges-France agents were arrested): 'This woman ALAIN helped the British, was arrested, denounced two men in mid-trial, without being tortured. Those two men died, one was executed. Those two deaths being caused by her, in agreement with the families of these who are no more, we are asking she not be attacked. Only, we insist she be removed from the Committees she belongs to, that she receive nothing from the Government, and that her local Town Hall be so informed.' (Seidel's documents for one of those men is included further below.)

She wrote up the barest report for herself: 'Condemned to death by the German War Council, 28 September 1943.' She spent the rest of the war in concentration camps in Germany.[242]

From SIS to a place in French history

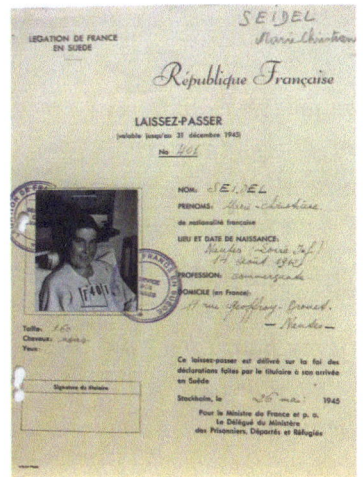
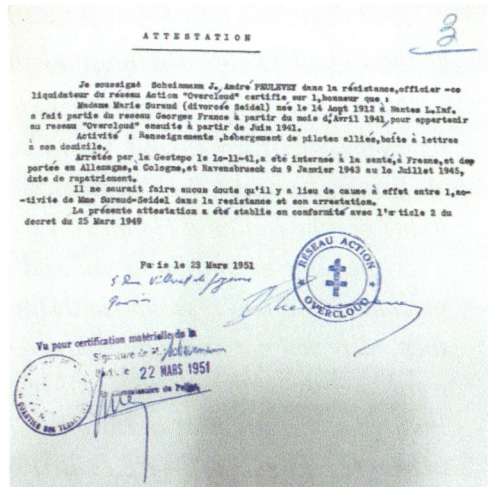

Marie-Christiane Seidel in hospital after being liberated from Ravensbrück and taken to Sweden by the Red Cross. André's signed testimony *de cause à effet* for Marie Suraud (divorced from Seidel) about her resistance activities, imprisonment and concentration camps.

André wrote *the attestation de cause à effet* testifying that her activities in the resistance led to her arrest and deportation. 'I, the undersigned Scheinmann J, André PEULEVEY in the resistance, *liquidateur* of the Action 'Overcloud' network, certify on my honour, that Madame Marie Suraud (divorced from Seidel) born 14 August 1912 in Nantes, was part of the Georges-France network from the month of April 1941, and then of the "Overcloud" network from June 1941. Activity: Intelligence, sheltering Allied pilots, her home a message center. ... There can be no doubt that there is a link from cause to effect between Madame Suraud-Seidel's activity in the resistance and her arrest.' Signed, J. Scheinmann, 23 March, 1951.

It is fascinating to wonder, but there is no hint, as to whether Marie-Christiane Seidel and André were close during the war, or grew to be so afterward.[243]

Dear Camarade,   *May 30, 1946*

How grateful I am to you for the good moments we passed together the other day, it is always pleasant to chat with you, we suffered the same tortures and we can understand each other and speak as good camarades.

And then I am a little late in getting back to you, because when I got here I had a punctured lung and am only now starting to recover.

Now I can't find the words to thank you for the decorations, I am happy for Mr. Marchais and Mlle. Cozannec, I thank you very much. As for me, I wonder if I was right to deserve all that. I am happy I didn't get the Légion d'Honneur, I would have been embarrassed to wear the same decoration as you and Mr. Legeay (because I hope he will have it.) You were so superior to me in work and in Resistance, and then, were you not and will always remain my Boss, I have no other word to describe the emotion and respect that your little red ribbon inspired in me, and it is carried with such dignity and honor. You want to have the insignia of the F.F.L. attributed to me, the one who sent me to find you, and know you, Avenue Mannaury remember, was a great wish of mine, but do I have the right to it?[244]

Now, let's talk about work. I am making a summary of the members of network members, I am going to ask you...'

Marie-Christianne Seidel gave enormous time and effort to profile and document dozens of resistors for André. She made short summaries for each, with their activities, their eventual fate, and if they had died as a result of their resistance – even if they broke and gave up others – pleading for them to receive honors or for their children to be freed from military service to return to keep the family farm, for instance.

More than a hundred P2 agents (fulltime paid status in the resistance, also awarded to those who were deported and/or died for their actions) to be registered with Overcloud are on the many lists in his archive. Some of the names appear on a plaque for the Johnny network. Others appear in the following list of Bête Noire sabotage agents arrested as a result of the parachute drop of the night of January 31-February 1, 1942, intercepted by the Germans. (The Le Tacs and André were meant to return on the plane but their plans were changed. André writes that the British 'knew something was wrong.')

Although in 1946 Marie-Christiane Seidel wrote to André, 'You were so superior to me in work and in Resistance' and wondered if she deserved the Forces Françaises Libres (designation as being in de Gaulle's military)

From SIS to a place in French history

she eventually achieved many distinctions with his help, including the FFL, the Ordre du Régiment with War Cross with Bronze Star, the order of the Army Corps with Vermilion Star, the Médaille de la Résistance with rosette (1946). [245]

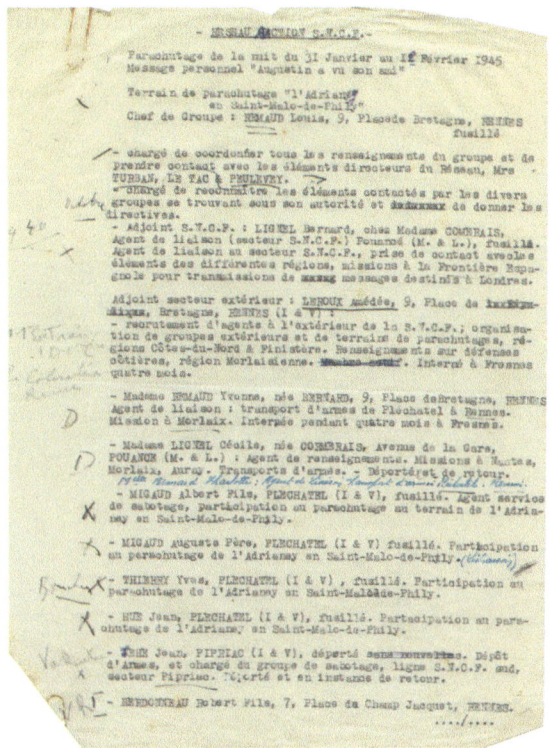

List of agents of André's first network at the SNCF, La Bête Noire, arrested as a result of the parachute drop into the Adrian dropping zone at Saint-Malo de Phily on the night of Jan 31-Feb 1. 1942. The code phrase disseminated on the BBC to alert the group that the parachute drop was going to proceed was 'Augustin a vu son ami' (Augustin saw his friend.)

List starts with Louis Remaud, who was 'in charge of coordination of his group's intelligence and in contact with the directors of the Network, Mrs. Turban, Le Tac & Peulevey.' (or, as the inked correction indicates, Le Tac, Peulevey and Mrs. Turban.)

Document from André's private archive.

'Réseau Action S.N.C.F'. Fate of Bête Noire agents, p. 1.
Of the 14 agents named on the first page of this 'Réseau Action S.N.C.F' list, p1: six died (if shot marked 'fusillé') three imprisoned, four deported and coming back or came back...

But who, during the war and immediate post-war years, wrote the story and created the official documentation of André? Madame Louis, the British, and Joël Le Tac all contributed documentation of his crucial role in their organizations, recorded in French official post-war government publications and archives.

André finally was registered to Overcloud by Joël Le Tac in 1947, after first being written into Georges-France by Madame Louis and then out of it and into CND Castille (Confrérie Notre Dame, started by Col. Rémy).[246] Although he had worked with GF/31 for a year before joining Overcloud, André's registration with Overcloud was 'technically correct' according to the way the French government decided to register agents with the last network in which they served, and André was operating with Overcloud after Groupe 31/Georges-France.

André (top row) and his agents signed into Overcloud by Joël Le Tac. His name Joseph Scheinmann is written in ink above the typed name André Peulevey. His 'function' is given as 'Head of the SNCF Sabotage Group', his 'real' military grade (rank) as 'Sergeant' (as he was in the Army 1939-1940.) His rank of Captain 'by assimilation' – because of his service in the resistance-is written in by hand.

André's dates with Overcloud (November 1941-February 1942) cover the entire three-month span of the Overcloud network's existence, as it is registered by the French Government. This seems worth discussion by historians.[247] While there had been preceding actions by Joël, there was no Overcloud network until André joined Bête Noire and the SNCF organisation in Brittany to Overcloud in November 1941. And it was André who could find the agents he had worked with for more than a year before that with Madame Louis for Georges-France (including those who were not arrested with her in October 1941). This accounts for his becoming *Liquidateur de Reseau*, instead of Joël Le Tac, although usually the head of network would fill that rôle.[248] Joël, however, signed the forms and wrote the 'history' of the network.

Réseau Overcloud file at Vincennes showing the Overcloud network's dates as those when André joined his networks to theirs – November, 1941 to February 1942; that it was created by Colonel Passy 'for the benefit of the British SOE' with Joël as leader, Colonel Passy/the BCRA and Gen Gubbins/ the SOE as contacts, its scope (right column) being Brittany and its Mission, 'Action' (upper left, Intelligence and Evasion crossed out.)

In 1957, Joël Le Tac wrote up a new affidavit *de cause à effet* for Joseph Scheinmann, since his original paperwork had been made out for Peulevey. By that time, Joël had 'manned up' to his work as *Liquidateur de Réseau* for Overcloud. He took over after André left for the US and before Joël turned the job over to his mom ... [he was, after all, its network head, 'Chef de réseau,' not just 'Chef de mission,' André's title and Joël's mom's, who took over after Joël.]

'Certificate of relationship of cause to effect between Resistance activity and Deportation:

I, the undersigned, Joël Le Tac Officer of the Legion of Honor, Companion of the Liberation, Officer Liquidateur of the Overcloud Action network, certify the connection of cause to effect between the Resistance activity of Mr. Joseph Scheinmann called André Peulevey and his arrest by the German police on the 5th of February 1942 at Rennes.

Organiser of an important intelligence network within the structure of the SNCF (French National Railroads), in November 1941 joined the Overcloud Action Network for technical logistics and communications. Arrested in February 42, he was deported to the Natzweiler-Struthof concentration camp and to Dachau.

[Signed] in Paris, 10 Sept. 57 Joël Le Tac'

Testimonial of cause and effect signed by Joël Le Tac. Joël doesn't mention the trip to London that André made with him and his brother ... From records for André at Caen, thanks to Pierre de Jaegher.

Although the politics of Gaullist post-war France were not simple to navigate, especially by a former agent of the SIS, André did not document that challenge. For comparison, the privileged Victor Chatenay, who liquidated his networks *Honneur et Patrie* and *Jade-Fitzroy*, and had worked for Dunderdale and Greene at their SIS office in London during his interlude from the Resistance, had no qualms about dropping names and hanging out the dirty laundry. 'Finally, after having met Guillet, Manuel, Franklin, Debesse, Passy, etc ... my network was recognized,' bellyaches Chatenay about challenges similar to the ones André must have encountered. Both were laboring to shove their SIS networks down the throats of the Free French at the helm of the provisional Gaullist government that had installed itself after the liberation of Paris. 'But [wrote Chatenay] ... how many difficulties, errors, negligence and incomprehensible malevolence I was to encounter. How many lost dossiers! ... little meanies, in the shadows, were sending the process of network registration off its tracks. How to explain that a dossier would disappear twice? Why these nasty maneuvers, why?'[249] André, more discreet and more diplomatic, never asked this (even rhetorical) question. He dealt with the reality.

Perhaps André was a successful *Liquidateur* because he was known to have been in the camps, as his greatest helpmeet, Marie-Christiane Seidel, had been as well. Chatenay credits one of his network leaders, just returned from the concentration camps, for accomplishing the task he found so excruciating.[250] 'For me, it was Providence that brought Commander Cotrelle back from Buchenwald ... Barely recovered, he had the courage to put the dossiers back into shape. And I must say loud and clear that I would have been incapable of bringing this enormous and necessary work to a satisfactory outcome. It is to him that honour is due for having [ensured] the rights of our agents better than anyone.'[251] I have not found anywhere that Joël Le Tac spoke of André for his job 'liquidating' Overcloud.

Despite the immediate and disastrous consequences of the betrayal of the Le Tac network, joining the brothers in their trip to London had this one good result in the long term: that André and his agents from all his SIS-affiliated networks, who otherwise might not have been recognized by the post-war French government because they had been working with the British, were officially acknowledged.

These details of the post-war recording efforts convey the amount of confusion and inaccuracy, not to mention possible ill or good intentions, and the politics of memory up to today, that were introduced into the recording process.[252] André registered those he knew from all his groups who were deserving into Overcloud, if they had not been recognized elsewhere, especially by Madame Louis, whose self-reported 'slightly deficient' memory led her to overlook a number of the agents of Groupe 31.[253] To be fair, she roamed throughout France collecting the reports for England from an agent in each region, as she did from André, rather than being out and about in town and country all over Brittany, as he was. 'It was only André who would have known the vast majority of the GF31 agents in the 'area', particularly as during 1941 he was bringing into the fold smaller disparate groups as well as recruiting new agents.'[254]

The date from April 1, 1941 for the beginning of the Georges-France network given in most of the French government documents is not consistent with what we know of Madame Louis, Turban and André working separately and together in the Resistance from fall of 1940.[255] International and national politics of the resistance no doubt played a role. It could be that the Gaullist government was not willing to acknowledge the network before April not only because of its origins with the SIS but also because of its close ties to the Deuxième Bureau, for which Madame Louis and others in its leadership had worked before WWII. A complicating factor is also that the official chronology of the network written up by Madame Louis has it originating in the earlier network 'Frise', and the cloud under which the history of Georges-France has been darkened since Louis' post-war disgrace.[256]

Document of and by Madame Louis from the Georges-France file at Vincennes showing the origin, name and date of the network headed by Madame Louis as FRISE, August 30, 1940 to January.

A depressing amount of documentation of André's rôle was presented in the German trial held in in November 1942 of Madame Louis and many Georges-France agents.[257] Even before the time of her arrest on October 24, 1941, we can assume the Germans were tracking him and everyone else named in what the Germans described as a 'mass of documents' taken from her apartment earlier in 1941. (When she reported this to the French government after the war, she only said that they had found and taken money and jewelry.) The documents she carried on her person at the time of her arrest added to those taken months earlier, so that the indictment by the German military court in the trial of Georges-France agents held in Paris runs to 24 pages for Madame Louis.

André is mentioned multiple times by name or agent number. On page 13 André appears as 'sub-agent named Peulevey' who obtained ID cards in the name of 'Mr. and Mrs. Perrin' for Louis and her paramour Pierre Gontier whom she had made her adjunct after she rescued him from prisoner of war camp at the very onset of the occupation of France. More significant contributions are given for André, on other pages of the trial, that the Germans credit to their interviews of Madame Louis.

Madame Louis's indictment in the German trial describes his contribution, based on her unforced testimony:

'...Another important agent, since arrested, was the interpreter André Peulevey, who, under the code name "31AQ" furnished from Rennes information on the tactical insignia, the épaulettes, the state of mind of the population, and above all, on the apparatus for surveillance of the German railroads in occupied France. He transmitted to Dame Louis ten or so reports among which there are some that concern coastal defenses etc. He is the one who also provided false ID cards in the name of Dumaine to Dame Louis. Another agent of Dame Louis in Rennes, named Martin, "31 AQ bis" handed in reports on airfields and naval forces. Then Dame Louis tried to enter into rapport with a high functionary of the railroads named Turban. ("Tutenglair")'...

French National Archives, SHD GR 17 P 131

Page 21 of the German trial indictment of Madame Louis.

Quite a tragic way to have his accomplishments brought to light. In fact, the German indictment of Louis and Gontier in the Georges-France trial attributes to Gontier much of the work that André did. Gontier himself told the Germans he took dictation from Dame Louis, probably from her agents' reports, including André's, as we can recognize.

'We were able to have all these details because the essential reports were able to be seized, either as originals or as copies, at dame Louis's place and at Gonthier's [sic] place ... dame Louis admits that she transmitted information transmitted by her sub-agents on the subject of German ships that were invalidated or sunk, on the morale of troops, on their numbers, their leaves, the results of the blockade, the delivery of foodstuffs, the places where the population was either Germanophile or Germanophobic ... Gonthier remembers taking dictation to write reports concerning the placement of B.C.A. guns and coastal armaments, the movement of troops, the entry and exit of the "Scharnhorst" and "Gneisenau" and the movement of ships of the German navy. He remembers also that, when the German-Russian war exploded, Dame Louis reported how many divisions were sent to the Eastern front.'

The Germans noted after the above: 'That information, as a whole, didn't all come from persons on trial here that we were able to indict for espionage, but from other sub-agents who fled or who are now awaiting trial.' (trial pp. 19 and 20) André states being convicted in two other network trials. Those trial documents have not been located.[258]

Beside suspecting Madame Louis for the nefarious disappearance of any monies that had been promised to her, Suzanne Wilborts was bitterly disappointed by 'our British friends' as André called them. He wrote to reassure her, on 14 November 1945: 'At the request of my British service, I gave over to the English the list of all my agents as of the end of October 1941, and who helped with escape. As it was true to fact I said that YOU, Miss Yvette (Marie José's birth name) and the regretted [late] Dr. your husband, that you were arrested for ESCAPE and Intelligence, which means that you and Yvette will each receive 40,000 francs and that you will have a pension from the English [in compensation] for the Doctor ... When I went to London I had already declared that you had spent more than 200,000 Frs that sum will probably be reimbursed by our English friends who are terrific [*extrèmement chic*]...'[259]

André was seeing things more benignly than some who knew the same 'English friends'. Chatenay writes of Greene in Paris in the fall of 1945, while he was working as *Liquidateur* (registrar) the network of Jade-Fitzroy: 'I am not surprised to find him to be a pitiless accountant who doesn't want to pay, nor even to reimburse, those who worked and spent money for the network.'[260]

Suzanne Wilborts continued to write to André about her desperation with the British. 'Recently, my friend General Audibert was seated not far from Major Green of the I.S. during an official banquet. Green, knowing him to be Breton, asked for news of us, my daughter and me, being surprised not to have heard. It seems he said nice things about us to the General. I therefore wonder, since they seem so well-disposed toward us, why I never received anything from them ... After your arrest I gave another 275,000 francs for the network to Roger Martin...'

As to why the British never made good on their immediate postwar reassurances of support for Wilborts and Seidel – no doubt among many others – Tim Austin attributes their 'dropping the ball' to the French government insisting, after the war, that the British discontinue their relationships with their former agents. Having so recently regained their sovereignty, the French may have feared that some of these former agents would become future agents as well. A foreign power organizing and compensating their citizens was no longer to be tolerated. We don't know if André ever updated his assurance to Madame Wilborts that they would help her financially because 'our British friends are very 'chic.'

Madame Wilborts, who started her resistance group at the very start of the occupation and who delivered babies at Ravensbrück with her daughter and others in some of the most heart-breaking efforts exerted by concentration camp prisoners during the war, wrote further to André on 18 June, 1947: 'Now, I am all alone. Life is very difficult. I do all the birthings here, which is quite tiring, as they almost always take place at night; my garden is what is mostly keeping me alive. I sell eggs and vegetables. I raise goats for milk. In the evenings, I write books. I'm on my 5th, but the publishers are the ones who see all the profits. Well, I'm not asking for anything but I find it a bit painful that I don't even get thanked.'

We know that Suzanne Wilborts and André remained good friends, from a letter we have that she wrote to him in 1949 to explain something disparaging that apparently he thought she had said about him. She explains how, under interrogation, in order to save him, she had made an honourable and courageous attempt to bamboozle the Germans by claiming that André was just a *poseur* (just posturing).

KER-AVEL 19 January 1949
ILE DE BREHAT CÔTES-DU-NORD

My dear Le Neveu [the nephew]

Allow me to tell you that you are just an old fool.

I am going to refresh your memory.

When during my interrogations, for the Germans, they talked to me of you, of your famous trip to London, I always denied it to their face: 'Ah! Peulevey! but he's half-cracked. That trip to London never existed except in his imagination, he was incapable of doing something like that. Boast about it, maybe, but execute it, never.'

That is simply what I was alluding to in my letter. It had no pejorative meaning, and was only a memory of a trick thus played on the Germans.

That being said, I am delighted to know that all three of you are happy, having a handsome boy.

As for me, if I had insisted on my vetting by grade it is because I have for my heart a disability pension of 'sous-lieutenant' and it would have been more advantageous to have a rank of Captain, and that times are tough! As well as the British having happily scooped up their 200,000 francs.

I send you my affectionate memories and friendly regards from Yvette, Sidonie.

Letter from Suzanne Wilborts to André recalling how she bluffed about him to the Gestapo.

Chapter 3
André reframes and reclaims his life

We share glimpses of his more personal struggles in recasting his social and professional identity, paying the costs, cutting his losses, deciding to leave Europe behind.

Even after enlisting and while serving in the French army, André was still an *apatride*/stateless until gaining French citizenship in 1951. Jorge Semprún, a Spaniard, was also in the 'Resistance' in France as part of a British network. He writes about being an Expat/*apatride* in the struggle and its aftermath.[261]

'I thought about all that could be said regarding these two words: return, repatriation. First of all, I hadn't returned to my homeland, in coming back to France. And then, if you thought about it, it was clear I would never again be able to return to any homeland. I had no native country anymore. I would never have one again. Or else I'd have several, which would amount to the same thing. Can you die – think about it – for several countries at once? ... As for me, I'd never thought of dying for my country ... So this idea had never entered my mind whenever I had occasion – rather frequently, those past few years – to think about my chances of dying. About risking my life, in other words. It was never a "homeland" that was at stake.'[262] [263]

As soon as he could leave Dachau for Paris, André took the road of his return, if not repatriation. A French government official tried to tell him he didn't need his back pay for the two and a half years he had been in Gestapo prisons and concentration camps, since the Germans had housed and fed him. (His pay for the 38 months of his captivity, finally awarded in 1948, was 63,732 francs.) [264]

As usual, André was galvanized by that absurd challenge: he ended up at the celebrated Plaza Athenée hotel as his temporary address. 'Chez Monsieur Paul' ('Mr. Paul's place') is where he can be reached, as noted on the first government document we have for him after his return. Like many other posh Paris hotels that had been used as Nazi headquarters, The Plaza Athénée was repurposed after the liberation to processing and housing the returnees from the concentration camps. Monsieur Paul was the name of its famous concierge.

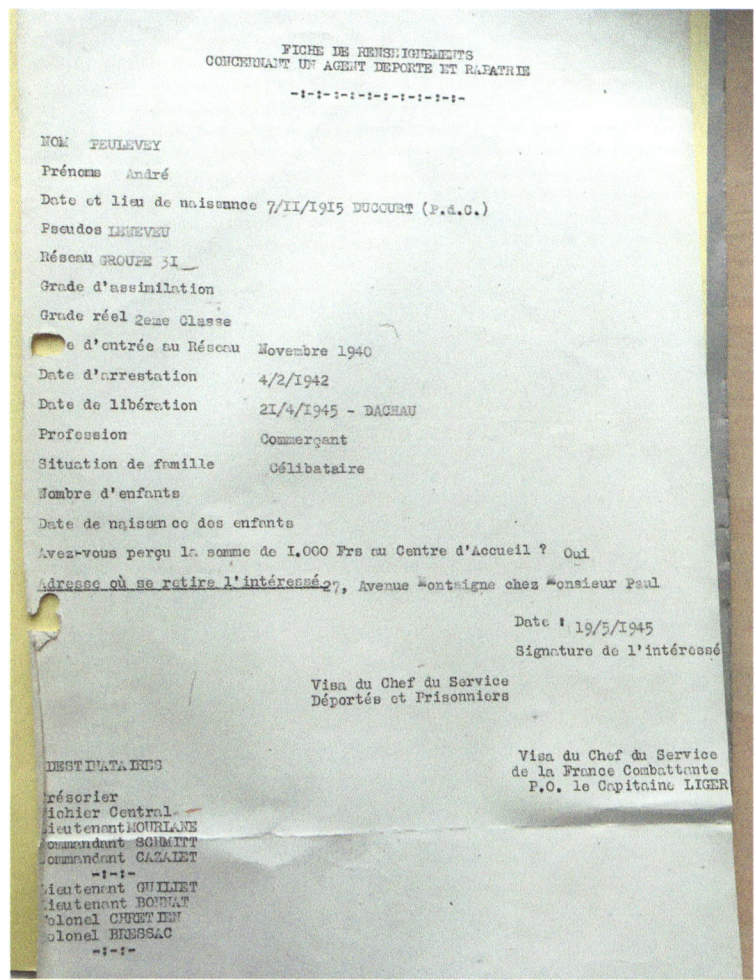

'Information sheet concerning a deported and repatriated agent' Underlined is 'where the party in question can be found: chez Monsieur Paul at 27, Avenue Montaigne,' the address for the Hotel Plaza Athénée. List of addressees, at bottom left.

In Paris, André joined many of the social and friendship organizations of Resistance Fighters, Aviators' Club, Officer's Club. He must have been trying to establish the security of a solid identity in the shifting sands of post-war France where he still was not a citizen and where his British-run networks were not those most favored by the Gaullist narrative of the French having liberated France (maybe with a little help from the Allies).

André's club membership cards from Paris, after the war.

Organisations and clubs he joined in 1946 – all at posh addresses – whose personalized invitations addressed to 'Mon Capitaine' and membership cards are part of his archive, some stamped with postage, include the Club du 18 Juin, (the name referring to the date of de Gaulle's historic appeal to French Citizens from London); Cercle Interallié de l'Aviation; Club des Officiers Français; Association Amicale d'Entraide des

Anciens Officiers Chargés de Missions-Action (sponsors: Cdt. Schmidt and Cdt. Depute listed on verso). There are meal and drink tickets from the D.G.E.R. (Secret Service) and an invitation to a 1947 reception with fashion show, raffle and auction. In 1951 he joined the Association des Français Libres – with a questionnaire to be filled out for the membership committee including who would provide recommendations ('Colonel Passy and Sir Dunderdale'), members of networks with whom you worked ('Mssrs. Le Tac, Moureau, Wilborts, Le Deuff, Poge etc.') and two members of the FFL who could recommend him, including Comte Albert de Pouzols Saint-Phar whom he identifies as 'Monsieur de Pouzols'. To questions about what he did in the resistance, he answered: Intelligence, Evasion, and Sabotage.

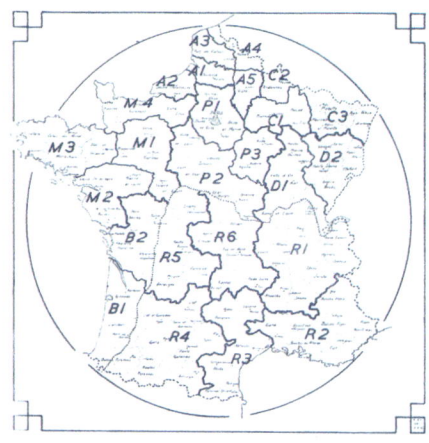

The people who sponsored André for memberships knew him from his work during the war, and after, as Liquidateur de Réseau: for example, his archives preserve the Cdt. Schmidt assignment to be Liquidateur for the railroad agents 'section SNCF' of Overcloud in early July 1945, and one from Cdt. Laverdet-LeGall on 25 August, greatly extending this responsibility to registering the entire region 'M' of French territory for Overcloud. Région M includes all of Brittany, the Pays de la Loire and Haute Normandie, from Le Havre in the north through Le Mans and Tours in the East and south to La Rochelle.

Map of the regions of France for Service 'Action,' Special Operations, including André's territory for registering Overcloud agents in Region M. Map from *Livre d'Or de l'Amicale Action*, to which André belonged.

In chilling counterpoint to, and perhaps as a cause for, these glitzy social and professional enterprises, André's archive shows that they were not merely frivolous or ambitious. In 1947, when his major responsibilities included registering an historic network for the French government, and he was still in the process of obtaining his birth certificate from Germany for the purpose of establishing French citizenship, the French police were tracking him for being of nationality 'to be determined.'

 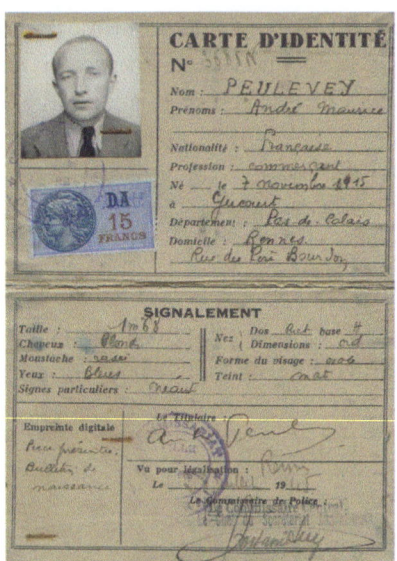

Left: Prefecture of Police Administration of Aliens. Joseph Scheinmann authorized to reside until 7 December, 1947. He must have lost the 'birth certificate' he had shown to get the ID card at right, dated July 28, 1945 for André Peulevey, French national. Box at lower left corner of ID lists a birth certificate as documentation.

While André was working diligently for at least five years to establish the identities, verify the service, and inscribe his agents under the Le Tac network Overcloud for pensions befitting their Fighting French roles, Joël Le Tac, who described André's enthusiasm for espionage as *désinvolture* – i.e. care-free, casual nonchalance – if that was ever correct, (doubtful!) immediately on return from the camps went to live at the Paris apartment of fashion designer Edward Henry Molyneux.[265] Molyneux had served de Gaulle in London during the war. Joël started working for him in January 1946, traveling the world to help present fashion shows, host parties, and increase the designer's business and renown.[266] Joël settled in Brazil, not to return until 1949 when he joined the French Secret Service and went into politics.[267]

While being immersed for five years in recording the history of his agents' contributions, André was transitioning back to business. Even as early as 1945-1946, he was entrusted with the job of provisioning for the 'Amicale Action' the fraternal association of the veterans of Special Operations run by de Gaulle's BCRA.[268] He also worked for his wife's family's brush business.

Investigating a career in the structures of the 'New Europe', he wrote a serious and elaborate application to be hired as provisioning officer for UNESCO. In that 1949 application, under the name Scheinmann, he writes that he again was doing what he had done before the war, 'buying and exporting costume jewelry, souvenirs, wine and liquors, toys...'

He started the three-page cover letter entitled 'CV', complete with specific names of addresses of previous employment, thus: 'I am the son of a storeowner. My parents owned three stores and employed thirty people. Therefore, I have always been closely associated with subjects of retail sales in the very difficult fields of shoes, ready-to-wear clothing, and sporting goods.'

For this job application, he received a recommendation from the man who had supported and facilitated his post-war efforts in being certified with the Resistance and taking back his birth identity. 'Commandant Laverdet-LeGal, Commander, head of the Service "Action," FC, certifies by this that Captain Scheinmann called Peulevey organised and directed the Cooperative of the Service "Action" from July 1945 to November 45. Very good buyer, excellent organiser, he succeeded in supplying the food for our cooperative perfectly, despite the absence of funding and the scarcity of all food supplies. Having achieved an appreciable benefit for our rest home, Captain Scheinmann left us as his own choice, free of any obligations. — Paris, 6 December, 1946. Head of the service "Action-FC" [France Combattante] Stamped with the seal of Service "Action."'

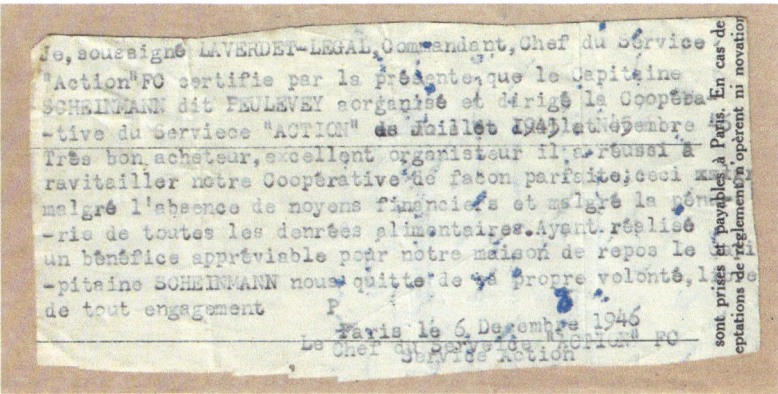

Commander Laverdet-Legal's 1946 recommendation that André used for his UNESCO job application. A carbon of the letter, spelling mistakes corrected, dated December 3, on full-size paper, is also in André's personal archive, with this piece pasted at bottom.

The agents of his networks after the war, who were French nationals, identified themselves in their statements as resistors; only a few identified what they were doing as espionage. One of those, Marie-José Chombart de Lauwe says she was invited to join the French Secret Services in 1946, as 'they no doubt wanted to benefit from my hardened experience of clandestinity.'[269]

Was André offered the same opportunity? André positioned himself with the French government after the war as a spy for France. He used the term agent for himself and for others in his networks. In his 'Report of Captain Peulevey' he uses the term CE, Counter-Espionage.

Would André have wanted to continue in intelligence for the other Allies? André received SPECIAL ORDERS from APO 887 on September 4, 1945 to a US base in the South of France, from 'Headquarters, Military Intelligence Service, United States Forces, European Theater' for 'Captain André Peulevey, 0419064, French Liaison Officer, attachd this Hq, WP Nice, France, for TDY[Temporary Duty Travel] ...to carry out instructions of the C[ommanding]O[fficer], travel by rail, GMT, and/or commercial or mil aircraft.' Upon completion of TDY, will return to proper station.' —Signed By Order of Colonel Ford: Charles B. Amyx, 1st Lt., AGD, Asst. Adjutant.[270] We do not know what André did under these orders.

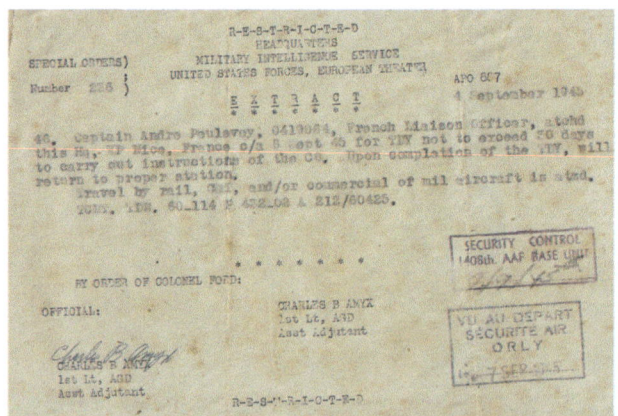

SPECIAL ORDERS from US Forces, September 4, 1945. The 1408th AAF base unit security control stamp with handwritten date 7/9/45 was Orly airport, in Paris, as seen on the French stamp. [If no room the following sentence can be dropped...] The American Air Force operated the airport from September 1944 and returned it to the French Government in November 1947.

André reframes and reclaims his life

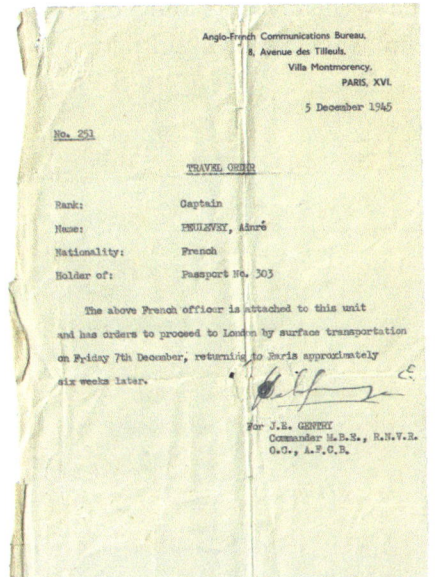

From the British: On letterhead of the 'Anglo-French Communications Bureau, 8 Avenue des Tilleuls, Villa Montmorency, Paris XVI, dated 5 December 1945:

'Travel Order Captain Peulevey French Passport No.303

'The above French Officer is attached to this unit and has orders to proceed to London by surface transportation on Friday 7th December, returning to Paris approximately six weeks later.

'[Signed] For J.E. Gentry'

Travel order to London from SIS.

From the French: Ordre de Mission issued to André on November 6 for travel to London from December 1, 1945 [1944] to January 10, 1945 with passport No. 303. Signed over the stamp at lower right by A.[André] Dewavrin – ('Colonel Passy') who was Directeur Général des Etudes et Recherches (French Secret Services) from April 1945 – April 1946.

Ordre de Mission from the French.

André received leave for a trip by car and rail from Rennes to Paris on January 21, 1946 with no assigned end date and with permission to adopt civilian clothing by the Service de Recherche des Crimes de Guerre Ennemis (Office of Research into Enemy War Crimes) in Brittany.

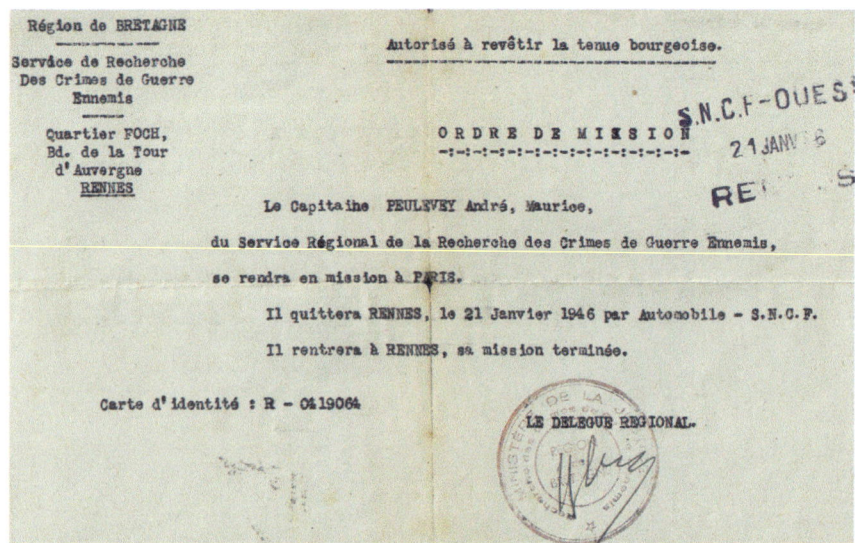

Orders from the French to investigate war crimes.

Why were these efforts not availing for future assignments? Were these trips just for debriefing and/or just for his research as *Liquidateur de Réseau*? Is it possible that his Jewish identity becoming known harmed his chances to join the intelligence community? Clues may have been lost with the papers discarded from his archive. [271]

His personal papers show he made his first official move to retake his original identity in November 1945. Commandant Laverdet-Legall, The Director of France Combattante issued a confirmation of the existence of an official file for 'Mr. PEULEVEY André coming from London as Chargé de Mission First Class

Captain on 4 February 1942.[272] His real name SCHEINMANN Joseph born the 28 January 1915 at Munich (Germany.)'

The delay in finalising his resistance documentation under his birth name was probably caused by four years' wait to receive a copy of his birth certificate from Germany. The delay in his identification also ensured that his own and his agents' honors and pensions would be awarded for wartime service.

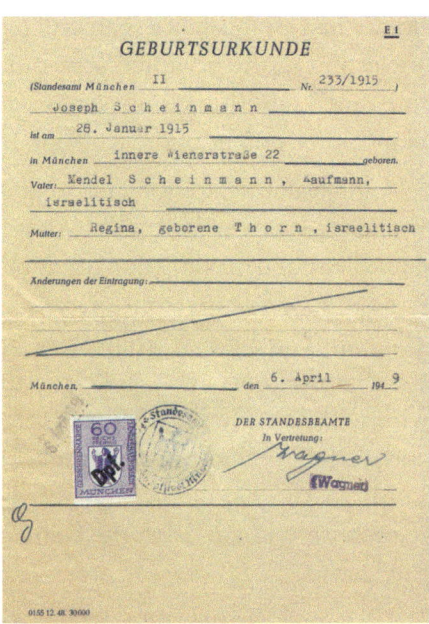

The first document found in André's archive in which his birth identity appears, since the beginning of the war: confirmation of his service and rank in the Resistance with his real name and identity, November 3 1945, signed by The Director of France Combattante Commander LAVERDET-LE GALL and A.Pons, head of 'Récupération Action.' Right: André's birth certificate provided by Germany in 1949, showing he was born at Wienerstrasse No.22 in Munich.

The transfer of his French records of the Resistance and his Legion of Honor and other decorations, from the name and identity of André Maurice Peulevey to Joseph Scheinmann were accomplished and noticed in French Government publications in the 1950's.[273] In 1951 the *Journal Officiel de la République Française* also announced that both his and his wife Claire had received naturalised French nationality.[274]

There is no evidence that the British know André's identity as a German-born Jew, but as a German he would have been able to serve Great Britain. Of 11,426 foreign nationals in the British Armed Forces in WWII, the largest group by far were the Germans – Jewish or political refugees.[275]

But the French, if he had he been found out, except by Laverdet-LeGall, a member of the Workers and Farmers Socialist party (PSOP), who worked on Joël Le Tac's first missions and also with Robert Simon of the Valmy network who transited to England on that trip in January 1942...[276]

France had established a shameful record of antisemitic initiatives, both in Vichy and in the occupied zones, and even some members of de Gaulle's war-time leadership group were suspected of ties to the dreaded *Cagoule* – France's equivalent of the Ku Klux Klan.

Collaborators, for a year or so after the war, were subjected to purges/vigilante justice – *l'épuration sauvage*. But as for its legal *épuration*, France's equivalent of denazification, to track down and punish collaborators, Jean Cassou, an influential resistor, calls it '*La Mémoire courte*' – short memory. The *épuration* has even come to be criticised as *la non-épuration*.[277] Going through the motions of judicial redress ended within less than a decade, with surceases and shortening of sentences for collaborating war criminals and traitors, including for example Madeleine Téry, who fingered Madame Louis to the Gestapo.[278] France, like the US, was moving quickly to reestablish relations with the Germans against their new cold-war enemy, the Soviets.

Bringing the question up to this day, is it possible that André is not included in any way in the official history plaques, including for Turban, at the SNCF railroad station where he worked in Brittany or in exhibits (including about the NNs) at the museums at Natzweiler, now that he is known to have been not only SIS, not only born German, but also a Jew?

This author has been told that the French government policy is to entrust (seemingly sequester) the memory of its Jewish political prisoners to Holocaust memorials.[279] Serge Barcellini writes that not highlighting political prisoners at Natzweiler who were Jewish is justified, because André and the other Jewish *Nacht und Nebel* and other secret Jews in the camp 'were not sent there not as Jews, but as political prisoners'.[280] Chombart de Lauwe had a different point of view: 'The concentration camp system was a whole, with different facets, in which genocide represents the most absolute crime against humanity. I reject the opposition made between resistor heroes and Jewish victims. There were great Jewish heroes of the Resistance, and [there were] non-Jewish victims...'[281]

This approach has only very recently been endorsed as official history by the French government, starting in 2023 with 'an upheaval of memory': the first visit by a French head of state ever to the Mt. Valérien, site of hundreds of executions by the Germans.[282] It is only recently that those executed there as resistors have been acknowledged to be Jewish or foreign born.²⁸³ And on February 21, 2024, Missak and Mélinée Manouchian, survivors of the Armenian genocide, were enshrined at the Pantheon, with great pomp and circumstance; the only speech, a long one, about 'Strangers/Foreigners in the Resistance' was given by Emanuel Macron.²⁸⁴ The event was greeted with a frenzy of self-acclamation, coming around again, not surprisingly, to the gifts of French values and history.²⁸⁵

Another point of view is that 'part of resistance's importance lay in this: that it unsettled people's thinking from the set ruts of ordinary long-established life and made them more ready to entertain new ideas; of which the idea of membership in some sort of supra-national organization was not the least important.' ²⁸⁶ Many, but not all, survivors of the resistance looked forward to a brighter future of entente among former enemies in their memoirs, and to their hopes for the formation of a new European Community.²⁸⁷

André was not so infatuated as some other survivors with bringing the Germans back onto the world stage. 'If they thought they could succeed, they would do it all over again,' he would often say. When he was back in Munich for the 50th anniversary of the liberation of Dachau, he was accosted on the street by a German who raged at him: 'They should have killed you all.' To the end of his life, he refused to sit on a stage or at a dais with a German dignitary.²⁸⁸

Not saving his parents was the greatest defeat that André suffered in the war, and in the end, lasted much longer than the victories of his career as a spy. If one looks into his eyes in the photo taken in Rennes after the war, one can see 'a still-flickering light from the extinguished star of our dead years...' as Jorge Semprún said of himself: '... sadness gripped my heart ... an essential part of me would never come back ... Finding myself alive once again, forced to ... project myself into a future unbearable to imagine, even a happy one...' ²⁸⁹

André took several months recuperation leave every year after the war before he left the French Army for the reserves, to deal with an enormous quantity and variety of documented ailments adding up to his being awarded 100% disability.²⁹⁰ His elevation to Officer of the Legion of Honor specifically mentions his status as a 'grand mutilé', those over 65% disabled. His archive contains a dozen or more medical exam reports.²⁹¹

His friend from the camps, Dr. Henri Rosencher, added a personal note to one of these reports that he had himself written: 'Mon Cher André, I will write more at length, wanted to send you as soon as possible the affidavit you asked me for. I was frightened by the number of illnesses that are crushing you. You must come home soon so that I can console and treat you. Courage! Hugs for Claire and Michel from us all. Fraternally yours, Henri.'[292]

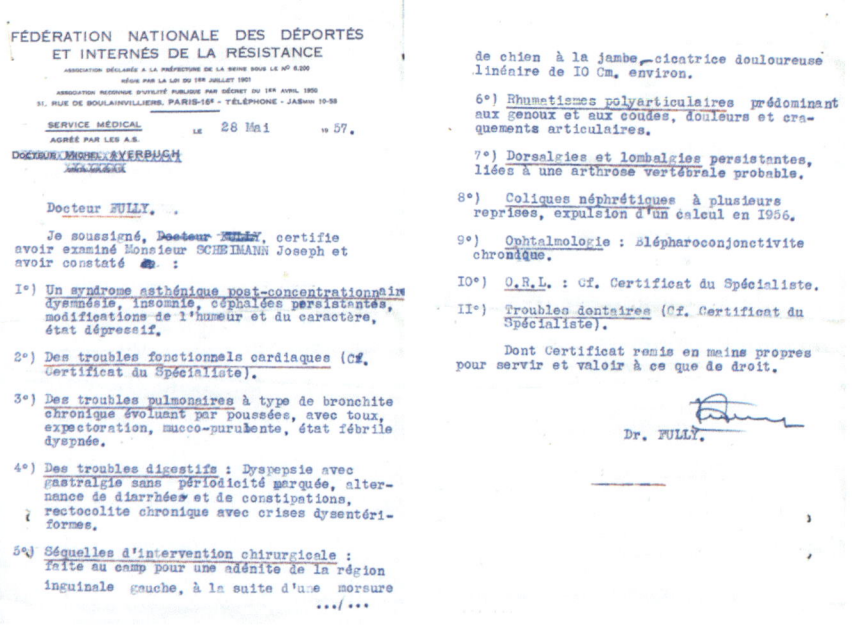

Dr. Fully's report on André's medical conditions in 1957, on letterhead of the Medical Service of the Fédération Nationale des Déportés et Internés de la Résistance includes '1) Post-concentration camp syndrome' and '5) ... a painful scar approximately 10 cm in length from a surgical procedure in camp following a dog bite.'

André left Europe and his career in intelligence with seemingly no regrets. 'I have no political ambitions and no longer take on noble causes, but I am happy to live in a country where men are free and can live according to their own convictions,' he wrote in a better time, in the United States.

However, there may always have been that other self that slumbered. He returned to Dachau for the 50th anniversary of its Liberation, where he was photographed schmoozing with his dear friend Henri Rosencher, the buddy he had made at Natzweiler under Rosencher's *nom de guerre*, Breuillot. Were they experiencing something similar to Semprún's return to Buchenwald? 'I realized that I was coming home. It was not hope I had to abandon, at the gate to that hell. On the contrary, I was abandoning my disappointments, the mistakes and failures of life. I was coming home, what I mean is, home to my world when I was twenty ... I was abandoning all the deadly despair that accumulates throughout a lifetime, to rediscover the hopefulness I knew at twenty, surrounded by death.'[293]

Henri Rosencher and André at the 50th anniversary of the liberation of KL Dachau. Right: André wearing the commemoration French political prisoner name badge.

We asked if André could have been as effective as he was, in building networks, had he been known to be Jewish. The same question can be asked of his work organizing for his comrades in the camps, and of other secret Jews there like Rosencher, who spied, fought and doctored for the British in North Africa and at the uprising in the Vercors before doing so at Natzweiler. Would this have been possible if they had been known to be Jewish, a most despised minority (like the Roma and Sinti) within a despised minority (the French) in the camps.[294]

'Do we not undergo metamorphoses throughout our lives, as if we hand off the baton from one state of ourselves to the following different one?'[295] When we ask ourselves if André lost or gained an identity in all those years of living as Peulevey rather than Scheinmann, and after the war when he eventually became once again Joseph Scheinmann, *commerçant (shopkeeper)* and once again lived in a country at peace, it seems that

André's identities ran a relay – with Scheinmann passing the baton to Peulevey and Peulevey passing it back to Scheinmann again.

André chose not to pursue avenues for credit if he found them superfluous, or knew other avenues to be more politically viable. André and most of his agents were registered as FFC (Fighting French Forces) and, if deported, DIR (Déporté Interné Résistant.) He may have not wanted them to feel they were missing something if he insisted too much on his FFL credentials. Most of his documentation is for the FFC, rather than for the FFL (Forces Françaises Libres). The FFL is defined as being 'elements constituting the regular army of Free France' and numbering 52,000 men and women.[296] For context, of more than 700,000 files on named individuals in the Resistance, the French government identifies 109,000 people as FFC and 70,000 as DIR.

In fact one of the French government documents for when his records for the DIR (Déporté Interné Résistant) attribution were changed to Scheinmann from Peulevey lists that the evidence presented included his 'attestation FFL.' Fabrice Bourrée and Laurent Laloup have also identified de Gaulle's 'handwritten certificate' for André in September 1945 as having been delivered to members of the FFL.[297] The 'Moustique' – the Free French parachutist badge he is seen wearing in Rennes and that the family still has – is an FFL insignia. And André's last medical leave, August 7, 1946, for three months, was by permission of the Commission Interministérielle de l'organe centrale FFL.

Medical leaves while he was still serving in the Army (11 months between June, 1945 and October, 1946) show that lavishing attention on the laborious process of collecting the first-person accounts of his comrades in arms, and second-hand ones where the resistors concerned had died in the camps or been executed may have taken its toll. The following years in which he continued to register his agents and regain his identity were mentally strenuous and the continual stirring of memories must have been crushing.

It was not always a matter of one-time correspondence: often, complaints and adjustments, address searches, and recriminations were involved. His agent Madame Seidel wrote of feeling such disgust at the incessant clamour of the agents and their families for funds, that she wished she hadn't come back from the concentration camps. André wrote back to share with her a philosophy that he tried to adopt to deal with the same strain: 'Don't be disgusted, what is happening is human and natural, and, since one has to live in the present and not in the past, one has to pass the sponge over it and seek to find pleasant things to be happy to have come back.'

André stayed in touch with fellow combattants of the shadows after the war and they remembered him fondly when this author looked them up. They include his dear friend after the war Claude Huard, with whom he visited often in Florida where they both had vacation residences; Yves Le Tac, faithful to his head of state Charles De Gaulle, who served the French in Algeria and was injured in his hospital bed in Paris in an assassination attempt by the OAS (Organisation de l'armée secrète); and Doctor Henri Rosencher of Paris, whose autobiography *Le Sel, la cendre, la flamme*, (*Salt, Ash and Flame*) describes his derring-do and unrelenting fight against the Germans from North Africa to the Vercors, three escapes from prisoner of war camps and his imprisonment at Natzweiler and Dachau, where he and André became friends.[298]

They had been through hell together without knowing each others' real names. Henri and André met again in Paris by chance for the first time after the war, in line with their wives on the Champs Elysées to see a movie. They embraced and then they said to each other: 'You know, I am not really Breuillot ... You know, I am not really Peulevey.'

The last time I saw André at his house in Padnaram Village, South Dartmouth, MA. André's last ID card: French nationality.

A Closer Look

Who Betrayed André?

> "Betrayals were the daily
> bread of the Resistance." [299]

Before moving on to those close to André whose indiscretions may have helped seal his fate, let's dispel any confusion that André's alias/nickname might lead to a traitor not connected to his networks named Roger Leneveu, whose alias was 'Roger Le Légionnaire,' Here is the portrait of Leneveu, who worked for the Gestapo, in every way a very different man than André:
'corpulent, bulging eyes, a slight Parisian accent, living at 10-12, rue de l'Ecluse, 5th floor, in Montmartre, always armed ... Prime target, Leneveu is said to have been cut down by resistor Joseph Le Ruyet [triple agent infiltrated into the Gestapo of Rennes] in Paris, before the Liberation.'[300]
André never speaks or writes of being armed.

When Joël Le Tac returned from England at the beginning of February 1942 he was caught with his agents' names and paperwork. Joël obviously felt free to allow his biography to contain this incriminating information, some 50 years after the war when many survivors of the camps had died, as well as relatives of people who died there or were eliminated by firing squad. The details are jarring.

'Apparently not aware that André and Turban and others in his orbit had been arrested the day before, on the 5th of February Joël Le Tac took the train for Rennes, arriving on the 6th at the apartment of one of the student staffers of the underground newspaper, *La Bretagne Enchaînée* (Brittany in Chains.)[301] In the apartment, the German police pull out their weapons. Joël can only drop his suitcases and ... burst out laughing. In his suitcases, the police discover ... a revolver, telescoping blackjack, dagger, annotated maps, aerial photographs of the Breton coast...'[302]

Then there was De Kergolay, Joël's Overcloud network radio operator, who gave up André's code name and continued to transmit under German orders, but without his security code, alerting the British he was transmitting under duress. The British then began transmitting back to him what they wanted the Germans to believe: it was a double-cross operation named 'Sealing Wax' to have the Germans believe the British thought 'Overcloud' was still in operation.[303]

Appraisals by Lt. Cpl. Warden of de Kergolay when he was in England for assignment with the Free French and trained at Special Training School No. 22 show the keenness of British Secret Services observations in view of what was to come. 'Kergolay does not seem so amenable to discipline as the others, and also seems to think he should be an officer. It would not hurt to keep an eye on his contacts during his leave.' (29 January 41) Some weeks later: 'I met Kergolay in the Services Club, Gordon Street 17.4.41 and asked him to have a drink with me. He told me that Forman (whom I knew as a student) had arrived back from France two days before, having been there for six weeks. He also told me that Le Tac had missed the boat back but that Capt. Berger thought there was no need to worry for his safety. Berger himself had also been back to France ... de Jonghe ... Although he is a conceited and tiresome person he seems to be most anxious to be off and do some work in France. How much he would tell if caught is another question.'[304]

The Le Tacs and their network Overcloud, including de Kergolay, were delivered (as well as by others) by henchmen of Double Agent Victoire, AKA La Chatte when her agents Robert Kiffer and Robert Goubeau were arrested with lists of Overcloud agent names in December of 1941.[305]

The Germans let the Le Tacs and André continue to operate. 'BOB suggested to LE TAC that he could find a secretary for them, being of course VICTOIRE ... They penetrated OVERCLOUD in December, 1941 but were prepared [and did] allow the LE TAC brothers, the organisers, to return to England a month later, before arresting them.'[306]

Thus the British observed, and André experienced, in both the cases of Overcloud and Georges-France, the divergent methods of the Gestapo and of the Abwehr, two of the multiple German agencies for counter-intelligence and repression. The Gestapo were wont to immediately arrest their suspects, as they did with Madame Louis, but the Abwehr tended to let their suspects run – as they did with some of her network's leaders including André, Turban, and others who were allowed to escape the first murderous blow to the Georges-France network – so as to have infiltrators identify more of a network's members and other of its leaders who took charge and rebuilt the networks after they had been breached.[307]

The betrayal of Georges-France (arrests in October, 1941) is attributed to Madeleine Téry, a contact recommended to Madame Louis by one of her pre-War Deuxième Bureau (French Secret Service) associates.[308] 'The arrest of the woman Louis and of Gonthier in mid-October 1941 was made possible by the fact that Gonthier tried to secure a woman in Le Havre for his intelligence work, a woman who informed the German authorities. Thereupon, Gonthier was followed and taken when he came to Paris, and Louis who got on the train with him in Rouen was arrested with him in Paris. On that occasion, a vast amount of documentation was seized that also dealt with other of the network's agents.'

Louis and Gontier's information was put to lethal use on a wide scale, with dozens shot, deported and imprisoned (22 shot at Mt. Valerien, November 27, 1942 after the trial ended; 14 deported and died in Germany; 14 deported who came home; 12 imprisoned for a year at Fresnes) and dozens more continuing to be tracked. André and many others were allowed to run on, but were doomed.

Other networks besides Georges-France with which André was associated were betrayed by the Abwehr's *'Vertrauensmann/V-Mann'* ('Confidence men'). The takedowns by infiltrators such as Roger Bardet and Jacques Humbert started in October of 1941 and went on into the summer and fall of 1942 at least.[309] Jacques Humbert, 17 years old, delivered the Le Dantec network.[310]

After the war, wrapping up the SIS networks for the 'Anglo-French Communications Bureau', Captain Deckers wrote to André on behalf of 'one of the persons named by Mrs. Lehmann, M. Jacques GENIES ... They were denounced by a person named Humbert, currently in prison in Rennes.' Among the arrests, Deckers indicates those of Lehmann, Taurin, Eric Peters (a painter) Bois-Gontier, Jobick Guillaume (nephew of Le Dantec) and an unknown Spaniard...'[311]

Other references to traitors are in the British document KV-4-344 LRC-RVPS 'Example of a typical case of an alien interrogated at LRC' about Jean Poumeau de la Forest that leads to Jean le Pollotec and VMs (German confidence men) Georges Kraft (alias Georges André) and Charles Ortet. These two infiltrated and knew the Overcloud members de Kergolay and Joël Le Tac, as detailed at greater length in Patrick Miannay's encyclopedic *Dictionnaire des Agents Doubles dans la Résistance*.(p.164.) The list of who betrayed André goes on...

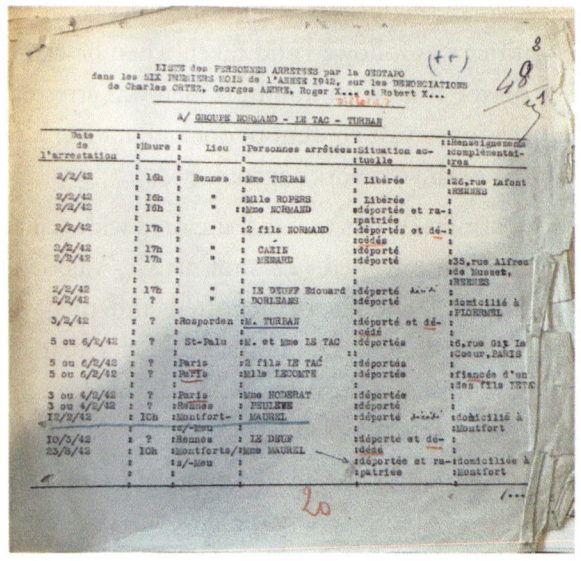

List of persons arrested by the Gestapo on denunciation of Charles Ortez, George André [alias for Kraft] Roger ____ X, Robert X...'__

Madame Turban
Miss Ropers
Madame Normand
2 Normand sons
Cazin
Menard
Le Deuff
Dorleans
Mr. Turban
Two sons and Mr. and Mrs. Le Tac
Miss Lecomte
Mrs. Hoderat
Peuleve
Maurel
Le Deuf
Mrs. Maurel

Robert Joseph Deckers (initially Intelligence Corps, transferred to SIS/MI6 in November 1942, assigned to Anglo-French Communications Bureau for SIS mop-up operations after the fall of Paris) drew up a schema of the August 1940-November 1941 networks aggregated into Georges-France – with Wilborts, Turban and Peulevey. Readers will recognize others from this book: Seidel, Eidem, Le Belzic, Legeay, D'Estienne d'Orves. André's personal archive of post-war correspondence includes Adam, Bocq, Menard, Jaunet among many others also included in Deckers' schema.

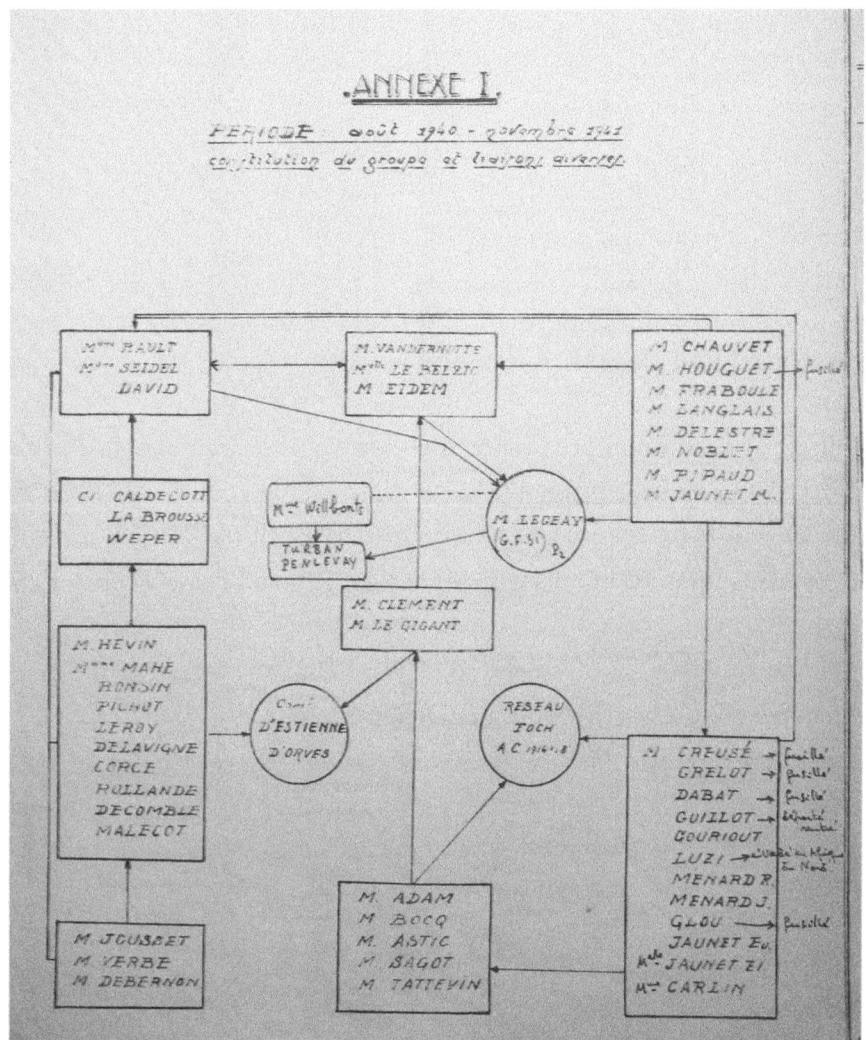

Deckers' post-war schema of August 1940-November 1941
groups and liaisons in the Georges-France network

Similar to 'a star around which celestial bodies gravitationally revolve, each with their own satellites, around a Boss, man or woman, are deployed a multitude of sub-networks that respond to its attraction.'[312] The fall of one network complicated, and ultimately doomed, the working of all the others.[313]

André's War Record

French Government Decorations:

Knight of the Legion of Honour: May 21, 1946 signed by De Gaulle; Reissued to Scheinmann, Joseph alias Peulevey, 11 April 1952, signed by General Paul Dassault. Entitles the bearer to wear the War Cross with Palm.

Officer of the Legion of Honour issued to Scheinmann, Joseph, 13 July 1961, signed by General Georges Catroux.

Médaille de la Résistance Officer with rosette (April 24, 1946)[314]

Croix de Guerre/War Cross with Vermillion Star and Palme February 25, 1946

Volunteer Cross

Medal of the Camps (Médaille des Déportés).

André's medals and parachute badges photographed by his son.

André's War Record

LEGION OF HONOR: KNIGHT, OFFICER

André's Légion d'Honneur case and medal when he was awarded his first rank of Chevalier/Knight, in March 1946, flanking his later citation for elevation to Officer 'for the grave disabilities from the deprivation and violence he suffered.'

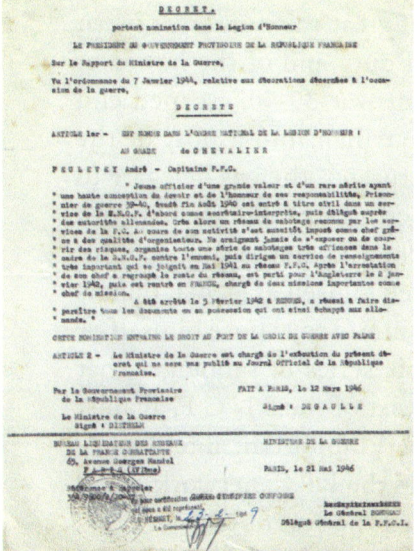 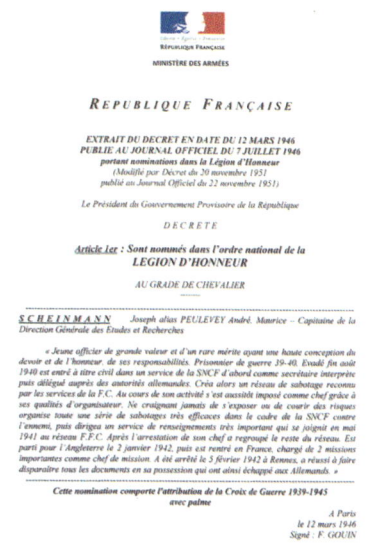

André's certified copy of his Knighthood of the Légion d'honneur and its official version today. Original translated in the text.

DECREE

carrying the nomination for the Legion of Honor

THE PRESIDENT OF THE PROVISIONAL GOVERNMENT OF THE FRENCH REPUBLIC

Upon the Report of the Minister for War,

In accordance with the ordinance of 7 January 1944, relative to the decorations awarded on the occasion of the war

IT IS DECREED

ARTICLE 1– IS NAMED TO THE NATIONAL ORDER OF THE LEGION OF HONOR WITH THE GRADE of KNIGHT

PEULEVEY André – Captain F.F.C. [Forces Françaises Combattantes/French Fighting Forces]

Young officer of great valor and rare merit having an elevated concept of duty and of the honor of his responsibilities, Prisoner of war 39-40, escaped end of August 1940 entered as a civilian into a post of the S.N.C.F. first as secretary-interpreter, then as delegate to the German authorities. Then created a sabotage network recognized by the services of the F.C. In the course of his activity immediately established himself as leader, thanks to organisational skills. Never afraid to expose himself or to run risks, organised a whole series of sabotages that were very effective in the context of the S.N.C.F. against the enemy, then directed a very important intelligence service that in May 1941 joined the F.F.C. network. After the arrest of his boss regrouped the rest of the network. Left for England on January 2, 1942, then returned to France, charged with two important missions, as head of mission.

Was arrested February 5 1942 at RENNES, succeeded in making all the documents in his possession disappear, thus depriving the Germans of them.

THIS NAMING BESTOWS THE RIGHT TO WEARING THE CROSS OF WAR WITH PALM

ARTICLE 2- The minister for War is charged with the execution of the present decree that will be published in the Official Journal of the French Republic.

By the Provisional Government

DONE IN PARIS, March 12 1946

Signed: DE GAULLE

The Minister for War

Signed: DIETHELM

BUREAU OF LIQUIDATING THE NETWORKS

Ministry for War OF FIGHTING FRANCE

65 Avenue Georges Mandel, PARIS XVI

PARIS, May 21 1946

Refer to 334/9600/d/JC-ST

Seen as certified to be a valid copy
that was represented to us LE VESINET on 23-2-1949

The Commissioner of Police (signed) (stamp of the Sureté Nationale local bureau)[315]

ORDER OF THE ARMY CORPS

DECISION No 30

Le Général DE GAULLE, Président du Gouvernement Provisoire de la République Française, Chef des Armées,

CITE A L'ORDRE DU CORPS D'ARMEE

PEULEVEY André Maurice   F.F.C.

" Prisonnier de guerre évadé, entre dans le réseau A I G L E en Octobre 1940, forme un réseau de Sabotages au sein de la S.N.C.F. devant fonctionner pendant 15 mois. S'est vite imposé comme chef, a travaillé en même temps comme agent local de renseignements d'abord, régional ensuite. Est entré dans le réseau F.F.C. en mars 1941. A repris à lui seul l'organisation après l'arrestation de son chef, a contacté de nombreux groupes, les a réorganisés en vue d'un meilleur rendement. Est passé en Angleterre, y a passé son brevet de parachutiste, est revenu chargé de deux missions très importantes dont il est le chef. Arrêté dès son retour, n'a jamais avoué de ce qu'il connaissait, malgré les coups et les tortures, est resté un an au secret, déporté en Allemagne, est libéré en avril 1945, est revenu le moral intact. "

CETTE CITATION COMPORTE L'ATTRIBUTION DE LA CROIX DE GUERRE 1939 AVEC

ETOILE D'OR

PARIS, le 13 Février 1946

Le Général DE G A U L L E, Président du Gouvernement Provisoire de la République Française, Chef des Armées
P.O. Le Général JUIN
Chef d'Etat-Major de la Défense Nationale
signé : JUIN

PRESIDENCE
DU GOUVERNEMENT PROVISOIRE DE LA REPUBLIQUE FRANCAISE

PARIS, le 25 Février 1946

COPIE CERTIFIEE CONFORME

MINISTERE DE LA GUERRE

FRANCE COMBATTANTE

Référence à rappeler :
334/8082   JC-ST

Le Capitaine C O U L B O I S
Chef du Bureau Liquidateur des Réseaux de la France Combattante.

André's Order of the Army Corps with War Cross and Gold Star.

Decision No. 30
General DE GAULLE, President of the
Provisional Government of the French Republic, Leader of the Armed Forces
CITES to the ORDER OF THE ARMY CORPS
PEULEVEY André Maurice F.F.C.

'Escaped prisoner of war, enters the AIGLE network in October 1940, creates a Sabotage network at the heart of the S.N.C.F. which was to function for 15 Months. Quickly acknowledged as leader, worked at the same time as intelligence agent, locally at first, then regionally. Entered the F.F.C. network in March, 1941. Single-handedly took over the organisation after the arrest of its leader, contacted numerous groups reorganised them to better effect. Went over to England, got his parachute certificate there, came back charged with two missions of great importance to lead. Arrested upon his return, never admitted to what he knew, despite the blows and torture, stayed a year in solitary, was deported to Germany, liberated in April 1945, came back with his morale intact.

THIS CITATION INCLUDES THE ATTRIBUTION OF THE WAR CROSS 1939
WITH GOLD STAR
Paris, February 13, 1946
By order of General JUIN
Chief of Staff of National Defense
signed: JUIN
Paris, February 25, 1946
Copy dated 23-2-1949 [316]

MEDAL OF THE RESISTANCE, WITH ROSETTE
and
CROIX DE COMBATTANT VOLONTAIRE

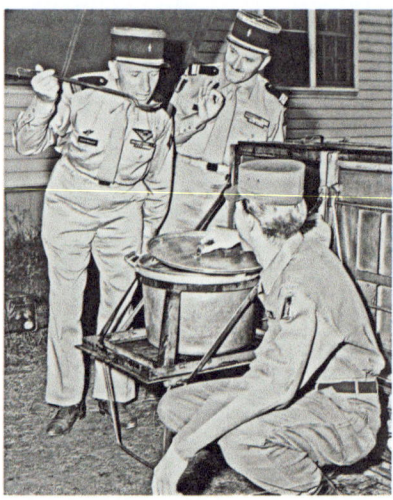

André continued to serve in the French Army Reserves as Lt. Colonel after he moved to the US. Here he tastes the cuisine at their base at Ft. Drum, NY. Photos of André's medals missing from the family's collection from Pierre Tillet, left, for the Medal of the Resistance with rosette and Wikimedia, right, for the Cross of the Voluntary Combattant.

The Medal of the Resistance, with Rosette, is the most rare of André's medals.[317] The Médaille de la Résistance avec Rosette was created by de Gaulle on 8 February 1943 to 'recognize remarkable acts of faith and courage' in the French Resistance in World War 2. The *Journal Officiel de la République Française, Annexe 17 May 1946* lists that it was awarded with rosette to Capitaine Louis Ledeuff (posthumously), Capitaine André Peulevey, Lieutenant Yvonne Le Tac, and Lieutenant Renée Louelle. Of 65,000 people given this award, 4549 received the award with rosette. Others who won this level of the award include Josephine Baker, Louis Aragon, and Pierre Mendès France. The black and red color symbolize mourning and blood

Trip and Training in England

From the archives at Kew[318]

Setting the stage:
Lieutenant Holdsworth who accompanied the Le Tacs and André proposed using the Channel for transiting information as well as agents a month before Joël was ferried to France on his first Overcloud mission.

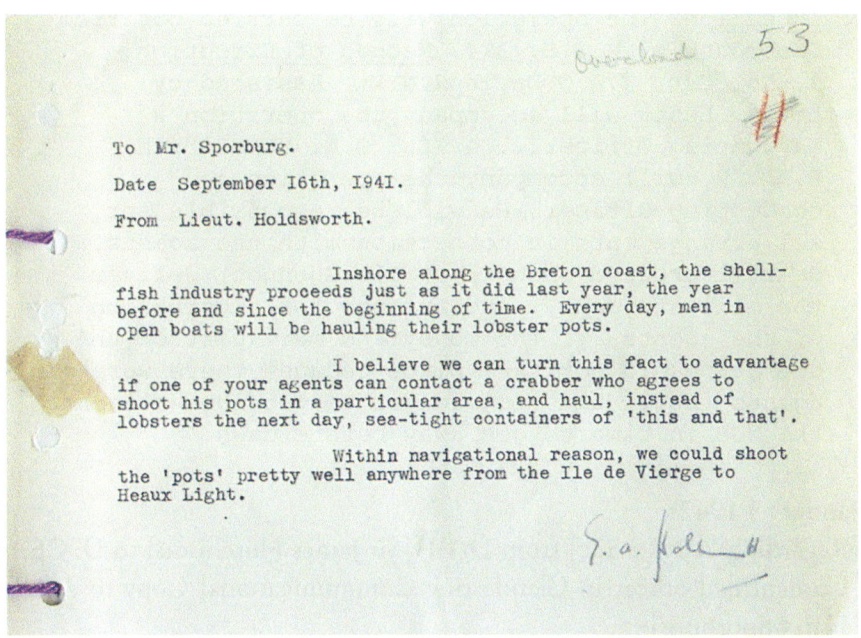

From the British National Archives at Kew, file for the Overcloud network: Gerald Alfred Holdsworth's plan for repurposing lobster pots along the Breton coast where André and the Le Tacs traveled courtesy of the British 'Secret Flotilla.' The Heaux light on the West was at the Ile de Bréhat, where Suzanne Wilborts started the network, La Bande à Sidonie; the Ile Vierge was East of the Ile Guénoc into the Channel off St. Pabu, the Le Tac home from where André left for England.

January 3, 1942:

SIS plan for the pickup of 'Operation Overcloud II (the Overcloud Group and Joël known also by that name on his second trip to England with the SOE) no later than January 7.'

> Operation Orders addressed to N.I.D.(C).[319]
> [Naval Intelligence Division (Head of SIS)]
> Charts: 2675a - English Channel, Western Sheet.
> 2644 - Ushant to Plateau des Roches Douvres.
> 1432 - Approaches to 1.
> 'Object: to include 3 or possibly 5 agents from the Ile Guennoc; the rendez-vous being at the Balancing Rock on the South-Eastern end of the island between 2359 and 0300...
> Intention: The operation will be carried out from Dartmouth by M.G.B. 314. Method of Execution: 3. Lt. Cdr. E.A.G.Davis R.N.R., Assisted by Lt. A. Letty will accompany the operation's Navigating Officer....4. Lt. G.A. Holdsworth R.N.V.R. will accompany the operation as conducting Officer. He will be responsible for all arrangements in connection with the agents. He will proceed onshore at Ile Guennoc, deliver the mail and money, and arrange for embarkation of the agents.... The money and mail part of the operation did not take place because there were 7 agents in all and took longer to get them all onto the MGB in time to get away before dawn.'

January 5 1942:

[Regarding Yves Le Tac] from D/RF [Sir James Hutchison] to D/CE.1 [Unidentified officer in Clandestine Communications] Copy to AD/S [Harry Sporburg]:

> A further OVERCLOUD operation, similar to that which brought S. (now to be known as Serveri [sic]) into the country, is expected to take place on the night of the 6th-7th instant. it is hoped to bring Back FABULOUS [Labit] and MAINMAST [Forman], also OVERCLOUD's elder brother .... OVERCLOUD's brother has been working for us since the fall of France, but hitherto has not been brought to England. ...I am extremely anxious

that he should avoid the R.V.P.S. Royal Victoria Patriotic School interrogation center for arriving foreigner vetting.]320

January 8, 1942:
Official report of Lt. RNVR Gerald Alfred Holdsworth about the arrival of Overcloud 2 (the second of Joël's trips under the auspices of SOE.)

Repeat Overcloud, Night January 6th./ January 7th, 1942

SECRET

To: Captain Piquet-Wicks
From: Lieutenant Holdsworth

We had obtained the day previously the Commanding Officer (Lieut. Curtis') approval to include one extra man in the party....A departure was made from the Lizard at 1700 hours and a landfall at the Ile Vierge 2230. A raid on Brest was observed to be in progress during the twentieth hour, at which time we were about 70 miles distant. ...Even before our boats had left the ships' side, a canvas canoe was observed approaching and flashing a blue light. On closing it with one of our dinghies, we were hailed by Overcloud himself: he had two men with him in his canoe and explained that there were four more waiting to be picked up on the island. Sub-Lieutenant Richards in one boat, Pierre and myself in the other, located them on the southern point....The necessity of completing the ferry operation in one trip oweing to the lateness of the hour, meant that four persons were obliged to crowd into one of the 9'6" dinghies, which in the groundswell, put her well below plimsoll marks. All however reached the M.G.B. without swimming. Overcloud, [Joël Le Tac] whom we rather expected would be returning to the mainland in his canoe, was insistent that he needed to accompany the others to H.Q. It was pointed out to him that as far as we knew he was not expected, and that it might be quite three weeks before we could return him, but he still thought it was urgent.

...

H.Q. must please provide us the opportunity to have the fullest conversation with Overcloud on this subject. Because M.G.B. 314 very wisely wished to withdraw owing to the galaxy of flashing lights, it was decided not to make a further return trip to the island to deposit the container [of demolition materials] and the Foldboat. We therefore made our departure at 0215...

Baths and breakfast were provided for the seven men, their papers collected and sealed for H.Q. inspection, transport arranged to Truro, where they were put aboard the 12:05 train in charge of Sergt. Peake and C.P.O. Pierre. [Signed] G. A. Holdsworth LT RNVR

January 11, 1942:
Just five days after their arrival on British soil, a 'MOST SECRET' report of a planning meeting for their return to France on January 11, 1942 in Captain Eric Piquet-Wicks office in London lists Le Tac as 'Joël' and André, is 'A.N. Other,' an S.I.S. cover name.

NOTES OF MEETING HELD (Stamped MOST SECRET)
at 4 p.m.
on Sunday, 11th January, 1942
in Captain Piquet-Wicks's Office.

Present: Captain Piquet-Wicks

Lieut. Holdsworth [Helford Flotilla]

Sub-Lieut. Richards [Helford Flotilla]

Lieut. G. McKenzie [Helford Flotilla]

Lieut. Bienvenue [alias for Raymond Lagier, BCRA]

Joël [Le Tac]

Pierre [Jean-Pierre Forman, BCRA, called Pierre by Passy]

Sgt. Peake [of Royal Victoria Patriotic School (MI 5)]

A.N. Other [André]

1. It was agreed that no reference should be made outside the meeting, to any of the Rendezvous proposed....

January 20, 1942:

Captain Piquet-Wicks of SOE confirms to Commander Dunderdale that

```
'it is possible for your agent and W/T operator
to be returned together with our OVERCLOUD party.
In this connection, I attach copy of a memorandum
despatched to our liaison with Captain Slocum.321
Lieut. Holdsworth asked specifically that an
effort be made for your man to visit him at the
same time as Overcloud (the Le Tacs) in order
that that may have the training necessary for the
successful completion of the proposed operation.'
```

January 21, 1942: Stamped SECRET:

```
    SEA OPERATION - OVERCLOUD
   The operation will be carried out by a fast
craft which will be provided by Capt. Slocum's
organization...
   The agents will travel to Lieut. Holdsworth's
address in Cornwall...
   Any equipment which will need to be landed will
be small and can be accommodated in the lashed
canoe...
   Lieut. Holdsworth - if required, Sub-Lieut.
Richards and their Chief Petty officer will
accompany the operation...
```

January 26, 1942:

Passy requested of Picquet-Wicks that the British allow their agent LaBaume, of the BCRAM 'to accompany our agent JOE to the embarkation point,' explaining that he is making the request 'to allow Lt. LaBaume and JOE to finalize definitively and in peace the last detail of the mission that it is difficult to do in London.'

January 27, 1942:

['Overcloud' is Joël, André is now 'Turquoise']

```
       'Overcloud'/'Turquoise' Arrangements'
   The following arrangements have been made with
Lt. Holdsworth and Captain Piquet-Wicks, and it is
hoped they will remain final:
```

1 TURQUOISE' agent and 2 'OVERCLOUD' agents will travel to Helford on the 9:50 p.m. train from Paddington on Wednesday, 28th January, for training on 29th January and embarkation on Friday, 30th January.

2) Lt. Goodfellow will accompany all 3 agents on this train. 2 sleepers have been booked for him and 'TURQUOISE', and S.O.E. will provide sleepers for the 2 'OVERCLOUD' agents.

3) Lt. Goodfellow will be required to provide tickets and sleeper ticket for himself and 1 agent. SOE will provide their two agents with the same.

4) Lt. Goodfellow should call at No.1 Dorset Square (Marylebone Road) with 'TURQUOISE' at 8:30 P.M. on Wednesday, 28th January, to collect the SOE agents and luggage, which is considerable.

5) On arrival at Truro, the party should proceed to the Red Lion Hotel for breakfast and telephone Lt. Holdsworth (Mawnan Smith 333) who will come and to fetch them.

6) Accommodations for the whole party will be arranged by Lt. Holdsworth at Helford.

January 29 & 30, 1942:

Report to De Gaulle's Section 'Action' of the departure of agents JOE (Service 'ACTION') and Yve (Service 'ACTION' and Commissariat of the interior).

The following report – HS 6/416 – submitted by Captain Bienvenue, alias for Raymond Lagier, to the Head of BCRAM (Bureau Central de Rensignements et d'Action Militaire) – the Secret Service of France Libre/General De Gaulle describes how 'Joe' and 'Yve' were taken to their point of departure on January 29, 1942.

André is mentioned as 'the English agent' and 'the agent' whose conducting officer was 'Goodfellow' – a Frenchman, Martin Robert de Lesseps, grandson of Ferdinand the Suez Canal developer. His 'Goodfellow' alias was the English name of his fiancée. Noted is that Thomas Greene insisted on going along too.

Trip and Training in England

The man who signed this first-hand report 'Severi' – was Fred Scamaroni. His career features in Piquet-Wicks' *Four in the Shadows*. In March, 1943 he was tortured and would die by suicide in the hands of the OVRA, the fascist political police in Corsica, after telling them his name was Severi, without revealing anything.

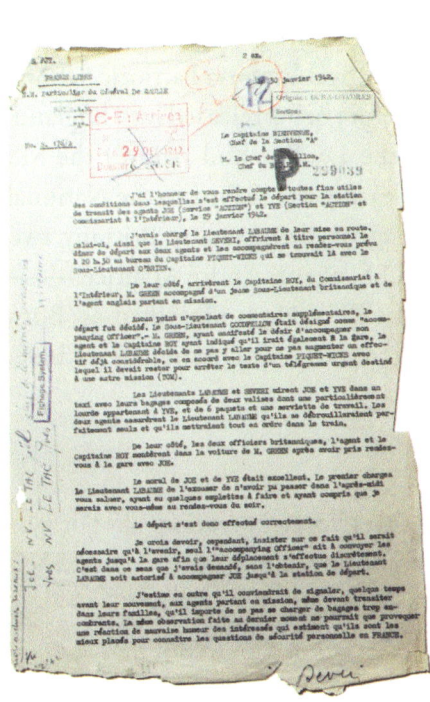

'Lieutenants LaBaume and Severi took them to the departure dinner before their meeting at 20:30 at the office of Captain Piquet-Wicks ... Arrived Captain Roy of the Commissariat of the Interior and Mr Green, along with Sub-Lieutenant [Goodfellow] and the English agent leaving on the mission. Sub-Lieut. Goodfellow was designated as the accompanying officer. Mr. Green expressed the wish to accompany his agent to the station.

'Lieutenant La Baume and Severi put Joe and Yve in a taxi with their baggage, which consisted of two suitcases- one of which, particularly heavy, belonging to Yve - six packages and a briefcase. The two agents assured LaBaume that they would be perfectly fine on their own and would organize everything on the train. For their part, the two British officers, the agent and Captain Roy got into Mr. Green's car, having agreed to meet Joe at the station.'

The signer concludes by recommending that, in future, their agents be accompanied by one of their officers, as had been planned for but was not done in this case, and that agents, even if returning to their families, not have so much baggage.

Report to De Gaulle's Section 'Action' of the departure of agents JOE and Yve and 'the English agent' (André) signed by the Lt. Severi, the alias for Fred Scamaroni, who had just returned from a mission himself. From the 28P3 Overcloud dossier, courtesy Fabrice Bourrée.

February 16, 1942:

A radio message was the first to alert the SIS to the arrests The British, who understood that de Kergolay was being used by the Germans, because the security check (element that would have been included to give the sender's 'all clear') was omitted in the coding. Their communications with the Germans were then used to manipulate them, in a pretense of continuing Overcloud, renamed for processing by the British 'Operation Sealing Wax.'

May 23, 1942:

In a MOST SECRET report of the investigation of Van Ackere, an agent infiltrated to England by the Germans, at Royal Victoria Patriotic School, where arrivals from abroad were vetted before being released into England, (except for known operatives such as the Le Tacs and André) the SIS whited out André's last name before releasing the record to the National Archives at Kew. It describes the 'three agents being sent to Brittany, two of them S.O.E. 'and the third was an S.I.S. agent, André Maurice ———————— Alias Henri Maurice LE NEVEU.' He is identified as 'Born 7.11.15' and described as 'height 1 Metre 68; hair chestnut; eyes blue; oval face; straight nose.'[322]

1943:

Another page from Kew about the Overcloud operation after it was renamed identifies André by his code name Turquoise. Entitled 'SEALING WAX' at center and above that at top left, 'Major Robertson:'

```
'I saw Captain Piquet-Wicks this morning and
discussed the SEALING WAX case with him....
   For a long time he operated with the Free
French an agent known to them as OVERCLOUD ...He
also brought his brother, Yves le TAC in with him
and they came into contact with two of  [blank
space for 'Dunderdale's'] agents, one of who was
called TURQUOISE. There were several operations
in connection with the case and the relevant dates
were as follows:
   October 13th/14th 1941: OVERCLOUD (Joe le TAC)
went back to France.
```

December 31st 1941 [An operation took place on which a W/T set, known as PLAICE, was sent out for OVERCLOUD. and a man called SEVRY @ FRED returned to England.]

January 6th/7th 1942: As a result of a sea operation OVERCLOUD and his brother came to England with several others including TURQUOISE.

February 2nd/3rd OVERCLOUD and his brother returned with TURQUOISE and with a wireless set called MAUVE which was to be used for TURQUOISE.'

(Documents from HV 6/12 at Kew Courtesy Nigel Perrin)

The very controversial Madame Louis

Madame Wilborts alluded cryptically to André that Madame Louis' pre-war activities were 'highly suspect'. Louis' FFL designation post-war may have been due in part to her having worked for French Intelligence Services – the Deuxième Bureau – before the war. From 1925 to 1937, according to the information in the German trial indictment for which it seems she cooperated, 'she occasionally played the part of informer to the Deuxième Bureau against the Communists.'[323] She may have continued to do so after the Vichy government took over in occupied France.[324]

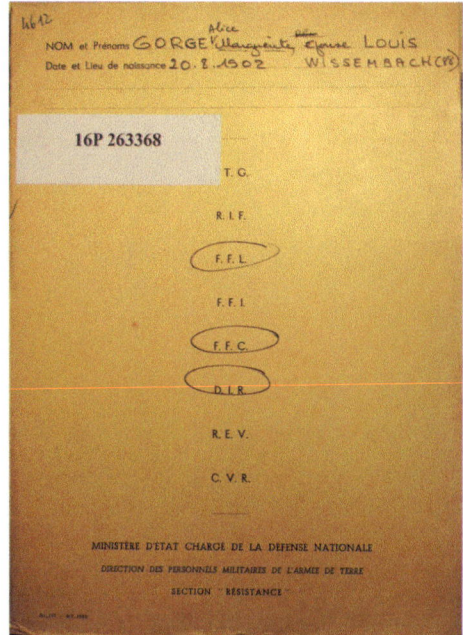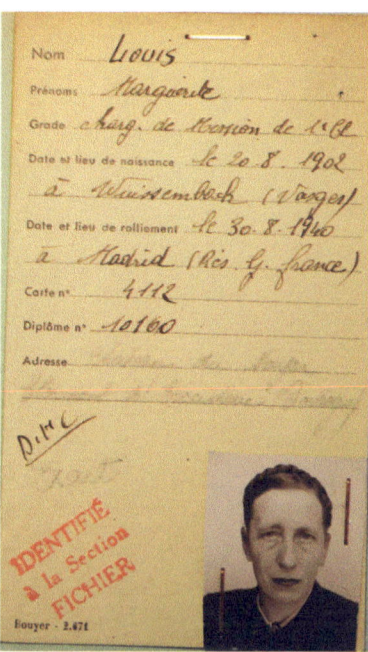

Madame Louis' ID from her dossier © Archives Nationales 16P263368

It is a puzzlement that we know nothing about André and Madame Louis ever connecting after the war. Did she ever ask him to help her find Groupe 31's agents? They were both working with Robert Joseph Deckers (initially Intelligence Corps then transferred to SIS/MI6 in November 1942 – and then after the liberation of Paris to the Anglo-French Communications Bureau for SIS mop-up operations). On November 9 1945, Deckers wrote from 8 Av. des Tilleuls to Lt. Mitchell of France Combattante: 'Following up on our conversation on the subject some time ago, I am sending some elements for text citations and a presentation of facts concerning the activity of Mme. Louis of Group 31, who has not applied for any honours. The importance of her work and her exceptional courage deserve, I believe, a request for the Legion d'Honneur. Perhaps the Medal of the Resistance could also be obtained for her. I would be infinitely grateful to you, if, as a personal favour, you would submit these requests on the appropriate official forms and in the required terms, and would shepherd them toward the goal...' [325]

Despite this tribute and the honors she did receive, several legal actions sullied the name of Madame Louis, post-war, and may have contributed until recently to the neglect of the Georges- France network.[326] Partial list: In 1956, she was removed from the directorship of the veterans association of the Georges-France network, due to her refusal to recognize some agents and insertion of others who could not be proved to have served; in 1957, the police in Limoges (dossier 45.680) investigated the suspicious death of her lover René Guichard (a young married man with children who was thought to have committed suicide or something – a bottle of poison was found at the foot of the ladder from which he was hanging in the barn attached to her place of business); at the end of 1957 to early 1958 she was fined for writing a check backed by insufficient funds; in 1958 she was investigated again, for her involvement with Colonel Zuccarelli in influence-peddling and racketeering of fraudulent promises to obtain trucking permits and Resistance testimonials. On 24 April, 1959 her right to wear the Légion d'Honneur with the rank of Chevalier (Knight) awarded to her on January 14, 1948 and all other French or foreign decorations was suspended for ten years, retroactively, due to allegations of selling influence and extortion.[327]

Marie-José Chombart de Lauwe, daughter of Suzanne Wilborts who had started *La Bande à Sidonie* before they were folded into Group 31 complained to André about Madame Louis' derelictions both during and after the war. 'Of the 27 deportees from the network, arrested on the coast between February and May 1942, 14 would not come back from the camps.³²⁸ Despite this heavy toll, we would have our network certified. We worked a lot with the English of the IS and the person in charge of vetting who was in Paris knows little of our activities, and what's more, has a penchant for trivializing them.'³²⁹

> EXTRAIT DU JOURNAL OFFICIEL n° 100
> du 29 avril 1959 - page 4671 -
>
> GRANDE CHANCELLERIE DE LA LEGION D'HONNEUR
>
> Décrets du 24 avril 1959 relatifs à la discipline des membres de la Légion d'Honneur et des décorés de la médaille militaire.
>
> Par décret en date du 24 avril 1959, pris en exécution des décrets des 16 mars et 24 novembre 1852, les peines disciplinaires ci-après ont été prononcées :
>
> Est suspendue pendant dix ans, à partir de la date de la notification du décret de l'exercice des droits et prérogatives attachés à la qualité de membre de la Légion d'Honneur et privée, en outre, pendant le même laps de temps, du droit de porter toute autre décoration française ou étrangère ressortissant à la grande chancellerie la nommée GORCE (Marguerite), épouse LOUIS. Chevalier de la Légion d'Honneur du 14 janvier 1948.

Suspension of Madame Louis' Legion of Honour was published on 29 April 1959 in the *Journal Officiel*, issue 100, p. 4671

Despite the German trial documents being closed for another 60 years, Suzanne Wilborts knew to blame Madame Louis for dozens of agents being seized by the Gestapo at the time of her arrest. These names mentioned in the German trial indictment included hers – 'Gisbons in St. Brieux' [Wilborts was known as Gibbons].

Suzanne Wilborts wrote on 10 April 1947 detailing difficulties being registered and the indignity of seeing others recognized who did not deserve to be, due to the Madame Louis' mishandling of the verification process: 'I don't think you'll get much from Group 31, Madame Louis always saying she got nothing from us, which is normal because she was arrested ... and she could after that know nothing of the activity of the group that now has picked up agents that never worked for it during the war.'

Max Eidem, head of the Comité Rennais des Etudiants, was one of those to whom Madame Louis had denied recognition. The arbiter who worked for the Liquidation Bureau decided after receiving this testimony: 'To conclude, the membership of Max Eidem not being in doubt, it is important to establish the nature and importance of the tasks that were assigned to him. Madame Louis, registrar of the network, calling herself insufficiently informed, (allegation formulated by Madame Wilborts) it would be useful to question Mr. Peulevey on this subject, as his position of secretary to the late Mr. Turban, regional director, would bring all guarantees that could be desired.'

When she wrote to André, 26 June 1947, about how much Georges-France agents suffered after the war from Madame Louis' selective amnesia, or from her not ever having known who her sub-agents were at all, Suzanne Wilborts also blamed Madame Louis for the British not fulfilling their promises of support.

'Last year, in June 1946, I received a visit from an officer of the I.S. [Intelligence Service] who came to find out what were my means of existence, my state of health, my pension, etc ... He seemed stupefied that I collect only 7,000 francs per year, as a war widow, plus a disability pension of 700 francs per month!! He told me not to torment myself for the future, that the British, knowing what they owe me, would take care of me. The agents of poor Jean Legeay each received a small sum. That is nice. But the guy who snared us, the one who sold out all the network, and who had never worked for the IS, also got 18,500 francs via Madame Louis! That is stupefying. You know she made herself so hated by Group 31, that she was fired from her job as President. She got herself demobilised as "Commandant" and her origin is completely suspect. I have come to ask myself if, by chance, they hadn't given her something for me. I know she harmed me as much as she could with the IS, but how to find out?'

There is no record of any criticism of Madame Louis by André.

André's Agents

André in his vast archive of documentation of his agents also preserved correspondence from many of the top government officials administering the registration of the networks of the resistance. Among the names of people writing to him as *Liquidateur du réseau* Overcloud, both sending and requesting information, or to whom he replied, are 'Le Médecin Colonel LORMEAU, Président de la Commission Nationale d'Homologation FFCI' (1948); 'Le Général DEJUSSIEU PONTCARRAL, Délégué Général FFCI' (1947); Le Colonel JOSSET, Délégué Général FFCI' (1947); Le Capitaine LIGER, Officier Liquidateur de la FRANCE COMBATTANTE (1945) and possibly Gilbert Renault/'Rémy' (1948).

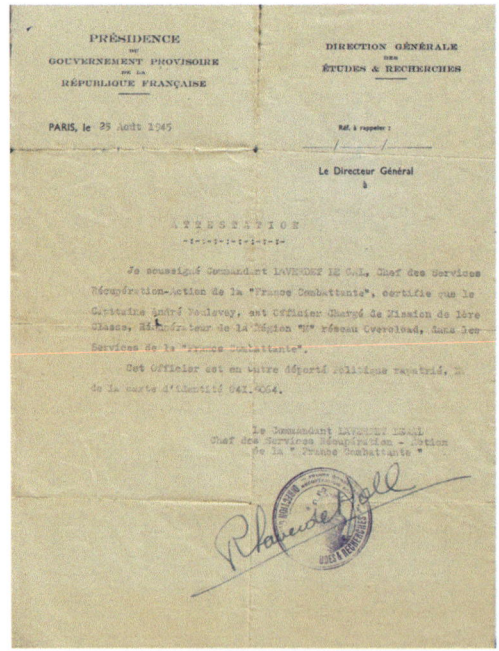

Paris, 25 August, 1945

Certification

-:-:-:-:-:-

I, the undersigned Commander LAVERDET LE GAL, head of Recuperation-Action of the "Fighting French" certify that Captain André Peulevey is an Officer, Mission Leader 1st Class, Registrar of Region "M" for the Overcloud Network, of La "France Combattante."

This Officer is furthermore a repatriated political deportee, ID card 041.9064 [Stamp and letterhead of the DGER]

One of the official documents in André's files certifying him as Overcloud Network Registrar ('Récupérateur, later 'Liquidateur'). This one from Laverdet Legal, 15 August 1945.

We could have included here the most documented (with up to 20 pages of testimony and photographs) of the most famous of his agents: Henri Lehmann (including a full page letter by Julian Kraehling, lawyer, who defended him in his trial by the Germans, testifying to his leadership role); André Ménard, Louis Remaud, Robert Nidelet, Madame de Saint Laurent (who left 10 children and was decapitated in Cologne for sheltering Englishmen), Jean Le Dantec, and André Tessier who contributed amazing documentation – including photographs of German defense lines, copies the letter of a teenager to his mother on the eve of his execution, and the memory that on '10 February 1941 at 4:15 in the afternoon, in Rennes, Place Toussaint, a German soldier was seen washing his car with a French flag, squeezing and shaking it out many times and laughing sneeringly.' ... These are just a handful of many agents documented in André's archive.

Albert and Auguste Migaud's are the graves in foreground of this moving photograph by Pierre de Jaegher of the Cemetery of Ivry-sur-Seine where resistors who were shot at Mt. Valérien are buried, including members of Georges-France, Groupes Lehmann and Le Dantec, and many others in André's history.

The very laconic ID for herself that Madame Seidel sent 'on request of Captain Peulevez, associate of Commander Joël Le Tac, both superiors' and her paragraph about agent Torqueau represent dozens of summaries she wrote up for André's agents in Brittany. Here, 'Mr. Torqueau of Nantes was part of the group for Intelligence and at first sheltered an Englishman. Then provided us with abundant information. He is the one who worked at the testing laboratory of the SMGO factory in Nantes; he gave us the miniature model of an anti-aircraft shell. His information was always very precise and he gave it unselfishly. He was not arrested, since it was only I who knew of him.'

That last sentence appears on more than a couple of Seidel's agent summaries.

Seidel summary for herself and for Torqueau, who 'was not arrested, since it was only I who knew of him.'

André's Agents

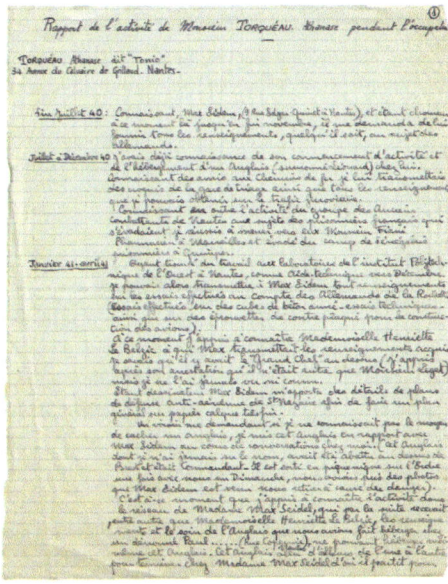

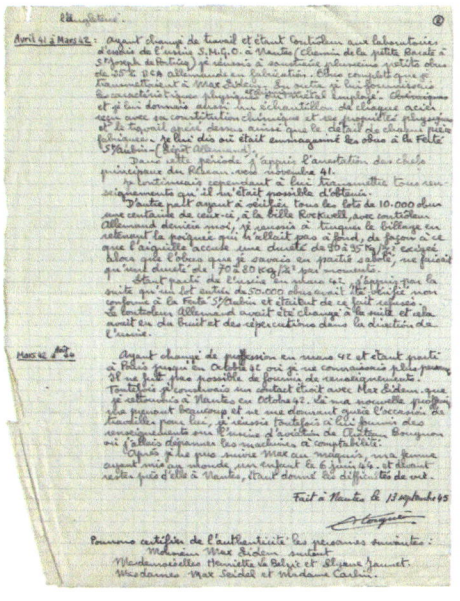

Anathase Torqueau's report of activities. His is not of unusual length for many documents in André's archive of his agents, though as Madame Seidel said, 'very precise'. He recounts stealing the chemical analyses, samples of steel and designs of each product produced in the munitions factory where he worked, reports where they were stored, and describes how exactly he sabotaged the shells with the German inspector right behind him.

Self-report of agent Anathase Torqueau's activity in the Resistance.

Here is a whole family, in Madame Seidel's careful and caring words over her signature, which are joined in André's archive by two long letters about the Marchais family.

'Madame Marchais, the wife of Monsieur Marchais, executed as outcome of our trial, continued on, after the death of her husband, to shelter freedom fighters, to centralise information, and to destroy all the mail that came through the post office which denounced French people to the Germans.

She was not arrested.'

'Mr. MARCHAIS André worked with us starting in December 1940; he sheltered several Englishmen among whom MacMillan and Harry Pool. It was at his place that I stopped off when I took drawings/maps or intelligence for Mr. LEGEAIS, to be turned over to LENEVEU. [André]

Arrested in the middle of the trial due to the denunciation of Madame Alain, he was sentenced to death. His attitude at trial was most dignified; he was executed at Cologne on 20 October 1942.

He left 4 children, two of them minors.

I ask that his son, Mr. Jean MARCHAIS, be exempt from military service, as he is supporting 4 children.

I further ask the Government's attention to giving Mr. MARCHAIS all posthumous awards to which he is entitled.'

'Mr. Jean MARCHAIS worked with his father, André MARCHAIS, who was executed in Cologne. He took care of collecting intelligence and having it passed on by Monsieur Legeais.

After his father's arrest, he continued to be part of the F.F.I. (Free French) where he accomplished missions that were greatly appreciated by Captain GUILLAUMAT Commander of the Free French of Saint-Brieux.

He was not arrested.'

Madame Seidel's signed summaries for the Marchais family: husband, wife and son. From André's private archive.

This glimpse of André's agents started with Madame Seidel's silence and courageous dedication to the agents in her networks while under interrogation. Her sister, Théotiste Epron, leaves an inspiring statement as well.

André's Agents

Report of Miss EPRON

'Report requested by Madame Seidel to be submitted to Captain Peulevez

It was in September 1940, that, living in Prefailles, my sister Mrs. Seidel asked me to collect all the information I could find about the coast of Pornic, Prefailles and surroundings. I alerted her to the numbers of the German regiments that were there.

In February 1941, my sister asked me to help her wash and mend the clothing of Englishmen she was hiding at her home. Then in July 1941, she asked me to come live with her, because she had too many men hidden there and she didn't want to have any woman who was a stranger come into her apartment. So I took over the management of her residence, greeting the Englishmen, fixing their food, doing all the housekeeping chores. When the Gestapo came to arrest us, I got Lieutenant Reece and Pilot Appolliard out, but unfortunately they came back and were arrested.

When someone would come to the house to bring maps or information to my sister, I was the one who took them. I was deported to Germany and ended up at Ravensbrück.

I only regret one thing, that I didn't do more.'

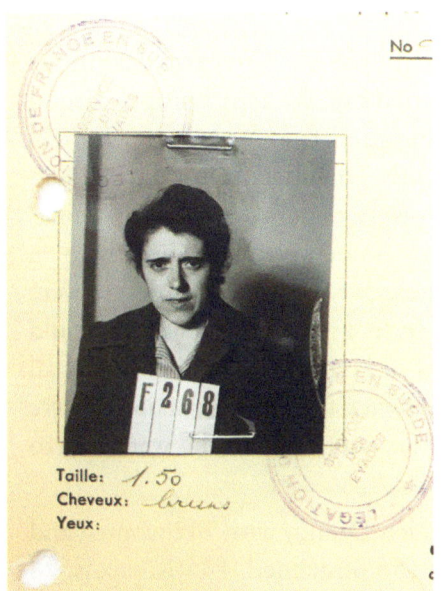

Théotiste Epron's photo ID after her rescue by the Red Cross and her statement that her sister Marie-Christianne Seidel asked for, to submit to André.

Records for the murder of Max and Regina in the Holocaust

Max and Regina were rounded up in July1942. 'Over two days in the summer of 1942, French police carried out Western Europe's largest wartime roundup of Jews, acting on orders from occupying German forces and their French allies. On July 16 and 17, a total of 12,884 Jews – men, women and children – were snatched from their homes in Paris and in neighbouring suburbs. Some were taken directly to an internment camp in Drancy, northeast of the capital. The rest were crammed into the Vélodrome d'Hiver, a stadium ... which would give its name to this sinister chapter in French history.'[330] Almost all those rounded up were sent to Auschwitz and the vast majority were murdered immediately, including Max and Regina, who were sent to Poland on Transport #11.

'Transport #11 on July 27, 1942, left Drancy with 742 women and 248 men, composed of 595 Poles, 156 undefined, 154 Russians, 28 German and no French,' as detailed by Klarsfeld, 2012. Of the 76,000 Jews deported from France through 1944 (42,000 deported to the extermination camps in 1942) only 2,500 survived.[331]

Regina Scheinmann was born 16/06/1888 in Jaroslav, Lwow, Poland, imprisoned 15/07/1942, died 27/07/1942 [sic] in Vernichtunglager Auschwitz (from the Memorial book of Düsseldorf).[332] Yad Vashem gives her names as Regina Thorn or Torn, Sheinman or Shinman, wife of Maksimilian, murdered in Lublinka, in a page of testimony given by her sister-in-law Nekhama Pomerantz in 1956.

See also Yad Vashem's central database from *Le Memorial de la deportation des juifs de France 1942-1944* by Serge Klarsfeld, Paris, 1978, and Germany's Bundesarchiv for Max Scheineman [sic] born 14/02/1890 Zycznick, Poland transport #11 from Drancy on 27/07/1942, died 10/8/1942 at Auschwitz (*Vernichtungslager* extermination camp) Birkenau.[333]

Records for the murder of Max and Regina in the Holocaust

Adela SARAGOUSSI 1918 · Allègre Saragoussi 1910 · Anna SARAGOUSSI 1914 · Bitty SARAGOUSSI 1909 · Gracia SARAGOUSSI 1897 · Isaac SARAGOUSSI 1883
Mathilde SARAGOUSSI 1922 · Samuel SARAGOUSSI 1919 · Moretka SARANGA 1916 · Moïse SARCGORODSKY 1875 · Vittorio SARDAS 1920 · Abraham SARFATI 1908
David SARFATI 1904 · Ludivica SARFATI 1921 · Norbert SARFATI 1921 · Rachel SARFATI 1916 · Roger SARFATI 1937 · Samuel SARFATI 1898 · Ernest SARMANN 1907
Estera SARNA 1890 · Georges SARNA 1927 · Ida SARNA 1929 · Mayer SARNA 1896 · Sarah SARNACKA 1902 · Elie SARTERSON 1897 · Theodore SARTSKI 1904 · Gimpel SAS 1904
Leonid SASLAWSKI 1897 · Chaja SASS 1888 · Jacob SASS 1902 · Markus SASS 1890 · Albert SASSON 1875 · Ernestine SASSON 1898 · Esther SASSON 1924 · Régine SASSON 1886
Samuel SASSON 1890 · Sarah SASSON 1911 · Joseph SASVARI 1896 · Nathalie SASVARI 1898 · Richard SASVARI 1894 · Victor SATTINGER 1899 · Michel SATZ 1910
Erna SAUER 1888 · Hortense SAUER 1885 · Johanna SAUER 1885 · Kathe SAUER 1899 · Liselotte SAUER 1903 · Settchem SAUER 1860 · Clara SAUERHAFT 1896
Dina SAUERHAFT 1921 · Getzel SAUERHAFT 1892 · Isaac SAUL 1896 · Joseph SAUL 1903 · Mazaltov SAUL 1879 · Menahem SAUL 1919 · Suzanne SAUL 1925 · Vidal SAUL 1878
Isaac SAÜL 1906 · Jacob SAULEMAN 1892 · Lucie SAULEMAN 1908 · Denise SAUPHAR 1920 · Jean SAUPHAR 1926 · Lybe Nusyn SAUTER 1894 · Isaac SAVARIEGO 1895
Azik SAVELEN 1922 · Albert SAWELSKI 1901 · Anatole SAX 1885 · Gustave SAX 1895 · Heinrich SAX 1903 · Kurt SAX 1904 · Olga SAX 1894 · Simon SAYAGH 1909
Idel SCAIANSKI 1901 · Zelman SCAIANSKI 1923 · Abraham SCAIANSKY 1911 · Issona SCAPA 1920 · Margot SCAPA 1924 · Gilbert SCERMANA 1886 · Clara SCHABLIN 1884
Frida SCHABLIN 1900 · Gerda SCHABLIN 1912 · Paul SCHABLIN 1884 · Pierre SCHABLIN 1913 · Isidore SCHABOLSKI 1905 · Marguerite SCHACHER 1898 · Max SCHACHER 1896
Amalia SCHACHET 1900 · Scheindla SCHACHNA 1868 · Abraham SCHACHNER 1896 · Bertha SCHACHTER 1906 · Erna SCHACHTER 1902 · Fanny SCHACHTER 1919
Herman SCHACHTER 1904 · Joseph SCHACHTER 1895 · Max SCHACHTER 1906 · Paul SCHACHTER 1901 · Dora SCHADOROFF 1890 · Georges SCHADOROFF 1887
Simon SCHADOROFF 1922 · Alfred SCHAECHTER 1900 · Haïm SCHAECHTER 1910 · Régine SCHAECHTER 1896 · Suzy SCHAECHTER 1928 · Isidore SCHAEFER 1886
Caroline SCHAETER 1890 · Sally SCHAFERMAN 1900 · Hersch SCHAFFEL 1910 · Anna SCHAFFER 1923 · Paul SCHAFFER 1924 · Sali SCHÄFFER 1901 · Walln SCHAFFIER 1923
Marcel SCHAFFRO 1922 · Moïse SCHAFIR 1893 · Samuel SCHAFIR 1935 · Sura SCHAFIR 1910 · Szefir SCHAFIR 1905 · Beila SCHAFRAN 1891 · Bernard SCHAINER 1924
Génia SCHAINER 1930 · Marie SCHAINER 1895 · Tobia SCHAINER 1898 · Maurice SCHALER 1927 · Rebecca SCHALER 1910 · Rachel SCHALIT 1892 · Rudolphe SCHALLER 1914
Mélanie SCHALMANN 1885 · Léonie SCHAMES 1924 · Marthe SCHAMES 1900 · Paul SCHAMES 1915 · Balcia SCHANDOR 1929 · Gitel SCHANDOR 1904 · Klara SCHANDOR 1927
Maurice SCHANDOR 1932 · Sophie SCHANGER 1892 · David SCHANZER 1901 · Max SCHANZER 1904 · Otto SCHANZER 1890 · Chana SCHAPIRA 1914 · Halfons SCHAPIRA 1911
Jacob SCHAPIRA 1908 · Aline SCHAPIRO 1918 · Anna SCHAPIRO 1898 · Gelta SCHAPIRO 1901 · Gisèle SCHAPIRO 1933 · Isaak SCHAPIRO 1889 · Leja SCHAPIRO 1910
Léon SCHAPIRO 1897 · Moses SCHAPIRO 1893 · Olga SCHAPIRO 1894 · Raphaël SCHAPIRO 1904 · Serge SCHAPIRO 1940 · Wladimir SCHAPIRO 1894 · Adolf SCHAPSE 1901
Anna SCHARC 1902 · Simon SCHARER 1902 · Bertha SCHARF 1922 · Chaja SCHARF 1895 · Charles SCHARF 1922 · Edgard SCHARF 1894 · Elisa SCHARF 1882
Esther SCHARF 1915 · Fajga SCHARF 1896 · Feya SCHARF 1896 · Joseph SCHARF 1892 · Joséphine SCHARF 1901 · Léon SCHARF 1929 · Maurice SCHARF 1906
Moses SCHARF 1909 · Osize SCHARF 1913 · Salomon SCHARF 1890 · Schaskiel SCHARF 1893 · Selma SCHARF 1892 · Sima SCHARF 1908 · Hélène SCHARFF 1890
Ilse SCHARFF 1920 · Israël SCHARFF 1898 · Julius SCHARFF 1879 · Ludwig SCHARFF 1878 · Sophie SCHARFF 1879 · Theodore SCHARFF 1876 · Alexandre SCHARFMAN 1894
Ita SCHARGEL 1890 · Bernard SCHARITON 1904 · Karolina SCHARL 1907 · Bruno SCHARLACH 1896 · Jacob SCHARLAT 1898 · Ignace SCHART 1891 · Hertch SCHARZSTEIN 1906
Samuel SCHASCHTER 1906 · Chaja SCHASGEZICHT 1901 · Myriam SCHASGEZICHT 1929 · Estelle SCHASZINSKI 1937 · Richard SCHATS 1883 · Berek SCHATZ 1898
Jacques SCHATZ 1902 · Loudmila SCHATZ 1896 · Nadine SCHATZ 1930 · Rosalia SCHATZ 1875 · Zilda SCHATZ 1896 · Elias SCHATZBERGER 1891 · Klava SCHATZKER 1892
Paul SCHATZKER 1889 · Benjamin SCHATZMAN 1877 · Conrad SCHAUER 1901 · Otto SCHAUER 1906 · Paula SCHAUER 1908 · Gustava SCHAUL 1906 · Albert SCHAVSINSKI 1899
Hans SCHAWAB 1901 · Frederic SCHAWARTZ 1922 · Wolf SCHAWARZ · Marcel SCHAWLOW 1925 · Regina SCHAYER 1905 · Genia SCHECHTER 1900
Marguerite SCHECHTER 1895 · Moses SCHECHTER 1888 · Bernard SCHECIMER 1895 · Augusta SCHEER 1903 · Wolf SCHEFER 1896 · Bernard SCHEIBOWITCH 1920
Simon SCHEIDE 1899 · Samuel SCHEIDER 1890 · Bella SCHEIDMANN 1928 · Herbert SCHEIGE 1908 · Hermann SCHEIMANN 1923 · Idel SCHEIMANN 1888
Hermann SCHEIN 1897 · Julius SCHEIN 1894 · Leo SCHEIN 1901 · Otto SCHEIN 1888 · Gitla SCHEINBACH 1909 · Salomon SCHEINBACH 1909 · Isaac SCHEINER 1889
Marcus SCHEINER 1873 · Moszek SCHEINER 1905 · Salomon SCHEINER 1939 · Sara SCHEINER 1896 · Bernard SCHEINFELD 1928 · Malka SCHEINFELD 1896
Rachel SCHEINFELD 1934 · Juda SCHEININE 1897 · Max SCHEINMANN 1890 · Regina SCHEINMANN 1898 · Joseph SCHEINOWITZ 1905 · Sara SCHEINOWITZ 1911
Michel SCHEKTER 1898 · Edwige SCHELESNIKOW 1897 · Gedalia SCHELESNIKOW 1896 · Jacques SCHELESNIKOW 1939 · Irène SCHELINGER 1898 · Jacob SCHELSOHN 1897
Adolf SCHELZER 1908 · Jean SCHEMAMA 1911 · Leopold SCHENFELD 1868 · Israël SCHENKEL 1886 · Jacob SCHENKEL 1890 · Markus SCHENKEL 1900 · Rosa SCHENKEL 1904
Sigi SCHENKEL 1931 · Dina SCHENKELT 1929 · Hélène SCHENKELT 1939 · Irena SCHENKER 1900 · Stephan SCHENKER 1932 · Nissim SCHENKERMANN 1896
Moszek SCHENKMAN 1901 · Fania SCHEPETOVSKI 1892 · Anna SCHEPS 1936 · Collette SCHEPS 1937 · Henriette SCHEPS 1903 · Léon SCHEPS 1900 · Heinrich SCHEPSER 1900
Abraham SCHER 1889 · Elie SCHER 1898 · Emile SCHER 1883 · Henri SCHER 1896 · Jacob SCHER 1898 · Jacques SCHER 1916 · Jules SCHER 1878 · Léon SCHER 1887
Martin SCHER 1899 · Sophie SCHER 1900 · Suzanne SCHER 1916 · Charlotte SCHERCKER 1928 · Abe SCHEREL 1905 · Alice SCHERER 1913 · Chaïm SCHERER 1900
Feiga SCHERER 1905 · Jacques SCHERER 1903 · Joseph SCHERER 1906 · Mathilde SCHERER 1894 · Moïse SCHERMAN 1902 · Schaïa SCHERMAN 1885
Scheindla SCHERMANN 1884 · Chaja SCHERMANN 1895 · Favella SCHERMANN 1893 · Herbert SCHERMANN 1914 · Léon SCHERMANN 1905 · Nathan SCHERMANN 1895
Victor SCHERMANN 1898 · Dora SCHERMANT 1938 · Gootzel SCHERMANT 1899 · Hélène SCHERMANT 1908 · Jeannine SCHERMANT 1932 · Annie SCHERMER 1898
Mozes SCHERMER 1895 · Louis SCHERR 1897 · David SCHERZ 1893 · Ida SCHERZ 1898 · Raymonde SCHERZ 1933 · Rose SCHERZ 1931 · Rudolphe SCHERZ 1912
Abraham SCHERZER 1890 · Armand SCHERZER 1923 · Esther SCHERZER 1926 · Hariski SCHERZER 1927 · Kalman SCHERZER 1918 · Nesia SCHERZER 1891
Simon SCHERZER 1930 · Ludwig SCHEUCHER 1926 · Ernest SCHEUER 1907 · Ruth SCHEUER 1910 · Samuel SCHEUER 1877 · Max SCHEURE 1895 · Recha SCHEURE 1891
Paul SCHGENAGER 1905 · Abram SCHIA 1892 · Adolphe SCHICHA 1888 · Selma SCHICHA 1903 · Hans SCHICK 1890 · Michel SCHICK 1917 · Leo SCHIDLOF 1908
Chie Benzion SCHIDLOVITCH 1912 · Moses SCHIDLOWSKY 1929 · Cécile SCHIEMENSON 1897 · Hans SCHIESINGER 1909 · Alla SCHIFF 1890 · Aron SCHIFF 1915
Edouard SCHIFF 1937 · Fanny SCHIFF 1887 · Hans SCHIFF 1898 · Hans SCHIFF 1900 · Hillel SCHIFF 1902 · Jacheta SCHIFF 1905 · Jacob SCHIFF 1909 · Kalman SCHIFF 1887

Section of the Wall of Names including Max and Regina Scheinmann at the Mémorial de la Shoah in Paris.
© Mémorial de la Shoah, Paris

Claire's Story

Prologue

Claire Dyment was born on New Year's Day of 1918 at the city of Międzyrzec Podlaski (מעזריטש *Mezri'tsh*), Lublin Voivodeship, Poland.[334] At the end of the 1930s approximately 12,000 inhabitants, or ¾ of its population, were Jewish. In 1939, during the Nazi-Soviet invasion of Poland, the city was overrun by the Wehrmacht. Fewer than 1% of the Jewish population of the city survived the Holocaust. The family history has it that Claire's father and her two younger sisters died at Warsaw in 1942/3, in 1941 her older brother Gedalliah in Auschwitz and her nephew Max in Sachsenhausen.

Family and first marriage

Claire was the 10th child and 5th daughter of Manisz Dyment b. 1876 and Rejzla Limoner b. 1880 both in Mezri'tsh. She was the last child born 'in Russia'. After 1918 the family moved to Leipzig and were there by 1920/23 where and when the last two children, two girls, were born. Her mother died in late November 1931. She left behind 10 of her 12 children (5 sons and 7 daughters). By 1935 members of the family emigrated to Israel (then the British Mandate of Palestine) and it is believed that at some time Claire also went there.

By sometime in 1938, Claire moved to Britain, probably by ship. On 26 June 1939 she married Francis Charles Jarrett (also born in 1918) of Poplar, London, who was then a lorry driver and motor fitter. In so doing, Claire acquired British National status. After the war began in September 1939 her husband was called up and joined the Royal Army Service Corps (RASC). In April 1946 Claire and Jarrett divorced. He married again and died in 1989.

Claire's War

Claire's WAAF Classifications & Ranks & Trades:

ACW2 – Aircraftwoman 2 – Clerk General Duties at enlistment

ACW1 – Aircraftwoman 1 – 'Acting' Sergeant – Clerk Signals by the end of 1943

LACW – Leading Aircraftwoman – 'Temporary' (war-time rank) Sergeant – Clerk Signals Linguist by the end of 1944

Claire Dyment Jarrett, Sergeant, wearing the RAF/WAAF eagle symbol on her uniform.

In December 1941 the British National Government introduced conscription for women. On 17 August 1942, Claire enlisted in the WAAF (Women's Auxiliary Air Force) – Service Number: 2130888.

She underwent her initial WAAF training – spit and polish, military discipline etc., and also testing for personal and technical skills – at RAF Bridgnorth from 28 August (No. 1 WAAF Depot, a first site for recruits – created on 6 Nov 1939) and then RAF Morecambe (No. 3 WAAF Depot). It is likely that she had already been marked for her final destination, probably from the time of her first interview. On entering the WAAF she made have undergone extra checks. Her service record carries a security note, in capitals, about not moving her without higher authority.

Claire's Postings.

On 9 October 1942, after 6 weeks, Claire arrived at RAF Kingsdown in Kent where she was placed on their staff roster[335]. Kingsdown was by then a major part of the RAF Y-Service signal intercept structure, collating intercepted German Air Force (GAF) – particularly fighter aircraft –

Radio Telephony (R/T) messages from a number of stations, called Home Defence Units (HDUs), on the south and east coasts of England.

> *Wireless operators, many of them civilians, but also service personnel – in particular WRNS (females-Navy), WAAF (females-Air Force) and ATS (females-Army) – tracked the enemy radio signals across the frequencies, carefully logging every letter or figure. The messages were then sent to Bletchley Park, then the HQ of the SIS/MI6 Government Code & Cypher School (GC&CS) to be deciphered, translated and fused together to produce as complete an intelligence picture as possible of what the enemy was doing.[336], The Y-Service Signals Intelligence (now known as COMINT) was an important integral part of Bletchley Park's operations to produce Signals Intelligence (now known as SIGINT). SIGINT was a vital part of the intelligence sent to the military services for day to day operations and to the relevant British Intelligence organisations, in particular the Combined Intelligence Section (CIS) in London which collated all the intelligence used for the planning of the D-Day Operation Overlord[337].*

After about a year at Kingsdown, on 10 August 1943, Claire was recorded as posted to 'Great Yarmouth' (Norfolk). This was actually a posting to RAF Gorleston – a Home Defense Unit/HDU on the North Sea Coast. At that location, she was one of the female operators involved in 'Operation Corona'. First discussed in concept in mid-1943 and described in official documents as a 'spoofing and jamming operation', Corona started from Kingsdown on the night of 22/23 October 1943 on a RAF bomber raid on the industrial centre of Kassel and caused immediate 'chaos in the enemy night defence organisation'. The operation persisted into 1945. Impersonating Luftwaffe operators, top level 'native' German linguists like Claire misdirected German fighter pilots in the midst of RAF bombing missions.[338,339]

In April 1944, after a short return to Kingsdown, she was posted briefly to RAF Coltishall (Norfolk, not far from Gorleston). It is thought that there she acted as an interpreter for the first arrival of the Polish Air Force, the 316 'City of Warsaw' squadron, newly operating with North American P51-B Mustangs.

On Sunday 4 June 1944 she is recorded as officially back at Kingsdown. This was the day before the original date for D-Day and Operation Overlord. It finally went ahead, successfully, on Tuesday 6 June.

The V1-flying bomb attacks on Britain started on 13 June 1944. On 20 July 1944 Kingsdown was accidentally hit by a stray V1 which caused some damage but no fatalities.

On 8 August 1944 Claire is recorded as having been posted to a station called RAF Canterbury. This planned move was designed to position VHF receivers closer to the continent as the battle moved further inland in France. This date was also the date of the start of the operations to finally break out of Normandy. The Falaise Pocket was closed on 17 August and Paris was liberated on 25 August.

It is still not clear to researchers where the 'Canterbury station' was but it is thought that this was *then* a cover name for the HDU site at RAF Hawkinge, near Folkestone, the original station of the operators who had moved to Kingsdown in the summer of 1945.

Claire (second from right, back row) at RAF Chigwell c. August/September 1945

Claire remained at 'Canterbury station' until 7 August 1945 when she had a short-term posting to RAF Chigwell in Essex prior to being officially released.[340] She was given a 'Category A' release – 'services no longer required and not liable for a recall' – on 14 September 1945, effective on 9 November 1 945.

She had indeed come some way from the time and place of her birth. She had given her country of refuge valuable service in a time of its very great need. For her war services Claire Dyment Jarrett was awarded the British War Medal.[341] Decades after her death on December 10, 1985 the Bletchley Park Veteran's Badge and the Government Communications Headquarters GCHQ Badge were created, to which she would have been entitled. Visitors may see a plaque for Claire Jarrett Scheinmann at Bletchley Park museum.

Her life would soon take a new and very happy turn with André till her death on December 10, 1985.[342] An amazing combined story of how two immigrants, from Germany to France and Poland to Britain, delivered most valuable service to British Secret Intelligence.

Dr T B Austin, MA, D.Phil (Oxon)

A preliminary version of this essay was presented in the March 2021 online newsletter of the Secret WW2 Learning Network and Operation Corona in the January 2021 issue. Thanks to Paul McCue for also featuring her on https://secret-ww2.net/resources/operation-corona-claires-story/

Claire and André post war.

Bibliography

Primary sources in public archives.

France:[343]

Archives Nationales (Pierrefitte-sur-Seine):
From 72AJ/3300-72AJ/3404 Dossiers individuels (Individual alphabetized listings of documentation) des membres de l'Amicale des réseaux Action (classement alphabétique).
72AJ/3383 PERROTIN-PIATTE includes 'Peulevey, André Maurice, né André Joseph Scheinmann'.
https://www.siv.archives-nationales.culture.gouv.fr/siv/rechercheconsultation/recherche/ir/rechercheGeneralisteResultat.=GENERALISTE&searchText=Andre+Maurice+Peulevey
Sûreté Nationale (French State police):
Intérieur. Fichier central de la Sûreté nationale : dossiers individuels de SA à SCH (fin XIXe siècle-1940). https://www.siv.archives-nationales.culture.gouv.fr/siv/IR/FRAN_IR_060295
19940474/118, Dossier 11459 Joseph Scheinmann 1933-1937 and 19940474/118, Dossier 11458 Joseph Scheinmann 1937-1939.
Service historique de la Défense (SHD), Vincennes:
GR 16 P 472792 (in SHDGR_16P_P.pdf) André Maurice Peulevey
GR 16 P 539178 Joseph Scheinmann DIR (Déporté et Interné Résistant) and FFC (Forces Françaises Combattantes.)
Service historique de la Défense (SHD), Caen:
AC 21 P 671359 Joseph Scheinmann Military records; Déporté Résistant attribution under # 109931123; documents dated 1954-1959.
Ordre de la Libération, Paris
Médaillés de la Résistance:
https://www.memoiredeshommes.sga.defense.gouv.fr/fr/arkotheque/client/mdh/medailles_resistance/detail_fiche.php?ref=3354093&debut=peulevey and

https://www.ordredelaliberation.fr/fr/
medailles?fulltext=Andre+Peulevey&items_per_page=10&sort_
bef_combine=nom_ASC#resultats-medailles

[This online record was requested to be updated to Scheinmann.]

Mémorial de la Shoah: Collection André Joseph Scheinman.

Fondation pour la Mémoire de la Déportation List of the NN convoy of 8/9 July, 1943 to KLNa: http://www.bddm.org/liv/details.php?id=I.114.

NB: Other interesting documentation, still unexplored, might be found in the département records and those of the prefectures of police.

Great Britain: (National Archives at Kew)

Documents are quoted in this book with acknowledgement that these archival references are Crown copyright, are being re-used under the terms of the Open Government Licence and are held at The National Archives, Kew, Richmond, TW9 4DU.

KV-4-344 LRC-RVPS 'Typical Case of an Alien Interrogated' —Jean Poumeau de la Forrest, who tried to represent himself as the Brits' best choice for a successor to the Le Tacs for organizing students and creating propaganda in Rennes. Includes much about André, Turban, Yves and Joël. https://discovery.nationalarchives.gov.uk/details/r/C11286236

KV6/12 'France: folders each dealing with a particular SOE operation whose security was in doubt, entitled SEALING WAX/OVERCLOUD ... relating to attempted infiltration By Van Ackere, also contains much information about the Le Tacs and company. https://discovery.nationalarchives.gov.uk/details/r/C11135805

HS6/602 SOE France-Liaison with Free French. Shows that in October 1941, De Gaulle was ready to assume closer relations and assert greater responsibility in planning internal resistance and the British were feeling the pressure and opportunity and a willingness to participate jointly in those plans. Includes briefing for letter from Hugh Dalton to De Gaulle. Includes the very interesting report from 'French Agent' possibly Yves Le Tac, H-1, who is listed as a member of the Intelligence Service of De Gaulle's general staff.

HS 6/416 Overcloud mission 1941-1942 including documents relating to the return of André to France.

Germany:

ITS Digital Archive, Arolsen Archives.

For Peulevey:

Personal file of PEULEVEY, ANDRE, born on 7-Nov-1915, born in GUCOURT, PAS-DE-CALAIS. https://collections.arolsen-archives.org/en/archive/1-1-29-2_01012902-030-460

Registry office card André Peulevey, Dachau, 1.1.6.7/ 10725079/ ITS Digital Archive, Arolsen Archives.
https://collections.arolsen-archives.org/en/document/128670644
https://collections.arolsen-archives.org/en/search/person/3215790?s=André%20Peulevey&t=2431394&p=0

List of names of the prisoner transport of 9 July 1943 from Fresnes/France to Natzweiler concentration camp including Peulevey, Le Tacs, others in their networks:
https://collections.arolsen-archives.org/en/document/3128969
from p. 11 of: https://collections.arolsen-archives.org/en/archive/1-1-29-1_8123400-8124400

United States:

US Holocaust Memorial Museum/USC Shoah Foundation Testimony of André Scheinmann https://collections.ushmm.org/search/catalog/vha24954; André Scheinmann papers https://collections.ushmm.org/search/catalog/irn74549; Mel and Cynthia Yoken interview on film, other TV interviews, author talk at Yom HaShoah, 2001: https://collections.ushmm.org/search/catalog/irn85372

USC Shoah Foundation – The Institute for Visual History and Education, André Scheinmann interview by Helen Sendyk, #24954 Boca Raton, FL, 1/21/1997. https://sfi.usc.edu/

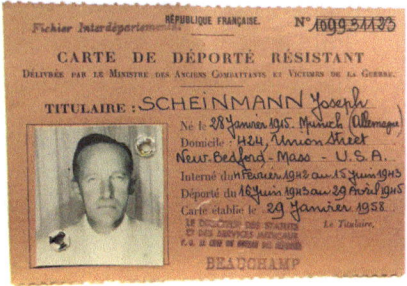 

Carte de Déporté Résistant applied for and received in 1958.

Publications referencing André by name or circumstance:

Amicale Action. *Livre d'Or de L'Amicale Action*. Paris: O.R.I., 1953. Full name of the association: 'Association Amicale d'Entr'aide des Anciens Officiers Chargés de Missions-Action et de leurs Collaborateurs recrutés en France.' Peulevey is mentioned in the Liste Générale Alphabétique and in the Liste par Départements, Seine-et-Oise: André Peulevey (mispelled Peuveley), 102, Boulevard des États-Unis, Le Vésinet.

Amicale des Anciens de Dachau [Fraternal Organization of the Survivors of Dachau, among whom André's comrades from Natzweiler: Leon Boutbien, Pierre Hentic, Roger Leroy, Pierre Rolinet...] *Allach, Kommando de Dachau*, Editions France-Empire 1986

Arte F: http://lescombattantsdelombre.arte.tv/#/marie-jose-chombart-de-lauwe/entre-les-lignes/ Marie-José Chombart de Lauwe gives her testimony about the network Georges-France, saying, 'I went to Rennes. And at Rennes, I was connected to the Georges-France network [described on screen as '*Réseau Georges-France 31; Réseau de renseignment et d'aide à l'évasion de prisonniers britanniques qui a oeuvré en Bretagne entre 1941 et 1942*' [Network for intelligence gathering and escape assistance for British prisoners, operating in Brittany between 1941 and 1942] ... Me, in Rennes, I was most often in contact with André who was the liaison, at the Café de l'Europe and the Café de la Paix, and I brought him the documents etc. And in an emergency, I would go to Louis Le Deuff, the radio operator, at the Place St. Sauveur in Rennes...'

_____, *Les Combattants de l'ombre: des européens contre le nazisme* (Fighters in shadow: Europeans against Nazism) shown 7/23/2013. http://www.arte.tv/fr/3885730.html Put into book form as *Les combattants de l'ombre* by Bernard George et Ambre Rouvière. ARTE Editions/Albin Michel, 2011

Campo. Ramón Javier. *Canfranc Nid d'Espions*, Biarritz, Atlantica, 2011. Illustrations pp. 194-195. (Originally published as *La estacia espía*, Barcelona: Peninsula, 2006.)

Chatenay, Victor. *Mon Journal du Temps de Malheur*, Courier de l'Ouest, 1967. Arrested February 11, 1942 in Brittany, his interrogators questioned him repeatedly about the Le Tacs and Le Neveu. Later worked in London SIS offices of Biffy Dunderdale and Thomas Greene.

Chombart de Lauwe, Marie José. *Resister toujours: Mémoires.* Paris: Flammarion, 2015. Much on the Brittany networks including Peulevey, 'mon contact privilégié' on pp. 71, 73, 219-221.

_____, *Toute une vie de résistance.* ["A whole life of resistance"] Paris: Graphein, 1998. The preface recounts that her mother's intelligence gathering network, "La Bande à Sidonie" was absorbed into the network "31 Georges France" and what she did for it and how it ended with their arrests, but mentions no names. Her experience of the prisons of Angers, la Santé, Fresnes, then Ravensbrück and Mauthausen, reflections on the official French memory of the Resistance, its non-Jewish and Jewish heroes, and of Nazism's Jewish and non-Jewish victims, and the need to recognize them in their particularity and together.

Coudert, Marie-Louise. *Elles la résistance.* ["They, the women of the resistance"] Paris: Messidor/Temps Actuels, 1983. Foreward by Marie-Claude Vaillant-Couturier. Portraits of two dozen women, including Marie-Jo Chombart de Lauwe, whose narrative includes her work for André.

Green, Sheryl. https://www.courageindisguise.co.uk/blog/introducing-joseph-scheinmann-aka-agent-andré 2024

Huguen, Roger. *Par les nuits les plus longues: Réseaux d'évasion d'aviateurs en Bretagne 1940-1944* [During the longest nights: escape networks for airmen in Brittany 1940-1944] Rennes: Ouest-France, 1986. References to André as Le Neveu and Peulevé and his network Réseau Georges France 31, pp. 38-39 and index.

Leroy, Roger, Roger Linet, and Max Nevers. *1943-1945: La résistance en enfer.* [1943-1945: Resistance in Hell] Paris: Messidor, 1992. Section about André entitled: 'One of Ours is an Interpreter!' p. 88; other portraits and passages of André Peulevey on pp. 154, 159 and 204-205.

Le Souvenir Français. *1942: Hommage aux combattants engagés au service de la France.* Numéro special joint à l'envoi de la revue 528, octobre, 2022. André Scheinmann biographical sketch, p. 58.

Le Tac, Monique. *Yvonne Le Tac: Une Femme dans le Siècle (de Montmartre à Ravensbrück).* Paris: Editions Tirésias, 2000, preface by Geneviève de Gaulle Anthonioz, pp. 123-130.

Lovinger, Robert 'One Man, One Cause' 6/27/1999 http://www.southcoasttoday.com/apps/pbcs.dll/article?AID=/19990627/LIFE/306279885&emailAFriend=1#sthash.c0b1GEHs.dpuf and 'He Saw the Best and the Worst of Mankind' 5/15/2001. New Bedford, MA: *Standard-Times*. Feature article and obituary. http://www.southcoasttoday.com/apps/pbcs.dll/article?AID=/20010515/NEWS/305159997&emailAFriend=1

Maradène, Georges. *Réponses à un questionnaire: La vie dans les camps de Natzweiler- Struthof et Dachau*. [Answers to a survey: Life in the camps of Natzweiler-Struthof and Dachau] Dions, 1995. Unpublished. 162 pages, unnumbered. About André on p. 23: 'To be noted, too, that the prisoner serving as our interpreter, who arrived with us on July 9 [1943] was a German Jew living in France, member of the Intelligent [sic] Service. The Germans would never know. He was liberated I think from Dachau and lives in the US.'

Picquet-Wicks, Eric. *Four in the Shadows: A True Story of Espionage in Occupied France*. London, The Adventurers Club, 1957, 1959. Picquet-Wicks was in on the planning of the Overcloud trip to and from England, and mentions the SOE/BCRA agents who were transported with it, but not André except as 'the other man' or 'the third man', pp. 157-159.

Ragot, Docteur André. *NN: nuit et brouillard*. Imprimerie Coopérative Chevillon, 1958 Vol.1: Natzweiler, Vol 2: Dachau.

Reynaud, Franck. Joël Le Tac, *Le Breton de Montmartre*. Rennes: Editions Ouest-France, 1994, pp. 109-111, 118,124-125.

Richards, Sir Brooks. *Secret Flottillas, Vol 1: Clandestine Sea Operations to Brittany 1940-1944*. Barnsley: Pen & Sword, 2011, pp. 115-117, 313-314.

Simon, Jean, ed. *Le Camp de Concentration du Struthof/Konzentrationslager Natzweiler: Témoignages*. Schirmeck: Essor, 1998. ["The Concentration Camp of the Struthof: Konzentrationslager Natzweiler: Testimonies"] Schirmeck: Essor, 1998. 'An American-French Interpreter at Natzweiler' interview with André Joseph Scheinmann, p. 78.

Spicer, Tim. *A Dangerous Enterprise: Secret War at Sea*. Barbreck, 2021. p. 101.

_____, *A Suspicion of Spies The biography of Wilfred 'Biffy' Dunderdale*. Barbreck, 2024

Tillet, Pierre. *Tentative of History of In/Exfiltrations into/from France during WWII from 1940 to 1945 (Parachutes, Plane & Sea Landings)* Mentions André and his Overcloud cohort. Spreadheet continually updated; see 6/1/1942 and 1/02/1942. http://www.plan-sussex-1944.net/anglais/pdf/infiltrations_into_france.pdf

Tremain, David. *Double Agent Victoire: Mathilde Carré and the Interallié Network*. Stroud: The History Press, 2018, p. 149.

USC Shoah Foundation – The Institute for Visual History and Education. Interview #24954 of André Scheinmann, 1/27/1997 at Boca Raton, Fl by Helen Sendyk, videography by Donna Schatz. Four video tapes of testimony and photographs. https://sfi.usc.edu/ to ask for access to: http://vhaonline.usc.edu/viewingPage.aspx?testimonyID=27014&returnIndex=0

US Holocaust Museum. *Registry of Jewish Holocaust Survivors*. Washington, DC. Lists survivors by camps, including 32 from Natzweiler when searching by 'Natzweiler-Struthof'. André's record: http://www.ushmm.org/online/hsv/person_view.php?PersonId=4987387

Wiki-Rennes. 'André Peulevey, Allemand juif, cheminot rennais, interprète auprès des Allemands, espion pour les Britanniques'. https://www.wiki-rennes.fr/André_Peulevey_,_Allemand_juif,_cheminot_rennais,_interprète_auprès_des_Allemands,_espion_pour_les_Britanniques

Yoken, Professor Mel and Cynthia. Video interview in French and English of André Joseph Scheinmann at New Bedford, MA, 13 November 1992. Transcribed and translated into English, unpublished. https://collections.ushmm.org/search/catalog/irn85372

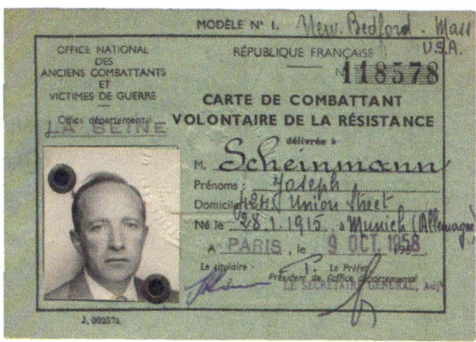

Carte de Combattant Volontaire de la Résistance, 1958 gives André's German birth, participation in the French Resistance, US residency – and the toll reflected in his eyes.

Other historical resources:

Books starred are by/about people André knew as a secret agent, or by survivors of the same camps/subcamps.

Albertelli, Sébastien. 'Les Services Secrets de la France Libre: Le Bureau Central de Renseignement et d'Action (BCRA), 1940-1944. Presses Universitaires de France. In *Guerres mondiales et conflits contemporains* 2011/2 (n° 242), pp. 7-26.

*Alizon, Simone. *L'exercice de vivre*, Stock, 1996. She was a member of Johnny network, aggregated to Georges-France/Groupe 31 by André.

Allen, Michael Thad. *The Business of Genocide: The SS, Slave Labor, and the Concentration Camps.* University of North Carolina Press, 2002

*Amicale des Anciens de Dachau. *Allach, Kommando de Dachau*. Editions France-Empire 1986

Aroneanu, Eugène. *Inside the Concentration Camps; Eywitness Accounts of Life in Hitler's Death Camps*. Westport: Preger, 1996

Ashcroft, Sir Michael. *Special Forces Heroes; Special Ops Heroes; Victoria Cross Heroes; George Cross Heroes.* Hachette Book Group.

Auda, Grégory, ed. *Dans les Archives Secrètes de la Seconde Guerre Mondiale, Les Chemins de la Mémoire Numéro Special Décembre 2015.* 'Mémoires et Patrimoine', www.defence.gouv. fr

Austin, Dr. T.B. 'SIS/MI6 and The Early Resistance in France: Georges France/Groupe 31 and Madame Louis'. Unpublished, 2022

*Bakels, Floris B. *Nacht und Nebel: Night and Fog* Cambridge: The Lutterworth Press, 1993. Prisoner no. 4381 at Natzweiler Concentration Camp, Prisoner 99718 Dachau Concentration camp.

Bailey, Roderick. *Forgotten Voices of the Secret War: An Inside History of Special Operations during the Second World War.* Ebury, 2008

Barcellini, Serge, 'Le gazage de 87 Juifs au camp de Natzweiler-Struthof' in *La Shoah: temoignages, savoirs, oeuvres*, edited by Annette Wieviorka and Claude Mouchard.

Belot, Robert. *La Résistance sans de Gaulle.* Fayard, 2006

Bemelmans, Ludwig. *The Blue Danube.* Illustrated by the author. NY: The Viking Press, 1945

Béné, Charles. *Du Struthof à la France Libre*. Raon-L'Etape: Fetzer, 1968.

Blanc, Julien. *Au commencement de la Résistance: Du côté du musée de l'Homme 1940-1941*. Éditions du Seuil, 2010

Bogarde, Dirk. *For the Time Being: Collected Journalism.* Viking, 1998

Bougeard, Christian. *Histoire de la résistance en Bretagne.* Editions Jean-Paul Gisserot, 1992/2002

Brandes, Sabine "Der Exodus der jüdischen Ärzte aus Düsseldorf re Dr. Sindler of the Maccabi Sports Club. https://www.aekno.de/aerzte/rheinisches-aerzteblatt/ausgabe/artikel/1998/04-1998/der-exodus-der-juedischen-aerzte-aus-duesseldorf Accessed 1/4/2023

Calet, Henri. *Les murs de Fresnes.* Paris: Editions de Quatre Vents, 1945.

Casalis, André H. *Le Réseau Johnny.* Lulu. https://www.lulu.com/fr/shop/andr%C3%A9-casalis/le-reseau-johnny/paperback/product-19qznvzv.html Accessed 1/10/2023

Cassou, Jean. *La Mémoire courte.* Mille et une nuits/Arthème Fayard, 2001

Caveney, Mike, Jim Steinmeyer and Noel Daniel. *Magic 1400's-1950s.* Taschen, 2013

Cobain, Ian 'Foreign Office hoarding 1m historic files in secret archive.' https://www.theguardian.com/politics/2013/oct/18/foreign-office-historic-files-secret-archive Accessed 1/20/2023

Cobb, Matthew. *The Resistance: The French Fight against the Nazis.* London: Simon & Schuster, 2009

Cole, Jonathan. 'Theatre of war: the drama of the Special Operations Executive' https://blog.nationalarchives.gov.uk/theatre-war-drama-special-operations-executive/ Accessed 1/20/2023

Cooke, Philip and Ben H. Shepherd: *European Resistance in the Second World War.* Barnsley: Pen & Sword, 2013

*Cowburn, Benjamin. *No Cloak, No Dagger: Allied Spycraft in Occupied France.* Barnsley: Pen& Sword, 2009

Cunningham, Cyril. *Beaulieu: The Finishing School for Secret Agents.* Barnsley, Pen & Sword, 1998

Davies, Philip H.J. *MI6 and the Machinery of Spying: Structure and Process in Secret Intelligence.* London: Frank Cass, 2004

De La Marck, D. D. Y. (2003). De Gaulle, Colonel Passy and British Intelligence, 1940–42. *Intelligence and National Security, 18*(1), 21–40. https://doi.org/10.1080/02684520308559245

De La Martinière, Joseph. *Les N.N.: Le décret et la Procédure Nacht Und Nebel.* Paris: FNDIRP, 1989

Dean, Martin. *Robbing the Jews: The Confiscation of Jewish Property in the Holocaust, 1933-1945*. Cambridge University Press, 2008

Des Pres, Terrence. *The Survivor: An Anatomy of Life in the Death Camps*. Oxford University Press, 1976.

_____, 'The secondary witness: an interview with Terrence Des Pres'. https://fortunoff.aviaryplatform.com/collections/24/collection_resources/9811/file/45008

*Douhéret, Léa. *Témoignage*. Cavaillon: Mistral 1993.

Duras, Marguerite. *The War: A Memoir*. NY: Pantheon, 1986.

Eisen, George. 'Jewish History and the Ideology of Modern Sport'. *Journal of Sport History, Vol. 25, No 3*, pp. 482-530.

*Fedération Nationale des Déportés et Internés Résistants et Patriotes. *Hommage à Charles Joineau*. 2000

Feig, Konnilyn. *Hitler's Death Camps*. Holmes & Meier, 1981

Finnemore, Sheila Ann. *Hidden from view: foreigners in the French Resistance 1940-1944*. https://etheses.bham.ac.uk?id/eprint/4824

*FNDIR, UNADIF, Bernard Filiaire. *Jusqu'au bout de la Résistance*. Stock, 1997

Fogelman, Eva. *Conscience and Courage: Rescuers of Jews during the Holocaust*. NY: Anchor, 1994

Fontaine, André and Gérard Molina, 'LAVERDET Raymond, alias Red, Le Gall, Ruis' biographical essay at https://maitron.fr/spip.php?article233747 Accessed 3/14/2023

Foot, M.R.D. and J.M. Langley. *MI9: Escape and Evasion 1939-1945*. The Bodley Head, 1979; Biteback, 2011

Foot, M.R.D. *Resistance: European Resistance to Nazism 1940-1945*. First published by Eyre Methuen 1976. McGraw-Hill, 1977 and Granada Publishing, 1979 have identical pagination for quotes.

_____, *SOE in France: an account of the work of the British Special Operations Executive in France, 1940–1944*. London: Her Majesty's Stationery Office, 1966

Frank, Jacob. *Himmler's Jewish Tailor: The Story of Holocaust Survivor Jacob Frank*. Syracuse University Press, 2000

Freeman, Paul. 'Chevalier Ernest Thorn "King of Illusionists"' Presented at the 7th European Magic History Conference, Turin, Italy, August 2017. Online as Final-version-Chevalier-Thorn.pdf courtesy of davenportcollection.co.uk

Vintage Chevalier Ernest Thorn documents courtesy of John Davenport, https://www.davenportcollection.co.uk/

Galitzine, Yurka N. Report, "Report on Atrocities Committed by the Germans Against the Civilian Population of Belgium, February 1945, by Hq. 21 Army Group" (78 pages) [C.D. Jackson Papers, Box 2, Atrocities – Paris (4); NAID #12005700]. The Dwight D. Eisenhower Presidential Library and Museum https://www.eisenhowerlibrary.gov/sites/default/files/research/online-documents/holocaust/report-of-atrocities.pdf, pp. 15-21 report by former prisoners about punishments, including p. 18 on the French first transport summer 1943 and treatment of NN prisoners.

Gilet, (Patricia), éd., *Le Livre blanc du BCRA*, édition électronique, Archives nationales, 2015. http://www.siv.archives-nationales.culture.gouv.fr/siv/IR/FRAN_IR_053686

Girard, André. *Bataille Secrète en France. With 167 satirical, emotional ink drawings by the author.* NY: Brentano's, 1944

Guttman, Israel. *The Heroism of the Jewish People in the Second World War.* Tel Aviv: The International Quiz on the Heroism of the Jewish People, 1985

Gwennhadhu (Erwan Rivi) *De Viris Illustribus* blog about Vichy resistors. https://devirisillustribusblog.wordpress.com/2023/01/10/

le-mysterieux-colonel-germain-ii-les-vychisto-resistants/#_ftn6   Accessed 1/10/2023

Harismendy, Patrick and Erwan Le Gall. *Pour une histoire de la France Libre*, Presses Universitaires de Rennes, 2012 – in particular the chapter: 'Elements d'une approche de l'histoire de la France Libre' by Christian Bougeard, subchapter 'L'apport des Bretons à la France libre: un bilan partiel'.

Hastings, Sir Max. Essay on the BBC's *History Extra* magazine: 'WW2 espionage: The spies who surprised me' published in 2015. https://www.historyextra.com/period/second-world-war/ww2-espionage-the-spies-who-surprised-me   Accessed 1/24/2023

_____, *The Secret War; Spies, Codes and Guerillas 1939-1945*. William Collins, 2016

Heiden, Konrad. *Der Fuehrer: Hitler's Rise to Power*. Boston: Houghton Mifflin Company, 1944

*Heilbronn, Max. *Galeries Lafayette, Buchenwald, Galeries Lafayette*. Paris: Economica, 1989

*Hentic, Pierre. *Agent de l'Ombre: Mémoires 1941-1945*. Éditions Maho, 2009; éditions de la Martinière, 2012

Hodgson, Lynn Philip. *Inside-Camp X: Camp X, the top secret World War II 'Secret Agent Training School' strategically placed in Canada on the Shores of Lake Ontario*. Blake Books Distribution, 2000

_____, http://www.camp-x.com

Hug, Chrystel. 'Alix Marrier d'Unienville' https://www.alliancefrancaise.london/Alix-Marrier-dUnienville.php   Accessed 1/19/2023

*Israël, Gérard. *Heureux comme Dieu en France* Robert Laffont, 1975

Jeffery, Keith. *The Secret History of MI6 1909-1949*. (First published in Great Britain as *MI6; The History of the Secret Intelligence Service, 1909-1949*.) Penguin, 2010, 2011

Karski, Jan. *Story of a Secret State*. Boston: Houghton Mifflin Company, 1944

Kedward, H.R. 'The Resistance in France' © H.R. Kedward, 2005 http://www.port.ac.uk/special/france1815to2003/chapter8/interviews/filetodownload,31504,en.pdf

Kemp, Anthony. *The Secret Hunters*. London, Michael O'Mara Books, 1986

Klarsfeld, Beate and Serge Klarsfeld. *Hunting the Truth: Memoirs of Beate and Serge Klarsfeld*. NY: Farrar, Straus and Giroux, 2018

Klarsfeld, Serge. *Liste par addresses des Juifs Arrêtés à Paris et Déportés – Tome 1*. Paris: FFDJF (Fils et Filles des Déportés Juifs de France) and Beate Klarsfeld Foundation, 2012

_____, *Le Memorial de la deportation des juifs de France 1942-1944* Paris, 1978
Online at https://klarsfeld-ffdjf.org/publications/livres/2012-Le-Memorial-67-pages/

Klemperer, Victor. *I Will Bear Witness: A Diary of the Nazi Years (Vol 1: 1933-1941; Vol. 2 1942-1945)*. First published by Random House, 1999 and republished since.

Knapp, Bill. *A Thorn in the Side: The Story of Johnny Hopper*. Lafayette, IN: Carbon-Based Books, 2007

Knout, David. *Résistance Juive en France*. Paris: Centre de Documentation Juive Contemporaine, 1947

*Lacaze, André. *Le Tunnel*. Julliard, 1978

Lacroix-Riz, Annie. *La non-épuration en France: de 1943 aux années 1950*. Armand-Colin, 2019

*Le Belzic, Henriette. *Henriette Le Belzic, résistante déportée (de novembre 1941 à avril 1945): Mémoires d'une Bretonne dans l'enfer concentrationnaire nazi*. Coop Breizh, 2018

*Le Corre, Guy. *Un cheminot rennais dans la Renaissance 1941-1944*. Paris, Editions Tiresias – A.E.R.I. 2003

Leff, Lisa Moses. *The Archive Thief: The Man Who Salvaged French Jewish History in the Wake of the Holocaust*. Oxford University Press, 2015

Lengyel, Olga. *Five Chimneys: A Woman Survivor's True Story of Auschwitz*. Academy Chicago Publishers, 1995

Levi, Primo. *The Reawakening*. First published in English by The Bodley Head, 1965

_____, *The Periodic Table*. Schocken Books, 1984

_____, *Moments of Reprieve*. Simon & Schuster/Summit Books, 1986

Lewis, Damien. *The Nazi-Hunters: The Ultra-Secret SAS unit and the quest for Hitler's war criminals*. Quercus, 2016

*Lewis, Mark and Jacob Frank. *Himmler's Jewish Tailor: The Story of Holocaust Survivor Jacob Frank*. Syracuse University Press, 2000

*Lie, Arne Brun. *Night and Fog*. W.W. Norton, 1990

L'Ordre de la Libération. *La Médaille de la Résistance Française.* 2023 https://www.calameo.com/read/0059649420dfce38c495c

Lormier, Dominique. *Les 100 000 collabos: le fichier interdit de la collaboration française.* Centre France Livres, 2018

Mackenzie, William. *The Secret History of S.O.E.: Special Operations Executive 1940-1945* London; St. Ermin's 2002

Macintyre, Ben. *The Spy and the Traitor: The Greatest Espionage Story of the Cold War.* London: Viking/Penguin/Random House, 2008

*Maisel, Phillip. *The Keeper of Miracles.* Pan Macmillan, 2021

Markstein, George. *The Cooler.* NY: Collier/Macmillan 1989. A work of fiction.

Mawsdley, Evan. 'Fifth Column, Fourth Service, Third Task, Second Conflict?' chapter in Cooke & Shepherd.

McLaughlin, Jeff. *Graphic Novels as Philosophy.* University Press of Mississippi, 2017. Also available at https://www.academia.edu/36476152/ See Shores.

McLoughlin, Jane. 'What Makes a European?' from the Observer, 1971, accessed BookBlast® Archive January 18 2023. https://bookblast.com/blog/book-blast-archive-what-makes-a-european-jane-mcloughlin-the-observer-1971/#more-1247

Miannay, Patrice. *Dictionnaire des Agents Doubles dans la Résistance.* Paris: Le Cherche-Midi, 2005

Michel, Henri. *Bibliographie critique de la Résistance.* Service d'Edition et de Ventes des Publications de l'Education Nationale. Brochure #6RB Institut Pédagogique National, 1964

Navelot, Philippe. *Numéro Spécial-décembre 2015-Dans les archives secrètes de la seconde guerre mondiale.* Les Chemins de la mémoire/Ministère de la Défense, Secrétariat général pour l'administration.

Neave, Airey. *The Escape Room: The fantastic story of the underground escape lines in Nazi-occupied Europe, and of Room 900, London, the secret office from which they were run.* Garden City, NY: Doubleday & Co., 1970

Noguères, Henri. *Histoire de la Résistance en France de 1940 à 1945: I, La Première Année Juin 1940-Juin 1941 & II, L'armée de l'ombre Juillet 1941-Octobre 1942.* Paris: Robert Laffont, 1969

O'Connor, Bernard. *Internment, Escape and Repatriation*, Vol. 1: 1939-1942 and Vol. 2: 1943-1946. Lulu, 2022. https://www.lulu.com/spotlight/coprolite/ and http://www.bernardoconnor.org.uk

_____, *Operations VIVACIOUS and BRANSTON: Anti-Nazi German Jew Robert Baker-Byrne's subversion and sabotage missions in Berlin and Lubeck before the end of the Second World War.* http://www.lulu.com 2021

Office of Chief of Counsel for the Prosecution of Axis Criminality. Nazi Conspiracy and Aggression. Washington, DC: U.S. G.P.O., 1946. Online at https://lccn.loc.gov/2011525363 For 'Night and Fog Decree, 7 December 1941, on the Punishment of Crimes against the Occupying Power in the Occupied Territories: Death or Secret Deportation to Germany...' NT_Vol-XXXVII Document 090-L, pp. 570-577. (Nuremberg trials)

*Ottosen, Kristian. *Nuit et Brouillard*, Brussels: Le Cri, 1994, originally *Natt og Tåke, Historien om Natzweiler-fangene*, Oslo, Aschehoug, 1989

Quinn, William W. Colonel, G.S.C. A C of S, G-2, 7th U.S. Army. (Foreword) *Dachau* (1945) download at https://www.eisenhowerlibrary.gov/sites/default/files/research/online-documents/holocaust/report-dachau.pdf Accessed 7/20/2023

Paillole, Paul. 'De l'Armistice à la Victoire, Large historique de ce que fut notre combat', *Bulletin de l'Amicale des Anciens des Services Spéciaux et de la Défense Nationale*, n°1, 1954

*Passy, Colonel. *Souvenirs: 2ième Bureau Londres*. Monte-Carlo: Raoul Solar, 1947

_____, *10 Duke Street Londres (Le B.C.R.A.).*

_____ Collected as *Colonel Passy: Mémoires du Chef des Services Secrets de la France Libre*. Editions Odile-Jacob, 2000

Perraud-Charmantier, A. *La Guerre en Bretagne: Récits et Portraits* Vol. I. Nantes: Aux Portes du Large, 1947

Perrin, Nigel. *Spirit of Resistance: The Life of SOE Agent Harry Peulevé DSO MC*. Barnsley: Pen & Sword, 2008

Perry, Michael Wiley. *Dachau Liberated: The Official Report by U.S. Seventh Army Released Within Days of the Camp's Liberation by Elements of the 42nd and 45th Divisions*. Seattle: Inkling Books, 2000

Pierre-Bloch, Jean. *Le temps d'y penser encore*. Paris: Simoën, 1977

_____, *Jusqu'au dernier jour*. Paris: Albin Michel, 1983

*Piguet, Mgr. Gabriel. *Prison et déportation: témoignage d'un évêque déporté*. Dijon: L'Echelle de Jacob, 2009

Pisar, Samuel. *Of Blood and Hope*. NY: Macmillan Publishing Co., 1979

Pitchfork, Graham. *Shot Down and on the Run: True Stories of RAF and Commonwealth Aircrews of WWII.* Bloomsbury, 2017

*Poitevin, Arthur. 'Le Journal de déportation d'Arthur Poitevin.' In *Bayeux et le Bessin 1940-1944.* Bayeux: Renaissance du Bessin, 1996

Pollack, Guillaume. *L'Armée du silence: Histoire des reseaux de Resistance en France 1940-1945.* Paris: Editions Tallandier/Ministère de Armées, 2022

_____, 'Dans l'ombre de la France occupée'. https://www.lamontagne.fr/vichy-03200/loisirs/dans-lombre-de-la-france-occupee_14285482/ Accessed 4/4/2023

Półtawska, W. 'Paroxysmal hypermnesia states observed in former prisoners after 30 years.' *Medical Review – Auschwitz.* August 11, 2017. Originally published as "Stany hipermnezji napadowej u byłych więźniów obserwowane po 30 latach." *Przegląd Lekarski – Oświęcim.* 1978: 20–24. https://www.mp.pl/auschwitz/journal/english/170040,paroxysmal-hypermnesia-states-observed-in-former-prisoners-after-30-years

Pressac, Jean-Claude. *The Struthof Album,* edited by Serge Klarsfeld. NY: the Beate Klarsfeld Foundation, 1985. Now online at https://klarsfeld-ffdjf.org/produit/the-struttof-album-version-anglaise-originale/ [Struthof misspelled on the website listing   Accessed 1/15/2023]

*Quellien, Jean (Préface) *Bayeux et le Bessin 1940-1944 Vie Quotidienne Résistance Déportation Libération & Journal de deportation d'Arthur Poitevin* Bayeux: Presses de la Renaissance du Bessin, 1996

Rémy. *Mémoires d'un Agent Secret France Libre Juin 1940-Juin 1942.* Paris: Aux Trois Couleurs, 1945

Riess, Curt. *Total Espionage.* New York: G.P.Putnam's Sons, 1941

Robertson, K.G. (editor) *War, Resistance and Intelligence: Essays in honour of M.R.D. Foot.* Barnsley: Leo Cooper, 1999

*Rosencher, Henri. *Le sel, la cendre et la flamme.* Paris: privately printed, 1985; Paris: Editions du Félin, 2000. (Best friend of André in the camps and later.)

Rowe, M.W. *J. L. Austin: Philosopher and D-Day Intelligence Officer* Oxford University Press, 2023

Ruby, Marcel. *F Section SOE: The Story of the Buckmaster Network.* London: Leo Cooper, 1988

*Salton, George Lucius. *The 23rd Psalm: A Holocaust Memoir*. Madison: The University of Wisconsin Press, 2002

Schoenbrun, David. *Soldiers of the Night: The Story of the French Resistance*. NY: E.P.Dutton, 1980

Seghers, Pierre. *La Résistance et ses poètes: France 1940-1945*. Paris: Editions Seghers, 1974

Semprún, Jorge. *Literature or Life*, Viking, 1997. Originally *L'ecriture ou la vie*. Gallimard, 1994

Sendyk, Helen. *The End of Days: A Memoir of the Holocaust*. St. Martin's University Press, 1992; Syracuse University Press, 2000

*Sheppard, Bob. *Missions secrètes et Deportation 1939-1945*. Bayeux, Editions Heimdal, 1998. His spoken testimony: https://www.iwm.org.uk/collections/item/object/80010223

Shiber, Etta. *Paris-Underground*. New York: Charles Scribner's Sons, 1943

Shores, Corry. 'The Minor Machinery of Animal Packs: Becoming as Survival in Spiegelman's *Maus*', *Graphic Novels as Philosophy*, edited by Jeff McLaughlin. University Press of Mississippi, 2017

_____, http://piratesandrevolutionaries.blogspot.com/2012/10/whos-real-paul-masson-personal-non.html

Skorr, Henry. *Through Blood and Tears: Surviving Hitler and Stalin*. Portland: Valentine Mitchell 2006

Smith, Andrew WM. 'Eclipse in the Dark Years: Pick-up Flights, Routes of Resistance and the Free French', *European Review of History*, 25:2 (2018), pp.392-414.

Sofsky, Wolfgang. *The Order of Terror: The concentration camp*. Princeton University Press, 1993

Soo, Scott. 'Resisting in France and la vie inventée,' University of Sussex Journal of Contemporary History, 1 (2000).

Speer, Albert. *Infiltration: How Heinrich Himmler Schemed to Build an SS Industrial Empire*. NY: Macmillan, 1981

Stafford, David. *Britain and European Resistance 1940-1945*. UK: Macmillan, 1980 and University of Toronto Press, 1983

_____, *Secret Agent: The True Story of the Covert War against Hitler*. Woodstock and NY: Overlook Press/Peter Mayer Publishers 2001

Stanley, Ilse. *The Unforgotten*. Beacon Press, 1957. The German Jew who brought 400 Jews out of the concentration camps, to November, 1938, when she had to leave Germany.

Steinberg, Lucien. *Jews Against Hitler (Not as a Lamb)* NY: Gordon & Cremonesi, 1973

_____, *Les Autorités Allemandes an France Occupée*, Centre de Documentation Juive contemporaine, 1966

Sullenberger, Captain Chesley 'Sully' with Jeffrey Zaslow. *Highest Duty: My Search for what Really Matters*. New York: Harper Collins, 2009

Suttill, Francis J. *Shadows in the Fog: The True Story of Major Suttill and the Prosper French Resistance Network*. The History Press, 2019

Tilly, Charles. *La France conteste*. Paris, Fayard, 1986

Todorov, Tzvetan. *A French Tragedy: Scenes of Civil War, 1944*. University Press of New England, 1996. The massacre of Guerry, in which Diana Mara Henry's Alsatian family were killed by the French Fascists.

Tooze, Adam. *The Wages of Destruction: The Making and Breaking of the Nazi Economy*. Penguin, 2007

Vich, Catherine. *Capitaine de frégate Honoré d'Estienne d'Orves (1901-1941) 276 GG2: Répertoire numérique détaillé, Sous-Série GG2-Fonds Privés*. Vincennes, Service Historique de la Dédense, Archives Centrales de la Marine, 2004/rev.2009

West, Nigel. *MI6: British Secret Intelligence Service Operations 1909-45*. New York: Random House, 1983

_____, *G.C.H.Q. The Secret Wireless War 1900-1986*. Hodder and Stoughton, 1987

Wieviorka, Annette. *Déportation et génocide: entre la mémoire et l'oubli*. Hachette/Pluriel 1992

_____, *La Shoah: temoignages, savoirs, oeuvres*, edited by Annette Wieviorka and Claude Mouchard. Cercil: Presses Universitaires de Vincennes, 1999

_____, *The Era of the Witness*. Cornell, 2006

Wieviorka Olivier. 'À la recherche de l'engagement (1940-1944).' In: *Vingtième Siècle, revue d'histoire, n°60, octobre-décembre 1998*

_____, *The French Resistance*. Cambridge, MA and London: Belknap Press of Harvard University Press, 2016

*Wilborts, Suzanne. *Pour la France*. Charles-Lavauzelle, 1946

Wilhelmson, Alexandra. 'The Adventures of a Stateless Prince: Francis Xavier of Bourbon Parma' *APORTES,* no100, año XXXIV (2/2019), pp. 181-238.

School group coming in to visit Natzweiler, 2016.
Photo © Diana Mara Henry, Natzweiler Press

Quadrant of a mysteriously marked up map of Paris from André's archive.

Endnotes

1. Link for researching the various categories of veterans of the resistance, their networks, the administrative entities for them in France: https://www.fondationresistance.org/pages/action_pedag/recherches-biographiques-sur-resistant_dossier-thematique-28.htm
2. 'Tired of Imposture' —p. 127.
3. The French have called the camp Le Struthof, the name of the farmstead and former ski area where it is located, to take away any negative connection to Natzwiller, the small town nearest to the camp, which the Germans called Natzweiler. This has set back scholarship about the camp, which was largely unknown to researchers until a couple of decades ago, when the French started to sometimes call it Natzweiler-Struthof. As Struthof, it is also often confused with Stutthof, the concentration camp in Poland. All German documentation calls it Konzentrationslager/KL Natzweiler, or KLNa and that is how it will be termed in this book.
4. Annette Wieviorka's quote from an unnamed 1948 'rarely read text' by Robert Antelme, in *The Era of the Witness*, p. 127.
5. Max and Regina were listed as of Polish Nationality in the Kempten files of the German Government's 'List of allied Nationals and other foreigners, German Jews and stateless etc. who were temporarily or permanently stationed in the community, but are no longer in residence'. (A document from the early post-war period when 'the so-called Allied Order required the German authorities to make investigations about foreigners in the respective administrative districts. The aim was to obtain the most comprehensive information possible on the fate of prisoners, forced labourers and refugees in Germany.' —Arolsen archivist explanation.) Einwohneramt, 2.1.1.1/ 69972995/ ITS Digital Archive, Arolsen Archives.
6. Tim Austin puts them on the Holland-America Line's SS Volendam leaving Boulogne on July 16 arriving in NY July 27, 2039, with Max returning on the same ship after the start of the war in September.
7. https://en.wikipedia.org/wiki/German_military_administration_in_occupied_France_during_World_War_II
8. USC Shoah Foundation – The Institute for Visual History and Education, André Scheinmann interview by Helen Sendyk, #24954 Boca Raton, FL, 1/21/1997 https://vhaonline.usc.edu/viewingPage?testimonyID=24954&returnIndex=0#

9   André would say he was arrested by the Gestapo because that is the agency best known by the public, but in his answers on official forms he credited the Feldgendarmerie. For a synopsis of the multitude of services of German repression in occupied France see: https://www.cheminsdememoire.gouv.fr/en/services-german-repression-occupied-france. At the top of that page, a photo of the SIPO, the service that sent the NN convoy to Natzweiler, and at the bottom, of the Feldgendarmerie.

10 Max, age 52 and Regina Scheinmann, age 54, with the address of their hotel at 19 Rue de Rivoli appear on p. 355 of the book by Serge Klarsfeld of the list by address of names of Jews arrested in Paris. The cover shows French policeman and SS officer working together. The book contains more than 37,000 names – about half of the Jews deported from all of France. It is not known who was Hermann Scheinmann, age 19, residing at the same address.

11 Sam Pisar, a survivor of the Bialystok ghetto and of Auschwitz, in his memoirs *Blood and Hope* sums up this aspect of his life as it might André's as well: 'Yes, your life has been a fascinating journey, Sam Pisar … Bravo! But where it really counted, the resurrection of loved ones, the departed that motivated and propelled you all these years, there you have failed, there you are bankrupt, unable to meet the debts you have incurred to your blood and to your past.'

12 The Official Secrets Act is quoted and referenced (TNA HS9/251/7, 13 July 1944) in O'Connor's *Operations Vivacious and Branston*.

13 Hastings, *The Secret War*, p. 262. 'In fact, a very effective resistor' is Wiki-Rennes appraisal online of what André accomplished in his pioneering leadership of the Resistance in Brittany that was just getting started when he jumped in.

14 '… students from all areas of study … originally worked on propaganda via publication of *La Bretagne Enchainée* … their action was small scale activism such as the release of tear gas in theatres projecting German films, bludgeoning notorious collaborators. Since we've met with them, an action branch was created under the leadership of *Ménard*, directly under my orders, and a propaganda branch, led by *Normand,* under the orders of *Yves le Corre* … About 100 students, young men and women, were in this group, six of whom were ready to do sabotage, other services being counterfeiting, photography, locksmiths, towing, car repair and chop shop for German vehicles.' Source: Joël report sent 29 December, 1941. Overcloud network file 28P3 25 at Vincennes courtesy Fabrice Bourrée.

15 'The ideal form of association for young people is clubs. One club in particular, stimulated by Ménard, meets regularly. Under cover of dances and music, these clubs have three goals: 1) get the agents together and supervise them 2) orientation for propaganda, action and sabotage 3)

identify individuals capable of acting for us. To that end, these clubs include members who are neutral and ignore the clubs' true goal...' — as above, Overcloud network 28P3 25 at Vincennes.

16 'Though, for many of the people who joined it, resistance was an adventure – almost a game ... for success, one had to be capable of silence ... to be inconspicuous, not to stand out in a crowd, never to attract a second glance, was the safest and most precious of a resistor's gifts; still more, of a secret agent's.' —Foot, *Resistance*, p. 15.

17 Members of the resistance in the specified 'Aryan' nations – France, Norway, Luxemburg, The Netherlands and Belgium – imprisoned under the NN decree, simply were made to disappear without a trace in the concentration camps, first in Natzweiler and Hinzert, later also in Gross-Rosen, Mauthausen, Sachsenhausen, Ravensbrück, Dachau and Flossenbürg, and finally only at Natzweiler, by its iteration of 7 June, 1943, a month before André's arrival there.

Nacht und Nebel became embedded in public consciousness as a description for the whole of the concentration camp experience when it was used as the title of the widely viewed 1955 Alain Resnais film, *Night and Fog* (*Nuit et Brouillard*, in French), with its text by Alain Cayrol – himself an NN prisoner. This metaphorical use of the phrase had the perhaps unintended consequence of consigning the WWII history of this very specific crime to obscurity.

The [U.N.'s] 1992 'Declaration for the Protection of All Persons from Enforced Disappearances' states that the 'systematic practice [of enforced disappearances] is by its very nature a crime against humanity'. 4th Preambular paragraph. Adopted 2010 by the General Assembly in resolution 47/133 https://www.ohchr.org/en/instruments-mechanisms/instruments/international-convention-protection-all-persons-enforced   Accessed 4/2/2023.

18 Linet, Leroy and Nevers, pp. 88, 154, 159, 204.

19 Sorting out propaganda from reality, the reader will realise that Leni Riefenstahl's title for her pro-Nazi film 'Triumph of the Will' more rightfully belongs to the accomplishments of the Resistance.

20 Fogelman, p.80.

21 Microfilm from US National Archives and Records Administration (NARA) Item #RG 238, e.174, No-1501; Location 190.12.24.1, box 31 of the series titled Nuremberg Organization (NO) Documents, March 15, 1947 - June 20, 1949 (Record Group 238).

22 In its official registers, 806 Jews were registered at Natzweiler with no name.

23 See Joineau, p. 43, 'Inequality of the races? ... Some of us were subjected to even greater martyrdom than the others. I see again my comrade Jacques

[Magrisso] stretched out on the ground, an enormous rock under his kidneys ... the SS and the *Kapo* grinding his body with their truncheons, tortured for hours, his body covered with wounds, his shaved head covered with crusts. Because, you see, his red triangle with the letter F [French] was sewn on top of a yellow star. Jacques was Jewish. A Jew of Turkish origin. And this "mixed blood" had pushed the expression of his inferior race so far as to fight for his adopted country, France. Jacques was a resistor, and a valorous one.' See https://maitron.fr/spip.php?article145164 for Magrisso's actions in the resistance and transit through the concentration camps.

24   Some of the Jews sent away from Natzweiler survived Auschwitz, whereas their mates thought they would never have survived had they remained at Natzweiler. Maradène, p. 42: 'On October 20 [1943] three of our Jewish comrades were sent to Auschwitz. Two would come back. From what they said it seems they were happier in that camp than they were at Natzweiler.' Jean Lemberger, one of the Jews sent away from Natzweiler, was twice sent to the gas chamber at Auschwitz and twice pulled out. Israël, pp. 303-304, 321. 'He said that if he came out, it was because he was not considered a racial prisoner but rather a political prisoner. Since he came through Natzweiler, he had a "dossier", he was known and in principle had to be tried in a German court ... He wasn't like those Jews whose destiny was to die for no reason, because they had done nothing. Those ones didn't even have the dignity of being recognized as an enemy ... He was made to leave the ranks of death and his striped clothing was returned to him. He was a political prisoner, a resistor who hadn't arrived at Auschwitz in a transport of Jews ... He knew that no one would ever fully know or entirely believe...'

25   Otto Bickenbach and his assistant killed at least 50 people at Natzweiler. Amnestied in 1955, he continued to practice medicine in Germany until his death in 1971, and his assistant in those crimes worked as a public health officer. https://www.dgim-history.de/en/biography/Bickenbach;Otto;1125 'The life of the bacteriologist Haagen did not end with the death sentence he received in France 1950. In 1965, he received a position in the West German institute for viral disease of animals (*Bundesforschungsanstalt für Virus-Krankheiten der Tiere*) in Tübingen. https://muse.jhu.edu/article/258052/pdf 'Although sentenced to life imprisonment, he returned to research in 1952 as a result of the amnesty in the former West Germany, and then worked as a published researcher. https://www.thelancet.com/journals/lancet/article/PIIS0140673605671991/fulltext Accessed 7/24/2023

26   *The Struthof Album*, published by the Beate Klarsfeld Foundation, 1985, a compendium of Nuremberg Trial documents on the gassing of Jews at Natzweiler.

27   Published in the German paper of his hometown, 10/07/1973, reprinted in *Le Patriote Résistant*, the journal of the Fédération Nationale des Deportés et Internés Résistants et Patriotes, and in Maradène, p. 10.

28	The companies which employed Natzweiler prisoners include Daimler Benz, Hermann Göring-Werke, Elmag, Hiller, Kempf, B.M.W., Bosch, Vornag, Züblin, Wüste, Messerchmitt, Adlerwerke, Hans Heymann, Metalwerke GmbH (Spaichingen), Württembergische Metallwarenfabrik Geislingen/Steige, Freidrich Krupp Eisenwerke, Lufag, Heinkel, Alfing Kessler, as well as numerous German local and national governmental entities including the *Wehrmacht* and the SS itself. It is only in recent decades that the extent of the National Socialist slave labor system has started to be studied, throwing new light on Albert Speer's 1981 very political 'tell all.' Researchers for the US Holocaust Memorial Museum have identified from 10,000 to more than 40,000 of them throughout the occupied territories.
29	Portraits and passages about André in Leroy et al., pp. 88, 154, 159 and 204-205. Also, Ragot recounts that prisoner 1416, a *Kapo* wearing the green triangle (for habitual criminals) wanted to interrogate Ragot. 'As I didn't want to answer, I told him I didn't speak German. He went to find an interpreter, a Frenchman who had arrived in July, whom he started to flatten to the wall with blows. So I gave vague answers, that seemed to satisfy him.' —p.18.
30	FNDIR, p. 101.
31	See Cobain.
32	'As the menace of Nazi Germany increased in the late 1930s, SIS began to prepare for the possibility of war. One move in 1938 was the establishment of Section D ... Section D's aim was simple – 'to plan, prepare and when necessary carry out sabotage and other clandestine operations, as opposed to the gathering of intelligence.' Section D became a Secret Service section, the SOE, separate from SIS. —from SIS official website. https://www.sis.gov.uk/our-history.html
33	Richards, p.116.
34	Picquet-Wicks, p. 158.
35	A mysterious character, he is said to have been the owner of the Northern Irish Whiskey Company 'Greene & Greene'.
36	Quote from p. 4 of André's 1999 handwritten CV for the author. 'The son of a Constantinople ship owner, Wilfred Albert Dunderdale was born in Odessa on Christmas Eve 1899. He was studying to be a naval architect in St. Petersburg when the Russian Revolution broke out in 1917. His father sent him to Vladivostock to take delivery of the first of a new class of submarines, built in America, and deliver it to the Black Sea. To transport a submarine, still in five separate sections, thousand of miles by rail across a country in the throes of a revolution was asking a great deal of a seventeen-year-old boy – but Biffy accomplished it ... The day before [World War 2] was declared Dunderdale was given the rank of Commander RNVR.' "Dunderdale, Wilfred Albert (1899-1990), intelligence officer". *Oxford*

Dictionary of National Biography (online ed.). Oxford University Press. 2004. doi:10.1093/ref:odnb/40173. ISBN 9780198614128.

37 Quote from p. 4 of André's 1999 handwritten CV for the author.

38 Diagram of SIS Organization, September 1939, in West's *MI6*. For more than a decade before war broke out, Dunderdale had been responsible for liaison with the French Secret Service (Deuxième Bureau) and also played a key role in extracting from Poland the Enigma machine that enabled the British to decode German military messages during much of the war. *The Dictionary of National Biography* entry by John Bruce Lockhart 'from personal knowledge' describes him as 'neat, dark, immaculately dressed, stubby in build, and always with a Balkan cigarette, in a long, black, ivory holder...' —pp. 113-114.

39 A topic worth researching further: funding the resistance, a comparative study of resources provided by the British to their mission heads. Cowburn writes that 'in the winter of 1941-1942 ... the [SOE] organizers of resistance were starting business in a modest way. For instance, when I left England I had been given the sum of only 26,000 francs, the purchasing power of which was about 100 pounds, and this for a stay of indefinite length.' —p.57.

40 The Anglo-French Communications Bureau was a cover for the SIS Office in Paris. Madame Louis claimed the SIS gave her 400,000 francs per month to distribute to her agents, starting at 3,000 francs each. (From her narrative at Vincennes.) Caroline Babois writes: 'I am very happy with your presentation of my father's letter and his photo. I find it very moving that JEG's letter contributes to proving André's absolute honesty.' To identify her father, she writes of John Edward Gentry: 'Worked in SIS sub-section P1c and became head of MI6's Paris Station right after the war, presumably because of his close relations with the Free French. She quotes Keith Jeffery, p. 397: 'After Dewavrin ['Passy'] had complained to Dansey about Dunderdale's hostility to de Gaulle, in February 1941 Menzies tried to calm things down by giving Dunderdale the primary task of collecting intelligence from the ports in German occupied France ... The maintenance of two parallel SIS French sections, while administratively inefficient, was a pragmatic solution to the intelligence opportunities which emerged after the fall of France.'

41 There is much debate about the actual number of summary executions of collaborators during the 'épuration sauvage' of 1944; Lormier estimates between 10,000 and 15,000 —p. 370.

42 Pollack characterizes de Gaulle's attitude toward Intelligence as 'incomprehension and disdain', seeing it as a device to assert his legitimacy and muscle in dealing with the English —p. 35.

43 Decree No. 366 of July 26, 1942 to recognize members of the resistance as part of the Forces Française Combattantes. According to Pollack, p. 65,

its preamble stated that 'The validity of activity is conditional on their acceptance by General de Gaulle, which recognition will open the door to the rights of those parties' although that is not included in the copy this author has.

44　The *Attestation* bears the stamp of the DGER, French Secret Service successor to De Gaulle's Free French BCRA in London. See Sebastien Albertelli: https://www.cheminsdememoire.gouv.fr/en/occupied-france-bcra-londres-alger-paris

According to Yann Fossurier on the SOE Forum, 19 June 2023, 'French SOE agents were asked by de Gaulle to leave the British special services in Sept./Oct.1944. Many of the were transferred to the newly-formed DGER (Direction générales des études et recherches.)'

45　Pollack, p. 50, his summary of file no. HS 6/318 regarding the SOE. There is even the case of Dufour, who in 1943 brought suit against de Gaulle for being tortured by his aide Captain Roger Wybot in the basement of 10, Duke St. in 1942 and forced to join the BCRA. The British settled the case with him for a sum that they would hardly have paid if he had not been their agent.- see Patrick Marnham, *War in the Shadows: Resistance, Deception and Betrayal in Occupied France*, Simon & Schuster, 2020.

46　Robertson, p.181. David Stafford quoting from John Le Carré's *A Perfect Spy*, (Coronet edition, 1987, p. 484)

47　From André's files at Caen the dates of his service are listed as 1/11/1940 to 21/6/1946 and his legal obligations are waived.

48　https://bletchleypark.org.uk/roll-of-honour/15670/   Accessed 3/20/2023

49　Mady speaking in 'I am André: A story of Triumph" Suzanne Richard documentary for New Bedford Cable access, shown 4/19/01, the year Yom Ha Shoah memorial program in New Bedford centered on a tribute to André.

50　One can listen to the *Horst Wessel Lied* in a recording made in 2018 (per archivist at the Imperial War Museum) at https://www.iwm.org.uk/collections/item/object/80033942

51　Sam Scheinman was declared a citizen of the U.S. in Superior Court of the City of New York on 22 May 1893.

52　The Volendam, via the port of Boulogne.

53　Dr. Adolf Sindler was a refugee from Galicia who relocated to Haifa in the 1930's after the anti-Jewish laws prevented his practice of medicine in Germany. http://aerzte.erez-israel.de/sindler/   Accessed 1/4/2023. See also Brandes and Eisen.

54　Tim Austin discovered a Ruth Weil, born in Düsseldorf 6 days after André, whose family was in jute and sack commerce. He found that she and her family went to Australia before making their US Declaration of Intention (for citizenship) on 2 June, 1942.

55 Zionism, the movement to reclaim Israel (then known as Palestine, the name the Romans changed it to 2,000 years ago) as a homeland for the Jewish people.

56 Two months after Hitler came to power, he opened Germany's concentration camp, Dachau, outside Munich, in March, 1933, for the punishment of his political enemies.

57 The Nord-Pas de Calais Mining Basin was declared a European Heritage site in 2012 by UNESCO.

58 Family photo albums show the Scheinmanns still taking vacations in Germany in the 1930s.

59 André's obituary by Robert Lovinger included this evidence of André's life-long passion for tennis: 'Mr. Scheinmann went into business here, selling toys and shoes, but he was best-known as a top-flight tennis player. A founder of the New Bedford Tennis Association, he created a number of tennis programs for young people.' One of his son's friends, when André took the two young men to visit Natzweiler on the same trip to compete in youth tennis tournaments in France, recalled to the author in 2022 that when he saw the camp he realised André had kept urging him to keep fit and keep working on his sport in case of having to survive a similar fight for his life.

60 At Munich, by agreement of Germany, Britain, France and Italy, the German annexation of the German-speaking part of Czechoslovakia was given the go-ahead on September 30, 1938. Neville Chamberlain, the British Prime Minister spoke of the pact as having assured 'peace for our time' and Munich has come to represent (the futility of) offering appeasement to aggressors.

61 https://www.wiki-rennes.fr/Bombardement_du_17_juin_1940 Identifies la clinique Saint-Yves as a hospital from which all staff, nuns and doctors pitched in to help.

62 https://www.bbc.co.uk/history/ww2peopleswar/stories/24/a7501024.shtml

63 In 1940 1.8 million French soldiers were taken as prisoners of war by Germany. During the coming months most of these men were deported into Germany for use as slave laborers. Nearly a million were still held in Germany in 1945 when they were liberated by Allied and Soviet forces. 'We Have No Place: The Captivity and Homecoming of French Prisoners of War, 1939-1947' James Quinn, Ph.D. thesis, University of Kansas, 2011

64 The French Army, like the French Foreign Legion, gave its fighters false identities if they had foreign names, so that if captured by the enemy they would not be thought to be traitors to the other side. In correspondence with the author, Aline Angoustures, Cheffe de la Mission histoire et exploitation des archives, OFPRA (Office français de protection des réfugiés et apatrides) wrote a long history and explication of the official

army practice of giving an alias – a 'nom de guerre, including that: 'This practice hides their identities and may protect their families from reprisals; it may also be a form of dissociation from domestic life.'= see https://www.ofpra.gouv.fr/

André, as others, were given the name, date and city of birth of a real person (a child who had died in infancy) their deceased parents' names, etc. He kept the name André to the end of this life, adding it to Joseph Scheinmann.

65 Pollack has an interesting spin on this: 'For the networks, recruiting is an absolute necessity and an eminently delicate question. The network is an elitist organisation. It's the network that chooses its agents.' However, André's planning shows he also chose his network and went to the top, with Turban, to do so.

66 Madame Louis' official report for the French government in the network file at Vincennes says the Georges France/Groupe 31 sent 53 weekly reports every Thursday, starting at the end of September 1940 via Canfranc, Pamplona, St. Sebastien, and Madrid. On the same page she states, 'I would bring it [the mail] to Oloron Ste. Marie every Friday for our network agents.' She also states that the network had radio transmitters at Excideuil and Caen but wasn't aware of how and when the transmissions were made. It is very possible that she did not know all of André and Turban's strategies either.

67 Radio programs broadcast by the BBC for French listeners.

68 'The French Army proposed to people who were from a former German country, parts of Poland, parts of Germany, Alsace and so on, to have another identity, because if the Germans caught you and considered you German, they would shoot you. So you had a choice. You could go to North Africa – not the European theater – or, you changed ID. So, I said, "I'll change ID." So I was called to the office, they told me "This is your name." ... They gave me a new paybook, they gave me an id-for which I had a father, a mother, I was born in a part of the country which I was familiar with, and that's it. So I had changed.' —André from the USC Shoah Foundation interview, clip used in 'I am André; A story of Triumph' Suzanne Richard documentary for New Bedford Cable access, shown 4/19/2001

69 ... Some of these two paragraphs taken from video interview of André by Mel and Cynthia Yoken.

70 For the air drop location sketched in the maps in his archive, André may have been working with Laverdet-Le Gall who was operating in the area at the time, or with Victor Chatenay, who was liaison network with the SNCF for the Jade-Fitzroy SIS network for which Pierre Hentic organised air and sea operations between Brittany and England. Hentic is in André's little black book.

71 'On December 22, 1940, Lieutenant Commander Honoré d'Estienne d'Orves secretly landed on the Breton Coast to establish one of the first Free France Intelligence networks, known as Nemrod. Betrayed by his radio operator ... he was executed on August 29, 1941. He was the first agent of Free France to fall to the enemy's bullets.' —Olivier Wieviorka, p. 1. A biography linking him and the de Lorgeril family, who were part of André's network. at: https://www.cheminsdememoire.gouv.fr/en/honore-d-estienne-dorves

72 'From almost the beginning of the occupation, Franz Stock was named as priest for Germans residing in Paris. In 1941, he was assigned to work as a chaplain in the Fresnes Prison, La Santé Prison and Cherche-Midi Prison in Paris. He was also a chaplain at the execution site at the Mont Valérien. These roles earned him the nicknames *L'Aumônier de l'Enfer* (The chaplain of Hell) and *L'archange des prisons* (The archangel of the prisons). He is said to have met with more than 2,000 prisoners before their executions, including the French Navy officer Henri Honoré d'Estienne d'Orves.' www.franz-stock.org

73 Marie-Jose Chombart de Lauwe, then serving as President of the Paris-based Fondation pour la Mémoire de la Déportation, letter of May 17.

74 https://www.memoresist.org/resistant/jean-baptiste-legeay/

75 'Father Legeay, (Christian brother condemned to death 28 March 1942) said to have facilitated the feeding of British aviators, would not have had the intention, in so doing, of harming the German occupying forces, wanting simply to apply principles of charity, which his order required of him. The French Ambassador (delegate of the [Vichy] government in the territories) believes he needs to underscore the clarion call to the population of Brittany so often tormented by British bombardments would be the execution of a priest, veteran of the 1914-1918 war, mutilated, decorated with the Croix de Guerre (War Cross) and the Military Medal...' Letter attached to the record of the German trial also including Théotiste Epron, Henriette Le Belzic, Brachu, Adam and Josephine Bocq, Le Gac, Alexandrine Tilly, Torty, Allain, l'Henoret, Loutrage, Roverch, Passiant, Marie Cozannet, Pennehoat, Marie de Saint Laurent, Le Bonniec, Marchais, among others whose names appear in André's agent lists. Thanks to Pierre de Jaegher for SHD file GR 28 P 844(52).

76 André at another point calls Madame Louis the head of the Georges-France/Groupe 31.

77 De Gaulle, 'though pursuing purely French policies ... was dependent on the British to an uncomfortably large extent. They provided him with the money without which all the resistance movements in France were bound to languish; they provided the wireless sets without which he would have no rapid communication with the field; they provided all the aircraft and almost all the ships that carried his agents to and fro. This made him all the more determined to have policies of his own.' —Foot, *SOE in France*, p 137.

78	See Smith: 'The Gaullists cooperated best with the British intelligence services (SIS), whilst they tussled more openly with the military aims of the SOE, and the desire of the independent F Section to ensure that co-operation to put it quite brutally – must be one-sided ... Claude Dansey was the Assistant Chief of SIS, and he split its French efforts into two streams: Wilfred "Biffy" Dunderdale led efforts to seek useful contacts and information from the remnants of France's pre-war Intelligence Service, whilst Kenneth Cohen was tasked with cultivating new contacts. The BCRA's aim was very much to show itself to the British as the main interface with the resistance, whilst the British maintained an open mind as to other possibilities, and sought to maintain their own networks in France not dependent upon the Free French.' —p.8.
79	Renaud, pp. 108-111. SOE memo of 6 September 1941 entitled OVERCLOUD gives the origin date for the name: 'This is to confirm our telephone conversation of this morning, when it was arranged that the code name OVERCLOUD should be allotted to a team of two- one organiser and one W/T [radio] operator – proceeding by sea to the coast of Brittany during the October moon period. This team is formed from members of the F.F.L.' The mission set up what is called 'the first réseau action in the occupied zone' — http://www.ordredelaliberation.fr/fr_compagnon/601.htm
80	Yves had been organizing propaganda, the underground press, and students in Rennes and Paris, from the beginning of the occupation, although his brother Joël, known by the name of their network, Overcloud, was the first to go to London.
81	Read the paper online or download at: ark:/12148/cb361410729.public at https://gallica.bnf.fr/ark:/12148/cb361410729/date
82	French National Archives file GR 16 P 539178. Yves' prescient political analysis pointed to the establishment of De Gaulle after D-Day and to his own service to De Gaulle as head of state during the war in Algeria.
83	Maybe Joël should have been as concerned about Raymond Cabard alias Bat A alias Fraichin file at Vincennes SHD GR16P99094 according to Pierre Tillet: 'arrêté ? déserteur ? interné à Marseille, déporté en Allemagne & porté disparu?' (arrested? deserter? imprisoned in Marseille, deported to Germany and reported as disappeared?)in HISTORIQUE 2ieme GM INFILTRATIONS EN FRANCE-rev108-31122023
84	'Joe' was the name for Joël Le Tac, 'Joe X' for his radio operator de Alain de Kergolay and 'Joe Y' for radio operator Pierre Moureaux. Quotes from Renaud, pp. 108-111.
85	For descriptions of this trip, mentioning André: Richards, pp. 115-116, 314; Huguen, pp.38-39 and index; Spicer, p. 101; Monique Le Tac, pp. 123-130; Picquet-Wicks, pp. 157-160.
86	In his 'Historique du Réseau des F.F.C. "Overcloud"' Joël specifies it included 1 intelligence service, called 31; 1 action service (connected the

B.C.R.A.); 1 evasion service (connected to Slocum and Holsworth); 1 sabotage service (in liaison with SOE "Bretagne Enchaînée"); 1 propaganda service (Captain Bozel) and lists two sub-networks: 'Bête Noire' in Brittany and 'Valmy' in Paris.

87   Monique Le Tac, pp.123-130. Yvonne, Monique's grandmother, was 60 when she, her sons Joël and Yves (Monique's father) and her husband were arrested. They constitute an early of example of what Soo described: 'The family as a site of subversion provided another means of recruitment, conceived new identities and opportunities for female political expression, and offered shelter to fugitives.' Andrée, Yves' wife, was the one who 'manned' the Overcloud network during January 1942 when André and Joël were in England...

88   Full name of the organization publishing *Gens de la Lune*: Association d'Entr'aide des Anciens Officiers chargés de 'Missions-Action' et de leurs collaborateurs recrutés en France. (Fraternal organisation of former officers of Special Ops missions and their collaborators recruited in France.)

89   The MTB and the MGB were the same type of boat, equipped with different armaments. André was actually on the MGB 314, as identified by Brooks Richards who crewed and wrote about the trip in *Secret Flotillas*. Piquet-Wicks called it an MTB, and as he was hosting the planning meetings that André attended, perhaps André got the designation there. Spicer fills the reader in on the hazardous conditions for all on board, and the extraordinary demands made on the navigator in particular, David Birkin, who had to sail across the German convoy line in the English channel 10 miles from the Breton shore, across the fierce currents running close to the coast, with its engine cut back to avoid detection and to avoid shoals and mines without radar which could be intercepted by the Germans.

90   Thank you to Nick Fox OBE in correspondence Feb.9 2023 regarding Sgt Peake: 'There was a Sgt George Peake (7686389) in the Intelligence Corps who served initially with 3 Field Security Section and was then posted to "special duties" – this was a euphemism for service with SIS, SOE or MI5. He later transferred to the Royal Marines. Coincidentally, there was a Sgt Peake who was a member of the Helford Flotilla (see below). This Sgt Peake was a Royal Marine and fluent Breton speaker. It may be that he is identical with Sgt George Peake, who was initially Intelligence Corps, as the Corps recruited many NCOs with language skills. He may well have been involved in the meeting due to his knowledge of maritime matters/ riverine skills/French coast etc. which would have been useful for the canoe insertion.'

91   Piquet-Wicks in *Four in the Shadows*: 'A lieutenant-commander came over to the group of six Frenchmen all busily drinking boiling coffee from large enamel mugs. "what a catch," he smiles at them. "Next time I'll bring a bigger ship, and run a ferry service."' —p. 160.

92 Translated by the author, retaining the French cadence and turns of phrase.

93 André further on says the radio operator was code-named Nelson. See below.

94 Pierre Hentic writes that in spring, 1942, he was introduced to 'Nelson,' a radio operator sent from London. 'Although working for a different outfit, he sent over a report on the blow to our network ... Nelson was French, but served in the British Navy most notably on a warship whose famous name became his alias. He tells us of his long patrols in the Mediterranean ... Nelson and I became good friends. I learned a year later that his name was Hamon." —p.171.

95 André was at that time living at 7 Rue de Rohan in Rennes.

96 The fateful return from England of André and the Overcloud mission is described at length by Sir Brooks Richards, one of the Navy (RNVR) men aboard the MGB 314 when it brought André's party over to England – 'they were met with hot tea, whisky and sandwiches.' Then: 'Three weeks later, on the night of 1-2 February, they went back to Ile-Guennoc, again using MGB 314. This time there were only three passengers, the Le Tac brothers and Peulevé [sic.] It was a bright, moonlit night. They embarked Yves and Peulevé in one Folboat, Joël went with the luggage and Peulevé's new suitcase set in the other. The operation proceeded without a hitch, though the tide was out and there was more than a kilometer (0.6 miles) of beach between their landing point and the Le Tac villa, across which they had to lug their two canoes and their baggage. Fortunately, it was very cold indeed and no sleepless German was loitering on the balcony of any of the requisitioned villas.

'But disaster was awaiting: de Kergolay had been arrested during their absence in England ... Peulevé was also arrested on arrival in Rennes; three days later Joël fell into a trap that had been set for him in the flat of a Resistance colleague in the same city, [Rennes] which was his chosen operational headquarters. Yves, whose propaganda mission took him to Paris, was arrested there two days after his brother, and wounded into the bargain. The Le Tac parents and Andrée, their daughter-in-law, shared the same fate. They were all deported but, miraculously, returned from concentration camps three-and a half year later. De Kergolay ... continued to operate his wireless set under enemy control until 1943, but he omitted his security check and SOE's RF section recognised the traffic as Funkspiel (deception) and handled it accordingly. De Kergolay was condemned for collaboration with the enemy after the war, but Yeo-Thomas ["The White Rabbit"] was able to clear him of the charges relating to OVERCLOUD and his life sentence was reduced. The extent to which OVERCLOUD was in contact with a whole series of organisations whose security was under systematic attack proved fatal: Georges France 31 had been penetrated.' —pp. 115-117.

97 Yvette Wilborts (Marie-Jo Chombart de Lauwe) explains in *Résister Toujours* that her mother and she continued in the Resistance after the arrests of most members of their networks: 'Thus, we continued to pay the price of liberty. The repression was growing. At the beginning of 1942, Turban, Peulevey, the Le Tac brothers and their wives fell into mousetraps ... We received a warning from London: "Group entirely uncovered by the enemy, cease all work." We floated for a moment. Then my mother sent back the following message: "Since the beginning of the hostilities we sacrificed our lives. Will continue to work as in the past." Examined in the cold light of today, this stubbornness was a strategic error, or worse, even though the network was heavily infiltrated, the file was already thick and out fate already sealed. But that message, that will to continue at whatever cost, summarized our state of mind perfectly.' —pp. 76-77.

98 Victor Chatenay, of the Jade-Fitzroy network, writes about his 'mistaken arrest' on February 11 and repeated interrogations starting on February 26, 1942 at the Hôtel Edouard VII by the Gestapo as to whether he knew Joël Le Tac, Le Vigan, Kergolay, Le Neveu —pp. 67,71. Another young man tells him in prison that 'he came over from England and that with two or three comrades, he headed that big resistance affair that the Germans call the Rennes or Turban affair, for which hundreds of persons were arrested. (I was told 800.)' p. 80. References to Sidel [sic: Seidel],p.38,;Yvonne Le Tac p.50; Morel, p.50; arrests in Rennes, p.62; Normand p.78; Turban, p.80; Le Tac, pp.71, 82.

99 'And so I couldn't be forced to give other people, I didn't know anything, and I cut down my activities to economic information. They wanted to know who I talked to in England, what information I gave them. I told them how much sugar was transported, I'm not an officer, I know nothing.' André Scheinmann interview, USC Shoah Foundation – The Institute for Visual History and Education.

100 André is playing off the Wehrmacht (Army) Military Intelligence Service – the Abwehr – against the Gestapo (Secret State Police) – all instruments of repression. He eventually was sent to the concentration camps under the auspices of the Sicherheitspolizei/SIPO (Secret/Security Police).

101 Helmut Knochen's bio in Miannay ps 163/164 details his participation in the Venlo incident and his assignment to Paris in June 1940 where he was assisted among others by Kurt Lischka. 'He was supported by the Geheime Feldpolizei (secret military police of the German Wehrmacht) and in his position as *Befehlshaber der Sipo und des SD* – head of the BDS/Sipo is installed at 72, Ave. Foch. He spearheaded the big police and intelligence affairs on French territory ... Condemned to death by a military tribunal in France in 1954 ... he was pardoned by de Gaulle in 1962...' More at https://www.cheminsdememoire.gouv.fr/en/services-german-repression-occupied-france

102 Two links point to the controversial interpretation of La Roque's politics that André and others identified as far-right wing. https://francearchives.gouv.fr/fr/authorityrecord/FRAN_NP_051336 and https://www.lepoint.fr/histoire/le-colonel-de-la-rocque-figure-tutelaire-d-un-fascisme-a-la-francaise-09-05-2019-2311747_1615.php#11

103 See Calet's very poignant book of inscriptions on the walls of Fresnes by prisoners of all nationalities and circumstances.

104 https://collections.arolsen-archives.org/en/document/82329122 and https://collections.arolsen-archives.org/en/document/82329123

105 See Fondation pour la mémoire de la déportation for the list of the 56 men, 'all Frenchmen,' sent in the first transport of NN prisoners to Natzweiler from France. http://www.bddm.org/liv/details.php?id=I.114.

106 'Indeed, resistors registered as FFC (Forces Françaises Combattantes) engaged in a network before Decree 366 of July 1942 have received the same rights as the FFL (Forces Françaises Libres/Free French).' —Fabrice Bourrée in email correspondence 11/14/ 2022. André spoke to the more common knowledge of the term Free French.

107 Dr. Lavoué made his roneo machine available for the printing of an underground newspaper, *La Bretagne Enchaînée* (Brittany in Chains) It was issued as a single two-sided sheet of which 3,000-5,000 were printed every two weeks between November 15, 1941 and January 1, 1942. The principals had been active in the resistance starting in June 1940: Etienne Maurel, Louis Normand, André Ménard and André Simon. Six issues are in the collection of the Bibliothèque Nationale de France, département Réserve des livres rares RES-G-1470 (1028) ark:/12148/cb361410729

108 See Nuremberg trial document in reference to Walde of the Abwehr's Foreign Intelligence Service: GB-278 *731-D Statement by Colonel Walde of the former German Air Force Inspection 17, 13 December 1945, concerning events after the escape of British Air Force officers from Camp Sagan in March 1944, in particular concerning a discussion in the Reich Security Main Office where reference was made to a previous discussion at Hitler's head- quarters... —IX-594; XI-172; XIX-476. See also the transcript at https://avalon.law.yale.edu/imt/04-10-46.asp

109 The complete list of prisoners on the transport, online at the Fondation pour la Mémoire de la Déportation, lists 'Peulevey dit le Neveu' among '100% French' NNs. Twenty-nine came back, 27 died. http://www.bddm.org/liv/details.php?id=I.114.#peulevey

110 Henri Gayot arrived at the KLNa in April 1944, for the five remaining months before the prisoners were moved to Dachau; the camp was overcrowded to as many as 8,000 prisoners in 12 barracks but chaos and typhus lessened the labor and cruelty had diminished with the change of Kommandants in May. Gayot drew some of his scenes from accounts of his campmates who had been there during the Kramer reign of (greatest)

terror and not all details may be accurate, although expressive of the situation psychologically. For more on Gayot and the man who wrote the text for his portfolio of drawings, Roger Laporte, who was in the second convoy of French NNs in July 1943, see https://portal.ehri-project.eu/units/us-005578-irn671442

111   Ottosen, 'L'arrivée des Français,' —p. 56.

112   'As far as survival is concerned,' Primo Levi once said about the concentration camps during an interview with Philip Roth, '... I maintain there was no general rule, except perhaps arriving at the camp in good health and speaking German.' The quote from Levi continues: 'Aside from that, chance determined the rest. I saw cunning people and idiots survive, brave souls and cowards, "thinkers" and madmen.' Quoted by Semprún, p 300.

113   https://collections.arolsen-archives.org/en/search/person/130432291?s=andre%20peulevey&t=532954&p=0 , records of André Peulevey preserved by the International Tracing Service/I.T.S. at the Arolsen Archives, International Center on Nazi Persecution, Germany   Acccessed 1/22/2023

114   Israël tells the story of Jean Lemberger, pp. 303-304, 321.

115   *Sicherheitspolizei*/SiPo/ Security Police was created in 1936 by SS leader and Chief of the German Police Heinrich Himmler to establish a close working relationship between the criminal police (Kripo) and the Gestapo. The Security Police was closely tied to the Sicherheitsdienst (SD), the SS intelligence service. The Security Police and the SD were combined into the Reich Security Main Office (RSHA) in September 1939. The Security Police were key perpetrators of the Holocaust. Security Policemen carried out mass shootings, coordinated deportations, and committed other horrific crimes. – https://encyclopedia.ushmm.org/content/en/article/the-security-police-sipo   Accessed 1/30/2023

116   I'm replacing 'Block' with barrack everytime André used the German word.

117   Ottosen, 'L'arrivée des Français,' p. 56.

118   See Bakels for an account of life at Natzweiler for such a *prominentem* prisoner from the Netherlands.

119   Various survivors mention different last names for Willi or Willy. Emails in 2014 and 2017 from René Chevrolet, in charge of Memory and Educational and Cultural Activities at the CERD: 'Willy Behnke was a Communist epolitical prisoner of the Nazis from 1933-1934. He spent a total of about 12 years in prison and in camp. He arrived at Natzweiler in the first transport May 21 1941. His registration number was 6. At the beginning of 1944, he became Lagerälteste. Many prisoners testified to his efforts to diminish their suffering. After the was he became a political leader of the RDA [East Germany] ... Willi Kratt was a political prisoner

born 21/03/1905. He was transferred to Natzweiler from Buchenwald on 14/03/1942. He also was at the Frommern subcamp. He was "freed" on 30/11/1944 to be incorporated in the sadly famous Dirlewanger Division much like many German political and criminal prisoners at the end of the war. The SS needed cannon fodder ... he was a *Kapo* and, like Willi Behnke, well-disposed toward French prisoners, according to witnesses.'

120 'Aleksandr Solzhenitsyn makes this pertinent observation about a crucial problem in the life of the camps, the elimination of informers. Indeed, it was with this that all resistance began, whether in the Russian camps or in the German camps. On which link must one exert pressure in order to snap the chain of servitude? S asks and he replies: "Kill the stoolie! That was it, the vital link! Make knives and cut stoolies' throats- that was it!"' —Jorge Semprún, *What a Beautiful Sunday!* Harcourt Brace Jovanovich, NY, 1982

121 See Perrin.

122 George McGovern talking about flying the B-24 Liberators in formation over Germany: http://new.wymaninstitute.org/2004/12/george-mcgovern-and-the-bombing-of-auschwitz/

123 See Béné on the only known successful escape from Natzweiler until the evacuations in September 1944. On August 4, 1942, five prisoners of various nationalities, who worked at the car repair shop and at the laundry, took an SS car, disabled the others, and with two dressed in SS uniform and the others stashed and hidden in the vehicle, saluted smartly going out the gate, without being stopped, in a thunderous rainstorm. Four escaped successfully, and made their way back to England to rejoin the war effort. One was caught and brought back to Natzweiler to be hanged on 5 November, 1942.

124 André's Natzweiler records at the US Holocaust Memorial Museum include infirmary forms that he was seen and tracked there for 40 days, from 17 November through 26 December.

125 Fritz Hartjenstein.

126 'A theatrical performance was born in the Frenchmen's clan ... Georges Briquet led the ball, playing director, casting director, producer ... Good will produced Fernandels by the shovelful, Maurice Chevaliers were found, Tino Rossis, even a Marie Dubas, puppeteers, an illusionist, clown-contortionists ... The party lasted three hours. To close out, a tour de France in Song ... and finally, sotto voce, of course, "La Marseillaise". That was simple defiance. It was Christmas. We had just reconnected with hope, we had become, for a few hours, human beings.' This is how the performance is related in *Allach, Kommando de Dachau*, p. 140 by the Amicale des Anciens de Dachau (Fraternal Organization of the Survivors of Dachau, among whom André's comrades from Natzweiler: Leon Boutbien, Pierre Hentic, Roger Leroy, Pierre Rolinet...)

127 Arthur Poitevin, a former KLNa prisoner who says he was not invited to a Christmas party in his barrack at Dachau, gives a bitter account. —p. 145.

128   Robert Wernick tells a similar story about Johnny Hopper saving Arne Brun Lie. https://robertwernick.org/articles/Johnny_Hopper.htm

129   The names of prisoners André cites at Dachau do not come up on the camp's website- but neither do his names ... or that of General Delestraint.

130   André must have been in the prisoner throng with Brian Stonehouse (SOE) at Dachau's liberation, as Stonehouse recounts (without the same humor) the woman journalist in uniform who was first through the gates. https://www.iwm.org.uk/collections/item/object/80009635 (Tape five)

131   The British never gave André a commendation or decoration for his year or more of service to the SIS and return of the funds he received from them.

132   The law regarding the looting ('spoliation') of property was passed on 21 April 1945 and reenacted with a new deadline of November 30, 1947. André and his lawyer, Maître J. Dutilleul of Béthune, worked diligently through 1945 and 1946 and received a favorable judgement in time. But the process of reclaiming the goods that a marshal had itemized in 1945 broke down once the apartment was discovered to be empty and the occupant, Mielloch, had moved several times, to Roubaix and on to other cities in France.

133   Renamed Bruay-la-Buissière to change its reputation and camouflage its history after a gruesome and scandalous sexual assault/murder case occurred in Bruay-en-Artois in 1972.

134   The list André wrote up on his *demande d'idemnité*: In the smoking room: Minister's desk, table, 6 chairs, armchair, upholstered armchair, bookshelves, armoire with drawers and shelving, standing ashtray, 2 bronze statuettes (gladiators and shotputters), 1 inkstand (dog upright in bronze), complete library of 3000 volumes including 500 rare books, sheet music, record player, 1 large and 2 small carpets, 1 chandelier, 1 bronze desk lamp; entry: coat stand, rug; kitchen: range, complete equipment, hot water heater, bathtub, table, buffet, ice chest; 25 decorative cushions, 2 dolls, 1 Vega typewriter, large new radio, 2 table cloths (1 made of green silk with black hem), 4 piece crystal set for bedroom, 1 room heater, 4 radiators. Also, 5 suits, four pairs of shoes, underwear, socks, health items, tennis equipment, gold ring, watch, gold fountain pen, 30,000 francs in cash. His estimated total: 800.000 francs.

135   André's lawyer, on 16 May 1946, characterized Mielloch as a 'person of bad faith' who had been interpreter for the *Kommandatur* (headquarters of the German occupation) of Bruay. The lawyer got an account on how the man Mielloch came to occupy the Scheinmann dwelling and to have their furniture: 'On the 22nd of November, 1940, Mr. [Max] Scheinmann, resident of Bruay, a Jew, had been alerted that he had to leave that very night. In order to protect his belongings, he contacted Mielloch, baker at Divion [about 2 miles from Bruay] and came to an agreement with him on the fictitious sale to him of most of the furniture including a dining

room set, a bedroom set, and office for the sum of 12,000 francs for which a receipt was immediately given. Mr. and Mrs. Scheinman were deported to Germany and with no news of them, their son assumes that they died in captivity.'

136 The British used the term 'E'/Enemy for what the Germans designated *Schnellboot*, or S-Boot, meaning 'fast boat' fast attack craft of their Navy (the *Kriegsmarine*) during the Second World War. See: Wilson, Steve: 'Enemy Boats' at Military.com and 'E-Boats' at the British Military Powerboat Trust website.

137 We have not researched these two proud assertions. According to Tim Austin: 'She was entitled to have received it at some point, but under what 'surname' did she receive it? It should have been in the reign of King George VI. He was King until 6 February 1952. She would not have been personally decorated by the King. If still serving when it was issued – unlikely I think – she may have been decorated in uniform by a RAF Officer. But it is quite probable that she received it later 'through the post' with a certificate.'

138 The term is given as *Prominente, Prominenten* in Michael, Robert and Karin Doerr's *Nazi-Deutsch: an English lexicon of the language of the Third Reich*. Westport: Greenwood Press, 2002.

139 'The resistance offered volunteers personal fulfillment. "Never were we freer than under the occupation," wrote Jean-Paul Sartre when the war was over ... through their struggle, resisters lived in harmony with their principles.' —Olivier Wieviorka, p. 117.

140 While André knew that he was working with an SIS network he made the history palatable to the French authorities. 'I know that having worked directly for the Intelligence Service, we are the poor relations of la France Combattante,' wrote Suzanne Wilborts, explaining her rôle in Georges France. ('The only survivor higher placed than I in our group in Brittany is the secretary and adjunct of Turban, André Peulevey, Captain...') André's two-page letter of reference is also part of her SAINT MARTIN Suzanne épouse [Mrs.] Wilborts file, 16P 530840.

141 Hans Sommer served as SS Obersturmführer (First Lieutenant) in the Sicherheitsdienst/SIPO during World War II. Collections: Office of Strategic Services, Central Intelligence Agency collection, National Security Internet Archive (NSIA) https://archive.org/details/nationalsecurityarchive?query=Hans +Sommer. Cäsar Lindemann (1921-1944) was a German Wehrmacht soldier who was stationed in occupied France during World War II.

142 Compare to prisoner Vladek in *Maus*, described by Shores: 'Vladek was changed so much by his experiences that his older "real" self died.' (Shores, 'Animal Packs', pp. 12 and 13)

143 Official historians of the British secret services during the war, such as M.R. Foot, Brooks Richards, Keith Jeffery and F.H.Hinsley wrote

with official sanction and under official and self-censorship. William MacKenzie's government-commissioned work was not published for 50 years. Limitations of their encyclopedic works become increasingly evident as a new generation of researchers have gained access. Even first-hand accounts by people who worked in top echelons of the Services, such as Airey Neave, Leo Marks, Maurice Buckmaster and many agents could be profitably revisited in the archives. See also 'Good thrillers, but bad history: A review of published works on the Special Operations Executive's work in France during the Second World War' by Mark Seaman, in Robertson.

144 'In the last few years, the knowledge of the Free French [under de Gaulle-the FFL and BCRA/SOE-RF] and of the Fighting French [Forces Françaises Combattantes, the interior resistance to which Andre belonged] has greatly progressed to a science entirely due to the opening of the archives and the commitment of young researchers...' Bougeard, in Harismendy.

145 Vera Atkins in conversation with and as recorded by M.R.D. Foot, *Resistance*, xii. Atkins was Intelligence Officer of F Section SOE and seen by many as the power behind Colonel Buckmaster who ran that section's network. Background of SOE contributed by Paul McCue: 'SOE was created from Section D of SIS, EH Dept of the Foreign Office and MI(R) of the War Office.'

146 Hastings, *The Secret War*, p.xxv

147 _____, p.xv: 'Those who killed each other were the most conspicuous, but ... outcomes were also profoundly influenced by a host of men and women who never fired a shot ... covert operations assumed an unprecedented importance.'

148 Interview #24954 of André Scheinmann, USC Shoah Foundation.

149 Same document as above.

150 'The family environment, especially the influence of a close relative, seems to be a deciding factor in the trajectory of many...' – Erwan Le Gall in Harismendy, p. 36.

151 'Many of the finest intelligence officers of all nations were Jews. The Third Reich paid heavily for excluding them from its secret services ... The nations that gathered and used information best in the Second World War were those committed to intellectual honesty and the pursuit of truth.' Hastings, *Secret War*, p. 556.

152 'Resisters tend to be out of step with their time – usually in advance of it ... Originality necessarily came high on any list of characteristics desirable in resistance ... Much in resistance was out of the ordinary; most of its best hopes lay in being as different, as unusual as could be.' Foot, *Resistance*, p. 13 and 14.

153 Shores in McLaughlin, 'Animal Packs', pp. 8-9. 'Jews under these conditions lost their normal fixed relational structures and had to adapt to a situation

of high variability in the composition and structuring of their social groupings ... In *Maus*, for example, we see how family relations become less binding than opportunistic temporary alliances between strangers.'

154 *L'exercice de vivre*, p.80. Jean Cassou, another resistor, coined the term 'absurd refusal' (*un refus absurde*) to describe the apparent absurdity of pitting oneself against the overwhelming German presence.

155 'Fifth Column, Fourth Service, Third Task, Second Conflict: The Major Allied Powers and European Resistance' by Evan Mawdsley, in Cooke and Shepherd, Chapter 1.

156 Foot, *Resistance*, pp. 67-68. 'Part of the historic importance of resistance, unknown to resistors at the time and not likely to have been much appreciated by them if it had been known, lay in this: that it provided several secret services with a field in which their counter-espionage departments could exercise.' Foot quotes 'an expert' definition of counter-espionage by 'C. Felix' in *The Spy and His Masters* (Secker & Warburg 1963), pp. 129-130: 'generally interpreted to mean ... a defensive operation against the enemy's intelligence operations. Quite the contrary, CE is an offensive operation ... The ultimate goal is to penetrate the opposition's own secret operations apparatus.' André was offered by the Abwehr to do this after his arrest and said he would have considered it (and become a triple agent) but for their demand he betray his comrades to seal the deal.

157 Christian Bougeard gives figures as high as 17.2% participation in de Gaulle's Free French for a region that constituted barely more than 5% of the population of France, and calls Brittany the 'first-ranked region of France.' From subchapter heading 'L'apport des Bretons à la France libre: un bilan partiel' (The Breton contribution to Free France: a partial balance sheet), in Harismendy, pp. 24-28

158 Benjamin Cowburn, *No Cloak, No Dagger*, p. 110.

159 Bougeard, in Harismendy, as above.

160 These identities were of infants who had died after being named and whose parents were also deceased.

161 'The network was known to the SIS as "Groupe 31" (Its full code 23031: 23 was the SIS country code for Spain.) The agreement to form the network was made with the SIS head of station, Leonard Hamilton-Stokes and his deputy David "Togo" MacLaurin, at the Hotel Continental in San Sebastian, after initial discussions with the British Vice-Consul there, Harold Goodman. Paloc, the network leader for Spain, received "George/s" as an alias and Georges France was used as one of the BBC's code phrases.' Robert Urbain Jean Paloc died 3/3/45 in concentration camp Flossenbürg after having been moved from Auschwitz and Buchenwald. Thanks to Tim Austin for this history

On the memorial list at Flossenbürg he is still falsely mentioned to have been a double agent for the Germans. https://asso-flossenburg.com/deporte/

paloc-robert/ According to Pierre de Jaegher, in correspondence with the author on 8/8/2023, that Memorial Association's online slur ' is a result of the slander spread by Madame Louis. Paloc was 'turned' and worked for the Germans,yes, but he immediately asked Bartoli [de Mandres who later became the network registrar when Madame Louis was ousted] to let London know what had happened. He played a double game that eventually was discovered and resulted in his being sent to concentration camp along with his radio operator, Flé. His dedication should never have been questioned.'

162 Thanks to Tim Austin for sharing the files from the French National Archives at Vincennes on Agnès Turban, born Agnes Ingham on 16 February 1905 in Mytholmrayes, Yorkshire.

163 Today, called Arts et Metiers/Sciences et Technologies — https://artsetmetiers.fr/

164 Scholars such as Professor H. R. Kedward have pointed out that the Resistance in France evolved from being a call for return to an earlier form of nationhood to being an 'investment in a struggle which would not only liberate the territory of France but change its social and political landscape ... There was both diversity and unity, leadership from the top and from the grass roots, organization from outside France and from within, and a potent mixture of motivations, political and non-political, military and civilian, national and local.' In this mix he highlights the role of women, and of 'foreigners, refugees and immigrants' who were 'marginalized in subsequent accounts. Today we are in no doubt that the western Allies did intelligence better than their enemies, partly because they gave free rein to superb civilian talent.'

165 Quoted in Davies, p. xi and attributed to Deacon, Richard. *C: A Biography of Sir Maurice Oldfield, Head of MI6* (London: Futura, 1985), p. 189.

166 Foot, in *Resistance*, describes at length and in detail the various kinds of 'railway go-slow in France, part of the general railway go-slow in western Europe,' and 'it was the permanent attitude of non-cooperation and go-slow of the railway staff, even when they were not on strike, that made it impracticable to clear up enough of the mess for the trains to run.' —pp. 44-45.

167 Lt. Colonel S.H.C. Woolrych in 1943 to the Secret Training Schools' students expresses the tactics André employed long before he attended such a school, if he ever did: 'The purpose of the Organization to which you and I belong is Subversion ... The Boche is an emotional creature who cannot stand too much dislike. All sorts of extra work can be created for him by over-caution and especially excessive zeal ... If the thing is properly worked he need never suspect that he is being made a fool of.' — Cunningham, pp. 147-148.

168 Shores, 'Animal Packs', in McLaughlin.

169	Wilborts explained in detail after the war, for the purpose of registering her agents of these networks, in a letter of 10 April 1947, in the Reseau GF 31 Historique folder at Vincennes, from Suzanne Wilborts to Max Eidem: 'At the beginning of the occupation, brother Jean LEGEAY of PLEHEDEL and I created a Resistance group known under the name of Bande à Sidonie; a group responsible mostly to save and lodge English refugees, or who fell into our area. When we were able to repatriate by direct motorboat, we would give them all the intelligence that we were able to collect, assigning them to give it, when they arrived in England, to the appropriate services. I would be thanked via the BBC, with the phrase: "Special message for Sidonie." I even sent [intelligence] directly to General de Gaulle in a plush duckie (a child's toy.)'
170	Same document as above.
171	Marie-José Chombart de Lauwe, *Résister Toujours*, p.71.
172	Tim Austin believes this visit from London was an agent of MI9, SIS section I.S.9, for which see Graham Pitchfork: *Shot Down and on the Run: True Stories of RAF and Commonwealth Aircrews of WWII*. Bloomsbury, 2017. p.11
173	'De Gaulle's relationship with his secret intelligence and subversive services, the Bureau central de renseignements et d'action (BCRA) headed by Colonel Passy, as well as with British intelligence ... in the light of the now declassified archives of the Special Operations Executive (SOE) and the BCRA ... reveal that de Gaulle failed to interest himself seriously in secret intelligence or subversion before the arrival of Jean Moulin in London in October 1941. De Gaulle's subsequent relationship with the BCRA and British intelligence was defined by an obsessive need for political control, which only served to compromise the BCRA's otherwise successful collaboration with British intelligence.' See De La Marck.
174	Jean Pierre-Bloch, *Le temps d'y penser encore*. Paris: Simoën, 1977 and *Jusqu'au dernier jour*. Paris: Albin Michel, 1983. Quoted in Ruby's *F Section SOE*, p. 217
175	https://www.sis.gov.uk/SIS website: 'At the Secret Intelligence Service (SIS) – otherwise known as MI6 – our mission is clear. We work secretly overseas, developing foreign contacts and gathering intelligence that helps to make the UK safer and more prosperous. We help the UK identify and exploit opportunities as well as navigate risks to our national security, military effectiveness and economy. We work across the globe to counter terrorism, resolve international conflict and prevent the spread of nuclear and other non-conventional weapons. We are here to help protect the UK's people, economy and interests.' (5/31/2018) 'We are SIS – the UK's Secret Intelligence Service – also known as MI6. Our people work secretly around the world to make the UK safer and more prosperous. For over 100 years SIS has ensured the UK and our allies keep one step ahead of

our adversaries. We are creative and determined – using cutting-edge technology and espionage. We have three core aims: stopping terrorism, disrupting the activity of hostile states, and giving the UK a cyber advantage. We work closely with MI5, GCHQ, HM Armed Forces, law enforcement and a range of other international partners. Everything we do is tasked and authorised by senior government ministers and overseen by Parliament and independent judges. People who work for MI6 come from all walks of life, with different skills, interests and backgrounds. MI6 is an organisation where integrity, courage and respect are central to what we do. We encourage and admire difference. Many MI6 staff are based overseas while others work from our headquarters in Vauxhall, London. Although our work is secret, everything we do is legal and is underpinned by the values that define the UK. We're #secretlyjustlikeyou (1/23/2022). For discussion of effects of too much and too little sabotage in occupied territory, see Stafford: *Britain and European Resistance 1940-1945*.

176   André Scheinmann interview #24954, USC Shoah Foundation. Suzanne Wilborts wrote in her post-war narrative for the French government: 'At that time the two [French and British secret] services competed for information. I was sent simultaneously agents of de Gaulle and of the I.S. but as, at that time, the French services were very poorly organised, so that intelligence was transmitted only every two weeks, whereas with the I.S., a bombing raid requested for a certain location would be executed by the RAF within 48 hours, I only wanted to work with the I.S.'

177   André's last name was no doubt removed by SIS when the SOE files were made public – which SIS documents never are.

178   Thank you to Nigel Perrin for this and many elements of the KV 6/12 file at the National Archives at Kew, and to Nigel West for identifying the initials D/R as SIS Director of Requirements, RF as République Française (Free French) and FR as SIS indigenous French Section.

179   Madame Louis' proposal for Turban to receive the Legion of Honour after his death included five points, the fourth being: 'When the head of the Head of Network [herself] was arrested he sent an agent to London to take orders for the reorganisation of the network.' —16 October 1946. 'Mémoire de Proposition' for André's Legion of Honour characterizes him as the head of the organisation after he was hired as interpreter to the German authorities.

180   From Report of Captain André Peulevey. SIS and SOE agents rarely worked together in a network. The short-lived relationship of André and the Le Tacs was unusual. BCRA (headed by Passy from July 1 1940) was de Gaulle's Bureau Central de Renseignements at d'Action (Central office for intelligence and operations) which had started as SR in 1940 and then became BCRAM – Militaire – until February 1942). SOE's French sections comprised SOE – RF, initially run by Picquet-Wicks, the branch

of the SOE that liaised with the BCRA, and SOE – F section, its British operations in France, run by Maurice Buckmaster. Everything after the Churchill-de Gaulle accords of August 7 1940 was set up to be paid for by the British in exchange for information, but the British did not owe them intelligence under the deal. http://www.france-libre.net/accord-franco-britannique/ Thanks to Tim Austin for this resource.

181 Overcloud Archives at Kew. SOE memo of 6 September 1941 entitled OVERCLOUD: 'This is to confirm our telephone conversation of this morning, when it was arranged that the code name OVERCLOUD should be allotted to a team of two- one organiser and one W/T [radio] operator – proceeding by sea to the coast of Brittany during the October moon period. This team is formed from members of the F.F.L.' The mission set up what is called 'the first réseau action in the occupied zone' -see: http://www.ordredelaliberation.fr/fr_compagnon/601.htm

182 The cover of folder at Kew 'HS6/416 SOE FRANCE 127: OVERCLOUD – Organiser and W/T op. taken to Brittany by sea 14.10.41 to contact the Resistance and organise sabotage, propaganda, requirements etc. Dates: September 1941 to January 1942'. Bozel was the alias of Jean Richemond (also spelled Richemont in Passy.)

183 Major General Sir Colin McVean Gubbins KCMG, DSO, MC Is identified by the Imperial War Museum in its description of his collection as SOE Director of Operations 1940-1942, Deputy for Operations 1942-1943 and Head of SOE 1943-1945. https://www.iwm.org.uk/collections/item/object/1030021611   Accessed 7/14/2023.

184 Document courtesy of Nigel Perrin, from KV 6/12 file from the British National Archives at Kew.

185 See Tillet. http://www.plan-sussex-1944.net/francais/pdf/infiltrations_en_france.pdf Spreadheet continually updated; look for dates 6/1/1942 and 1/2/1942 for André's passage to the UK and return.

186 The author wrote to the SIS in 2023 via the contact form on their website in preparation for this book, asking them to release their files on André. To date, no answer has been received. She also corresponded with Lady Margaret Thatcher and received from Mark Worthington and Miranda Granger of her private office considerate replies showing others had been involved in researching the request, but no information was sent.

187 See Campo, pp. 194-195. Thanks very much to Tim Austin for bringing this resource.

188 April 5, 2018 in email correspondence with Olivier Wieviorka. Also, in this context, Churchill's conception of a 'detonator strategy,' in which a large number of well-prepared 'patriots' would support a relatively small British force. —Mawsdley in Cooke & Shepherd, pp.15-16.

189 Pollack, p. 54.

190 London's rivalry with de Gaulle in supporting their own resistance networks was designed 'to counterbalance, from France, the influence of the Gaullist Resistance, which accounted for a large share of the general's legitimacy,' historian Thomas Rabino confirms.' —Olivier Wieviorka, p. 137 quoting Rabino, *Le Réseau Carte: Histoire d'un réseau de la Résistance anti-allemand, antigaulliste, anti-communiste et anticollaborationiste*. Perrin, 2008.

191 Passy couldn't possibly be referring to Joël Le Tac, who was sent on two sabotage missions in the first part of 1941 – 'Savanna', in March, and 'Josephine B', in May.

192 Passy, *Souvenirs: 2ième Bureau*, p. 212

193 Noguères, in conclusion of the first volume of *Histoire de la Resistance en France*: 'all the resistors, to tell the truth, was not a lot of people.' —pp. 498-499.

194 Bougeard, in Harismendy: 'The precocity of the Bretons' engagement in the FFL [Forces Françaises Libres/Free French] is remarkable, since they were 30.1 per cent of those who signed up in the first wave, in 1940, and again in the second great wave, in 1943.' p 27. Bougeard brings out the area's muted response to the sinking of the French fleet at Mers-el-Kebir by the British, despite the loss of numerous Breton sailors; the massive public attendance at funerals of downed British aviators such as the 2,000 in attendance at Lanester on 30 December 1940; and that: 'Throughout the war, the flower-adorned tombs of British aviators became places for patriotic meditation.' —pp. 16-18.

195 *ibid.* 'In the movie theaters, when the newsreels were played, shouts and whistles break out when Hitler comes on the screen ... At Brest and in Lorient, in October 1940, the Germans complained about these reactions, and in Rennes, the cinemas were closed as early as from July 8 to 11, for the same reason...' See also Olivier Wieviorka, pp. 13 and 14, for the walking demonstrations André describes.

196 'Denise is keeping the accounts for the network [Jade-Fitzroy] which is growing by leaps and bounds and spending money. But Greene wants an accounting. And when she was arrested, the books were discovered and disasters befell our agents. ... The crime remains. It's not a career that requires one keep records.' —Chatenay, p. 211

197 Chatenay, p. 227.

198 Chatenay, p. 309

199 'Character, not class, made people into resistors, or collaborators, or would-be neutrals...' —Foot. *Resistance*, p. 11.

200 Passy, *Souvenirs; 2e Bureau Londres*, p. 232

201 André could speak volumes in one word, or expand as much as he felt the person listening could bear. His 1999 or so conversation with my father, who was serving in Patton's Third Army and moving toward the Rhine

while André was being moved to Dachau, gave me an enthralling and dazzling display of how much more he could share than he ever indulged in with someone with less experience, whom he wanted to meet on their level of understanding. Beside sharing their passion for Churchill (for my father that included Churchill jokes – I never heard any from André...) these seemingly pacific and family-oriented businessmen relished the drama of history that brought them so close together in military victory.

202 As André explained to the boy, Britain was alone in the war before the Allies entered the war at her side – Russia when Germany broke the non-aggression pact with Russia and the US after the attack at Pearl Harbor. 'London at that time was the heart of the World.' (Cowburn, p. 143.)

203 KV 6/12 courtesy of Nigel Perrin. According to Richards, pp. 97-99, Gerry Holdsworth came out of Section D of the SIS. In the summer of 1940 he was asked 'to create better-organised facilities to enable SOE to conduct its own sea-transport operations to Brittany, as he had recommended.' This included setting up a base on the Helford river, that opens into Falmouth Bay, and taking over the 'Ridifarne' retreat to serve as a shore base for operations. Thanks to Nick Fox for this further about the Helford Flotilla: This was set up in November 1940 by RN Lt Gerry Holdsworth (at Helston, Cornwall) to mount clandestine operations to Brittany for SOE and, I believe, for SIS too. He requisitioned two refugee vessels and formed a crew of twelve. Later, the 'Inshore Patrol Flotilla' as it was called had eight Breton fishing vessels and two larger trawlers, working from a base-ship 'SUNBEAM II', a square-topsail auxiliary schooner. Clandestine sea communications with Brittany carried on until autumn 1943 when owing to bad weather and arrests of contacts in France, the sea line closed down. The Heaux light on the West was at the Ile de Bréhat, where Suzanne Wilborts started the network, La Bande à Sidonie; the Ile Vierge was East of the Ile Guénoc into the Channel off St. Pabu, the Le Tac home from where André left for England.

204 The British sent over VAN 1 air drop to Overcloud on December 13th: 2 tents, 6 sleeping bags, 2-7-seater rubber collapsible boats with paddles and pumps, camouflaged, 2 water buckets, 8 ground sheets, 16 enamel plates, 8 knives, forks, spoons, enamel mugs, meth.cookers, matches, soap, dish cloths, tin opener, 6 cooking sets; and food including tinned meat, tinned bacon, sardines, baked beans, milk, jam, tea, sugar, coffee, cocoa, biscuits ... but when Joël made requests, the BCRA harshly reprimanded him for treating them as 'simply providers of merchandise.' Yet, when he was in London, six weeks later, he and his bosses asked the British for miniature cameras with film, a microphone with battery and wires, and a pistol silencer, RAF maps of the region, RAF flares, and a portable radio ... Yves Le Cor (alias for Yves Le Tac) on the other hand requested to bring back with him a radio, a stenotype machine and 500 stencils, and to be sent as soon as possible two typewriters, an electric Ronéo (mimeograph), as much

white paper as possible, more stencils, and a second stenotype machine. (Overcloud files at Kew)

205   Joël received the Ordre de la Libération, the highest honor of the Resistance, while Yves Le Tac received, like André, the Médaille de la Résistance with rosette. See all the family's awards at: https://www.ordredelaliberation.fr/fr/medailles?fulltext=le+tac&items_per_page=10&sort_bef_combine=nom_ASC#resultats-medailles

206   Renaud reports Joël's claim to have received 250,000 francs for his return in February,1942 (probably from the Free French.) p.124

207   'Alien Personnel in UK Forces' per National Archives file HO213/55 totaled 39,183 in Dec.1944/March 1945, of which 196 French nationals, 3,240 Germans and 1,831 Austrians.

208   See Cole.

209   Mady speaking in 'I am André; A story of Triumph' Suzanne Richard documentary for New Bedford Cable access, shown 4/19/01.

210   Holdsworth had already broached this subject more fully in an October 18 message to Captain Piquet-Wicks (copies to Admiral Holbrook and Mr. Sporborg) after the arrival of the Le Tacs in London on their first SOE-assisted mission Overcloud.

211   See Cunningham, various chapters and pages.

212   Cunningham, p. 95: 'Paul Dehn, the propaganda expert, is also known to have taught codes, ciphers and secret inks.'

213   See Max Hastings: At Beaulieu, 'Gubbins and the senior staff had already decided to prepare a number of self-contained packages or modules, each of variable length and complexity, ... to meet whatever demands would be made ... for superficial or in-depth training of agents of various sorts. There were at least seven modules, Agent Management, Enemy Organizations and their functions, Communications and Codes, Security and Resistance to Interrogation, Criminal Skills including Railway Sabotage, Propaganda Warfare and Black Propaganda, and Fieldcraft and Living off the Land, i.e.survival training.' Cunningham: 'The curriculum included such subjects as murder, arson, train-wrecking and other forms of sabotage, robbery, safe-cracking and key making, burglary and housebreaking, forgery and "black" propaganda, blackmail, false pretenses and "casing" premises ... Indeed, the German counter-espionage agencies called Beaulieu "the Gangster School." ' The first Beaulieu instructor in criminal skills had been released from jail for civilian service to teach his specialties of burglary and safebreaking —pp. 63-64 and 72.

214   Hastings, *Secret War*, p.264. 'SOE – "the racket" as many of its staff irreverently referred to it ... established training schools in sabotage at Stevenage, black propaganda at Watford, fieldcraft at Loch Ailort and guerilla techniques at Arisaig.'

215   Email correspondence from Bernard O'Connor, 1/23/2023/ SIS 'students' attended SOE training schools. Whether they joined a group with non-SIS students is not known. If they did, they would have been given a fake name, have worn army fatigues and normal PE kits etc and almost certainly not have talked much about their background with other students. Brickendonbury Manor was purchased before the war started as an SIS training school and was used for that purpose until SOE was formed in July 40 which then took over the training. Brickendonbury became a specialised industrial sabotage training school when other properties were requisitioned … So – by Jan 42 there were many other STS where C/SIS agents received their training…

216   Email correspondence from Nick Fox, 1/23/2023

217   SIS training schools, about which not much is known, and its Section D (Special Ops) were transferred to the Special Operations Executive / SOE that was formed at Churchill's command at the beginning of the war. SIS' own website says 'Until the middle of the war, training of SIS officers and agents had, to say the least, been haphazard. But, as the Service continued to expand at a rapid rate, the need for more systematic training was recognised.' https://www.sis.gov.uk/ and https://www.sis.gov.uk/our-history.html #secretlyjustlikeyou

218   HS 6/416 National Archives, Kew.

219   On the other hand, a 'MOST SECRET' memo of the RAF on the Training of Special Agents at Kew, dated 15 January 1942 concerns 'the training of the Specials, which … is of a somewhat sketchy character. Quite frequently the men arrive at Ringway and have to get in from two to five descents within a very short space of time … when men have made six or seven descents … their chances of making safe landings is considerably greater than after they have made two or three…'

220   Passy, *Souvenirs: 2e Bureau Londres*, pp.138-141

221   'I unearthed only recently from an SOE file (HS7/51 UK National Archives) – that SOE processed **all** SIS personnel requiring parachute training at their (SOE's) STS 51 (Dunham House and Fulshaw Hall) establishments in Cheshire … trainees then came under No. 1 Parachute Training School at RAF Ringway – jumps from tethered balloons were made in Tatton Park, Cheshire and then drops from aircraft were made into Tatton Park from Whitley aircraft flying from Ringway (now Manchester International Airport).' Thank you to Paul McCue in correspondence, 4/27/2024.

222   André Scheinmann interview #24954, USC Shoah Foundation.

223   For SOE training designed by SIS instructors, see for example Sheppard.

224   Bailey, p. 45.

225   Renaud, p. 124.

226 André Scheinmann interview #24954, USC Shoah Foundation.

227 Bailey, p. 35.

228 André Scheinmann interview #24954, USC Shoah Foundation.

229 'By the Provisional Government of the French Republic, Done in Paris, March 12, 1946 Signed by de Gaulle.'

230 However, the woman who was known to André as the head of Network 31, Marguerite Görge alias 'Madame Louis' had all their most important agent names, regional and district heads, with them upon their arrest when Gontier was followed and they were seized in October, 1941. The Germans must have been watching them all since then although they were arrested three months later.

231 Hastings, *The Secret War*, p.xxvii.

232 Pollack, whose work was conducted with the support of the French Army Ministry, asserts the historic facts he has derived from the opening of the French archives, p.11.

233 As Monique Le Tac, Yves' daughter has noted, André's private archive 'will certainly serve as a reference and documentation of the Résistance in Brittany.' Correspondence with the author, 2/14/2023.

234 Pollack also questions both the French and British memory of women agents. He claims that female Communist agents are 'ignored' by the French and that the British focus on female agents of the SOE is 'evidence of the persistence, up to our day, of a gendered perception of the norms of war.' —pp. 420-421.

235 See Rémy (Gilbert Renault) 'leader of the Confrèrerie Notre-Dame -ND/Castille network', *Mémoires d'un Agent Secret*, pp. 17-19.

236 Letter from André' at Le Vésinet to Monsieur le Colonel Josset, General representative of the FFCI on 16 June, 1947. 17P185 file at Vincennes.

237 Chombart de Lauwe, *Résister toujours*, pp. 71,73, 219-220. His list of Overcloud agents attached was signed André Peulevey under the heading: Chef de réseau (Network head.)

238 'They were of every class, category and size,' writes Picquet-Wicks about the Free French who joined the S.O.E. 'Frequently they were ... the little people of France. Less frequently was the élite – by birth- to be found, although when such elements did materialize their heroism was of the highest.' —p.21
'Another member of the Overcloud network was the Baroness Marie Anne Geneviève d'Affry de la Monnoye, widow of Charles de Saint-Laurent 'died 12 November 1944 at Ravensbück, at the age of 49. [after imprisonment at Aachen, Gelsenkirchen, Breslau.] She was the mother of ten children.' —Le Belzic, p 51.

239 Honoré d'Estienne D'Orves' wife was Éliane De Lorgeril, whose brother was Charles Hubert De Lorgeril, the husband of this 'Madame la Comtesse.'

The countess' full name was Odette Marie Jeanne Guilhe La Combe De Villers, born Feb 4, 1904 in Rennes, died July 19, 1999. She was the recipient of the Croix de Guerre 1939-1945. Glimpse the castle at: https://www.lorgeril.wine/en/home/

240 She writes her name as Marie-Christiane but the government historical sites online today spell it Marie-Christianne.

241 Her voluminous file 21 P 679 103 under the name Marie Albertine Suraud at the Service Historique de la Défense at Caen includes testimony that André Peulevez [sic] was implicated in the same case, for which she was arrested 10 November 1941, that her status as Déportée Internée Résistante was established by the statement *cause à effet* by Mr. Peulevey, network registrar, that the German tribunal in Berlin condemned her to death on 28 September 1943 for espionage, high treason, and aid to the enemy that she was held at the Prison of La Santé in cell 101 from 10 November 1941 and then at the prison of Fresnes in cell 333 from 9 October 1942 to 8 January 1943; that she was kept in solitary for 18 months.

242 Le Belzic writes that 'Madame Seidel never appreared at the trial, as she spent the entire span of her internment [in France] at the Hôpital de la Pitié, she was expecting a child.' 'Born in 1912, shopkeeper's assistant, "résistante de la première heure" (Resistor from hour one) [Seidel's] sentence was commuted to forced labor. She was deported to Ravensbrück.' —pp. 8, 9, 25,27.

243 Her birth certificate as Marie-Albertine Caroline Suraud adds that she married Helmuth Max Paul Seidel in 1932 and was divorced in 1946.

244 https://www.ordredelaliberation.fr/fr/historique.

245 Joël received it, but not Yves. https://www.tracesofwar.com/persons/96875/Le-Tac-Jo%C3%ABl.htm. Accessed 8/28/2023.

246 That document was signed by Madame Louis on October 24, 1946. It is unclear why or who indicated in a handwritten note where his entry is crossed out that Andre 'passed to Castile CND networks' [Confrèrerie Notre Dame.] André was not a member of CND/Castile although Suzanne Wilborts went on to be, after André was arrested.

247 Pierre Tillet has mined the British National Archives for his encyclopedic contribution to the history.

248 Pollack asserts the 'amicale' – cohort group of former-agents would choose the Liquidator —p. 44. Research for this book indicates that some of the groups were still too amorphous with many agents murdered, not found, or just returning from the concentration camps and others scrambling with the necessities of life to be able to regroup so quickly, if at all. As they formed in time they could take action, such as the Georges-France agents did when they dismissed Madame Louis. Cdts. Schmidt and Laverdet-LeGall assigned André to be Liquidator, with Joël's endorsement or recommendation as the record shows.

249 Chatenay, p.271.

250 Chatenay's SIS network was Jade-Fitzroy for whom Pierre Hentic organised air and sea operations between Brittany and England. Hentic is in André's little black book, on the M page with Maho (Hentic's alias) crossed out. Recent French tributes to André (such as by Le Souvenir Français and Wiki-Rennes) also include André in the Turquoise-Jézequel network, though this author has found no documentation of that connection.

251 Chatenay, p.271.

252 'After the war, when the Nation wanted to recognize the services rendered by the Resistors, legislators found themselves in a situation without precedent and with no jurisprudence. They therefore had to build in an atmosphere deprived of serenity, from scratch, a new legal structure that as a result is sometimes lacking and even incoherent.' —Centre Historique des Archives https://www.aeri-resistance.com/html/bureauresist.htm

253 An example of this is how, headed by a man who had worked for MI6 in the decade before the outbreak of war, the Le Dantec group, that worked with André, was first registered by Germaine Tillion into the Musée de l'Homme group, then its Breton section that worked with La Bande à Sidonie and Turban into Georges-France, while the members of its Paris organization stayed registered with the MdI'H. Then a Colonel Legrand tried to get the FFC to separate le Dantec's group from G-F 'when he observed how Madame Louis worked. But by then it was too late.' -Thanks to Pierre de Jaegher for this account. Many Le Dantec group members and documentation in André's personal archive.

254 Correspondence from Tim Austin.

255 Laverdet-Legall's attestation for André's action in the Resistance from October, 1940.

256 Pierre de Jaegher is adamant that she made up this first network, Frise, out of whole cloth and that it never existed. She was however working in the Georges-France network, at least collecting and helping to courier the information to London (de Jaegher says through Palloc) from 1940 on.

257 Service Historique de la Défence, Vincennes, folder GR 17 P 131 for the German trial of Madame Louis.

258 It has been suggested that the André's trial documents were sent to Germany for his final disposition as an NN, where they could still be found or may have been destroyed under Allied bombing.

259 Madame Seidel, who documented for André the network she belonged to headed by Father Jean Baptiste Legeay, of Nantes, who was decapitated by the Nazis in Cologne in 1943, wrote to André on 30 May, 1946: 'I still have nothing from the British but that would help me a lot as funds are, as for everyone, really going down.'

260 Chatenay writes of Greene in Paris in the fall of 1945, while he was working as Liquidateur (registrar) of Jade-Fitzroy: 'I am not surprised to find him to be a pitiless accountant who doesn't want to pay, nor even to reimburse, those who worked and spent money for the network.' —p.260

261 Semprún's family fled Spain for France during the Spanish Civil War and was expropriated when the Fascists were victorious.

262 Opus. cit above, p.112

263 The French who were subsidised by Britain show some necessity to underline their patriotism. For example, André Carduner about his networks: 'Ils étaient "SIDONIE " Ils étaient "SHELBURN" Ils étaient la FRANCE.'

264 Settlement sheet he kept of his post-war compensation from the Caserne de Reuilly shows André was awarded '57,500 francs for 4 years and 15,721 for residential indemnity, taxes withheld'. With the 1,000 francs given to him on return from Dachau, and an advance received from the D.G.E.R. deducted, total compensation [finally] awarded in February, 1948 came to 63, 732 francs for back pay from February 5, 1942 to April 29, 1945.

265 Renaud quotes Joël Le Tac on his return from the camps: 'He [Molyneux] loaned me a suit. After three days, as I was hanging in, he invited me to a dinner he was hosting at the Lido. I found myself seated at Marlene Dietrich's table. I had three years' back pay, so I took advantage ... I had spent it all in two months...' That year 1945 was also when Joël Le Tac entered into the 'aristocracy' of the Resistance, 'l'ordre de la Libération,' with the rank of 'Compagnon.' —p. 137. In the summer of 1941 for his two first BCRA sabotage missions in France, Savanna and Josephine B, Joël had already been awarded the 'Military Medal with the profile of George VI on on side and the phrase "For Bravery on the field" on the other, by General Gubbins.' —p.93.

266 Renaud, p.135

267 They were both agents rated 'P2': 'agent qui basculé dans la clandestinité ou tout autre agent qui était P0/P1 qui est arrêté, fusillé etc. Cela correspond à l'engagement total.' ('Agent who crossed over into clandestine life or all other P0/P1 [part-time agent] who was arrested, shot, etc. It meant total engagement.') —Yves Chanier, webmaster for the site http://cnd-castille.org/

268 Bureau Central de Renseignments et Action. André is listed in the 1953 commemorative volume, *Livre d'Or de l'Amicale Action.*

269 Chombart de Lauwe, *Résister Toujurs*, p. 220.

270 André's number 041.9064 is the number that appears on the Attestation of 25 August 1945 certifying that 'Captain André Peulevey, is Officer Chargé de Mission de 1ère Classe, Récupérateur for Région "M" of Réseau Overcloud, in the service of "France Combattante." This Officer is,

moreover, a repatriated Political deportee, whose ID card No is 041.9064." [Signed by] Commandant Laverdet Legal, Chef des Services Récupération-Action de la "France Combattante."'

271 The author does not know how the selection was made to discard documents from his archive before they were shared with her.

272 Excellent biography of Laverdet LeGall, from his unpublished autobiography, at Le Maitron, Dictionnaire Biographique Mouvement Ouvrier Mouvement Social: https://maitron.fr/spip.php?article233747

273 *Journal Officiel de la République Française*: No 158./dimanche 7 juillet, 1946, p. 1438, announcements for 'ordre national de la Légion d'honneur "par décret du 12 mars, 1946": Peulevey (André) Capitaine; No. 276/jeudi 22 novembre 1951, p. 15777: 'Au grade de chevalier: Au lieu de "Peulevey (André Maurice), capitaine" Lire: "Scheinmann (Joseph) alias Peulevey (André Maurice), capitaine."' [With the rank of Knight: Instead of "Peulevey (André Maurice), capitaine" Read: "Scheinmann (Joseph) alias Peulevey (André Maurice), capitaine."]

274 Ibid., No. 279/dimanche, 25 novembre, 1951, p. 11707 'portant naturalisation, réintégration ... de la nationalité française' for 'Scheinmann, *née* (born) Dyment (Claire) and Scheinmann, Joseph'. His elevation to the rank of Officer of the Legion of Honour was published in the promotions section of the Journal Officiel of 18 July 1961.

275 Thanks to Steven Kippax for this valuable document and insight.

276 Note the disrespectful and grudging depiction and innacurate real name of André in Joël Le Tac's biography, although he bragged about how he met André, 'the 'boss' of the Rennes railroad group, the man in charge of FER 1': 'In reality, Peulevey is the name under which he works. In reality, his name is Schweiderman. He's a strange boy' [born three years before Joël.] Renaud, p. 110.

277 Annie Lacroix-Riz' term.

278 Madeleine Angèle M. Téry (1901-1990) was married to Norbert Haouisée de la Villeaucomte.

279 'Reclaiming identity: efforts to overcome the "Malaise of Memory" at the Natzweiler concentration camp' accounts for many of its identified Jewish pillars of the community and everyday heroes. Presentation by Diana Mara Henry at 'Memorialization Unmoored – The Virtualization of Material Mediums of Social Memory, A Yale Genocide Studies Program/Consortium for Reflections on the Aftermath of War and Genocide Symposium, March 8-9, 2018.'

280 Barcellini is Contrôleur Général des Armées et Président Général du Souvenir Français (Inspector General of the Armies and President of The French Memory). https://le-souvenir-francais.fr/notre-mission/ 'The malaise of memory ' is how Serge Barcellini described marginalization of

the Jews at Natzweiler. Separate and much smaller than the CERD, the museum of the camp Natzweiler itself is located in one of its remaining barracks and includes a display about its NN prisoners including a photo of Polish expat to France, Jewish bundist Aaron Skrobek, AKA David Kutner, along with one of Joël Le Tac.

281   Chombart de Lauwe, *Toute une vie de résistance*, p. 181

282   Historian Denis Peschanski's *bouleversement mémoriel*. — https://le-souvenir-francais.fr/loeil-de-lhistorien-denis-peschanski/

283   *Juifs, communistes, étrangers, immigrés, militants et combattants, ils étaient le visage même de ce que le projet nazi et celui de la collaboration voulaient détruire.-* ('Jews, communists, foreigners, immigrants, activists and fighters, they were the very face of what the Nazi project and the collaboration wanted to destroy.') 2/20/2024 Antoine Grande, https://www.linkedin.com/in/antoine-grande-8971a2106/

284   *Étrangers* can be translated as aliens, foreigners, or strangers...

285   Denis Peschanski writing for Le Souvenir Français claims for example that 'the trajectory of Missak Manouchian demonstrates the universalist dimension of all the combattants' involvement, in a convergence of identity around the values inherited from the French Revolution and the Enlightenment.' (... *l'itinéraire de Missak Manouchian permet de montrer la dimension universaliste de l'engagement de tous ces combattants, convergence identitaire autour des valeurs héritées de la Révolution française et du siècle des Lumières.*) Link cited above.

286   '... within Europe some thoughtful people began to reconsider the wisdom of the policies of entire national independence that most European states had pursued since 1848 ... The governments in exile in London, Belgium and the Netherlands agreed, in principle, during the war, on the Benelux customs union; of which some of the key principles were hammered out in the maquis of the Ardennes. From this grew eventually the European Economic Community; with all that implies for the future of the continent and the world.' Foot, *Resistance*, p.77; his sources given there.

287   The commanding Officer of the MGB 314 that took André to London and back, Dunstan Michael Carr Curtis, became a delegate to the European Parliament, spending 25 years there as an influential promoter of a European identity for Great Britain.

288   Dirk Bogarde, who served in the British army at the liberation of Bergen-Belsen concentration camp wrote in the *Daily Telegraph*, 26 November 1988: 'I just leave the elevator if a German enters.' Prince Yuri Galitzine, who wrote the report for SHAEF when Natzweiler was first discovered, wrote: 'For many years, I just could not bear to be in the same room with a German and it made me absolutely shake.' Kemp, p.97

289   Semprún, pp. 115, 119, 120.

290　André's first leave, from the Service de Santé/Health Department D.G.E.R. was signed on June 13, 1945 – certifying that 'his state of health requires a three-month rest period in the country.' In October 5, 1945 the Corps du Service D.G.E.R. granted him 30 days 'permission de convalescence' to go to Roscoff (in Brittany) and 'authorized to dress in civilian clothing.' On 26 February 1946 the internist Plarget at the Hôpital Tenon in Paris stated that his health required a three month stay in Switzerland, which received a favorable ruling from the Doctors' Council the same day and a stamp from the Prefecture of the Police. On June 21, 1946 the Centre de Libération du Département de la Seine Rive Gauche granted Officier 'permission libérale' with authorization to wear civilian clothing from June 22 to July 21. On August 7, 1946, he was assigned 3 months by the Commission Interministérielle de l'organe central F.F.L. (Forces Françaises Libres)

291　In a 'definitive' decision for 101% disability André's first 'infirmity' is listed as 'Syndrome de Targowla': 'Varieties of traumatic war neuroses, with delayed emotional paroxysmal hypermnesia (unusual power or enhancement of memory, typically under abnormal conditions such as trauma) suffered by former prisoners of nazi camps.' Considered to be the most widespread consequence of survivors of the death camps, the most typical, and the most enduring. Psychasthenia (multiple symptoms including fear, anxiety, obsessions, phobias, depersonalization, and physical symptoms such as tics, headaches, and fatigue). phobias, nightmare are consequences observed years after return to freedom...' https://www.medecine-des-arts.com/fr/article/targowla-syndrome-de.php See also: Półtawska.

292　Letter and report in André's personal archive.

293　Semprún, p.30.

294　Jews constituted 20% (more if including secret Jews and those who died in the gas chamber) of the population of Natzweiler.

295　See Shores on the creativity and originality of the forger, like André: http://piratesandrevolutionaries.blogspot.com/2012/10/whos-real-paul-masson-personal-non.html

296　The definition for these is given at https://www.aeri-resistance.com/html/bureauresist.htm , including for the FFL as being 'elements constituting the regular army of Free France' and numbering 52,000 men and women.

297　In the book *Ils furent des hommes:Essais et documents* by Conrad L. Flavian (Paris: Nouv. éd. latines, 1948) the exact same handwriting message appears without the decorations on André's, as if a personal message.

298　André mentions his debt to Henri Rosencher in the Yoken interview: 'He was one of the oldest prisoners and he was a doctor. And he immediately warned everybody not to eat! Because temptation was tremendous! The Americans came, there was food! So he told people, he took away food from them! And also I listened to him and I didn't eat much. Because you had to go very slowly for 2, 3 weeks, to gain gradually, gradually, get used to food again. Because more people died the first week than the week before. The one week after liberation, more people died than in the last week in camp! ... I did it very gradually. I disciplined myself. And from then on, I never ate much. I can discipline myself very well. I don't eat much. I never do much ... But even things I like! You know, when you like something, you tend to eat more! I stop! I like, say I like cheese cake, I could eat 2 or 3 slices, I eat only one slice.

299 Michel, p. 131.

300 Miannay, pp. 174-175.

301 The printing of 'Brittany in Chains' was facilitated by Dr. Lavoué, to whom André was shackled on their transport to Natzweiler in the first French *Nacht und Nebel* convoy. That irony that must not have escaped either of them or of the other members of their networks from Brittany, a baker's dozen of whom were in that transport of 56 men.

302 Renaud, p.125.

303 This was so effective that the Germans sent an infiltrator, Van Ackere, to follow up in England and give fake accounts about the network as if it were still operating. In an MI 5 report of their interrogation at the Royal Patriotic School where unknown foreigners were kept on arrival in Great Britain (from the Van Ackere folder at the National Archives at Kew) MI 5 identifies André as 'An agent from C. whose code name was TURQUOISE also traveled with the two brothers.' ('C' was the code for the Director of Secret Intelligence Service, who during World War II was Major General Sir Stewart Graham Menzies.). '... we were informed by a Dept at M.I.6 under Commander _____[Dunderdale blanked out] that this party had been taken by the enemy.'

304 HS 9/834/3 De Kergolay (closed up to 2022) See Miannay for the chronology of his betrayal, release by the Germans, escape to Spain in 1943, imprisonment after the liberation of France and trial that ended with his sentencing in 1946 to twenty years of forced labor, until the intervention of Yeo-Thomas led to his liberation in 1948 —pp. 160-161.

305 She was subsequently focused by the Abwehr on the betrayal of the Interallié network – the 'Lucas affair' – her most notorious contribution to betraying the Resistance. Victoire was arrested, as an agent of Interallié, in mid-November and offered her services (and her body) to the Germans the next day.

306 'SECRET- Extract from the 'VICTOIRE SUMMARY March 1944'. Original in P.F.64216 CARRE Vol. 6 Summary, pp.36.45.112 —National Archives at Kew.

307 Also: Annex of Archives nationales 72/AJ/82 (dossier n°3, pièce 10) a list by names of traitors arrested by the Secret Services of Vichy.

308   According to Pollack, Madeleine Téry's villa was occupied by officers of the Abwehr, among whom Commander Kaltenhauser of the Abwehr. She apparently traded the betrayal of Gontier for the Abwehr's release of her son-in-law from imprisonment in Germany. He was returned to France and freedom in January 1942 —p. 169

309   See Miannay for Humbert and hundreds of other 'confidence men' – infiltrators who volunteered and were hired outright – or resistors that were arrested and turned.

310   https://fusilles-40-44.maitron.fr/spip.php?article168887 provides a biography of Le Dantec.

311   Correspondence in André's archive. On the list of members of the Groupe Le Dantec are named as traitors, beside Humbert: Gabriel Grec, Herton, Knoblaugh, Planat, Tessuas (as best the handwriting can be deciphered.)

312   Pollack, p.324.

313   Turban succumbed in the hell of Natzweiler, sometime between April and May 10, 1944 (dates on different documents differ.)

314   65,000 Resistants received this honor, per *Le Souvenir Français Lettre No. 83*, Mai 2023. The honor was created by a decree by de Gaulle in London on 9 February 1943 and the higher award of the Médaille de la Résistance with rosette on 2 November 1945 for 'those notable for the importance of their service or the gravity of the risks run.' Only 4572 were awarded the rosette and officer designation. Thanks to Pierre Tillet for this background, see also: https://www.ordredelaliberation.fr/fr/en-savoir-plus-sur-la-medaille-de-la-resistance-francaise

315   The 2023 'official version' of this document from Service Historique de la Défense, Centre des archives du personnel militaire, DEVA/BRA 'section des fonds Citations', Caserne Bernadotte, 64023 Pau CEDEX (obtained courtesy of Fabrice Bourrée) does not include the mention of signatures by de Gaulle and Diethelm, but instead says it was signed by Gouin. On the other hand, in the modern 'official' record, the elevation of Joseph Scheinmann 'Captain of Forces Françaises Combattantes – Réseaux "Georges France and Overcloud" to the Rank of Officer, War of 1939-1945, Déportés-Résistants' are noted to have been signed by Charles de Gaulle on 13 July 1961, but changes him from Captain, FFC to Captain DGER…

316   These two awards appeared in the *Journal Officiel de la République Française* No. 158, 7 July 1946. These documents from André's archive are stamped as a 'copie conforme'/certified copy of the originals. Fabrice Bourrée has pointed out that there is an error in this official, signed, copy, and that the award was for 'Etoile Vermeil' -vermillion star – which is also noted on a government document when André's records were updated in the 1950's.

317   https://www.ordredelaliberation.fr/fr/medailles?nom=peulevey&prenom=&alias=&lieu_naissance=&departement_ce=All&pays=&annee=All&mois=All&posthume=

All&sex=All&items_per_page=10&sort_bef_combine=nom_ASC&type_recherche=1#resultats-medailles. Peulevey to be updated to Scheinmann, per assurances from its director.

318   Documents held at The National Archives, Kew, Richmond, TW9 4DU are quoted in this book with acknowledgement that these archival references are Crown copyright, are being re-used under the terms of the Open Government Licence.

319   During the war, the men of the SIS organization Naval Intelligence Directive – C (Clandestine) had been put in uniform with the RNVR, Royal Naval Volunteer Reserves.- Conversation with Roderick De Normann, February 2023.

320   D/RF [Sir James Hutchison] to D/CE.1 [Unidentified officer in Clandestine Communications] Copy to AD/S [Harry Sporburg]. (Annotations of initials courtesy of Nigel West.) It seems that Yves was a British Agent before his involvement with the BCRA. The SIS documents are not available to explore. Continuing in Intelligence and Special ops for De Gaulle in Algeria, Yves would not have wanted to publicize that.

321   'NID(c) was that part of SIS (headed by Frank Slocum, who was seconded to them from the Admiralty) which organised the small boat flotillas that serviced the SIS (later somewhat reluctantly shared with SOE and MI9) that both landed and picked up agents and escapees. They were not part of the Naval Intelligence Division but naturally liaised with them.'(SOE FOrum discussion 1 May 2024.)

322   National Archives, Kew – KV 6/12 folder

323   P. 7 of the Trial. Vichy's Deuxième Bureau, amazingly, continued counter-espionage against the Germans during the first two years of France's puppet government. Officials of the Vichy Deuxième Bureau, headed by Colonel Rivet, 'transmitted the name of enemy agents to law enforcement which arrested them and turned them over to military courts. Nearly 800 of these V-Mann (as the Abwehr called them) were thus arrested between July 1940 and March 1942, and nearly 400 of those were sentenced to a variety of punishments. Fifty received a death sentence of whom 15 or so were actually executed. —From gwennhadhu/Erwan Rivi's De Viris Illustribus blog 'Le Mystérieux colonel Germain (II): 3. L'épopée des vichysto-resistants. See also Paillole.

324   Madame Louis' ID from her dossier at the Archives Nationales 16P263368 gives her registration with the FFL (Forces Françaises Libres/Official Armed Forces of the Free French under de Gaulle), the FFC (Forces Françaises Combattantes/Interior Resistance) and the DIR (Déporté Interné Résistant). After the war the FFC became FFCI – Forces Françaises de l'Intérieur.

325   Dr. Tim Austin has broken ground with a first history of Groupe 31 that he characterizes as a most early, woman-led, SIS-funded network of escape, intelligence, and resistance. In regards to her post-war path, Tim points out: 'In 1949 Marguerite was awarded an initial 75% disability pension (for 5 separate conditions totalling 110%) which later rose in 1958 to 100% (for 8 conditions totalling 285%) ... her highest ranked condition, at 60% was *syndromπe neuro-psychique des Déportés-Résistants*.'

326 Pollack includes Georges-France, pp. 65, 165, 167-169
327 Service Historique de la Défense record for Toussaint Zuccarelli under Reseau Georges France: SHD GR P 4 418/4. Suspension of Madame Louis' Legion of Honor was published on 29 April 1959 in the *Journal Officiel*, issue 100, p. 4671.
328 Chombart de Lauwe, in *Résister Toujours*: 'At 21, it's not the same person standing before the mirror. Yvette, the young girl barely out of adolescence has become Marijo, survivor of the camps, who saw more of humanity than many will ever know.' —p. 201
329 ibid.
330 France 24. Holocaust: Vel d'Hiv Roundup, the Last Witnesses https://webdoc.france24.com/holocaust-vel-dhiv-roundup-last-witnesses/ accessed 12/25/2022.
331 https://klarsfeld-ffdjf.org/publications/livres/2012-Le-Memorial-67-pages/ Accessed 12/25/2022.
332 https://gedenkbuch-duesseldorf.de/memory-book/scheinmann-regina/ Accessed 12/25/2022
333 https://www.bundesarchiv.de/gedenkbuch/ Accessed 12/25/2022
334 'Since the 16th century it had been home to a large Jewish community. The town became part of the reborn Republic of Poland whose independence was confirmed through the Treaty of Versailles in June 1919.'- Tim Austin
335 In joining the Y-Service Claire became, in essence, affiliated with the SIS like André.
336 Bletchley Park: Hut 3 – Intelligence and Hut 6 – Decryption.
337 This 'fusion' of Y-Service messages with the high-grade ENIGMA decrypts was vital in the deciphering process. The 'Traffic Analysis' (numbers, times, places) of the Y-Service messages was also an important added value to that done for the ENIGMA messages. A lot of intelligence could be worked out from what the radio operators were saying to each other and their locations could be tracked down using radio direction-finding equipment. But most of the important messages were in code or cipher and had to be decrypted. – Based substantially on information from Bletchley Park.
338 Female operators were used first on the night of November 25/26 1943.
339 In November 1941 WAAFs and WRENS at Gorleston helped in the first capture and sinking of an E-Boat: S41.
340 RAF Chigwell had been a Barrage Balloon-making base until late 1943 – staffed with WAAFs – when it then became a secret radar development station. In particular it trained and equipped RAF mobile units (GCI – Ground Control and Interception units) that were landed on the Normandy beaches with the first waves. After the war it continued its radar service in the Cold War.
341 So noted on her service record.
342 She is buried next to him in the Jewish cemetery of Tifereth Israel in New Bedford, MA.
343 For further mentions of Peulevey, also see Overcloud files 28 P 3 25 and 17 P 185, the 'procès' – trials – of Seidel, Téry, Ross, des Bretons, Bête

Noire, Overcloud; GF historique (history), Réseau GF 31 états nominatifs (individual agents), Réseau Johnny; individual files for Saint Martin Wilborts, Marie Seidel, Yves Le Tac, Joël Le Tac, Henriette Le Belzic, Le Dantec, etc...

344   Max Hastings, *The Secret War: Spies, Codes and Guerillas, 1939-1945*, p. xxvi.

345   *The Scarlet Pimpernel*, by Baroness Orczy, published in 1905, was about a brilliant impostor – an apparently foppish Englishman who spirited members of the French nobility out of France to England during the French Revolution's reign of terror.

346   *The London Gazette*, 21 February, 1947, p.878 records Oscar's naturalisation as a British citizen. The 20 June, 1947 issue, p.2818, records his name change to John Gerald Stephens.

347   'SIS first acquired the MI6 nickname' in 1941. (Davies, p. 17) 'Where GCHQ specialises in gaining intelligence from communications, MI5 and MI6 both deal with human intelligence. MI5 focuses their efforts within the UK and MI6 focuses on gathering intelligence outside the UK.' See https://www.sis.gov.uk/our-history.html for the 'official' history.

348   André wrote 'Johny', the spelling used in the French National Archives lists. Not all these networks are *homologués* – officially recognized by the French government – for various reasons. 'I know that, having worked directly for the Inteligence Service, we are the poor relations of La France Combattante (the Fighting French.).' —Suzanne Wilborts file at Vincennes.

349   For more information: https://sfi.usc.edu/

350   FCO was a ministerial department from October 1968 to September 2020. It merged with the Department for International Development to create the Foreign, Commonwealth & Development Office (FCDO).

351   'Le Struthof' was inaugurated as a French National monument by De Gaulle in 1960. Konzentrationslager Natzweiler was declared a European Heritage site on March 1, 2018. This designation included not only the main camp but also more than a dozen of its slave labor subcamps. A majority of the 52,000 prisoners registered at Natzweiler were never at the main camp.

352   Carl Henry filmed his trip to Alsace in 1927; his films are available at the US Holocaust Memorial Museum in DC – https://collections.ushmm.org/search/catalog/irn1000069. He passed through Alsace again during his service as Warrant Officer with the US Third Army in 1944, writing the day books – essentially the first history – of the 305th Engineer Battalion companies A, B, and C of the 80th 'Blue Ridge' Division. Frontseattowar.com highlights his contributions and all 500 of his letters to his wife Edith Entratter are online under his Special Collection at the Du Bois Library, UMass Amherst: http://scua.library.umass.edu/henry-carl/

353   KZ-Gedenkstätte Neckarelz http://www.kz-denk-neckarelz.de/en/

354 Romain Blandre, Professeur d'histoire/géographie. Correspondant du Mémorial de la Shoah académie Strasbourg. Professeur-relais au CERD-Struthof, has drafted a detailed consideration of Simon's contribution to the history: 'Jean Simon, passeur d'histoire et de mémoire.' (Privately available.)

355 http://www.judaisme-alsalor.fr/perso/gyfeder/index.htm. When the author visited the gas chamber in 1991, the French government employee guide said they were not allowed to speak about the identity of the people who were killed there. Now finally the Roma and Sinti who perished there from phosgene gas experiments are remembered there as well.

356 https://www.youtube.com/watch?v=zNak-fgzLyg Attorney Steven Draisin and Shimon Samuels of the Wiesenthal Center placing the wreath during memorial ceremony at the KLNa; Charles Osgood's report.

357 https://www.natzweiler-struthof.com/Natzweiler-StruthofTestimonials.htm

Acknowledgements

André confided his memoirs to me in 1994. I continued to study his career for 22 years after his death in 2001. This book is thus, also, the story of an enduring friendship. I have come to appreciate him more as I discovered the background of his career you see here. When I pulled back the curtain, he surprised me, but he never changed. 'While scepticism about the secret world is indispensable, so too is the capacity for wonder: some fabulous tales prove true.'[344]

Revealing the secrets of another human being is an awesome challenge. Future scholars who study the history of André and his comrades will want to deal with the impasses and limitations which I could not overcome, but they will never again have the honour of being the first to bring his story to light. At my last seeing him, he begged me to publish his story – for his comrades. You will meet these amazing people as well.

Stuart Leasor, publisher, whose interest in the story of André is as great as mine, has my profound gratitude for his patience, understanding and lucid guidance. He is utterly wise, skillful, and kind.

I owe an incomparable debt to André's son Michel for introducing me to André. When we met, my life took a different direction – I moved back to the East Coast, bought a house near André's in Padanaram Village, South Dartmouth, Massachusetts, and began a journey of discovery into André's daring career: espionage, resistance and rescue that rivals the Scarlet Pimpernel for wit and derring-do.[345] André shared his photo albums with me, as did his son, and those family photographs add so much to his story. All uncredited images come from the family.

André's family's continued interest in the project, including Phil Scheinman's family film, buoyed my spirits. Zoe Scheinman, with her special flair for genealogy, unearthed Oscar Gerald Scheinmann, a 'serving officer in His Majesty's Forces.'[346] André's cousin Edmond Thorn, who witnessed the famous incident of André spilling tea in the lap of Claire, shared how precious was André's mentorship. Edmond introduced me to their remarkable great uncles, the illusionists of world stature known as

Chevalier Ernest Thorn (born Moses Abraham Thorn) and Henry Darvin (Heinrich Thorn). It seems that the illusionist gene runs in the family...

Michel shared his father's priceless personal archive in 2018. Nestled in tissue paper in a box of hundreds of letters and documents were André's translator's ID from when he worked with the Germans; his MI6 (popular designation of the Secret Intellingence Sevice/SIS) boss' signed letter of reference attesting to his trip to England, his new missions and code name Turquoise, and a receipt for the half-million francs he returned to the SIS after the war. Other treasures were his 'little black book' from after the war with the Paris phone number and contact information for his famous SIS handler 'Uncle Tom' Greene and for Wilfred 'Biffy' Dunderdale, head of a French section of SIS.[347] Also in his previously unrevealed archive were hundreds of his French agents' letters that André had saved, addressed to him as 'Cher camarade, Cher Le Neveu, Mon Capitaine...' where one can read about their service for the early resistance networks in Brittany: Johny (Johnny), La Bête Noire, Aigle, Georges-France/Groupe 31, La Bande à Sidonie, Le Dantec, Frère Legeay, Lehmann, Alexandre...[348] These letters came to him because, as 'liquidateur de réseau,' (post-war network registrar) for his last network, Overcloud, André was in charge of listing his agents for French government honors and pensions.

I owe a debt of gratitude to Chaim Mazo for his generosity from an earlier stage of the project. Professor Mel and Cynthia Yoken were infinitely gracious to share the video of their historic interview that André so obviously enjoyed participating in, speaking with them in both French and English. Branka Milosevic and Charles Pinto were angels for me. Their encouragement will never be forgotten. Likewise Teresa Gerade's tremendous gift of cataloguing more than 500 books in my library on these subjects, and great technical advice.

I had been working alone through the decades until Tim Austin reached out to me about our mutual interests and made his time and talents available to illuminate the substance and intricacies of André's involvement with the British. Dr. T.B. Austin is now a family historian who has been involved in three publications to date on aspects of his family history: Madeline Goold's *Mr. Langshaw's Square Piano*; J.M. Hughes' *Edmund Sharpe, Man of Lancaster*; and Geoff Brandwood's *The Architecture of Sharpe, Paley and Austin*. He also contributed to *RF is for Real Friends* by Chrystel Hug of the Alliance Française, London. He most recently substantially contributed to the biography of his uncle: *J. L. Austin: Philosopher and D-Day Intelligence Officer*. Tim's research into his uncle's intelligence work led him to take an interest in the relatively unknown origin and history of the very early WW2 SIS network Georges-France/Groupe 31. It was my incomparable good fortune that he decided to work with me on the story of André.

Sharing his insights about the incalculable importance of the new opportunities for research and of new directions from the archives, Tim took me to Kew and shepherded me through research at the British National Archives there. He introduced me to the literature and scholars of the secret history of WWII. With patience and insight, he reviewed with me almost every name in these pages of people who were in contact with André. They came to life with his help. 'Claire's Story,' the narrative Tim composed based on a two-page government employment record, resulted in her being inscribed on the Roll of Honour at Bletchley Park, in 2021. An honour long overdue.

So many authors contributed documents for this book, or leads to them; because I was working alone and with no funding, I am enormously grateful to them for sharing. I have tried to be as exact and thorough as possible with the captions and credits; if mistakes have been made, they are mine, and, with and apologies proffered here and now, all possible amends will be made. All photographs and documents courtesy of others are copyrighted by their authors and permission for any use must be obtained from the individual sources and the lending institutions. All translations from the French are my own.

The USC Shoah Foundation The Institute for Visual History and Education is gratefully acknowledged for allowing us to use the photo of André from interview #24954 and the transcripts of his testimony, 1/27/1997 at Boca Raton, FL by Helen Sendyk, videography by Donna Schatz.[349] Documents held at the British National Archives at Kew are quoted in this book with acknowledgement that these archival references are Crown copyright, and are used under the terms of the Open Government Licence.

Institutions such as the US National Archives and Records Administration, Arolsen Archives International Center on Nazi Persecution in Germany, the Foreign & Commonwealth Office and the

National Archives of the UK sound so imposing and anonymous; yet individuals among their personnel have understood my financial and time constraints, and have been, through the decades, not only helpful but encouraging.[350] I do not name them to protect their time and the details of their generosity but I am very grateful to each one who provided me with leads and documents beyond the scope of my limited questions.

On the subject of Natzweiler concentration camp where André was interned from July 1943 to September 1944, pages of thanks are due to so many who contributed to my understanding, writing and speaking on the subject. My metamorphosis from photographer/photojournalist to independent scholar had already begun ten years before I met André – when I first set foot on that bitter howling mountaintop where he and thousands of others – mostly political prisoners from all the countries of Europe – were imprisoned, starved, worked and tortured to death.[351] Georges and Claude Bloch first took my father and me there in 1985 during our visit to my paternal grandfather's home towns in Alsace.[352] I returned in 1991, 1998, 2016, and 2018.

Congresswoman Elizabeth Holtzman first impressed on me the importance of my research on Natzweiler. The two first Directors of the museum at the camp, the Centre Européen du Résistant Déporté/CERD, Valérie Drechsler-Kayser and Frédérique Neau-Dufour, were both generous in time and encouragement. René Chevrolet, head of the CERD's Documentation and Historical Research, and Sandrine Garcia have answered a hundred questions and provided amazing chunks of invaluable information available nowhere else. At the memorial museum of the BMW slave labor subcamps in Germany, 'Natzweiler on the Neckar', I have to thank Dorothée Roos and Arno Huth.[353] They received me ever so graciously when I visited and continue to partner and encourage my research.

Jean Simon wanted to enlist me for assistance on his historic anthology, *Le Camp de Concentration du Struthof – Témoignages*.(Le Struthof is the name by which Natzweiler has been known in France.) Although I was unable to join him on that project, his hospitality and his devotion to the site and history of the camp were unforgettable and inspiring.[354] Georges Yoram Federmann provided a home away from home for me at his office in Strasbourg and tour of sites of Jewish heritage as well as sharing his enduring passion for honouring the memory of the Jews who died in Natzweiler's gas chamber.[355] Stephen J. Draisin, in 1989 managed to place a plaque, the first memorial at Natzweiler, to honour the memory and continues to inspire me to reclaim the hidden memory of Jews at the KLNa.[356]

Robert Abzug of the University of Texas at Austin endowed me with his research files about Natzweiler for his book *Inside the Vicious Heart* almost at the beginning of my work on the camp. Konnilyn Feig's admiration and Martin Gilbert's respect for my subject and study galvanized me to keep on, as did that of other academics, including Professor Michael Dietrich, Professor Johannes-Dieter Steinert, and Professor Ellen W. Kaplan, who created a writing and learning module for her class at Smith College to dramatize the story of André.[357] Ken Waltzer invited me to speak at the Jewish Studies Association conference in 2009; my presentation, 'Life Was Not Beautiful: Memoirs of the KLNa', included André's, of course.

I continued to refine and reflect on André's story by presenting at conferences, including at Monash University, 2015; the University of Salzburg and the Hebrew University in Jerusalem, 2016. The second part of this book came into focus for my presentation on the theme of 'Strange Bedfellows/Unexpected Allies' at the German Studies Association's 7th Program Summer Workshop, Freie Universität, Berlin. That same year. David Simon, director of the Genocide Studies Program at Yale, invited me to present at the symposium, 'Memorialization Unmoored' in 2018, which led to my presentation at 'Traversing The Gap: Relevance As a Transformative Force At Sites Of Public Memory' – the 2019 Mellon Conference at the 9/11 Memorial & Museum.

The history of André in the resistance is enriched immeasurably by contributions of those who knew him then: Monique Le Tac, Yves' daughter; Mari-Jo Chombart de Lauwe, perhaps his youngest agent; and his many comrades at Natzweiler including Max Nevers, Georges Maradène, and Henri Rosencher who shared their memories as well. Camp fellows with whom I corresponded, including the great writer Boris Pahor, Arne Brun Lie, Gilbert May, Charles Joineau, Eugène Marlot have my debt of gratitude and affection. These and other prisoners at Natzweiler and its subcamps are remembered at: http://www.dianamarahenry.com/natzweiler-struthof/httpwww.natzweiler-struthofsecurity.htm

Generous French scholars, historians, curators and government leaders, too numerous to all be named, include Pierre Tillet, Denis Peschanski, Pierre de Jaegher, Sabah Chaib, Aline Angoustures, Annette Wieviorka, Olivier Wieviorka, Romain Blandre, Laurent Laloup, Serge and Beate Klarsfeld and Serge Barcellini, whom I first met on my third visit to Natzweiler in 1998, and who is now Président Général du Souvenir Français and Contrôleur Géneral des Armées. In 2022 André was included in Le Souvenir Français' special edition spotlighting 'One hundred heroes of the French Armed Forces 1942.' Thierry Chaunu, President of The American Society of Le Souvenir Français created a moving graveside tribute ceremony on Veterans' Day 2022 in honor of André Joseph Scheinmann, French Resistance Hero. Thierry introduced me to Alain Dupuis, President Federation des ancients combatants, and they valiantly pitched in to identify André's decorations. Fabrice Bourrée, who contributed to my research as early as 2018, was also watching over it in the last stages of going to press from his perch as Responsable du service de la médaille de la Résistance française for the Ordre de la Libération.

Authors of thrilling books on the Resistance and/or Secret Services, including Damien Lewis, Sharon Spinos, Matthew Cobb, Nigel Perrin, David Tremain, Lord Ashcroft KCMG PC., Lynn Philip Hodgson, Francis J. Suttill, Nigel West and Tim Spicer have my gratitude for their sustained interest and valuable contributions. Several of them also shared voluminous files from the Archives; this trans-Atlantic assistance was invaluable. So has been the fellowship of Caroline Babois née Gentry, Peter Mahood, Dr. Andrew W.M. Smith, Dr. Martin Dean, SOE Forum participants Steven Kippax, Phil Tomaselli, Colin Cohen, Alan 'Fred' Judge, Martin Briscoe, Alan Watson, Colonel (Retired) Nick Fox OBE, David Blair, Bernard O'Connor, Roderick De Normann, Sheryl Green and Mike Bluestone; The Secret World War Two Learning Network with Paul McCue, Ashley Barnett and Martyn Cox whose warmth and generosity are so appreciated – and there are many others. Even Baroness Margaret Thatcher, via Miranda Granger and Mark Worthington of her Private Office, and those at SIS who protested not being able to disclose, were helpful. Thank you.

Index

Please note: Documents from participants of the time and post-war include many name variants. We have tried to account for all known spellings. In some cases, no first name was available. In others, different first names may represent the same person.

ANDRÉ'S NAMES AND ALIASES

Agent from C 331
A.N. Other 250
André's numeric codes
    31AQ 6, 20, 67, 76, 85, 92, 165, 166, 184, 185, 211
    99421 3, 180, 184
Le Neveu 6, 18, 68, 88, 165, 167, 169, 179-181, 183, 214
Martin 165, 185, 211
Mispellings (in books and documents):
    Pauleveyv 19, 20
    Peulevé 68, 124, 279, 307
    Peulevez 262, 265, 325
    Peuveley 278
    Schweiderman 74, 328
Peulevey, André Maurice / André 2, 3, 6, 8, 14-16, 20, 24, 31, 36, 42, 45, 48, 53, 57, 79, 85, 88, 102, 106, 124, 133, 159, 161, 163, 167, 176-181, 188, 192, 193, 196, 200, 202-208, 211, 220-225, 229-231, 238, 240, 242, 245, 246, 254, 260, 274, 277
Scheinmann, Joseph / Scheinmann, André Joseph 2, 5, 6, 7, 24, 29, 30, 45, 149, 168, 176, 179, 200, 203, 206, 207, 208, 220, 221, 224, 225, 229, 230, 240, 277, 281
SIS Agent 180, 181, 211
Turquoise 7, 182, 183, 191, 251, 252, 254, 255

ANDRÉ'S FAMILY

Darvin/Darwin, Henry / Heinrich Thorn 338
Scheinman, Dr. Sydney 11, 12
Scheinmann, Mady / Rosa / Madeleine 1-13, 24, 29, 30, 42, 48, 149, 192, 301, 322, 343
Scheinmann, Max (Mendel) and Regina Thorn/Torn 5, 10-13, 25, 29, 30, 39, 173, 174, 266-269, 295, 296, 312
Scheinmann, Michel / Michel 9, 149, 150, 228
Thorn, 'Chevalier' Ernest / Moses Abraham Thorn 284, 285, 338
Thorn, Edmond 337
Thorn/Torn Jacob / Kuba and Madeleine 10, 25, 30, 147, 174
Torn, Josef 175

SCHEINMANN, CLAIRE DYMENT JARRETT (ANDRÉ'S WIFE)
birthplace: Międzyrzec Podlaski, Poland 269
Bletchley Park, Roll of Honour 23
British War Medal 273
first husband: Francis Charles Jarrett 269
her work: Operation Corona, SIGINT/Signals Intelligence 23, 271, 273
Home Defense Unit / HDU 271, 272
parents: Manisz Dyment, Rejzla Limoner 269
RAF stations: Bridgnorth, Morecambe, Kingsdown, Great Yarmouth /Norfolk/ Gorleston, Coltishall, Canterbury (Hawkinge/Folkstone), Chigwell 270, 271, 272, 273
WAAF / Women's Auxiliary Air Force 270, 271

ANDRÉ'S WORLD
apatride 178, 216
Army, French / German / Austrian / Polish 5-7, 23, 30, 32, 36, 38, 43-46, 47-55, 64, 90, 114, 128, 129, 130, 146, 165, 173, 174, 176, 179, 216, 227, 246
Au Soldeur Americain / The American Bargain Center 41, 148
Bruay en Artois / Bruay la Buissière 5, 11, 40, 41, 148
Düsseldorf 29, 33, 266
Horst Wessel Lied 29
infantry 6, 43, 45, 47
Jew, Jewish 10-16, 24, 29-46, 51, 63, 64, 73, 107, 135, 136, 144, 150, 174-179, 224-226, 229, 266, 269

Kempten (German city) 5
Loewy, Max 39
Maccabi (sports club) 33
Munich 5, 30, 39, 44, 135, 167, 179, 224, 225, 227
Padnaram Village, South Dartmouth, Massachusetts 231
Palestine, British Mandate 36, 37, 269
passport 5, 19, 44, 223
tennis 24, 33, 42
UNESCO 221
visa 11, 12, 41
Weil, Ruth 33, 34, 40

ANDRÉ'S FRENCH ARMY SERVICE
Béthune 45
draft / mobilisation 32, 44, 45, 47
hospital 6, 47-53, 70, 83, 109, 117, 119, 120, 124, 126, 136, 138, 142, 144, 203, 231
Indochina 44
Lille (André) 40, 45, 165
machine gun 47, 51, 61, 101, 134
parachute badge / 'moustique' / parachute wings 48, 161, 166, 195, 196, 230, 245
POW (Prisoner of War) 6, 53, 68, 163, 167, 177, 211, 231, 242, 245
Reserves 7, 19, 23, 44, 47, 167, 227, 246

ANDRÉ'S RESISTANCE WORLD SEE ALSO **LOCATIONS IN FRANCE & AGENTS** AND **RESISTANCE NETWORKS, OTHER OPERATIVES**
Action / Service Action / Service 'Action' 6, 74, 75, 181, 183, 203, 205, 208, 221, 252

airbase / Air Force Base / airfield 55, 58, 59, 65, 163, 164, 211
alias / pseudo 6, 18, 88, 165, 167, 176, 185, 188, 235, 238, 240, 250, 252, 253
Amicale Action 219, 220
anti-aircraft (gun) 59, 60, 61, 262
Aussweis / laissez-passer 11, 57
Ave Maria (by Gounod) 98
battleships, German - Gneisenau, Scharnhorst, Prinz Eugen, Bismarck 65, 84, 85, 212
Berlin 60, 69, 341
code / cipher 3, 67, 74, 78, 83, 92, 96, 149, 156, 166, 191, 196, 205, 236, 254, 271
Cologne 69, 261, 264
Comité Rennais des Etudiants 15, 72, 74, 75, 259
counter-espionage / CE 165, 176, 222, 248
courier 51, 59, 70
demonstrations 61, 62
drop / airdrop / dropping zone 66, 71, 86, 182, 195, 204, 205
E-boat 149
escape / evasion 6, 12, 16, 51-55, 66-69, 73, 87, 88, 95, 100, 104, 111, 119, 124, 125, 131, 133, 136, 140, 152, 167, 177, 181-183, 187, 199, 207, 212, 219, 231, 237, 242, 284
espionage / Intelligence 6, 12, 18, 20, 21, 23, 55, 57, 70, 71, 73, 76, 81-85, 88, 91, 92, 95, 101, 147, 149, 164-167, 172, 175-193, 196, 199, 203, 205, 207, 208, 212, 219-224, 228, 237, 238, 242, 245, 248, 256, 257, 259, 262, 271, 273
execution 15, 56, 66, 67, 93, 97, 98, 117, 133, 135, 140, 164, 166, 168, 178, 226, 243, 261, 264, 298, 333

film / movie / newsreel 14, 24, 61, 62, 68, 75, 91, 97, 166, 187, 193, 231
Free French 6, 8, 17, 43, 55, 62, 64, 66, 70, 72, 100, 121, 137, 143, 150, 154, 180, 181, 185, 186, 189, 190, 191, 194, 195, 208, 230, 236, 254, 264
Fresnes (prison) 7, 88, 102, 166, 189, 237
gas / gas mask 13, 47, 75, 165
Gens de la Lune (publication) 79, 80
guillotine (beheading) 69
gun 48, 51, 174, 194, 212
Hamburg 60, 164
hostages 61, 68, 99, 177
hotbox (train) 164
Houdini 87
interpreter / translator / translation 13, 14, 54, 57, 64, 65, 71, 73, 163, 167, 177, 179, 211, 242, 271
interrogation / torture 7, 15, 11, 36, 85-90, 92, 93, 98-101, 153, 154, 166, 178, 189, 193, 195, 197, 202, 213, 214, 245, 249, 253, 264
Kesselring, Lt. (German) 99
Kraehling (defense lawyer) 261
La Bretagne Enchainée / Brittany in Chains (underground newspaper) 72, 74, 75
Lindemann, John Cäsar Bruno Richard Capt. (German) 166
Liquidateur (*de réseau*) / Registrar (of a network) 7, 13, 21, 199, 200, 203, 207-209, 213, 219, 224, 260
Luftwaffe (German Air Force) 14, 23, 58, 271
machine gun 47, 61, 87
MacMillan and Harry Pool, (downed fliers) 68, 264
Marseillaise / God Save the King 96, 140

Mauve (radio operator code name) 255
Michelet / Michel 164
mine-sweeper 64, 65, 164
Molyneux, Edward Henri 220
morale 33, 35, 51, 58, 61, 122, 128, 129, 130, 138, 157, 212, 245
Nelson, warship / code name for radio operator Hamon 83
P0, P1, P2 (agent categories) 178, 204
Paris 7, 10, 11, 12, 19, 20, 21, 24, 25, 42, 49, 60, 66, 67, 74, 76, 81, 84, 85, 88, 89, 94, 99, 101, 102, 115, 141, 146-149, 165, 167, 172, 179, 180, 183, 188-191, 197, 208, 211, 212, 216-224, 231, 235, 237, 238, 243, 245, 257-260, 266, 267, 294
pilot 23, 43, 58, 59, 61, 69, 77, 149, 190, 203, 271
Plaice (radio operator code name) 255
propaganda 37, 45, 72, 74, 75, 100, 157, 180, 182, 183
radio (equipment, operator) 3, 7, 69, 70, 73, 74, 83, 85, 86, 88, 92, 99, 166, 168, 171, 194, 236, 278, 304, 305, 307, 316
Rauch, Lucien 18, 19
Red Cross 53, 61, 69, 79, 100, 102, 147, 203, 265
Rennes 6, 14, 15, 18, 20, 49, 50, 51, 53-63, 67, 68, 71, 72, 73, 74, 75, 77, 78, 85, 86, 93, 94, 101, 148, 161, 163, 165, 166, 167, 177, 178, 179, 183, 185, 196, 197, 208, 211, 224, 227, 230, 235, 237, 243, 261
reprisals 68, 99, 111, 177
resistance / resistor / underground 1, 6, 7, 9, 11-22, 37, 51, 56, 57, 59, 61, 63, 67, 69, 70, 74, 77, 99, 100, 104, 108-112, 117, 120-125, 130, 137, 143, 144, 147, 153, 154, 157-160, 167, 168, 171, 173-197, 198-215, 216-227, 230, 235, 246, 257, 260, 261, 263
sabotage 6, 14, 55, 57, 59, 60, 61, 69, 70, 73, 75, 77, 87, 99, 100, 107, 127, 163-165, 167, 171, 178, 180-183, 187, 190, 191, 196, 197, 204, 242, 263
Saint-Malo de Phily / 'Adrian' dropping zone 205
Senegal 63
Société Nationale des Chemins de Fer / SNCF / S.N.C.F. / French National Railroads/Chemins de Fer 6, 14, 18, 54-59, 63, 64, 75, 163-167, 177, 179, 182, 183, 205-208, 219, 226, 242, 245
Sommer, Chief Adjutant (German) 166
Stuttgart 69
submarine / submarine base 43, 55, 59, 60, 64, 91, 140, 163, 164, 196
suicide 104, 105, 111, 155, 253, 257
Todt (German organization) 60, 164
troop transport 167
U-boat 14, 60, 65, 96
Untermenschen 63
Upper Silesia 164
Walde, Captain (Abwehr) 101
wirecutter 164

LOCATIONS IN FRANCE

8 Avenue des Tilleuls, Paris 223, 257
69 Avenue Victor Hugo, Paris 147
Angers (prison) 87, 166
Avenue Victor Hugo, Paris 147
Bordeaux 19, 167
Bréhat 67, 68, 71, 165, 247
Brest 60, 65, 76, 84, 85, 163, 164, 249

Brittany 6, 14, 17, 49, 54, 55, 57-60, 64, 66, 67, 70, 72, 74, 76, 84, 163, 164, 176-179, 183, 186-189, 194, 196, 201, 202, 207, 209, 219, 224, 226, 235, 254, 262
Café de Flore 76
Café de la Paix, Rennes 68, 179, 188
Café de l'Europe, Rennes 68, 179
Carantec 165
Clos Béranger 66
Dinard 164
Fouquet's 188
Groslay 66
Hotel Caulaincourt 89, 197
Hotel Edouard VII 88, 89, 91, 101, 197
Hotel Lutetia, Paris 147
Hotel Paris Rivoli 10
Hotel Plaza Athénée, Paris 217
Ile de Bréhat 71, 247
Ile Guennoc 248
Ile-et-Vilaine (département) 56
Ivry-sur-Seine (cemetery) 261
Lannion 163, 164
Le Mans 219
Le Vésinet 10
L'Isle-Adam 66
Loire (river) 50
Lorient 60, 163, 164
Maxim's 188
Mont Valérien 67
Nantes 68, 69, 123, 165, 167, 202, 203, 262
Place Saint Sauveur, Rennes 68, 179
Ploermal 67
Pornic 265
Prefailles 265
railroad stations in André's network: St. Brieux, Morlaix, Auray, Plechatel, Pouancé, Lannion, Chateaubriant, Mordelles, Montfort s/Meu, Rosporden, Paimpol, Landerneau, Lorient, Brest, Vannes, Quimper, Quimperlé, Quiberon 60, 85, 163, 164, 183, 249, 258, 264
Rieucros 10
Romainville (prison) 99, 177
Rue Boissy d'Anglas 92
Rue de Saussaies 166
Rue Gît Le Coeur, Paris 81
St. Jacques 164
St. Malo 60, 164, 183
St. Pabu 76, 77, 84, 247
Tréguier 68
Vannes 163, 164, 183

FRENCH GOVERNMENT PERSONNEL, FUNCTIONS, ORGANISATIONS, SERVICE TITLES AND HONOURS
SEE ALSO **PERSONNEL BASED IN ENGLAND**

Audibert, General 213
Bloch, Jean-Pierre 180, 289, 317
Blum, Léon 42
Bozel /St. Bozel, Captain / Jean Richemond/Richemont 183, 306, 319
Bureau Central de Renseignments et d'Action / BCRA / BCRAM (M for Militaire) 6, 17, 70, 74, 171, 180-182, 185, 186, 189-193, 207, 220, 250, 251, 252
Catroux, General Georges 240
Combattant Volontaire de la Résistance 246, 281
Corps d'Armée / Army Corps (medal) 7, 18, 168, 205, 244, 245
Cotrelle, Cmdr. 209
Croix de guerre / War Cross 7, 205, 240, 244, 245
Dassault, General Paul 240

de Pouzols Saint-Phar, Comte Albert 219
Debesse 208
Dejussieu Pontcarral, Pierre 260
Déporté Interné Résistant / DIR 7, 202, 230
Deuxième Bureau 184, 210, 237, 256
Forces Françaises combattantes / FFC / FFCI 7, 22, 165, 183, 187, 199, 230, 242, 245, 260
Forces Françaises Libres / FFL / F.F.L. 8, 66, 100, 161, 168, 204, 205, 219, 230, 256
Foreign Legion 110, 176
France Combattante / FC 163, 164, 221, 224, 225, 257, 260
Franklin 208
French Air Force 70
Guillaumat, Comdr. 264
Guillet 208
Josset, Colonel 260
Journal Officiel de la République Française 225, 246
Laval, Pierre 98, 99
Laverdet/Laverdet-Legal/Laverdet-LeGall, Raymond Léon Albert / Red, Ruis 187, 219, 221, 224, 225, 260
Légion d'Honneur / Legion of Honour 7, 18, 168, 197, 204, 208, 225, 227, 240-242, 257, 258
Liger, Capitaine 260
Liquidation / *Liquidateur* (registrar) / Récupération / Récupérateur 7, 13, 21, 199, 200, 203, 207-209, 213, 219, 224, 225, 259, 260
Lormeau, Medecin Colonel 260
Manuel 208
Médaille de la Résistance / Medal of the Resistance 7, 168, 205, 240, 246, 257
Médaille des Déportés 240

Ordre de la Libération 275, 288
Pétain, Marshal 6, 64
Schmidt, Commandant 219
Service de Recherche des Crimes de Guerre Ennemis (Office of Research into Enemy War Crimes) 224
Vichy 6, 10, 23, 99, 150, 226, 256

RESISTANCE NETWORKS, OTHER OPERATIVES

Aigle 6, 180, 182, 184, 245
Alexandre 6, 200
Alliance 124, 125
Baudoin 190
Berger, Capt. 236
Cartigny 190
CND / Castille / Confrérie Notre Dame 199, 206
Georges-France / Group(e) 31 / GF31 / Network 31 6, 20, 67, 70, 85, 92, 93, 165-167, 177, 178, 180-185, 202, 203, 206-211, 236-239, 256, 257-261, 278, 282
Jade-Fitzroy 208, 213
Johnny / Johny / Jonny 6, 165, 180, 204
Kopernic 190
La Bande à Sidonie 6, 68, 178-180, 247, 257
La Bête Noire [The Black Beast] 6, 55, 74, 75, 178, 180, 182, 184, 205
Manouchian, Missak and Mélinée 227
Overcloud 6, 7, 17, 21, 55, 70-72, 75, 86, 165, 167, 181-186, 190, 194, 196, 199, 200, 203-209, 219, 220, 236-238, 247-255, 260
Renault 190, 199, 260
Turquoise-Jezequel 7, 182, 183, 191, 251, 254
Valmy 78, 183, 225

AGENTS / SECRET AGENT / SPY / SPECIAL OPERATIVES WITH AN ASSOCIATION TO ANDRÉ

Different first names may or may not represent different people. Many spelling variants exist.

Alizon, Simone 176
Barbe, Raoul 102
Bartoli de Mandres, André 316
Bernon 163
Bidaux, Abbé André 102, 123
Bocq, Adam 238, 304
Bois-Gontier 237
Bozel, Capt. 183
Brachu, Maurice 304
Comité Rennais des Etudiants 15, 72, 74, 75, 259
Conte, Andrée 68, 79, 306, 307
Cozannec, Marie 204, 304
Déan 165
De Kergolay, Alain Raymond Marie / de Kergolec 74, 168, 194, 236, 238, 254, 305, 307, 308, 331
De Saint Laurent, Marie Anne Geneviève d'Affry de la Monnoye 261, 304
d'Estienne d'Orves, Count Henri Louis Honoré 66, 200, 238, 292, 304, 324
Devaux 201
Dorleans 238
Eidem, Max 72, 238, 259, 317
Epron, Theotiste / Mme. Moïse Moscovitch 264, 265, 304
Forman, Jean / BCRA / called Pierre by Passy 78, 236, 248, 249, 250
Guillaume, Joseph 'Jobic' 237
Hentic, Pierre / Maho 278, 286, 303, 307, 311, 325, 326
Hoderat, Mme. 238
Ingham, Agnes 177, 238, 316
  See also Turban, Louis
Jaffré 163
Jaunet (two people) 238
Labit, Henri 78, 248
Lacaze, André 287
Lavoué, Joseph 101, 102, 117, 125, 126, 309, 331
Le Belzic 238, 287, 304, 324, 325, 334
Le Bonniec 304
Lecomte, Mlle 238
Le Dantec, Jean 6, 178, 180, 237, 261, 332, 334
Le Deuff / Le Deuf, Louis 68, 102, 164, 179, 219, 238, 246, 278
Le Gac, Francois 304
Legeay, Frère Jean-Baptiste / Legeais, Logeais 69, 123, 178, 180, 202, 204, 238, 259, 264, 304, 317, 326, 338
Lehmann, Henri 6, 178, 180, 237, 261, 338
Leroux 164
Leroux, Amédé(e) 163
Le Tac (group) 17, 18, 76, 77, 82, 84, 87, 89, 99, 102, 180, 181, 183, 196, 204, 209, 220, 236, 238, 247, 251, 276, 277, 279, 318, 312
Le Tac, Andrée 68, 79, 306, 307
Le Tac, Joël André / Overcloud 17, 68-74, 76-79, 86, 99, 165, 166, 180-184, 189-191, 194, 196, 205-209, 219, 220, 225, 235-238, 247-251, 262, 280, 305, 307, 308, 320, 322, 327, 328, 334
Le Tac, Yves / Yve / Le Cor/ Le Corre 17, 72, 75, 77, 79, 165, 180, 181, 191, 196, 219, 231, 248, 252, 253, 276, 307, 308, 321, 322, 334

Le Tac, Yvonne 68, 77-80, 246, 279, 308
L'Henoret 304
Lignel, Bernard 164
Lorgeril, Comtesse de née Odette Marie Jeanne Guilhe La Combe De Villers 200, 201, 324
Louette, Rina 68
Madame Louis / Mme. Louis See Madame Louis and her connections / Gorge, Marguerite Alice
Marchais, André (Albert) 204, 264, 304
Marchais, Jean 264
Marchais, Madame 264
Maurel, Etienne 102, 238, 309
Maurel, Mme 238
Ménard, André 75, 261, 296, 309
Menard, Paulette 238
Mevel 163
Migaud, Albert 261
Migaud, Auguste 261
Morel, Pierre 308
Moureau / Moureaux, Pierre 99, 219, 305
Nidelet, Robert 261
Normand, Louis 102, 238, 308, 309
Normand, Mme and two sons 238
Norman, Gaby / Normand, Gabrielle 68, 75, 102, 238
Palloc /Paloc, Robert 315, 326
Pennehoat, Louis 304
Peters, Eric 237
Poge, Maurice 102, 219
Remaud, Louis / Remault 75, 205, 261
Ropers, Jeanne 56, 238
Roverch, Augustin 304
Seidel, Marie-Christianne / Marie-Christiane née Marie Albertine Suraud 202, 203, 204, 209, 213, 230, 238, 262, 263, 264, 265

Simon, André 309
Simon, Robert / Valmy 78, 183, 225
Taurin 237
Tessier, André 261
Tilly, Alexandrine 304
Torqueau, Anathase 262, 263
Torty, Robert 304
Turban, Louis / 'Tutenglair', '31AP' 54-60, 64, 65, 68, 70-72, 85, 92, 102, 163, 177-182, 185, 205, 209, 211, 226, 235, 237, 238, 259, 308
See also Ingham, Agnes
Wilborts, Suzanne née Saint Martin / Sidonie Gibbons / Gisbons 67, 68, 71, 75, 178, 179, 212, 213, 214, 219, 247, 256, 257, 258, 259, 313, 316, 318, 321, 325, 335
Wilborts, Yvette / Chombart de Lauwe, Marie-José (Mari-Jo) 67, 68, 69, 178, 179, 200, 222, 226, 238, 257, 278, 317, 341

Not mentioned in this book but documented in André's personal and/or government archives:

Berdonneau, Denise
Berdonneau, Robert
Berthon
Bicherel
Birais
Bodiou, Yvonne
Boucher
Bourges, François
Brodin, Emile
Cabon, Charles
Callac
Catte, André
Chevalier, Mme
Dalibot, Pierre
Daniet

De Saint-Cossis
Derrien, Yves
Deslandes
Dramart
Duclos, Henri
Faludi
Favrel
Fleuriot de Langle
Frahier, Christiane
Grassin
Guillemin
Herin
Hue, Jean
Kerleau
L'Henoret
l'Huillier
Le Barzic, Jean
Le Barzic, Yves
Le Bonniec
Le Marchand, Joseph
Le Poder, Georges
Le Tac, Henriette
LeBrun, Marie
Leroy, Albert
Lignel, Cécile
Lonette, Renée
Lontrage
Marchais, René
Maurel, R.
Normand, Pierre
Patient, Alice
Pellen, René
Perrot, Jeanne
Poitel, Lucien
Remaud, Charlotte
Remaud, Francois
Remaud, Yvonne
Rocape
Rouerch, Augustin
Rousso, Jacques
Simon, André
Téhé, Jean

Thierry, Yves
Vaillant, Jacques
Vedet
Verrier, Jacques

ANDRÉ'S CONCENTRATION CAMP WORLD

Amicale des Anciens de Dachau 278, 282, 311
Appel / roll call 109, 111, 112, 118, 129
Aussenkommando / subcamps 7, 14
badge (color) / triangle 15, 103, 139, 151, 152, 229
barrack / Block 15, 105, 109, 111-123, 126-128, 136-145, 152
Bickenbach, Dr. Otto 13
Blockältester (Prisoner boss of a barrack) 119-123
Bourbon-Parme, Prince Xavier 16
Briquet, Georges 138, 139
Capello, Dr. Y (Joseph) 144
Condor Legion 136
crematorium (Natzweiler) 103, 104, 109, 112, 140
Delestraint, General Charles 122, 125, 143, 144
dog / German Shepherd 16, 11, 102, 130, 151, 172
Ehrmanntraut, Franz, SS Rottenführer (Corporal) / 'Fernandel' 11, 13, 116, 123, 132
experiments (medical) 13, 136
Frère, General Aubert Achille Jules 125
gas chamber (Natzweiler) 13, 103, 107, 108, 135
Gayot, Henri 11, 104, 110, 112, 118, 133
Haagen, Dr. Eugen 13
Hartjenstein, Fritz 311

Himmelfahrtskommando (work detail ascending to heaven) 126
Holzmann (company) 136
Huard, Claude 231
interpreter / translator / translation 13, 15, 16, 103, 105, 106, 115, 120, 124, 126, 129, 137, 148
Kapo (prisoner boss) 11, 15, 109, 112-120, 124, 126, 129, 130, 136-138, 151
Kartoffelkommando (Potato work detail) 111
Kommandant 11, 69, 90, 97, 103, 114, 115, 118, 132, 143
Kommando 14, 15, 107, 111-116, 118, 120, 123, 125-130, 132, 136, 141, 146, 152, 166
Kramer, Josef, Kommandant (SS) 11, 105, 107, 118, 132
Kratt, Willi (*Lagerkapo*) 13, 114, 115, 127
KZ-Gedenkstätte Neckarelz 14
Lagerkapo 113, 126
Leber, Karl 139
Lemberger, Jean 12, 107
May, Gilbert 12, 16, 341
NN / Nacht und Nebel / Night and Fog 7, 15, 11, 100, 101-125, 126-132, 135, 137, 140, 144, 157, 166, 226
Nuremberg 15, 13, 32, 297, 298, 309
Pelletier, Jim 129
Peulevé, Harry (SOE)
See Concentration camps / Oranienburg
Piguet, Monsignor Gabriel 16
proeminentem (various spellings) 109, 153
Revier / infirmary 16, 109, 111, 117, 141, 142
Rosencher, Henri / Breuillot 12, 17, 228, 229, 231

Schillio, Pierre 12, 144
Schonung (rest) 109, 117
Schroeder, Jakob (*Kapo*) / Big Jake / Big Jak / The Tamer (Le Dompteur) 15, 16
secret Jew 12, 16, 226, 229
Seuss, Wolfgang, SS 103
Skrobek, Aaron / David Kutner 328
slave labor 14
Sternenfeld, Dr. 141
Strassenbaukommando (Road construction work detail) / *Strassenkommando* (Road work detail) 115, 124, 132
strophantin (medication) 141
Stubenältester (senior barracks prisoner) 142
Stubendienst (room orderly) 140
Syndrome de Targowla 330
typhus 7, 13, 110, 136, 141, 142, 145, 172
Weberei (weaving workshop) 126, 127
Weiss, Martin Gottfried 143, 144

CONCENTRATION CAMPS / KONZENTRATIONSLAGER / KL

Only the ones mentioned in this book. Some of these are also known as extermination camps.

Allach 7, 14, 133-140, 166
Auschwitz 12, 13, 76, 107, 147, 266, 269
Bergen Belsen 107, 132
Buchenwald 68, 114, 209, 229
Dachau 5, 7, 12, 14, 45, 79, 133-144, 145, 159, 166, 172, 179, 208, 216, 227-229, 231
Flossenbürg 297, 315
Lublin / Majdanek 10, 13, 79, 269

Natzweiler / KLNa / Struthof 7, 9, 11-16, 81, 101-125, 126-132, 133, 135, 138, 151, 157, 166, 172, 179, 189, 196, 208, 226, 229, 231, 293

Oranienburg 124, 140

Ravensbrück 68, 77, 79, 200, 203, 213, 265

Sachsenhausen 269

PERSONNEL BASED IN ENGLAND (FOR THE BCRA, SOE, SIS/MI6)

Appoliard / Appolliard (pilot) 265

Atkins, Vera 171

Birkin, David 306

Bushell, Art, Capt. 194

Chatenay, Victor 188, 191, 198, 208, 209, 212

Churchill, Winston 17, 185, 186, 189

'C' / Major General Sir Stewart Graham Menzies 331

Cohen, Kenneth 305

Curtis, Dunstan Michael Carr 249

Davis, R.N.R. Lt. Cmdr. E.A.G. 248

de Gaulle, Charles / General de Gaulle/ de Gaulle 18, 21, 22, 43, 55, 57, 66, 67, 70-72, 123, 139, 185, 186, 189-191, 204, 218, 220, 226, 230, 243, 245, 246

de Lesseps, Martin Robert / Goodfellow 191, 252, 253

Deckers, Robert Joseph 237-239, 256, 257

Dehn, Paul 193, 194

Dewavrin, André / Colonel Passy 57, 186, 189, 195, 207, 208, 219, 223, 250, 251

Dunderdale, Wilfred 'Biffy' 6, 18, 20, 21, 82, 86, 181, 191, 193, 208, 219, 251, 254

Galitzine, Prince Yuri 285, 329

Gentry, John Edward 7, 19, 184, 223

Greene, Thomas H. / 'Uncle Tom' 6, 7, 18, 20, 21, 83, 88, 147, 148, 180, 184, 188, 191, 193, 208, 212, 252

Holdsworth, Gerald Alfred 'Gerry', R.N.V.R. / 'Holsworth' 82, 183, 189, 192, 247-252

Hutchison, Sir James 248

Jepson, Selwyn, Capt. 197

LaBaume (accompanying officer, BCRAM) 251, 253

Lagier, Raymond / Lieut. Bienvenue (BCRA) 195, 250, 252

Letty, Lt. A. 248

McKenzie, Lieut. G. (Helford Flotilla) 250

Mitchell, Lt. (France Combattante) 257

Molyneux, Edward Henri 220

Nasmyth-Shaw, Cautley, Wg Cdr. 195

Nelson 83

Peake, Sgt. George (RVPS, MI5) 82, 250

Piquet-Wicks, Eric Stanley 17, 183, 192, 249, 250, 251, 253, 254

Pool, William Harry (Canadian) and MacMillan (British) (downed fliers) 68, 264

Reece, Lt. [Mayo J.] (pilot) 265

Richards, Sir Francis Brooks 17

Robertson, Maj. 254

Roy, Captain 253

Scamaroni, Fred / Sévéri / Serveri / Severi /Sevry 248, 253, 255

Sheppard, Robert Marcellin 196

Slocum, Frank, Capt. 183, 251

Sporburg, Henry Nathan 'Harry' 248

Williams, Lawrence P. 191

Wills, James Ernest Elder 191

Yeo-Thomas, Forest Frederick Edward 307, 331

BRITISH GOVERNMENT OPERATIONS AND LOCATIONS

1 Dorset Square, London 252
Anglo-French Communications Bureau 19, 223, 237, 238, 257
BBC 78, 90, 117, 205
Blackpool 83
Buckingham Place, London 21
Camouflage Section (SOE) 191
Caxton Street, London 21
Cornwall 251
Foldboat 250
handler / accompanying officer 18, 21, 82, 191, 253
Helford (England) / Helford flotilla 250, 252
Manchester 84
MGB 314 / MTB (M.G.B. in documents) 17, 81, 82, 84, 248, 249, 250
MI5 250
MI9 185
'MOST SECRET' 250, 254
Naval Intelligence Directive / NID 248
Navy 69, 149
Ringway (air base) 166, 195, 196
RNVR / R.N.V.R. Royal Navy Volunteer Reserves 17, 19, 82, 249, 250
Royal Air Force / RAF 23, 58-61, 65, 103, 149, 195, 270, 271, 272, 273
Royal Army Service Corps / RASC 269
SIS/Secret Intelligence Service of Great Britain (known in France as IS, the term used by André) / MI6/British Secret Service 6, 7, 12, 13, 17-23, 64, 70, 71, 76, 82, 85, 88, 91, 95, 147, 171, 173-197, 198, 208, 209, 210, 223, 226, 236-238, 248, 254, 257, 259, 271
SOE / (SOE RF and SOE F sections) 6, 17, 22, 23, 70, 171, 180-185, 191, 193, 197, 207, 248, 249, 251, 252
Truro (England) 82, 250, 252
Truro / Red Lion Hotel 252
Women's Auxiliary Air Force / WAAF 270, 271
Y-Service Signals Intelligence/ SIGINT / COMINT 271

US PERSONNEL, LOCATIONS, OTHER

1408th AAF base (Orly airport) 222
Amyx, Charles B. 222
B-24 (American bombers) 124
Ford, Colonel 222

WWI-WWII LOCATIONS, EVENTS AND PERSONS

The Allies /Allied 14, 43-46, 61, 96, 99, 114, 124, 132-134, 136, 140, 158, 163, 166, 185, 202, 203, 218, 222
Anschluss 44
Beer Hall *Putsch* 5, 11, 38, 174
Berlin 60, 69
Blitzkrieg 43
Bloch, Jules 42
Blum, Léon 42
D-Day 23, 123, 124, 185, 271, 272
Danzig 44, 45
drôle de guerre / phoney war 47
épuration (purge of collaborators) 226
Fascism 46, 174
Fascist 46, 253
Franco 46, 136, 137

Gleiwitz 45
Italy 46
Kristallnacht 44
Pilsudski, General 30, 175
Poland 5, 11, 13, 30, 35, 38, 45, 46, 130, 139, 173, 266, 269, 273
Red Cross 53, 61, 69, 79, 100, 102, 147, 203, 265
Rhineland 43
Roma and Sinti 229
Spain, Spanish 46, 73, 136, 137, 184
Sudetenland 5, 44, 130
Tobruk 99
Treaty of Versailles 43, 114
World War I / War of 1914 11, 33, 36, 38, 40, 43, 49, 114

HISTORIANS, WITNESSES AND ARCHIVES
SEE **ENDNOTES FOR MORE**

Abzug, Robert 108, 341
Austin, Timothy Bowes / Dr. T.B., MA, D.Phil (Oxon) 23, 213, 273, 282, 295, 301, 313, 315, 316, 317, 319, 326, 333, 334, 338
Babois, Caroline née Gentry 19, 300, 342
Barcellini, Serge 226, 282, 328, 342
Bloch, Jean-Pierre 180, 289, 317
Bogarde, Dirk 329
Cassou, Jean 226, 283, 315
Centre Européen du Résistant Déporté/CERD (museum) 11, 14, 104, 110, 112, 118, 310, 328, 335, 340
de Jaegher, Pierre 184, 208, 261, 304, 315, 326, 342
de Kerillis, Henri 44
De Normann, Roderick 333, 342
Fondation pour la Mémoire de la Déportation 179, 276, 304, 309

Fox, Colonel (Retired) Nick, OBE 195, 306, 321, 321, 342
Hodgson, Lynn Philip 194, 286, 342
Kedward, Rod 177, 286, 316
Le Tac, Monique 72, 77, 78, 279, 305, 306, 324, 341
McCue, Paul 273, 314, 323, 342
Miannay, Patrick 238, 288, 308, 331
National Archives - France 17, 21, 171, 211, 305, 316, 335
National Archives - Great Britain 17, 171, 181, 247, 254, 276, 318, 319, 322, 323, 333, 339, 340
Noguères, Henry 186, 288, 320, 355
O'Connor, Bernard 288, 296, 322, 342
Perrin, Nigel 255, 311, 318, 319, 321, 342, 320
Pollack, Guillaume 185, 290, 300, 301, 303, 319, 324, 331, 332, 333
Rémy, Colonel / Gilbert Renault 199, 200, 206, 260, 324
Semprún, Jorge 216, 227, 229, 291, 310, 311, 327, 329, 330
Tabouis, Geneviève 44
West, Nigel 21, 318, 333, 342
Wieviorka, Olivier 177, 185, 292, 304, 313, 319, 320, 342
Yoken, Professor Mel and Cynthia 82, 105, 107, 277, 281, 303, 328, 330

POLITICAL ENGAGEMENT/ HISTORY

anti-semitism 37, 226
Balfour Declaration 36
British Mandate 36, 269
Communism, Communist 32, 73, 115, 120, 121, 126, 127, 137, 151, 154, 186, 256
Dugesclin 45

European Community / European
   Economic Community 172, 227
Geneva Convention 61, 127
gun (ownership) 48, 174
Herzl 37
Inquisition-Spanish 36
Jabotinsky 37
La Cagoule 226
Masada 36
Napoleon 45, 123
non-aggression pact 5, 46
Pinchas 37
Surcouf 45
Zealot 36, 45
Zionism / Zionist 36, 37

TRAITORS, DOUBLE AGENTS, INFILTRATORS (ALLEGED / ACTUAL), DOUBLE CROSS OPERATIONS

Bardet, Roger 237
Carré, Mathilde Lucie Bélard / 'La Chatte' / 'Victoire' 236, 281, 289, 331
de Lafforest/de la Forest, Jean Poumeau (V-Mann) 238, 276
Goubeau, Robert / Bob Edgar(d) 236
Grec, Gabriel 332
Herton 332
Humbert, Jacques 237, 331, 332
Kiffer, Robert 236
Knoblaugh 332
Kraft, Georges / Georges André (V-Mann) 238
Leneveu, Roger / 'Le Légionnaire' 235, 264
Le Pollotec, Jean 238
Ortet, Charles (V-Mann) 238
Planat 332
Sealing Wax 236, 254, 276
Téry, Madeleine Angèle Maria, wife of Norbert Haouisée de la Villeaucomte 226, 237, 331
Tessuas 332
Van Ackere 254, 276, 331
Vertrauensmann / V-Mann ('Confidence man') 237, 238, 333

MADAME LOUIS AND HER CONNECTIONS

Gontier/Gonthier, Pierre 211, 212, 237
Gorge, Marguerite Alice/ Madame Louis / Mme. Louis 67, 70, 92, 184, 185, 205-212, 226, 236, 237, 256-259
Guichard, René 257
Zuccarelli, Colonel Toussaint 257